Pagan & Witch Elders of the World
Past & Present
Pagans, Witches, Wiccans, Druids and Magicians Preparing the Path for the 21st Century

Revised Edition

Tamara Van Forslun
The Witch of Oz

Copyright © 2024 Twisted Souls Press LLC All rights reserved. No part of this book may be used or reproduced by any means, graphic, electronic, or mechanical, including photocopying, recording, taping or by any information storage retrieval system without the express written permission of the publisher.

ISBN paperback: 978-0-6457386-7-4
ISBN ebook: 978-0-6457386-6-7
ISBN hardcover: 978-0-6457386-8-1

Contact Twisted Souls Press LLC
www.TwistedSoulsPress.com
P.O. Box 1774
Ogden, UT 84402
twistedsoulspress@gmail.com

The author of this book does not dispense medical advice or prescribe the use of any technique as a form of treatment for physical, emotional, or medical problems without the advice of a physician, either directly or indirectly. The intent of the author is only to offer information of a general nature to help you in your quest for emotional and spiritual well-being. In the event you use any of the information in this book for yourself, which is your constitutional right, the author and the publisher assume no responsibility for your actions. Any people depicted in stock imagery provided by Thinkstock are models, and such images are being used for illustrative purposes only. Certain stock imagery © Thinkstock and Freepik.
Cover Photograph of Lord Raymond "Robat" Buckland with permission from photographer Gregory C. Ford.
All Interior Photos taken by the author or with permission from Elders or owners of the rights to the photos.
Cover Design by Sabrina RG Raven www.sabrinargraven.com

"What is needed now, more than ever, is leadership that steers us away from fear and fosters greater confidence in the inherent goodness and ingenuity of humanity!"

- US President - Jimmy Carter

About the Author
Lady Tamara Von Forslun - The Witch of Oz

Tamara Von Forslun In Egypt

Tamara Von Forslun, dubbed by Raymond Buckland "The Witch of Oz" in the early 80s, has been involved in the Craft since the 1970s and teaching Wicca and Witchcraft for over 50 years, she is considered one of the world's respected Pagan and Witch Elders and is the Founder and Creator of Australia's first legal Neo-Pagan Church "The Church of Wicca" (Australia August 1989), Arch Priestess of the Aquarian Tabernacle Church in Australia (1991). Traditional Initiated Witch Coven of Draconis (1970). An Alexandrian High Priestess (1978); High Priestess Elder of the Clan of Boskednan International since (1978); Ordained High Priestess of the Fellowship of Isis by Lady Olivia and Lord Lawrence Durdan-Robertson (1981); Accepted as Elder of the Grey Council of Wizards & Sages (2019). International Author and Lecturer, Teacher, Naturopath & Herbalist, Traditional Witchcraft Ritualist; Oracle High Priestess; Wiccan Marriage and Funeral Celebrant.

Tamara has travelled the world and met with many of our Elders. Along the way all that she has learnt, she has passed on freely to those who would listen and learn. Tamara, now at the end of her earthly cycle still being a teacher travels the world continuously and has revealed all she has ever learnt as a student of Magic, Witchcraft, Shamanism, Wicca, Tarot, Australian Aboriginal Magic, the Goddess, and Herbal Medicine in her books, also being lucky to have been born in an age where she has met with and befriended many of today's Elders of the Pagan Community.

Contents

About The Author – Lady Tamara Von Forslun
Thank you to all the Elders
What is a Pagan or Witch Elder

13th Century
    Angela de la Barthe 1230-1275
    Dame Alice Kyteler 1280-1325

14th – 15th Century
Abramelon The Mage 15th Century
    Jeanne d' Arc 1412-1430
    Agatha Southeil 1470-1488
    Ursula 'Mother' Shipton 1488-1561
    Cornelius Agrippa 1486-1535

16th Century
    Agnes Waterhouse -1503-1566
    Agnes Sampson -1591
    Dr. John Dee 1507-1608
    Johannes Weyer 1515-1588
    Edward Kelley 1555-1597

17th Century
    Catherine Monvoisin 1640-1680
    Maret Jonsdotter 1644-1672
    Isobel Gowdie – 1662
    Moll Dyer – 1697

18th Century
    Sir Francis Barret 1773-1856
    Joan Whytte 1775-1813
    Tamsin Blight 1788-1856
    Marie Laveau 1791-1881

19th Century
    Eliphas Levi 1810-1875
    George Pickingill 1816-1909
    Charles Leland 1824-1903
    Sir James George Fraser 1854-1941
    Arthur Edward Waite 1857-1942
    Dr. Margaret Murray 1863-1963
    Aleister Crowley 1875-1947
    Gerald B. Gardner 1884-1964
    Dion Fortune 1890-1946
    Adrian Reinman 1892-1967
    Lady Margaret DeLille Quin 1894-1995

20th – 21st Century
    Ross "Nuin" Nichols 1902-1975
    Dr. Frederick LaMotte Santee 1906-1980
    Israel Regardie 1907-1985
    Cecil Williamson 1909-1999
    Eleanor Bone 1910-2001
    William G. Gray 1913-1992

Stewart Farrar 1916-2000
Rosaleen Norton 1917-1979
Lady Olivia Durdan Robinson 1917-2013
Sybil Leek 1917-1982
Lady Sheba 1920-2002
Lord Lawrence Durden-Robertson Baron Riadh/Robertson of Strathloch 1920-1994
Doreen Valiente 1922-1999
Monique Wilson "Lady Olwen" 1923-1982
Francis King 1924-1994
Idries Shah 1924-1996
Vivienne Crowley 1925 –
Rhiannan Ryal 1921-
Alex Sanders 1926-1988
Madge Worthington 1926-2018
Patricia Crowther 1927-
Dolores Ashcroft Nowicki 1929-
Carl Llewellyn Wesche 1930-2015
Leo Martello 1930-2000
Grandmother Elspeth 1930 -
Frederick LaMond 1931 - 2020
Donata Ahern 1932 -
Laurie Cabot 1933 -
Raymond Buckland 1934-2017
Nybor 1936 -
Jack L. "Dafo" Bracelin -1983
Pete Pathfinder Davis 1937-2014
Marylyn "Motherbear" Scott 1937 -
Nelson White 1938-2003
Marion Weinstein 1939-2009
Michael York 1939-
H.R.Giger 1940-2014
Lady Elizabeth Patterson
Oberon Ravenheart-Zell 1942 -
Nicki Scully 1943 -
Richard Lance Christie 1944-2010
Abby Willowroot 1945-2018
Rev. Paul Beyerl 1945 -
Mama Donna Henes 1945 -
Margot Adler 1946-2014
Maxine Sanders 1946-
Dr. Jacque MacKenzie 1947-
Amber K 1947-
Rev. Robert "Skip" Ellison 1948-
Zsuzsanna Z Budapest 1948-
Morning Glory Zell Ravenheart 1948 - 2014
Selena Fox 1949 -
Isaac Bonewits 1949-2010
Andras Corban Arthen 1949-
Carol Garr 1949 -

Janet Farrar 1950-
Patrick Mc Collum 1950 -
John "Apollonius" Opsopaus 1950 –
Kat Tigner 1950 -
Raven Grimassi 1951- 2019
Starhawk 1951-
Donald Michael Kraig 1951-2014
Simon Goodman 1951-1991
Ellen E. Hopman 1952-
Morgana Sythova 1952 –
Professor Jack Montgomery 1953-
Prof. Ronald Hutton 1953 –
Pete Cropley 1953 -
Jesse Wolf Hardin 1954 -
Sallie Anne Glassman 1954 -
Velvet Reith 1954-2017
Phyllis Curott 1954 -
Sam Webster 1954 -
Dorothy Morrison 1955 -
Tamara Von Forslun 1956-
Scott Cunningham 1956-1993
Silver Ravenwolf 1956 -
Edain McCoy 1957 – 2019
Melissa "Rose" Anderson 1959-
Patricia Talesco 1960-
Rev. Vic "Mama" Wright 1961 -
Talyn Songdog 1963 -
Gavin Bone 1964 -
Belladonna Leveau 1965 -
Christopher A. LaFond 1966 -
Peter Brabyn 1967 –
Utu Witchdoctor 1968 -
Christian Day 1969 –
Toni Rotonda 1971-
Kristoffer Hughes 1971 –
Laura Golzalez 1973 -
Jason Mankey 1973 –
Alfred Willowhawk
Brian Cain 1975 –
Adam Barralet 1979 -
Kat McDonald
Shane Orthmann
Annie Waters
Sama Morningstar
Deidre Arthen
Eric Levanthal Arthen
Moira Ashleigh
Katlyn Breene & Bob Gatrix
Christopher Penszak
Luisah Teish

    Jeff McBride
    Antonion Batistessa
    Rebecca "Kundra" MacNess
Pagan Elders Past & Present (Alphabetical Order)
Dates to Remember
Merry Meet, Merry Part, and Merry Meet Again

Thank you to All the Elders!
May our Ancestors Bless You All, As You Have Blessed Us!

I have been ever so lucky to have been born in an era where since the 50s the majority of our Elders have stepped forward to forge a pathway for the Seekers, to make it easier stepping out of the Shadows in their endeavor and sacred calling to seek their Truth. Alas many of our Elders have also passed from this realm into the Summerlands, and now remain one of the Shining Ones of our Traditions. Many who are still with us constantly walk the Dragon/Serpent Lines (Leylines) of our Paths meeting and greeting all the new Seekers of the 21st century, and many of which I am lucky to be able to call my friends, brothers, and sisters.

I would like to thank all my dear friends and fellow Elders of the World that have helped me in putting together this remarkable who is who in the community "Pagan & Witch Elders of the World – Past and Present" book. Hopefully, it honors all the Elders of our history past and present. Some famous, some infamous, and some not very well known at all, as they have done or do their work behind the Shadows and closed doors and seek no notoriety for their immense work. Although I have over 500 names mentioned in this book, I only really had room to cover 150 Elders in more detail, and even that detail is limited due to the space. As a book can only contain so much information, and many of our Elders have their own bio-books out or plan to, but if you are interested in finding out more about a certain Elder and or their Tradition you can look them up and find out more or visit their websites. Hopefully this gives you a chance to get to know your Elders whilst they are still with us and show them your honor and respect for all they have done, as many are now in their 60s, 70s, 80s and even 90s and many still going strong with the heart of the Gods, and the faith and assistance of the Pagan Community world-wide.

I hope that this book becomes a legacy where new Seekers of the old ways acknowledge, honor, REMEMBER and know the Pagan and Witch Elders. This book contains a fraction of the vast lives and works of our Elders, the great people of our Traditions that gave their hearts and souls to clearing the way for the millions of Seekers who claim to be a part of the world of Magic in the eclectic Traditions of the Occult, Magic, Ceremonial Magick, Paganism, Neo-Paganism, Witchcraft, Wicca, Voudoun, Heathenism, Shamanism, Druidism, Hellenics, Kemetics, Baltics, Afro-Caribbean's, Eclectics and all the other New Age terms that people have adopted as an ancient insight and awakening into a new world of Pagan and Occult Traditions in the 21st Century. I have not mentioned many of their personal negatives as I feel that detracts from who they really are, we all have our secrets and our pitfalls that caused negativity and some harm. Let us not judge others as the religions of the one God have done. This is not what I am concentrating on, "An It Harm None!"

In Australia those that acknowledge themselves as an Earth Centred Religion (Pagan) have grown since 2006 – 2019 by 28% and are now one of the top 5 religious paths for Australians. In the US, the movement has moved forward in leaps and bounds and grown so incredibly, again with thanks to the Elders. It is estimated that in 1990 there were a total of 680,000 Neo-Pagans, including Wiccans, where that number had skyrocketed to 1.5 million. ReligionLink compared data from the 2008 ARIS survey with that of the 2001 survey. They state: "Specifically, the number of Wiccans more than doubled from 2001 to 2008, from 134,000 to 342,000, and the Pagans in the United States in 2008." Based on this and subsequent surveys, Religioustolerance.org provides a more current estimate. Oddly, however, they conflate all modern Pagans under the generic category of "Wicca" rather than "Paganism", as should be the case. Thanks to Oberon Zell who shared these facts from the US with me. Here are the figures from these surveys. Below are displayed in a line graph, with a projection for next year.

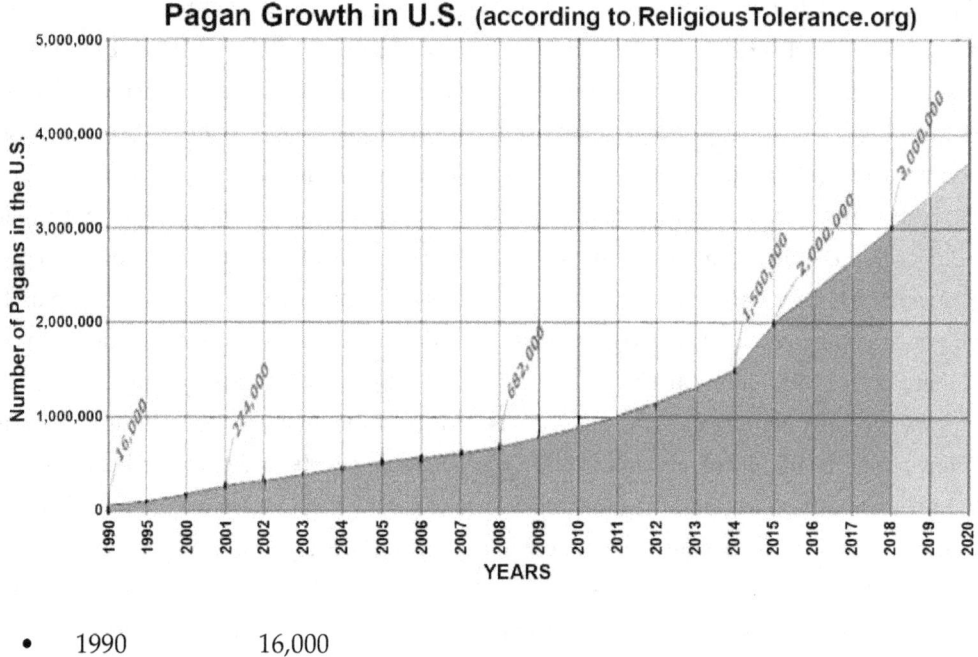

- 1990   16,000
- 2001   274,000
- 2008   682,000
- 2014   1,500,000
- 2015   2,000,000
- 2018   3,000,000
- 2020   3,600,000 (projection)

Now imagine how many there are of us worldwide, maybe it is time for a world Census.

This is the reason why we need to honor our Mentors and Elders and thank them for everything that they have done, especially through times that were 100% harder than they are today in the 21st Century. All religions have their mentors who are acknowledged in a way as martyr's, saints, leaders of inspiration, guru's, enlighteners, and spiritual mentors. We too have them, and many are still alive today.

So, let's start the legacy to honor and acknowledge all of our Elders, let us band together with all our differences as a large Fellowship all on a different path but with the end goal in mind, being at One with the Divine Feminine and Divine Masculine. Let us a form a Panel to select an Elder, to become the World Elder of that year, my vote for the year has to be my dear friend and sister Selena Fox, for all the hard work she has done over 50 years, and also to my brother Oberon Zell Dragonheart, for 50 years of service to our community.

By going with the statistics at 3 million practitioners as of 2018, modern Paganism (including Wicca) is now the second-largest religion in America after Christianity (70.6 million in 2014, which is declining by one percentage point per year), and the fastest growing in terms of percentage! By comparison, in 2014, there were 1.9 million Jews, 0.9 million Muslims, 0.7 million Buddhists, and 0.4 million Hindus in the US. The growth and acknowledgment of our Pagan Traditions has grown experientially with thanks and dedication to the Elders of our world that have forged forward and cleared the way for all the Seekers up to the 21st century and for those that follow.

As Oberon Zell states in his "2020 Vision": Just about every sixty years over the past few centuries at least; there has occurred a cultural Renaissance in Western Civilizations. Each of these periods has seen a similar flowering of the arts, poetry, music, drama, literature, culture, sciences, social movements, and 'utopian' communities. Those who come of age in their teens and twenties during one cycle become wise Elders/Wizards/Sages in their 70s and 80s next time around, tasked with mentoring of the next generation of young heroes-as in the stories."

The amount of support I have received has been astronomical with so many friends and Elders who are so busy themselves, (well those that are still alive, with many having one foot in the tomb and the other still in the womb) who gave their time and support to help me in the creating of this book with as many of the World Pagan Elders as I could possibly fit within its pages. The Elders who are alive range in ages from 60-97 years of age, with a few young up-an-coming Elders (Eldlings as I call them or Tweenagers) who are from the ages of 30-50, who have taken the lead as young teachers and guides for our community. There will be many who did not get a mention in these pages due to either not receiving permission from them or contact, or not knowing of them, but if there are Elders out there who have helped in making a difference please forward their names and bios onto me so when I revise this book in 5 years (Goddess Willing) or on my website, they can also be added to this book of acknowledged Elders who we must all honor no matter what their differences, for the courage and hard work that they have achieved to awaken Our Truth, and kept it alive helping others to realise their Truth as Pagans, and to bring the ancient knowledge to the Seekers of the ancient world into the light of the 21st Century.

I shall endeavor to set up a website for the "Council of Pagan Elders International" so more can be added throughout time and also keep it updated even after I am gone from this beautiful world. Through this Facebook page we can endorse Elders and eventually nominate and vote the Pagan Elder of the Year Award as stated before. This way our larger community can see where we are changing and growing and know who to acknowledge and thank. It will also give you contacts that may be in your area of living or interest, that you may want to touch base with the Elders to assist you in your journey.

Thank you for all the hard work and for the constant fighting that has been done with the establishment and the many barriers that were placed up due to ignorance and lack of true knowledge and understanding that you all helped to knock down. Thank you to all "Pagan & Witch Elders of the World – Past and Present" either who have passed on (as we have lost many in the last few years and undoubtedly will lose many more over the next decade,) or who are still present in this world, and if you get the chance to meet one of these special Elders, even the new younger Eldlings of tomorrow, please walk up to them and hold out your hand and "THANK" them, or better still give them a big healing hug, as they need this acknowledgement and also a little of your energy, for they did more and are still doing more than you will ever truly realise, as much of the Elders work is done behind the scenes. Honour them whilst they are still alive and honor them also through remembrance when they have left this mortal world, knowing that they will return.

"None Greater Than The Elders of the World.
Merry we Meet, Merry we Part, and Merry We Meet Again".

To find out more about the 2020 Vision put on all your posts.
#Iampaganandivote or for contact go to:
www.2020VisionAwakening.com
or
www.facebook.com/2020-Vision

What is a Pagan or Witch Elder?

So, what is a Pagan Elder?

Dictionary definition:

- One who is older than another or others, an elderly person.
- A forefather/foremother, a predecessor, one of a former generation in the same family, class, or community.
- An honorific title earned by a person who has through years of experience and training, and connection with experience, age, intuition, and intuitiveness, can transmit this knowledge to the younger generations, the Seekers of the same knowledge, given with the wisdom of the Elder.

Since the dawn of time there has always been some form of Paganism, although it may not have been known by that title. We have through history heard terms like, Pagan, Neo-pagan, Wizard, Shaman, Cunning Craft, Shamanka, Sorcerer, Sage, Magi, Magician, Witch, Wiccan, Druid, Heathen, Hellenics, Kemetics, Baltics, Afro-Caribbean's, Eclectics and Enchantress, and many more New Age terms that I have not yet understood or know. Pagan traditions also include anyone from all cultures and countries that choose an Earth-Centred Tradition as their faith or religion. These are each differently a study of the Invisible within the Visible and working with the electromagnetic energies of the unseen world to make changes in the physical, mental, astral, psychic, and spiritual planes. Witchcraft (originally and correctly written as Wicchecraft) is not just a tradition of the world but has been in every walk of life worldwide since the beginning of mankind.

Originally there were never any covens, as this was a wording that The Roman Catholic Church connected with Witches to meet the quota of a group of people that can be persecuted. Covens did come into effect in the 18th-19th centuries due to the growth of the Pagan movement. Traditionally there was only a solitary Witch or Shaman who was a selected child from the village, who was adopted by the Witch or Shaman of the village and trained their whole life to take over from the existing Elder, who was the spiritual Clan Mother or Clan Father, this child was usually someone who was rejected by the community due to having either disfigurement, dwarfism or was highly gifted.

They were taught everything that was needed to help and aid their village and the people of the village. They had to learn and understand the changing of the seasons, the movement of insects or birds, the Magic and medicine of all plants as Good or Bad Medicine, the Magic and ritual of planetary and Luna cycles and much more, as their communities' lives depended on this knowledge. This training did not take just a few years as though going to university, it took a lifetime to learn, remember, study and master, to discover new medicines and Magic that the old Shamans and Witches of old did not find themselves during their lifetime.

They could listen in the stillness and understand what all of Nature was telling them, this gave them a power over the people, and set them apart as the Wise One, Sage, Magi and Medicine Man or Woman, the Witch of the village or tribe.

As humanity changed and villages grew, the patriarchal side of mankind began to despise all the power that these Pagans and Witches held, and so took it against themselves to fight this ancient way of life, and bring their science and knowledge into the future, as false and evil. They then created schools and colleges of study that were only accessible to men, and all women were forbidden. The male establishment became so patriarchal that women were pushed aside of their skills and made to step backwards allowing men to take the lead on everything in life. Where women had the compassion, some men had the ego and misogynistic views that eventually brought the world to a destructive evolutionary world of industrial contamination without the true essence of nature being the provider of all that is healing and beneficial, man had turned their backs on nature due to greed and ignorance.

When this great change occurred, and things began to become dark and less connected from the emotions of life to the greed of having more or being better than the neighbor, the pat on the cigar smoking back of the bully became acceptable and a new step in man's evolution. But they too wanted some Magic in their lives and so religion was formed out of the controlling desires to spread and touch the world, where armies may have failed, religion conquered, when conjoined with the armies. They later formed great secret societies and lodges such as the Freemasons, The White Brotherhood, and The Golden Dawn and more. But these ritualistic orders were nothing more than modern versions of the ancient schools and teachings that were strongly associated with nature.

When the Roman Army came to power and formed their very own Roman Catholic Church, this is when the world changed for the worse. The Roman Catholic Church took control of everything and anything, and if it was not in compliance with the churches wishes then it was heretical and evil and had to be either destroyed or converted. The first plan of attack was to try and convert the heads of state, the Kings, and Queens of the countries that they had to conquer. Usually when the heads of state were converted, and hopefully their people also followed in their faith even when it was detrimental to their own way of life.

Firstly was the attack from the medical society that attacked women and their herbal knowledge and more natural forms of healing, and then the Church following in a wave of destruction of over 600 years of destroying all cultures, faiths and traditions of the ancient Pagan world that they had come into contact with, and if you did not bend a knee to their ways and renounce your past Pagan ways, you and nearly everyone associated with you (who they saw as also being tarnished with your sin) was taken, tortured and murdered in some barbaric method by the Inquisitors.

With over 600 years of torture and murder of over 9 million men, women, and children; the Roman Catholic Church has now grown to one of the most financial formidable institutions (businesses) in the known world, due to every soul who was ever persecuted, lost their lands and belongings due to being confiscated by the church and the courts. This was the foundation of the Catholic church's wealth and its misogynistic ways that devastated the world and built its foundation of wealth from the blood of millions of innocent victims through bigotry, misogyny, lies, deceit, conquer and fear.

It is through this constant persecution that the Magical side of the world became so hidden and secretive due to the fear of one's life and the lives of those around them. We were no longer free to honor and worship our true ancient and Pagan deities as our ancestors and everyone's ancestors did for thousands of years. Laws against Witchcraft were so severe, and unchallenged until the law against Witchcraft was repealed in England in 1951. This was the incredible time that everyone came out of the broom closet (so to speak) and began exploring their spirituality as they deemed fit for themselves and their Truth. It was slow at first, but the floodgates had opened and all forms of new and ancient styles of religious freedom began to emerge all over the world, it was an explosion of freedom and Awakening excitement, it was Magical!

The Tradition known as Witchcraft, came out as well and they wanted to defend and protect themselves, so cautiously they called their religion Wicca, taken from the Anglo-Saxon word Wicche, and slowly the Covens of the world were formed and opened up their doors to the public, and to those they felt were of genuine interest in returning back to the ancient ways as their ancestors.

The Pagan and Witch Elders of the world are the ones who stood out front in the public eye and were ridiculed and mocked by the general public and by their own, who felt they were nothing but egotistical people wanting to grandiose their own lives as demigods and Goddesses to their people. The truth of the fact is that the Elders had to have a strong form of ego to be able to come "out" and confront the establishment and the laws, sacrificing much in their lives. It took courage, and much determination to fight this battle, and with the grace and strength of the Gods and Goddesses, become a shining beacon to the masses who were also being called by the Light of the ancient deities and the path of old, the Shamans and Witches of old, as they are our Shining Ones.

ALL our Elders NEED to be honored and RESPECTED by the Pagan, Wiccan, or Witch world for all they have offered and given in sacrifice to bring forth this ancient knowledge into the new world of the 21st Century, they should not be judged with a Christian mentality, but looked up to for their valued efforts forging forward with courage and determination. To put themselves out there as a target to the non-believers as well as the believers. If it was not for them, the Craft would not have thrived into the massive Faith that it has become today. The sad thing is that some Seekers are lazy, and do not wish to study the old ways, but just sit back and read books, and believe everything that is on the internet as ANCIENT AND TRUE. The internet is a wonderful source for information but none of us can get out of a book or a webpage what we can gain from the fellowship of a spiritual family who are dedicated in working together as a Covenstead/Clan/Church/Fellowship and led by a truly trained and knowledgeable Elder who can teach us directly.

Many of the Pagan, Wiccan and Witchcraft community may never have even heard of some of these Elders, as their work and deeds have been done behind the shadows, so as to not gain much attention to themselves but for their very mission and goal at that time. They all need due respect for their efforts and dedication. I have also added what I feel may be the Elders of our future, (young Eldlings as I call them or Tweenagers) those that we can still look forward to because of their dedication and knowledge in stepping forward and taking lead, as they often share to any who ask. Many of our 20th century Elders have died or are preparing for their last Magical Walk on Mother Earth. Let us Honour all Elders now and give them the respect that they are due. As they are the Mentors and Shining Ones of our Paths, Traditions and Circles.

I have placed all the Elders in this book by their Dates of Birth, not the importance of each Elder in order, as they will each mean something different to each one of us, they consist of the last 700 years up to the 21st century who we owe everything, including our religious freedom to these people who fought, and for many who are still fighting for that religious freedom and equality that is being offered today. Honour all Elders, even the fools, for even the foolish among mankind may possess a truth that we sometimes cannot see or understand.

> "May the Pagan and Witch Elders of the World; Past, Present and Future watch over us and guide us as our Shining Ones, None Greater!"

Dame Alice Kyteler
Accused Witch
1280-1325

Medieval Portrait of Angela de La Barthe

Angela De la Barthe born in 1230 in Toulouse, France. Where many of the locals of the time said that she was a simple woman, but with a strong character. Angela always stood her ground for what she believed in, she was not afraid of a fight, and always said what she thought and believed. Through my studies and research, I have found that she was never probably a Witch, nor was she associated with any of the arts such as Herbal medicine, spells, or psychic involvement either. She

gets a mention here as one of the first to suffer in history from the Inquisition.

It seems as though she was just another poor soul who was falsely accused of being in league with the devil as a Witch. The Inquisitor Hughes de Beniols, who was the supreme chief of the Toulouse Inquisition targeted her. In her trial records she was accused of having sexual intercourse constantly with the devil and at the age of 16 gave birth to a monster child with a wolf's head and a serpent's tail, this baby fed on the lives of other babies that were supposedly slain by Angela. The Inquisition records also state that some babies were dug up from their graves and fed to her demon child.

Under extreme and lengthy torture Angela unwillingly confessed to all that she was accused of (to stop the consistent torture). She also added to her statement that she met regularly with the devil and attended his evil Sabbats just to rub salt into the wound. Angela was found guilty of being in league with the devil as a Witch, and was put to death at the pyre, and was burned to death by all the town who came to witness (as they had to attend, for if not in attendance could be seen as a show of guilt as also being in league with the devil). She left this world engulfed in flames at Saint Stephen's Church in Toulouse, France. Most of her story was very doubtful as it was later found out that because she had shunned advances from a local scholar, who had then claimed that she was in fact a Witch.

The fact is that Witches, real Wicches were not of the Christian persuasion, and thereby had no belief in a devil or demon, and only honored the living Earth as their Mother, The Divine Feminine and the Divine Masculine.

Dame Alice Kyteler
Accused Witch
1280-1325

Portrait of Dame Alice Kyteler

Dame Alice Kyteler was a lady of influence and wealth and was born in Alice's House in County Kilkenny, Ireland as the only child of a wealthy Flemish family of merchants who had settled in Ireland in 1274. Alice was sadly the first person recorded in Ireland who was accused and condemned for Witchcraft. During this accusation she fled the country and went to England, leaving behind much of her fortune and took only what she could carry with her to escape the atrocities of the Inquisition. In her quick leaving, her house maid, Petronilla de Meath was flogged and burnt to death as a co-conspirator at the stake on the 3rd of November in 1324.

Dame Kyteler had quite a name for herself as she was married four times.

- William Outlaw 1280-1285, who was also a merchant and moneylender, as the son of the Mayor of Kilkenny. Together they had a daughter Rose.
- Adam Blund 1302-1308, they lived in Callan, and he was also a moneylender.

- Richard Valle 1309-1316, who was a great landowner of County Tipperary. He mysteriously died in 1316, whereby Dame Kyteler took legal proceedings against her stepson, Richard for the recovery of her widow's dowry.
- John Poer 1316-1324.

In 1302, Dame Kyteler and her second husband Adam Blund were briefly accused of murdering her first husband. She received a great deal of resentment from the locals but due to her acquired vast wealth that she had accumulated and, in her skills, also as a money lender. Her charges were eventually dismissed. But again, when her 4th husband John le Poer fell ill in 1324, he expressed the suspicion to his family and friends that he was being poisoned by her. After his death, his children and together with the children of her previous three husbands banned together and accused her publicly of using poison and sorcery to murder them, and also of taking extreme favoritism of her first-born son, William Outlaw.

Dame Kyteler was also accused along with her supposed followers of:

- Denying the faith of the Christ and the Church.
- Sacrificing of animals to devils and demons at crossroads.
- Holding sabbaticals at night-time in churchyards, and performing black masses and honoring Satan, all in use to overpower the Church.
- Using and making of potions to kill or control Christians.
- The possessing of familiar (Robin Artison) who was a lesser demon of Satan.
- Poisoner and murder of four husbands.

The new Bishop of Ossory, Richard de Ledrede was a fanatic and was obsessed with the laws of the Church as he wanted to be higher than a Bishop, and he was filled with Christian morality. When Dame Kyteler's case was brought before him in 1324, he seized the opportunity to try and make a spectacle of her, being a Lady of influence and standing to confront the issues of Witchcraft. So, he issued her arrest, but Dame Kyteler had powerful friends and asked for their assistance. The bishop himself was then jailed and questioned by Sir Arnold de Poer (her first husband's brother), the Seneschal of Kilkenny. On the Bishops release, Alice had found that she had an enemy, who again took it as his mission to use church law to have Dame Kyteler arrested and tried again. The Chancellor insisted that she be excommunicated 40 days prior to her arrest, which gave her sufficient time to flee to Roger Utlagh, whereas the Chancellor was accused of harbouring heretics.

In the Bishops retelling of her Maid Servants confession, he writes:

"On one of these occasions, by the crossroads outside the city, she had made an offering of three cocks to a certain demon whom she called Robert, son of Art (Robertum filium Artis), from the depths of the underworld. She had poured out the cocks' blood, cut the animals into pieces and mixed the intestines with spiders and other black worms like scorpions, with a herb called milfoil as well as with other herbs and horrible worms. She had boiled this mixture in a pot with the brains and clothes of a

boy who had died without baptism and with the head of a robber who had been decapitated ... Petronella said she had several times at Alice's instigation and once in her presence, consulted demons and received answers. She had consented to a pact whereby she would be the medium between Alice and the said Robert, her friend. In public, she said that with her own eyes she had seen the aforesaid demon as three shapes (praedictus daemon tertius), in the form of three black men (aethiopum) each carrying an iron rod in the hand. This apparition happened by daylight (de die) before the said Dame Alice, and, while Petronella herself was watching, the apparition had intercourse with Alice. After this disgraceful act, with her own hand she (Alice?) wiped clean the disgusting place with sheets (kanevacio) from her own bed."

Dame Alice Kyteler fled to England, which saved her life, and she was not heard of again as she lived a quiet life with no contemporary records about her. The bishop did keep the trial going and for those that did not have the means to flee (27 supposed co-conspirators), were all tortured and put to death by the Bishop of Ossary.

Abramelon the Mage
Magician & Alchemist
14th-15th Century

15th Century Sketch of Abramelon the Mage

During the 14th to the 15th Centuries, the middle east abounded in esoteric and occult teachings and the greatest of these teachers was a Mage known as Abramelon. He through his travels combined religions and occult teachings of ancient Babylon, Egypt, Mesopotamia, Persia, Greece, Britain, and Syria, which also made it quite confusing for the conventional reader. Through this intermingling he formulated ancient and sacred texts of training which spread throughout the then known world.

His masterpiece Grimoire known as "The Book of Abramelon the Mage", was created as an epistolary novel where he speaks of the passing of his divine knowledge of the Kabbala and Magic to Abraham of which was passed to his son, Lamech and speaks of how he came by this sacred knowledge.

Abraham's writings begin with the death of his father, who gave him instruction along with Sigils and powerful symbols of Magic, in which it is necessary to acquire the Holy Kabbala before his last days. Abraham was so hungry for this sacred knowledge that he travelled to Mayence to study under a Rabbi, named Moses, who was well-versed in these great studies. Abraham studied under him for four whole years and commented that his former training was filled with many flaws and errors.

After this long intensively arduous study he decided to travel again for the next six years, eventually ending up in the country and birthplace of true Magic, Egypt. It was there in Egypt that Abraham met with Abramelon the Mage, an Egyptian Mage who lived away from the cities, in the desert sands outside the town called Araki. His humble home was situated on top of a hill that was surrounded by lush green palm and olive trees surrounded by the dry desert sands, an oasis that stood out for miles. Abramelon's key lesson was about the "Fear of God", and urged Abraham to be exact, devout and sure in his life as a spiritual person, to be always humble, and to acknowledge and remove all sin and to live a simple life with no possessions, as a sign of wealth is abhorred by God.

Abramelon taught Abraham the ancient Egyptian Magic of Tehuti and Seshat, "The Books of Life and Death" now called the Magic of the Kabbala and parts thus converted into the Tarot. When Abraham made certain promises to him to give up all false dogma's and live the way of Truth.

Abramelon gave to Abraham two Sacred Grimoires that he had to copy from, in his own hand of write, the cost for this was 10 gold coins, of which he distributed to 72 poor persons (as in the 72 Genii of the Mercury zone) in the neighboring town. Abramelon left Abraham to copy the Grimoires as he went to the town to share the gold coins, of which he returned 15 days later. The following morning Abramelon instructed Abraham to confess his life sins and promise to serve and fear the Higher God, and the Higher Mother Goddess. These two Grimoires formed the greater knowledge of the Holy Kabbala and highlighted the most elaborate ritual therein known as "The Abramelon Operation", which gives the proper ceremonial side of the ritual to gain all the knowledge and to have contact with The Shining Ones, (The Angels). This Ritual also gave the Mage the power to bind all demons and evil beings. The other Grimoire was of the Magic Squares of the Shining Ones and the Planets called Kameas, the Magical Sacred Squares of Tehuti Thoth. (Which is covered in my book "The Shining Ones – Angels of Heaven and Earth").

Medieval Sketch of Abramelon the Mage.

The system known as the Kabbala became so widespread and popular not only by Jewish Rabi's but created a whole new tradition in the 19th-20th centuries, 100's of years later and sprouted such well-known organizations as The Hermetic Order of the Golden Dawn and the Mystical Temples of Thelema of Aleister Crowley. The original teacher and writer of these traditions and systems of Magical belief is the High Priest of Aset and Assur, and later became self-proclaimed God of Egypt and Greece, Tehuti Thoth (known to the Greeks as Hermes Mercurius Trismegistus) which was later called the "Hermetic Corpus" which is a series of sacred "Books of Life and Death" that are the basics of Tehutism, Hermeticism and now in the 21st century called the Tarot.

Jeanne d'Arc Pucelle
High Priestess
January 6th, 1412 - May 30th, 1430

Jeanne d'Arc 1505 Manuscript

Jeanne d'Arc was born of the 6th of January 1412 in a small village which was part of the French Duchy of Bar, to Father Jacques d'Arc and Isabelle Romee in Domremy. Jeanne's parents were simple folk as small farmers and owned 20 hectares of land, which they supplemented the farming work with her father's position as a village tax collector and also heading the local watch.

Despite being surrounded by pro-Burgundian lands the family remained loyal to the French Crown and its governments. Jeanne's village was raided and burnt to the ground twice when she was just a child, where the family had to rebuild again. Jeanne never had any schooling and was quite illiterate, due to her parents needing her to help with working on the farm, this is why she could not read nor write. Jeanne did later learn to sign her name with the help of others. The D'Arc family were not religious in the Christian sense and were known as People of the Earth (Pagans). Jeanne always spoke of her many visions that she had of God, and these visions were heard of far and wide, where many came for miles to meet this young child of God and hear of her visions.

Jeanne's Birthplace and Home

When Jeanne was born, the French King was Charles VI, and he suffered with outrageous bouts of insanity and was often too ill to rule, which gave way to his brother Louis, the Duke of Orleans, and the King's cousin 'John the Fearless', Duke of Burgundy often they disputed and argued over the regency of France as they both wanted to be king and be the guardians of the royal children. With orders from the Duke of Burgundy the conflict escalated with the assassination of the Duke of Orleans in 1407. It was around this time with all the conflict within France, that King Henry V of England took advantage of all this internal warring and decided to invade France in 1415, winning a dramatic victory at Agincourt on the 25th of October, where he captured many of the northern towns of France.

In 1418 Paris was taken by the Burgundian armies, who massacred the entire Court of Armagnac and along with 2,500 of the loyal followers. The future French King Charles VII assumed the title of Dauphin (Heir to the throne), at the tender age of fourteen, after all four of his older brothers had died mysteriously in succession. His first act as Dauphin was to oversee a peace treaty with the Duke of Burgundy in 1419, which ended in disaster when Armagnac partisans assassinated John the Fearless during a meeting under King Charles's guarantee of protection. It was the new Duke of Burgundy, Philip the Good, who blamed Charles for the murder and entered into an alliance with the English. It was this alliance with the allied forces that conquered much of France. It looked as though France would be lost.

At the tender age of 16, Jeanne became a Pucelle, a leader and High Priestess of a great following "The People of the Earth". Jeanne asked a relative, Durand Lassois to take her to the nearby town of Vaccouleurs, where she petitioned the garrison commander, Robert de Baudricourt for an armed escort to bring her to the French Court and King Charles at Chinon. Baudricourt's sarcasm and laughter at this silly uneducated young girl did not deter Jeanne. Jeanne, with courage in her faith returned again a year later accompanied by two of Baudricourt's soldiers, Jean de Metz, and Bertrand de Poulengy, who supported her as a Pucelle. According to Metz who was told by Jeanne "I must be at the King's side ... there will be no help (for the kingdom) if not from me. Although I would rather have remained spinning [wool] at my mother's side ... yet must I go, and must I do this thing, for my Lord wills that I do so."

Under the guidance and protection of Metz and Poulengy, she was permitted a second meeting, where she made the prediction about a military reversal at the Battle of Rouvray near Orleans several days prior to messengers giving their report to the King. According to the "Journal du Siege D'Orleans", which portrayed Jeanne as a miraculous figure, Jeanne came to know the battle through "grace divine" whilst shepherding her flock of sheep in Lorraine and used this divine revelation to persuade Baudricourt to take her to the Dauphin. He then after receiving verification of the defeat, granted Jeanne an escort to visit Chanon. Baudricourt suggested to her to dress disguised as a male soldier to be safer whilst going through the hostile Burgundian territories, this fact that later swayed the charges against her later with the charge of "Cross-dressing", although others around her say it was a safety measure and it was the people of the village of Vaucouleurs who provided her with the male clothing for her disguise, to maintain her safety, and at the same time her beautiful long fair hair was cut short.

Upon arriving at the Royal Court of Chinon in 1429, when she was aged just 17 and the King was 26, at her meeting she made such an impression on the King during this private meeting with Jeanne where she spoke of Divine assistance. It was during this time that Charles' mother-in-law Yolande of Aragon was planning to finance a relief expedition to Orleans. Jeanne asked the King for permission to attend with the army and wear protective armor, provided by the Royal government through donations of special items for her sacred gold armor, and a white horse, sword, banner and alongside with other specialised items. Jeanne always viewed herself by the Grace of God to be the only source of hope for the King and all of France that was close to total collapse. Stephen W. Richey explains:

"After years of one humiliating defeat after another, both the military and civil leadership of France were demoralized and discredited. When the Dauphin Charles granted Jeanne's urgent request to be equipped for war and placed at the head of his army, his decision must have been based in large part on the knowledge that every orthodox, every rational option had been tried and had failed. Only a regime in the final straits of desperation would pay any heed to an illiterate farm girl who claimed that the voice of God was instructing her to take charge of her country's army and lead it to victory.

Upon her arrival on the scene, Jeanne effectively turned the longstanding Anglo-French conflict into a religious war, a course of action that was not without risk. Charles' advisers were worried that unless Jeanne's orthodoxy could be established beyond doubt—that she was not a heretic or a sorceress—Charles' enemies could easily make the allegation that his crown was a gift from the devil. To circumvent this possibility, the Dauphin ordered background inquiries and a theological examination at Poitiers to verify her morality. In April 1429, the commission of inquiry "declared her to be of irreproachable life, a good Christian, possessed of the virtues of humility, honesty and simplicity." The theologians at Poitiers did not render a decision on the issue of divine inspiration; rather, they informed the Dauphin that there was a "favorable presumption" to be made on the divine nature of her mission. This was enough for Charles, but they also stated that he had an obligation to put Jeanne to the test. "To doubt or abandon her without suspicion of evil would be to repudiate the Holy Spirit and to become unworthy of God's aid", they declared. They recommended that her claims should be put to the test by seeing if she could lift the siege of Orléans as she had predicted."

Jeanne's advice convinced other commanders to become her supporters, and they believed that she indeed was the Voice of God. Jeanne saved thousands of lives and turned the tables of the war on the Burgundians and the English. The English armies withdrew and headed north on the 18th of June eventually joining up with a unit of reinforcements under the command of Sir John Fastolf. Jeanne urged the Armagnacs to pursue, and pursue they did nearly decimating the English army, capturing and or killing the majority of their commanders, except Fastolf who somehow escaped with a small band of his close soldiers, where he eventually became the scapegoat for the humiliating defeat. Jeanne and her entire family were ennobled by King Charles VII on the 29th of December as a reward for her services and guidance.

From that day she became "The Maid of Orleans" and was considered The Heroine of France and the people. Jeanne led the French armies to multiple victories, with her always at the front of the armies and bearing her personal banner, the English feared her power, believing that she was indeed a messenger from God. Whilst all this notoriety was being conveyed upon her, a conspiracy was being plotted against her between the Burgundians and the English, the Burgundians knew she was too powerful in France and so they plotted a kidnapping where she was captured on the 23rd of May 1430 by a group of French nobles who had allied themselves with the English. Jeanne was handed over to the English and put on trial led by the pro-English bishop Pierre Cauchon, where she had been charged with a multitude of charges. The whole trial was a farce and politically motivated. After Cauchon declared her guilty, Jeanne was, after weeks of torture burned at the stake on the 30th of May 1431, dying terribly at the tender age of nineteen.

It was not until much later in 1456 where an inquisitorial court that was authorized by Pope Callixtus III, examined all the trial documents and immediately debunked all the charges and pronounced her innocent and forthwith declared her a Martyr of the Church.

Jeanne became a symbol of the Catholic League in the 16th century, and in 1803 she was declared a national symbol of France by the decision of Napoleon Bonaparte. Jeanne was beatified in 1909 and canonized in 1920 by the Roman Catholic Church. Documented witnesses at her execution by fire, said that she was displayed before all to see and tied to a tall central pillar at the Vieux-Marche in Rouen, where she asked two of the clergy, a Friar Martin Ladvenu and Friar Isambert de la Pierre, to hold a crucifix before her, this is where they grabbed a soldiers lance and tied a crucifix to its end and held over Jeanne's face, she was also given a smaller one which was placed in her dress near her heart. After the fires had turned to ash, the English commanded that the coals be raked to expose her charred remains, and she was again on two further occasions torched to stop the collection of her remains or any relics. Jeanne's remains were cast into the Seine River, after which the executioner Geoffrey Therage had later stated that he believed her to be a saint and feared his soul was now damned.

Prison of Jeanne's Last Days, now called the Jeanne d'Arc Tower

In the words of Stephen Richey, "She turned what had been a dry dynastic squabble that left the common people unmoved except for their own suffering into a passionately popular war of national liberation."

Since the death of Jeanne there have been two sealed jars that have been found, one in 1867 in Paris with an inscription "Remains found under the stake of Jeanne of Arc, virgin of Orleans." They consisted of a charred human rib, carbonized wood, a piece of linen and a cat femur – explained as the practice of throwing black cats onto the pyre of witches. The other jar concealed and hidden held by a family who were ancient followers of the Pucelle and High Priestess Witch, contained the charred remains of a thigh bone, carbonized wood, ash, and a small amount of melted gold (from the crucifix).

The only other relic, which was a ring presented to Jeanne by King Charles VII, which had passed through the hands of a cardinal, a king, an aristocrat, and the daughter of a British physician, was sold in March 2016 at a Lloyds of London auction for 300,000 pounds.

Agatha Southeil
Witch
1470-1486

Medieval Painting of Agatha Southeil

Agatha Southeil was born in 1470, and also known as "Little Aggy". She was an orphan, and a street urchin who was homeless and did whatever she could to survive. Whether it was stealing food or goods, money, begging in the streets or the prostitution of her young abused and dirty body. Southeil was an outcast who was shunned by most because of her unethical displays of morals and foul language and being very unclean. Her innocence was taken from her at an exceedingly early age due to having nothing else to offer for food, so she offered only what she had left, her body.

Southeil became pregnant at the tender young age of 15 and being unwed and with no-one to take care of her, she was branded and accused by certain women as a prostitute and witch. When she became pregnant and begged for help the town turned against her, even though still being a child herself, and it was gossip mongering that spread that she had slept with the devil, and the very child within her belly was the spawn of Satan himself.

Southeil ran and hid from the village and lived in a nearby cave in Knaresborough, of where a few good folk would bring her food and water to help her and her unborn baby. In time she gave birth, many say to a deformed female child that she named Ursula. As history would eventually call this child "Mother Shipton" a powerful Seer, who became a great Oracle, prophetess and Witch of her time in all of Great Britain. Southeil died not long after giving birth to Ursula. When she died, she was buried at the back of the cave, which is now a major tourist attraction for many, that has a plaque out the front of the cave.

Ursula was taken in by a family who lived near the cave, who lived the old ways as People of the Earth but kept to themselves. They took care of Southeil accepting her.

Southeil had a bad young life and died before ever knowing her daughter, but knew what it was to love someone, unconditionally. Although she died being only 16, she has been remembered for all the suffering of what an orphan of the time had to go through just to survive, and how society even then shunned her and abandoned her, proclaiming that she was a whore of the devil, instead of blaming some male within their community who took her body and made her pregnant, it was probably he that spread the rumor of her being a witch. Southeil was not a witch, but she gave to the world an immensely powerful Witch in her daughter Ursula.

Ursula "Mother" Shipton
Witch Oracle Elder
1486-1561

Medieval Sketch of Mother Shipton

Agatha Southeil (accused Witch as in the previous chapter) at the age of 16 gave birth to Ursula Southeil in a cave in Knaresborough who was reportedly born disfigured and her body also deformed, but these falsities and accusations were all fabricated and untrue by a writer, Richard Head who eventually owned up to it later in his life. Shipton was taken in by a kind family who lived nearby the Cave of Agatha Southeil, her mother, who were 'People of the Earth' (Pagans).

Shipton was always protected by her newly adopted family, but it was hard to stop the gossip of the villagers who believed that she was the spawn of the Devil. Many villagers spoke of strange sounds and large thunderous noises that came from the cave where the child constantly played. Those that passed too close to the Cave always spoke of the pungent odor of sulfur and brimstone (the devil's tools), such an exaggeration. As Shipton grew, people became aware of her gifts and also her gentleness and caring compassionate nature for others. She grew into being the Sage of the nearing villages, where people would come for miles to seek her abilities as an Oracle (a Seer) and Herbalist, also requiring her healing techniques and to ask for certain spells to be done. She was a gifted Seer and the Witch of the village and became famous for her accurate predictions which included the Great Plague of London, the attack of the Spanish Armada and the Great Fire of London. Shipton became so popular that she feared the talk of being a Witch and so in the town square where they held a large festival celebration with a Bale fire, she placed her wooden staff erect in the fire and when the villagers saw that the flames had no effect on it, said to all: "Look and see that if this has not burned, then know that I too will not be burnt."

People feared but also respected her for the great and varied knowledge that she held, and even though her reputation as the Village Witch grew as she aged, a carpenter from York named Toby Shipton fell in love with her gentle ways and they were married in 1512 (gossip spread that she had used Magic and a love-potion to lure him because of his good looks). They never had children and remained together in quite a comfortable manner due to the many visitors that required her knowledge and Magic, and for her services she was comfortably rewarded.

Although motherless she eventually became the Mother of the People, and she was called Mother Shipton, like the ancient Witches of old they were the Mother of the People although having no children of their own. Her Magical powers and abilities to foresee future events as an Oracle and acclaimed Witch spread to all the neighboring towns and she became immensely popular with people travelling for many miles just to have an audience with Mother Shipton. At first her visions and prophecies were local but in time she grew too ambitious with her Oracles and prophecies including the whole country, even to figures of the court of Henry VIII. Mother Shipton also predicted that Cardinal Wolsey (known in the far north as a Mitred Peacock) would on his way to see York, never actually reach it, and in the year of 1550, after he fell out of favour with the king, Wolsey set out to find refuge and was nearing York when a messenger Lord Percy, arrived with a Royal Summons demanding that he return to London to face charges of high treason.

Mother Shipton had some famous prophecies as an Oracle foretelling of the execution of Mary, Queen of Scots, the accession of Lady Jane Grey, Drakes defeat of the Spanish Armada, the Great Plague of 1665, and her most famous was of the Great Fire of London of 1666. Mother Shipton was a learned woman and wrote many of her prophecies in rhyme and in poetry, which was a thing that many Witches of the time did. In these mystical verses she foretold of great iron ships that would travel the world, motorized vehicles that would transport people across the land faster than horses or carriages, she also foresaw submarines, flying machines and communication devices that connected people all around the world.

There have been many false prophecies that were written by other people, and not by Mother Shipton, these I do not mention due to their fraudulent deceptions of lowly people pretending to have known Mother Shipton. There was a published book edited and (written) by Richard Head in 1684 which was supposedly written by Mother Shipton, but later it was revealed that he invented her prophecies and falsified it, as many of her prophecies were false and not by her but by others looking for fame. Mother Shipton died at the hands of the Inquisition and was hanged in the year of 1561 and was said to be buried in non-consecrated ground on the outskirts of York, at Clifton. Mother Shipton shall forever be remembered throughout history as one of England's greatest Wicches, Oracles and Prophetesses who only helped people that sought out her skills.

Mother Shipton's Cave

Cornelius Agrippa
Arch Magician, Occultist & Alchemist
September 14th 1986-February 2nd, 1535

Medieval Sketch of Cornelius Agrippa

Born Heinrich Cornelius Agrippa von Nettesheim, in Cologne. At the mere age of 13 he was so advanced intellectually that he matriculated at the University of Cologne in 1499 and graduated in 1502. Between 1502 -1507 and 1511-1518 he received degrees in medicine, Canon and Civil law. Agrippa connected with the school of Albertus Magnus at Cologne where he pursued his interest in Natural Philosophy and Natural History of Pliny the Elder. Eventually just taking the name Cornelius Agrippa. During his life the cultural crisis was ongoing in the Renaissance, and with his comprehensive fascination and study throughout his life of Magic, Witchcraft and all the Occult Arts. Wrote in his three books on Occult Philosophy called "De Occulta Philosophia libri tres" in 1510, but then decided to rework his writings in 1530.

Agrippa was well known and respected by many as the Archimagus (Arch Magus). His personal mission was to overturn many sciences and prove the relevance of Magic as a Natural and

True Science. He continually wrote as two separate entities each debating the pros and cons of all sciences whether mystical or natural. He was excellent at debating with his lower mortal self and his higher self, something that we should all do even in this day and age. All of Agrippa's writings are clearly defined in a broad philosophical, religious, and moral standing of the social significance of the learning of his era. His personal mission was to prove "True Magic" in the fields of Neoplatonic metaphysics, Witchcraft and Hermetic theology of Tehuti Thoth, and tried to offer mankind a wonder of knowledge to restore human cognitive and practical capabilities.

He wrote in such a manner that he wanted his reader to search through his writings and find and be awakened by the hidden meanings underlying the writing and erratic juxtapositions of his works. This allows the reader to open their inner and higher mind enough to see the invisible within the visible and allow his true inner esoteric meaning to reveal themselves to the worthy reader. His method, his exceptional knowledge in a disguised manner, which was typical of the traditions of the time, was so important for many of the Renaissance intellectuals by merging the two sciences, the intellectual side of learning with the Arts of Magic.

Agrippa, with his interest in ancient wisdom established a secret society called "Sodalitium", which was a secret Magic Circle and Initiatory Brotherhood which attracted many famous and infamous people from all over Europe. He honored women, especially high-ranking women such as Princess Margaret of Austria and Burgundy, daughter of Emperor Maximilian as the figurehead of strong women. He praised all women and dedicated his works to Princess Margaret.

Agrippa taught much about the Judaic Kabbala which attracted much interest from local professors, academics, and teachers at the university and also of the local parliament. He came to join the "Collegium" of theologians, where he tried to espouse his teachings, but many saw it as nothing more than a darker side of the Kabbala, especially being in Christian schools. He was actually denounced publicly as a "Judaising Heretic" by the Franciscan monk Jean Catilinet who was the provincial superior for the whole of Burgundy, where he preached in the presence of Princess Margaret at the court of Low Countries in Ghent. This charge put an end to his public teaching and speaking career and ruined his hopes of eventually obtaining Margaret's favour.

Agrippa in 1509 returned to Germany, and met with the Abbot of Sponheim, Johannes Trithemius at the monastery of St. Jacob and after spending nearly a week of intense discussion and sharing the interest of "Natural Magic" and its important role in contemporary present-day culture. This meeting greatly impacted Agrippa where he finished his compendium on Magic titled De Occulta Philosophia and was dedicated to Abbot Trithemius commitment, who received a copy of the manuscript and praised him for his great work. In the following years Agrippa was in Metz 1518-1520 as the city orator and advocate, in Geneva 1521-1523 he practiced medicine and finally in Frieburg until 1524 as the city physician. He kept on with his writings and teaching of his philosophies and built his reputation as an Occult Philosopher, he became highly respected by scholars from all works of life.

Due to this public attention he drew to him the religious authorities of the Inquisition and was arrested and accused of heresy at Lefevre by three monks. His defense was strongly sarcastic, Lefevre d'Etaples, became so anxious to the promise of becoming Agrippa's ally. Agrippa as an attorney defended many women and saved them from their fate of torture and death thanks to his powerful allies and friendships with the great families of the known world.

Agrippa in the spring of 1524 was offered a position as healer and physician to the Queen Mother of Louise of Savoy. But his outspoken ways eventually alienated him from the court and his position became less favorable. Where he was stripped of his pension and forbidden to leave France. Eventually he was allowed to leave France, and he accepted the office as the Imperial Historiographer at the court of Princess Margaret of Austria, as governor of the Low Countries, in Antwerp. It was here that he dedicated his life to the publishing of all his writings, and it was in Antwerp by Michael Hillenius in 1529, and in 1530 by Johannes Graphaeus, another printer. After his many writings and travels speaking on behalf of his Occult Philosophies, he decided to return back to France in 1535 where he was arrested on the order of Francois 1. Shortly after his release thanks to his friends in high places, he went to live in Grenoble where he died in 1536 of consumption.

Works by Agrippa

- *Opera*, 2 *volumes, Lyon, per Beringos Fratres*, (n.d.). (The imprint of this edition is false since the Bering firm had ceased publishing several decades prior. Zambelli (1972: 149–50) suggested attributing it to the publisher Tommaso Guarino of Basel in 1580]. Repr. Hildesheim-New York: Olms, 1970.
- *Apologia Adversus Calumnias Propter Declamationem De Vanitate Scientiarum et Excellentia Verbi Dei, Sibi per Aliquos Lovanienses Theologos Intentatas. Querela Super Calunnia ob Eeandem Declamationem per Aliquos Sceleratissimos Sycophantas Apud Caesaream Maiestatem Nefarie ac Proditorie Illata*, 1533.
- *De Arte Chemica (On Alchemy)*, edited by Sylvain Matton, with a Seventeenth-Century English Translation, Paris and Milan: S.É.H.A and Arché, 2014.
- *De Beatissimae Annae Monogamia, Ac Unico Puerperio Propositiones Abbreviatae Et Articulatae Iuxta Disceptationem Iacobi Fabri Stapulensis In Libro De Tribus Et Una ... Defensio Propositionum Praenarratarum Contra Quendam Dominicastrum Earundem Impugnatorem ... Quaedam Epistolae Super Eadem Materia Atque Super Lite Contra Eiusdem Ordinis Haereticorum Magistro Habita*, 1534.
- *De Incertitudine et Vanitate Scientiarum et Artium Atque de Excellentia Verbi Dei Declamatio Invectiva*, [Antwerp, 1530], in Opera, II, pp. 1–314.
- *De nobilitate Et Praecellentia Foeminei Sexus*, edited by Roland Antonioli and Charles Béné, translated by Odette Sauvage, Geneva: Droz, 1990.

- *De occulta Philosophia Libri Tres*, Cologne, 1533. Photomechanical reprint, edited by Karl Anton Nowotny, Graz: Akademish Druck- und Verlagsanstalt, 1967.
- *De occulta Philosophia Libri Tres*, edited by Vittoria Perrone Compagni, Leiden and Cologne: Brill, 1992.
- *De originali Peccato Declamatio*, in Opera, II, pp. 550–65.
- *De sacramento Matrimonii*, in Opera, II, pp. 536–49.
- *De Triplici Ratione Cognoscendi Deum*, edited and translated by Vittoria Perrone Compagni, Ermetismo e cristianesimo in Agrippa. Il "De triplici ratione cognoscendi Deum", Florence: Polistampa, 2005.
- *Dehortatio Gentilis Theologiae*, in Opera, II, pp. 482–91.
- *Dialogus De Homine*, edited by Paola Zambelli, Rinascimento, II s., 5 (1965), App. I, pp. 295–304.
- *Dialogus de Vanitate Scientiarum Et Ruina Christianae Relligionis*, edited by Paola Zambelli, Rinascimento, II s., 5 (1965), pp. 249–94.
- *Expostulatio Super Expositione Sua In Librum De Verbo Mirifico Cum Ioanne Catilineti*, in Opera, II, pp. 492–98.
- *In Artem Brevem Raymundi Lullii Commentaria*, in Opera, II, pp. 315–451.

Agnes Waterhouse
Mother Waterhouse - Witch Elder
1503-July 29th, 1566

Medieval Sketch Agnes Waterhouse

Agnes Waterhouse was affectionately known as 'Mother Waterhouse' (the title Mother was given to all Witch High Priestesses and Elders of the time and has now just made a resurgence) and was the first woman publicly accused and executed of Witchcraft in England. Agnes along with two others, her daughter, and a friend (Elizabeth Francis and Joan Waterhouse) all belonged to the same village, Hatfield Peverel. After much torture Agnes confessed to being a Witch and that her familiar was a cat (which she later turned into a toad) that she called Satan (words of the Inquisitors not hers). This creature originally belonged to Elizabeth to cause illness to William Fynne who died on the 1st of November 1565, also for using sorcery to kill a neighbor's livestock, caused further illness to others, and also bringing about the death of her husband.

Waterhouse was accused of several offences using Witchcraft, and Joan her eighteen-year-old daughter was also accused of Witchcraft and luckily not found guilty, it was Joan's testimony that sealed the fate of the other two who were convicted, and it was Agnes who was hanged as England's first executed woman of Witchcraft.

There is a full account of the recordings from the trial of Agnes Waterhouse that was published and written by John Phillips in a pamphlet titled, "The Examination and Confession of Certaine Wytches at Chensforde in the County of Essex before the Quenes Majestes Judges the XXV! Daye of July anno 1566". It was lacking quite a bit but does outline the testimonies of the three accused women.

Mother Waterhouse was loved by many as a great healer and advisor to the community, due to being proficient in herbal medicine where she cared for all the ill, it shows that despite her being called Mother Waterhouse and admired by many that the church was far more fearful and that no-one of the time dared to speak against the church, rather speak ill of a person who was a healer and Sage to her village and to all those that sought for her healing remedies. The strange thing at the time, that many who chose the old ways of herbs and potions were classed as heretics by the then medical fraternity which were all male, as women were not allowed, nor smart enough to learn or know the deep mysteries of healing and medicine. It was the male medical establishment that tried to stamp out all their competition of midwives and herbal healers, and it was the church who joined with them and followed by added the heretical act as adding a bit of flamboyant colour and propaganda.

This trial in Chelmsford was typical of the many trials of English Witchcraft with an abundance of absurd charges always with the mention of a familiar and the marks to suckle her familiar, called the makes of the devil. All who were accused were firstly starved, tortured to confess, had their entire families threatened with death, and then under confession were put to death to save their families.

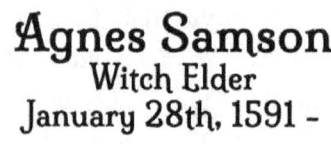

Agnes Samson
Witch Elder
January 28th, 1591 -

Medieval Portrait of Agnes Sampson

Agnes Sampson through town documentation showed that she died on the 28th of January 1591, but there were no known documents that showed her actual birth date. Agnes lived at Nether Keith which was a part of the Scottish Barony of Keith, East Lothian. It was told by most of the townsfolk and surrounding towns that she had great healing powers and was a midwife, and a natural herbal Apothecarian. She was famously known as the "Wise Wife of Keith" and the "Wicche of Keith".

It was in the spring of 1590 where news of the great Witch hunt of the Inquisition was instituted in Copenhagen, Denmark. Due to the perplexed nature
of the trials on witchcraft and sorcery, but across the pond in England, King James, hearing of these events decided to set up his own tribunal into these matters. It was in 1590 that England, prominently Scotland where the trials were swift and many of the trials were honored by the presence of King James in person who questioned all the accused

heretics personally. His interest increased in time as his faith in Christianity heightened and also increased due to becoming more popular with the people of Christendom. It was during these deep investigations that Sampson who was accused by Gillis Duncan, was arrested along with many others, and questioned about her involvement in the raising of storms. She was arrested, questioned, continually tortured, and resisted for as long as she could but as was stated at her Inquest:

"This aforeaside Agnes Sampson which was the elder Witch, was taken and brought to Haliruid house before the Kings Maiestie and sundry other of the nobility of Scotland, where she was straitly examined, but all the perswasions which the Kings maiestie vsed to her with ye rest of his counsell, might not prouoke or induce her to confesse anything, but stood stiffely in the deniall of all that was laide to her charge: whervpon they caused her to be conueied awaye to prison, there to receiue such torture as hath been lately prouided for witches in that country: and forasmuch as by due examination of witchcraft and witches in Scotland, it hath latelye beene found that the Deuill dooth generallye marke them with a priuie marke, by reason the Witches haue confessed themselues, that the Diuell dooth lick them with his tung in some priuy part of their bodie, before hee dooth receiue them to be his seruants, which marke commonly is giuen them vnder the haire in some part of their bodye, wherby it may not easily be found out or seene, although they be searched: and generally so long as the marke is not seene to those which search them, so long the parties that hath the marke will neuer confesse anything. Therfore by special commaundement this Agnis Sampson had all her haire shauen of, in each parte of her bodie, and her head thrawen with a rope according to the custome of that Countrye, beeing a paine most greeuous, which she continued almost an hower, during which time she would not confesse anything vntill the Diuels marke was found vpon her priuities, then she immediatlye confessed whatsoeuer was demaunded of her, and iustifying those persons aforesaid to be notorious witches."

Also stated:

"Item, the saide Agnis Sampson confessed before the Kings Maiestie sundrye thinges which were so miraculous and strange, as that his Maiestie saide they were all extreame lyars, wherat she answered, she would not wishe his Maiestie to suppose her woords to be false, but rather to beleeue them, in that she would discouer such matter vnto him as his maiestie should not any way doubt off. And therupon taking his Maiestie a little aside, she declared vnto him the verye woordes which passed betweene the Kings Maiestie and his Queene at Vpslo in Norway the first night of their mariage, with their answere eache to other: whereat the Kinges Maiestie wondered greatlye, and swore by the liuing God, that he beleeued that all the Diuels in hell could not haue discouered the same: acknowledging her woords to be most true, and therefore gaue the more credit to the rest which is before declared."

— *News from Scotland*

According to the official account, King James had not been convinced of Sampson's guilt prior to this last confession, but afterwards changed his mind. Sampson was taken to the scaffold on Castlehill, where she was garroted then burnt at the stake. Edinburgh Burgh

Treasurer's accounts itemize the cost of Agnes Sampson's execution, giving the date as the 16th day of January 1591 and the cost as £6 8s 10d. Even today the naked ghost of a shaved and bald Agnes Sampson, after her torments roams Holyrood Palace lands still in contempt of her execution, where she is often seen reaching out to many, and scaring those who she deems a non-believer.

Medieval Sketch of Agnes with the Devil

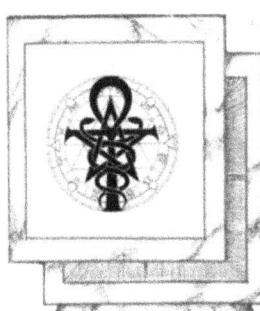

Dr. John Dee
Occultist and Magician
1507-1608

Medieval Portrait of Dr. John Dee Ashmolean

John Dee was born in 1507 in Tower Ward, London, to Rowland Dee of Welsh decent, and Johanna Wild. His father Roland was a mercer and courtier to King Henry VIII, John Dee also claimed to be a descendant of Rhodri the Great, the Prince of Wales and constructed a pedigree showing his descent. John as a child showed he had a superior talent with mathematics, he became an original fellow of Trinity College, Cambridge, on its ceremonial founding by Henry VIII in 1546. Dee travelled extensively and was a great collector of many artefacts and collectables of mathematical and astronomical instruments, he even collected items of great occult significance, which were his private passion. In 1552 on returning to London he met with Gerolamo Cardano and during their time together investigated a perpetual motion machine as well as a Magical gemstone that had specific Magical properties.

Dee eventually became a member of the 'Worshipful Company of Mercers', following his father's footsteps. In that very same year, he was arrested and charged with "calculating" for having cast horoscopes of Queen Mary and these charges were later expanded to treason against Mary. John appeared in the Star Chamber and exonerated himself, although he was freed and found innocent, he was turned over to the Catholic Bishop Bonner for religious examination. Due to his long history of being secretive and his involvement in certain aspects of the occult it seemed to have added much fuel to the fire and his chances of being exonerated were doubtful. His entire life he kept defending himself and always seemed to clear his name, but it became quite repetitious of religion and society to be publicly against John Dee.

Dee was so concerned with ancient artefacts and old manuscripts, books and texts that he presented to Queen Mary with a visionary plan for the preservation of all old writings and artefacts and with hoping for permission and grants to Found the first National Library, but his expensive proposition was denied, so he ventured on his own collection and expanded his own personal library cum museum at his home in Mortlake, where he spent a fortune on acquiring books and manuscripts from all around the known world. He became known as a world collector and became so famous for his undertakings that his center of learning outside of the known universities became the greatest in all England and attracted scholars from all over the world to learn and study and to assist with his collection, many also gifting to him some of their relics and books.

When Queen Elizabeth was crowned in 1558, John became her loyal and trusted advisor on all aspects of the arts including astrological, esoteric, and scientific matters, where he actually through divination of the stars chose her coronation date himself astrologically. John served as an advisor from the 1550s through to the 1570s, where he still continued on his voyages of discovery and provided great knowledge of technical assistance in navigation and ideological backing in the creation of the "British Empire".

Dee claimed to have occult knowledge of a great treasure and of ancient valuable manuscripts in the Welsh Marshes, kept at Wigmore Castle, so he wrote to William Cecil, the 1st Baron Burghley (Lord Treasurer) in October 1574, knowing that William's ancestors came from this area.

John Dee devoted his entire life to the research and study of Alchemy, Divination and Hermetic Philosophy (Tehuti Thoth Philosophy). In this era, he became one of the most learned people in the known world. He spent the last thirty years of his life in the world of Magic and spent his time attempting to commune with the Shining Ones (Angels) in order to learn the Angelic Language as a universal language to bring everyone and everything together, both Heaven and Earth.

Dee believed strongly and prophesized that man was heading down the path of self-destruction and with them would destroy the entire world through religion, ignorance, and industry, (when you look at the world today you can see where man is heading). He felt it was his mission to try to prevent this catastrophe and bring about the re-apocalyptic unity of mankind before it was too late. John believed that all his differing forms of knowledge were all different facets of the same quest, his search for a transcendental understanding of the divine forms which are the invisible within the visible, which Dee called "pure verities".

Shakespeare modelled the character of Prospero in The Tempest on Dee.

Dr. John Dee Works:

- *Monas Hieroglyphica,* 1564
- *Euclid's Elements (Preface to Billingsley's Euclid),* 1570
- *General and Rare Memorials Portraying to the Perfect Arte of Navigation,* 1577.
- *On the Mystical Rule of the Seven Planets,* 1582-1583.

Johannes Weyer
Witch Elder
1515-1588

Medieval Sketch of Johannes Weyer

Johannes Weyer was born in 1515 in a small town called Grave in the Duchy of Brabant in Habsburg, Netherlands. He attended Latin schools from an early age in Hertogenbosch and Leuven and at the early age of 14 then went to live and study with Agrippa the Mage in Antwerp, but in 1532 Agrippa and the young Johannes had to leave Antwerp, and settled together in Bonn, Germany under the protection of Prince-Bishop Hermann von Wied, as some believed they were in a homosexual relationship. (Agrippa completed his work on demons in 1533 and perished two years later when on a trip to France).

From 1534, Weyer studied medicine in Paris and later in New Orleans (which lured him because of the Magic and Mystery of the city). Johannes after much study grew to become an expert in the field of medicine and psychiatry, although he does not seem to have ever received any doctorates or notifications from any Universities. He eventually went back to his hometown Grave, where he was appointed the Town Physician of Arnhem in 1545. His strong belief in Magic and Witchcraft, especially demonology and being a prominent student of Agrippa.

In this recognized position of office, he was asked advice on Witchcraft in a 1548 court case against a fortune teller. He profoundly defended this young lady, and she was saved from the gallows. Johannes in 1550 moved to Cleves where he became the court doctor to Duke William the Rich, through mediation of his good friend humanist Konrad Heresbach.

Weyer published several books on the Occult, Witchcraft, Demonology, and Magic. One of his most intriguing books "Praestigiis Daemonum" written and published in 1563, was a full point-by-point rebuttal of the infamous book of hate known as the Witch hunters "Hammer" handbook, titled the "Malleus Malificarum" written by two Dominican monks Sprenger and Kramer who under authority of the Pope led the Inquisition throughout the entire known world. This incredible book includes interesting and documented reports of Agrippa, Faust, and Trithemius. Sigmund Freud says that this book is one of the ten most significant books of all time.

As an appendix to this incredible and dangerous book, Weyer added a catalogue of demons which he called "Pseudomonarchia daemonum". He referred to his source as "Liber officiorum spirituum, seu Liber dictus Empto, Salomonis, de principibus and regibus daemoniroum" (Book of the offices of spirits, called "Empto". 'Salomonus' is all about the princes and kings of demons), which includes the many names of demons, showing evidence that it was much older than the time of Johannes and 1563. For a concise and detailed comparative of the two books, "Livre des esperitz" (The Book of Spirits), see Jean-Boudet's "Les who's who demonologiaues de la Renaissance et leurs ancetres medievaux". Where Boudet includes a detailed comparison, and in fact adds a lot of what Johannes Weyer's Book lacked and was missing.

He eventually retired from medical practice in 1578 and was succeeded by his son, Galenus Weyer. After his full retirement he completed a massive medical grimoire on a subject unrelated to Witchcraft. He died on the 24th of February 1588 at the grand old age of 73 in Teckleburg, He was buried in his hometown in the local churchyard, which sadly no longer exists today. All church buildings, and tombstones from the graveyard have been removed but the bodies still remain underground with no markings at all.

Weyer's works include medical and moral works as well as his more famous critiques of Magic and Witchcraft:

- *De Praestigiis Daemonum et Incantationbus ac Venificiis (On the illusions of the demons and on Spells and Poisons),* 1563.
- *Pseudomonarchia Daemonum (The False Kingdom of the Demons),* an appendix to *De Praestigiis Daemonum,* 1577.

- *Medicarum Observationum Rararum Liber* (A book of medical observations on rare, hitherto undescribed diseases), 1567, translated into German as *Artzney-Buch Von Etlichen Biß Anher Unbekandten Unnd Unbeschriebenen Kranckheiten*, 1580
- *De Lamiis Liber Item De Commentitiis Jejuniis*, (A book on witches together with a treatise on false fasting),1577, translated into German as *De Lamiis, Das Ist: Von Teuffelsgespenst Zauberern Und Gifftbereytern, Kurtzer Doch Gründtlicher Bericht*, 1586
- *De Ira Morbo*, (On the disease of anger)1577., translated into German as *Vom Zorn, Iracundiae Antidotum: Buch. Von Der Gefehrlichen Kranckheit Dem Zorn, Und Desselbigen Philosophischer, Und Theologischer Cur Oder Ertzney*, 1585
- *De Scorbuto Epitome*, (On scurvy), 1564
- *Histoire Disputes Et Discours Des Illusions Et Diables, Des Magiciens Infame, Sorcieres Et Empoisonneurs: Des Ensorcelez Et Demoniaques Et De La Guerison D'Iceux: Item De La Punition Que Meritent Les Magiciens Les Empoisonneurs Et Les Sorcieres*, 1579. 1885 translation printed aux Bureaux du Progres Medical, Paris France. Two volume set.

"About 40 people at Casale in Western Lombardy smeared the bolts of the town gates with an ointment to spread the plague. Those who touched the gates where infected and many died. The heirs of the dead and diseased had actually paid people at Casale to smear the gates in order to obtain their inheritances more quickly." – From The Deceptions of Demons, 1583.

Weyer was one of the first to outwardly criticize the Malleus Malificarum and the Witch hunting trials by the Catholics and also the Civil authorities; he was the first person to use the term "mentally ill" or melancholy to designate those who had been falsely accused of Witchcraft. Today in a place of pride the Church of Tecklenburg displays a plaque in memory of Weyer, and in 1884 erected a tower in his honor, the Wierturm. The Dutch Human Rights organisation for health workers is named also after him. Also, alongside his mentor, Heinrich Cornelius Agrippa, he now appears as a character in the modern video game Amnesia, The Dark Descent.

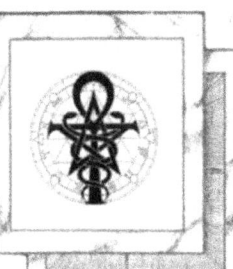

Sir Edward Kelley (Talbot)
Witch & Magician
August 1st, 1555-November 1st, 1597

Medieval Sketch of Edward Kelley

Edward Kelley was born on the 1st of August 1555. His life and adventures of his early life was very secretive, but his claim was that he was a descendent from a family of Ui Maine in Ireland, which is one of the oldest and largest kingdoms in Ireland. According to Dr. John Dee who did his horoscope charts and kept the notes that Dee had in his personal almanac. Edward never spoke of his life prior to Dee but it is assumed that he may have studied under the name of Talbot at Oxford University, he was quite proficient and highly educated in Latin and some Greek.

There are records that Kelley had served sentence for counterfeiting and forgery in the town pillory and was whipped publicly in Lancaster Square. He had both his ears cropped (a common punishment during the Tudor Dynasty). John Weever says, "Kelly (otherwise called Talbot) that famous English alchemist of our times, who flying out of his own country (after he had lost both his ears at Lancaster) was entertained with Rudolf the Second, and last of that Christian name, Emperor of Germany."

In many writings he first worked as an apprentice Apothecary. Eventually he along with Dee were renown as Alchemist's changing lead into gold, conversing with The Shining Ones (Angels), he loved married women, especially the display of wife swapping as a past time.

Kelley was a very colorful and outspoken character during the English renaissance where his knowledge and high claims as a Master Alchemist, where he could turn base metals into gold. He was also an Occultist and self-declared spirit medium, who worked with John Dee as Spiritual and Magical Investigators. Together they travelled, being highly paid for the summoning of spirits and angels for all who asked, and their fees were remarkably high.

Dee had for years prior to meeting Kelley, been trying to commune with the Shining Ones but was not successful even after employing dozens of mediums, scryers and crystal gazers, who all seemed to be frauds. It was Kelley who proclaimed that he had the knowledge and skill in making this contact, and in their first meeting in 1582 impressed Dee with only his first psychic trial. Kelley became Dee's official scryer and together they spent many years focusing their time and energy into these 'spiritual conferences', "Seances", and included many Prayers for Enlightenment. Luckily for Kelley from 1582 – 1589 his life and bond was closely tied between himself and Dee. It was Dee's mission in life to connect the ecumenical knowledge of alchemy and angelic contact that would heal the diversified and immense rift of Christendom.

Kelley eventually married a widow, Jane Cooper of Chipping Norton. He never had children to her but accepted her children as his own and was always classed as an exceedingly kind and gentle stepfather to them. Kelley due to loving the Latin language hired a tutor for her to learn the language so they could communicate with each other in Latin, and she could assist him in his writings.

Dee was acquainted with Prince Albert Laski, who was a Polish nobleman who was interested in alchemy. In September of 1583, Dee, Kelley and Lasky with their families left England for Europe where Dee sought the patronage of Emperor Rudolf II in Prague and also King Stefan of Poland in Krakow, but he failed to impress either of the monarch's. Dee and Kelley lived a very nomadic life travelling central Europe, never staying in one place awfully long. Together they continued their spiritual pursuit of the angelic communications, but Kelley was far more interested in alchemy than just mere scrying.

Together they did find a mutual interest in necromancy (the awakening of the dead), which caught the attention of the Catholic Church and on 27th March 1587, they were summoned to the Vatican and forced to defend themselves before the hearing of the papal nuncio, Germanico Malaspina, the Bishop of San Severo. Dee responded the interview with elegance and tact, but Kelley always on the defensive, infuriated the nuncio by arguing that one of the main problems with the Catholic Church was "the poor conduct of many of the priests". In a letter by the nuncio, he stated that he attempted to throw Kelley out of the window. Thanks to Dee they were both freed by arguing that they were investigating death as with the true faith of Christ in mind.

Due to finding the patronage of Count Vilem Roznberk, also known as Lord Rosenberg, who was wealthy beyond most, rose from an extremely wealthy family. He too had an interest in alchemy and spent a king's fortune trying to acquire the means of turning a base metal into gold. But he never did quite perfect this. By 1590, Kelley was living such an extravagant life where he had received several estates and large sums of money from Rozmberk. On these immense estates that Kelley acquired he was able to access some silver and gold mines, of which he took advantage of, and still working on his alchemy until certain noblemen thought that he actually was able to produce gold through alchemy.

King Rudolph II knighted him on the 23rd of February 1590 as Sir Edward Kelley of Imany and New Luben. King Rudolph later had Kelley arrested in May 1591, and he was imprisoned in the Krivoklat Castle just outside of Prague. He was accused of killing an official named Jiri Hunkler in a duel, but many believe that it was due to the fact that the king did not want him to leave with all his knowledge of alchemical secrets. Because at the time Queen Elizabeth I was trying to convince him to return back to England. Rudolph was a strong believer in Kelley's ability to turn base metal into gold, eventually he was released and restored to his former status.

Kelley again failed to produce gold for the King, which he had promised he could, eventually he was again imprisoned, but this time in Hnevin Castle in Most. Kelley's wife and stepdaughter attempted several times to have him released by means of an imperial counsellor, but sadly Kelley died as a prisoner in late 1597 through injuries that he had received whilst trying to escape the prison castle.

Kelley's Writings:
- *Tractatus Duo Egregii De Lepide Philosophorum Una Cum Theatre Astronomiae*, 1676.
- *The Alchemical Writings of Edward Kelley*, 1893.

Kelly believed that all angels communicated in a sacred language known as Enochian, and both Dee and Kelley claimed the language was given to them by Angels. Some believe that Kelley invented it, see for example the introduction to "The Complete Enochian Dictionary" by Donald Laycock.

Catherine Mon Voisin
Witch
1640-1680

Medieval Sketch of Catherine Mon Voisin

Born Catherine Deshayes in 1640, who as a young lady married Antoine Mon Voisin, a jeweler with an established jewelry shop in central Paris, but due to his lack of business knowledge and skill he ended up becoming bankrupt, this is when the well-educated Catherine shined the brightest and she decided to handle the family affairs on her own. Catherine had much basic knowledge also of natural medicine and was well renown as a midwife and provided many women with abortions, more well-known were her abilities as a Seer, Clairvoyant, and a gifted fortune teller. Mon Voison's spiritual gifts eventually led her to becoming one of the most wanted and yearned for mystical and Magical people in the second half of the 17th century in Paris. Someone that was being watched very closely by many, especially the Roman Catholic Church.

Mon Voison's special gifts made her a very wealthy and a powerful woman which influenced the known world of the occult and Magic, and later in the court of King Louis XIV, the famous king whose golden palace brought him immortal fame and countless concubines. Mon Voison became one of his lovers and this led to a dark scandal at the court where she became involved with intrigue and mistrust. Because of her psychic gifts and power, she became admired by everyone as she claimed her abilities were a gift from God, she went on to claim that she received these gifts when she was nine years of age.

In her young adult years, she loved to study and learn and through her fascination with spirituality and Magic she learned about physiology, anatomy and used her medical knowledge to read people's faces and hands to foretell the future of the person enquiring. Catherine had achieved a great fortune and enough monetary success that she created a special spiritual sanctuary as her workplace for her fortune telling. She also spent a king's ransom on her appearance, with the finest of clothes that were embroidered with the finest gold and silver throughout her garments. As her image increased so did her clientele, throughout the nobles and the courts of kings and queens throughout Europe.

It was in the year of 1665 that she attracted the attention of a priest of Saint Vincent de Paul's order and the Congregation of the Mission who questioned her abilities as being a gift from God and instead believed they were gifted to her from the devil. When facing the professors and priesthood at Sorbonne University, she gracefully explained how her gifts worked. Because of her eloquence and detailed explanation, she was freed. This then gave her license to be grander and more theatrical and so made her rituals and ceremonies more lavish by even adding a theatrical "Black Mass" to her set of skills, where she herself used in the theatre a living altar (Madame de Montespan) for the spirits who were worshipped. This ritual was performed by both Catherine and the priest Etienne Guibourg who performed this mass for the mistress of King Louis XIV of France, Madame de Montespan.

Medieval Sketch of Catherine & Priest Performing Ritual

Some of her clients were: François Henri de Montmorency-Bouteville, (the Duc de Luxembourg), Françoise-Athénad's de Rochechouart Montespan, (the Marquise de Montespan and king's mistress), Olympe Mancini (the Comtesse de Soissons), her sister Marie Anne Mancini (the Duchesse de Bouillon), and the Comtesse de Gramont (known as "La Belle Hamilton"). Having such a grand clientele helped her immensely in surviving more oppressions and much criticism, but when she became part of an affair as one of the greatest scandals in the life of King Louis XIV her life changed drastically and put her life in danger.

Mon Voison had become remarkably close to Madame de Montespan who asked her to perform many black masses as she was seeking greater power and influence from the king through Satan. These masses were performed in a house on Rue de a Tanniere. During one of these meetings Montespan received a special potion and aphrodisiac which was to be given to the king. Montespan was so jealous of the king and his many affairs, that she wanted him 100% or not at all and kept asking for poisons from Mon Voisin. It was getting worse when the king became infatuated with the young Angelique de Fontanges in 1679, Montespan asked Mon Voisin for a poison to kill the lovers, she refused many times, but it seems that eventually she was talked into it. The poison was made, and the plan set, but the plan failed as the target of the poison hit Louis' sister-in-law the Duchess d'Orleans instead, and also several others at the same time.

Mon Voisin was accused and arrested of these crimes as a poisoner. During her many hours of torture, she never gave the names of clientele nor spoke of the people who attended her rituals and ceremonies. Montespan was not connected to the poison as she was a trusted concubine of the king. But at a later time, evidence was presented by Mon Voisin's daughter, Marguerite, that proved Montespan was a part of the poisoning, which at first the king did not believe her and as Louis wrote in his letter to la Reynie in Lile, on August 2nd, 1680:

"'Having seen the declarations of Marguerite Monvoisin, prisoner in my Chateau of Vincennes, made on the 12th of last month, and the examination to which you subjected her on the 26th of the same month, I write you this letter to inform you that my intention is that you should devote all possible care to elucidate the facts contained in the said declarations and examinations; that you should remember to have written down in separate memorials the answers, confrontations, and everything concerning the report that may hereafter be made on the said declarations and examinations (to the judges), and that meanwhile you defer reporting to my royal Chamber, sitting at the Arsenal, the depositions of Romani and Bertrand until you receive orders from me. Louis."

Mon Voison, after much torture and long trials, was burned at the stake in the heart of Paris at the Place de Greve on the 22nd of February 1680. It was never recorded what happened to her daughter. As for Montespan she was never charged for the crime and died as a 65-year-old woman in May 1707.

Maret Jonsdotter (Big Maret)
Witch
1644-1672

Medieval Sketch Maret Jonsdotter

Maret Jonsdotter (also see Jansdotter) was born in 1644 in Sweden and was the first person in Sweden accused of Witchcraft, to this day she was the most famous of the Swedish Witches that was persecuted in that country of sorcery in the great Witch hysteria called "Det Stora Ovasendet" (The Great Noise) of 1668-1676, and it was her trial that unleashed the beginning of the atrocities of the witch hunt in Sweden, due to the monies that could be made, which eventually accused, tortured and murdered 283 people in those eight years and made many people very rich.

She was known as "Big Maret" as she had a younger sister with the same name as hers and she was called "Little Maret". There was no proof that she was ever involved in Magic and Witchcraft, but in the autumn of 1667 a local young shepherd boy, Mats Nilsson in the town of Alvdalen in Dalama claimed that he saw a girl lead his goats over Eastern Dalalven by walking on water at Hemmansang by Asen. The silly boy had tended the family's herd of sheep with this same girl for years, and they had a fight where she had beaten him up. Gertrud Svensdotter (meaning daughter of Sven) was only twelve years old.

So as to not lose face with his family he had told them that Gertrud had done these things assisted by the devil. Gertrud was then arrested and interrogated by the local priest, Lars Elvius, who encouraged her to say that she did indeed walk on water, and that she had done so by the use of Magic, which had been gifted to her by the devil. After much discussion with the priest, Gertrud was instructed to change her story to protect herself and so said that she lived with her parents in Lillhardal in Harjedalen, where a neighbor's maid had taken her to meet with the devil, this maid was Maret Jonsdotter. With the priest's instruction Gertrud made a detailed confession she claimed that, in 1663, when she was eight, Märet had taken her on a walk. They had passed a sandpit, and then came to a three-way crossroads, where Märet had cried out: "Thou Devil, come forward!" She claimed that Satan had then appeared in the shape of a vicar. They dined, and the following night, Märet had come to Gertrud and smeared her body and one of her father's cows with a red oil, after which they had flown away through the chimney and all the way to Satan.

Since then, the shepherd boy came forward and confessed that he had a vision in the woods where he was suddenly sucked up into the sky and looking down saw Gertrud sit in Blockula with several children that she had taken (children that had gone missing in the area) among them was his little sister, during this he also heard the voices of an angel and a devil discussing how many children and people they in their respective kingdoms, and it was Gertrud who took many to them. He only testified to this once and was given full praise by the priest and the community for revealing this whole evil affair.

This was the commencement of the famous witch trials known as the "More Witch Trials" where Märet Jonsdotter was the first casualty and victim amongst seven other victims that Gertrud had pointed out as witches, all this commenced in September 1668. Due to immense fear at the time even her younger sister pointed the finger at her claiming that she had made her ride backwards on a cow where her name had been written in a large book of the devil, even her younger brothers Oluf and Joen confessed the same things about their sister Märet.

Widow Karin, however, was released. Of the many people who were put on trial for sorcery in Härjedalen in 1668–72, seven people were executed. Gertrud Svensdotter was to witness the execution of the condemned in Mora on 19 May 1669. In 1670, she was called upon by the priest to recall her story for his guest in the vicarage. She married in 1673 to Lars Mattson (21), another of the witnesses of the witch trial. She died of unknown causes in 1675, buried one week after having given birth to a son, who also died.

The witch hysteria continued to rage throughout Sweden until the execution of Malin Matsdotter in Stockholm in 1676. In 1677, to avoid any further witch trials, the government ordered the priests to declare, through the churches, that all witches had now been expelled from the country forever.

Isobel Gowdie
Faery Witch Queen
-1662

Medieval Portrait of Isobel Gowdie

Isobel Gowdie (birthdate not known) is renowned as being the "Queen of Witches". Actually, she was known as the Faerie Queen of the Wicches. Gowdie was noticeably young as a housewife when she was tried for acts of witchcraft. The detailed confession was given without any form of torture at all. She openly spoke of her involvement with Witchcraft for at least fifteen years. In fact, her detailed confession takes one deeper into the folklore of Witchcraft at the time, of which the European and British witch-hunts and persecutions were nearing their end.

During her confessions she named her supposed coven of Witches including Janet Breadheid and Katherine Sowter, who were also tried alongside herself. Isobel openly spoke of flying to her sabbath meetings and how she had encountered the Horned God, but the court recorder changed the words from Horned God to devil as instructed at a church in Auldeame, and in a ceremony renounced her Christian baptism and faith and was baptized with her own blood which left the mark of the Horned God on her right shoulder, (a birthmark).

Isobel was imprisoned for a period of six weeks and with many confessions she claimed so many absurdities, even stating that if she passed by Christians, she would kill them unless they blessed themselves to keep them safe. Gowdie always spoke of being entertained by the King and Queen of the Faeries, which was in the sacred land of Elphane, the land of the elves "Under the hills". She claimed that it was the Faeries that taught her their Magic, not the devil, they also taught her how to climb corn straws where she chanted "Horse and Hattock, in the Lord's name". She also had the Magical ability to change into different animals of her choosing as a shapeshifter, how to change the weather and whip up storms and strong winds.

The only official records were of her arrest, imprisonment, and confessions, but never anything about her being executed. But it was her trial that eventually became the new wave of persecutions in Scotland during the reign of King Charles II from 1660-1685, and it always confirmed that Witchcraft was a post-Christian satanic cult instead of the true aspect of it being a surviving ancient religion of Nature and the Goddess of pre-Christian Europe that did not believe in the devil of the Christian pantheon. It was this widespread religion with no name that the Catholic authorities had been attempting to stamp out as evil since the end of the 15th century. It was these poor young girls' confessions that have survived through history and used in several novels, poems, and sonnets, even put into a symphony by Scottish composer James MacMillan.

Moll (Mary) Dyer
Witch
-1697

The Rock Moll Dyer Was Frozen to Death on

Mary Dyer, well known as Moll Dyer, as Moll is another term for Mary, she is a well-documented and quite a 17th century legend in Leornardtown, Maryland where she lived. Not a great deal is known about her early years, but she became quite famous in her later years when she was accused of Witchcraft and was chased out of her home by a raging mob of townsfolk in the winter months. She was so terrified she just kept running, and sadly her partially frozen body was found a few days later, as she had been frozen solid to a large rock (as pictured above, as there is no known image of her).

Many still believe that the land surrounding her cabin home is still haunted by the lost and wandering spirit of Moll Dyer, many of the townsfolk avoid this area of the land still believing that Mary had cursed the land, where even today crops will not grow, and it is documented as a place where there is a highly unusual number of lightning strikes. There was a reported sighting of a hunter whilst hunting along the Moll Dyer's Run around 1970 where he noticed an extraordinarily rich and dense fog patch that was cylindrical in shape, which had light emanating about a foot down from the top. This light crossed the stream eastward and moved across the wind instead of with the flow of the wind, then suddenly turned and went south. He believes that this was the spirit of Moll Dyer.

It is hard to know all the documented cases of this region as this story has survived where the archives of the local courthouse have not, due to a fire that destroyed the courthouse and archives in 1831, where everything was lost. The only evidence that still exists is:

- Immigration records show that Mary (Moll) Dyer and Malligo Dyer were transported to Maryland in October 1677 on a ship commanded by Captain Thomas Taylor.
- A great epidemic occurred in Southern Maryland from 1697-1698.
- On the 18th of August 1892 edition of St. Mary's Beacon (Edition 604, Volume LII), Joseph F. Morgan wrote that Moll lived in the area for many years and that her cottage was burnt to the ground whilst "Cotton Mather held sway in the land of Puritans". Mather was born in 1663 and died in 1728. This story has been reprinted in the "Chronicles of St. Mary's", which is available from the St. Mary's County Historical Society.
- There were several trials of witchcraft in Maryland which started in 1654 and continued up until 1712. There was a Rebecca Fowler of a neighboring Calvert County who was hanged as a witch on the 9th of October 1685 (Maryland Historical Magazine XXXL p. 271-298).

The Washington Times has called her "perhaps Maryland's best-known bit of witch-lore". According to legend as stated above Moll Dyer was found near frozen to a large boulder that she rested against as she died, which left indentations of both her hands and knees in the boulder. In 1972, this 875-pound boulder was lifted and moved from the woodland ravine near Moll Dyer Road to the Leonardtown Courthouse lawn in front of the old 1876 jailhouse, which now serves as the St. Mary's County Historical Society building. The rock remains there to this day as a sign of their local legend, also believing that it was cursed by Moll Dyer to anyone who neared it, and many have experienced dizziness and sometimes fainting.

Thomas Jarboe in 1994 conducted a series of interviews with locals including her descendants of the Dyer family. According to their truth Moll Dyer is said to have come from Ireland, Virginia, Kentucky, New England or Connecticut and lived in the area since the 1600s. She was a widow, who was disappointed in love, and was the mother of two sons. It is believed that she was a Catholic and that she came to Maryland as it was more religiously tolerant than many of the other colonies which were very fanatical of their faith and their ways.

Sir Francis Barrett
Occultist, Kabbalist and Alchemist
1773-1856

Medieval Portrait of Sir Francis Barrett

Barrett was born in 1773. Not a great deal is known of Barrett of his early years, but Barrett's parents being humble folk were married in the parish of St. Martin's in the Fields on the 29th of September 1772 and he was born in the following year of 1773.

Barrett was an Englishman and in later years publicly claimed that he was a devout student of the Arts, metaphysics, chemistry, and the natural occult. Known publicly as an eccentric who gave to any who asked lessons in the Magical Arts in his apartment where he devoutly worked at translating the Holy Kabbala and many other ancient religious or Magical texts into English. His main translation was Philosophy of the Universe circa 1735, from German in 1801. Francis X. King was his biographer who wrote a detailed life and history of Barrett.

Barrett's famous book, which is one of my personal favorites is called "The Magus" where he showed his interest in wanting to revive the interest in all Occult fields. This manuscript was actually a compilation almost entirely of the works of Cornelius Agrippa's Three Books of Occult Philosophy, the Fourth Book of Occult Philosophy, attributed to Agrippa, and also Robert Turners 1655 translation of the Heptameron of Peter of Abano. The book The Magus later influenced Eliphas Levi. The Magus was an in-depth book that covered the areas of Witchcraft and the natural Magic of herbs, stones (crystals), magnetism, talismanic Magic, alchemy, the Elements and numerology, also mentioned biographies of famous Occult adepts throughout history.

This book was a form of advertisement for Barrett to lure the correct interested people into forming and working together in his Magic Circle where he writes in the Magus (Vol. 2, p. 140) refers to an unknown Occult school which was Founded by Barrett.

According to the advertisement:

"The Author of this Work respectfully informs those that are curious in the studies of Art and Nature, especially of Natural and Occult Philosophy, Chemistry, Astrology, etc., etc., that, having been indefatigable in his researches in those sublime Sciences; of which he has treated at large in this book, that he gives private instructions and lectures upon any of the above-mentioned Sciences; in the course of which he will discover many curious and rare experiments.

Those who become Students will be initiated into the choicest operations of Natural Philosophy, Natural Magic, the Cabbala, Chemistry, the Talismanic Arts, Hermetic Philosophy, Astrology, Physiognomy, etc., etc. Likewise, they will acquire the knowledge of the Rites, Mysteries, Ceremonies and Principles of the ancient Philosophers, Magi, Cabbalists, and Adepts, etc.

The Purpose of this school (which will consist of no greater number than Twelve Students) being to investigate the hidden treasures of Nature; to bring the Mind to a contemplation of the Eternal Wisdom; to promote the discovery of whatever may conduce to the perfection of Man; the alleviating the miseries and calamities of this life, both in respect of ourselves and others; the study of morality and religion here, in order to secure to ourselves felicity hereafter; and, finally, the promulgation of whatever may conduce to the general happiness and welfare of mankind."

Barrett stated in his writings that he did not believe that real Witches had the power to torment or kill by enchantment, touch or by using a waxen image that came from Satan. He always claimed that if the Devil wanted to kill guilty men of deadly sin, he did not need an intermediary such as a Witch. He always stated that true Magic came from the higher self and the inner man who always longed for the external in all things.

Joan Whytte
Faery White Witch Elder
1775-1813

Medieval Portrait of Joan Whytte

Ms Joan Whytte was born in Bodmin, Cornwall in 1775, she was one tough little girl and never scared of a fight and throughout her life she was regarded as a brawling scrumpet, always fighting the locals verbally and physically, using foul language, and this got worse as she got older. She was often called the "Fighting Faery Woman" or the "Whytte (White) Witch of Bodmin".

Whytte was famous for her psychic predictions as a clairvoyant, and people came from near and far seeking her divine services as an Oracle, Seer, diviner and also a great healer. The one Magical power she was acclaimed in having was for her healing practices called "Clooties" or (Clouties), which was an ancient form of Traditional Magic using strips of cloth taken from the ill person and they were tied to a tree or a holy well as a form of Sympathetic Magic, such that when the cloth rotted, the disease was believed to have died as well.

Whytte always spoke her mind and feared no-one, she hated deceivers and liars and later in life she was very outspoken and became a very bitter and angry person due to having a rotten tooth abscess that became poisoned and because of the poison going through her bloodstream, it caused her to often rant and rave causing physical and abusive fights where she often exhibited great strength. The locals started believing that she was possessed by the devil. Through her public outbursts she was eventually arrested and jailed in Bodmin Jail for brawling (not for Witchcraft). Sadly, Whytte died in jail of bronchial pneumonia at the age of 38, brought on by her already ill abscess and the toxins sent through her body from the abscess.

Sadly, her bones have been disinterred and have been used ever since for seances and other various uses. Later, her bones were displayed at the Witchcraft Museum in Boscastle, Cornwall. When having her skeleton on display at the museum the staff started to experience a lot of disruptive influence put down as the disruptive poltergeist spirit of Ms Whytte. The museum brought in a reputable and well-known Witch to advise them, where she said that Wytte's spirit wished to be laid to rest properly in a burial ground, and she was removed from the museum and a formal funeral service where Joan Whytte was laid to rest in a peaceful wooded area in Boscastle, and her gravestone reads:

"Joan Whytte Born 1775. Died 1813 in Bodmin jail. Buried 1998. No longer abused".

Joan Whytte's Headstone

Tamsin Blight
The White Witch of Helston
1788-August 16th, 1856

Medieval Painting of Tamsin Blight

Tamsin (Tammy Blee) was born in Cornwall, England and during the end of the 18th century, Thomasine Blight (which is her correct known name) achieved great success and acknowledgement as Britain's most famous Hedge Witch, also as a Conjuror in West Cornwall. Her fame spread wherever she travelled to Redruth and when she was forced out of Redruth she went to Helston and her notoriety escalated there. Her famous abilities and gifts were in the removing of hexes, curses and spells that had been cast on people. This started to make her a good little fortune.

Blight was also a well-known Oracle and Seer and foresaw many events in future history, her claim to fame was also the ability to commune with the spirits and angels through the use of alchemical herbal hallucinogens.

She became a popular conjuror by the time she married James Thomas in 1835, where she was widely acclaimed as a "Cunning woman of the Arts". Together with James until the 1850s they formed an astonishing double act of Magic, where people came from great distances to hear what was on offer. Many of the locals also came to see her for either healing or cursing their livestock, even maidens that were in need of a good husband came for her spells. Blight was an excellent herbalist and a great healer, and her remedies were distributed through all of Britain which became a very viable business, especially as she added her talismans, charms and Spellcraft, which were individually made by her for the querant. The incredible amount of skill and knowledge that she had made her able to help any and all who inquired.

Through her eagerness and openness to help everyone with her gentle soul and good heart she started to draw attention from the Church and became a target for their bigotry.

This stress and worry about the church was too much for their marriage and so James and Tamsin separated when she also discovered that he preferred and had an affair with a man in the neighboring town of St. Ives. He was reported to the local magistrate, and with the fear of being arrested he fled Cornwall, and Blight never saw nor heard from him again.

There is a famous old Cornish folktale which was called "The ghost of Stythians" tells of the tale of Blight where she conjured a spirit in the Stythians Graveyard of an old woman, who recently died, for a male relative of hers who wanted to know where she hid her fortune. This great magical ritual where a charmed Magic Circle was formed around the male relative with a long incantation. Where she summoned the elementals and the spirits. During this ceremony crashing and strange sounds came from the neighboring forest accompanied by moans and groans, where witnesses claimed they were coming from the old woman's grave. They fled in fear and no treasure was ever found (that we know of anyway).

Blight was one of the lucky ones, that she was never targeted by the church authorities, and lived a successful life as a Witch and Conjurer, but mainly as a town Sage who healed with the Magic of herbs and as an Oracle of the Gods. Tamsin died peacefully on the 6th of October 1856.

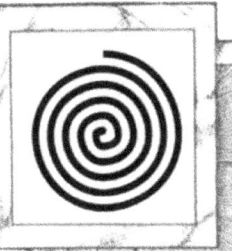

Marie Catherine Laveau
Voodoo Queen of New Orleans
September 10th, 1791 – June 15th, 1881

Portrait of Marie Laveau

Marie Catherine Laveau was born on 10th September 1791 as the illegitimate daughter of Charles Laveau, a wealthy white planter and Marguerite Darcantrel, a negro Creole and free person. It is also believed by some historians that Marie's mother and Grandmother were also voodoo practitioners. There is no other more famous in all of the south and in particular New Orleans, if not the world, even more famous than Andrew Jackson, Jean Lafitte, Huey P. Long and a few others.

Louisiana is well known for its voodoo which arrived in the US on board the slave ships that came from the coast of West Africa. These stolen Pagan people who were People of the Land, were torn away from everything they knew, and took with them the one thing that could not be taken from them, their deep knowledge of their local plants and herbs, their spirits, and the power to heal and to destroy.

When they arrived after a lengthy journey, and not understanding the language, were taken off the ship, christened by the local Christian priest and given a Christian name and told never to use their old pagan names again, they were taught English and the Christian faith do they could toe the line.

This new religion was only a copy of their own belief system but with different names. It was this new religion that they married in with their old Pagan religion along with that old knowledge of Paganism, Naturalism, Spiritualism, herbalism, Magic, and voodoo combined with Christianity. This was also dangerous as at that time all forms of music and dance were signs of the devils work at hand, so when the slaves began their own rituals and ceremonies with drumming, prayer, chanting, animal sacrifices along with dances together they brought about the effects of invoking the spirits for communication and ritual.

Laveau was one of these practitioners and was also highly praised and respected by her community that she eventually chosen by the people became the Queen of Voodoo and the chief practitioner of the whole of New Orleans and the entire South. Laveau was married on the 4th of August 1819 to Jacque Santiago Paris, their lavish ceremony was at the St. Louis Cathedral on Jackson Square, where the service was performed by Father Antonio de Sedella. Marie and Jacque's life together although very loving was short lived whereas Jacque died of an undiagnosed illness one year later. His mysterious death spread gossip throughout the French Quarter of New Orleans where many had presumed that Laveau had caused his death, but there was no evidence to convict her.

After his death Ms Laveau was known as the Widow Paris but focused her attention on taking up as a hairdresser to the wealthy women of New Orleans. This opened the doors for her to hear all the gossip of the elite whites, as well as their servants and slaves who by that time believed Laveau to be the most powerful Voodoo Priestess ever known.

Laveau was a clever person as she knew what it would take to benefit her and her career not only as a hairdresser but also as a High Priestess of Voodoo. Everyone was astounded at how much knowledge she knew about everyone and everything, believing that it was her ability to commune with the spirits that gave her this power of seeing and knowing, little did they know it was the gossip from her clients at her saloon that gave her the fame she needed. Her great abilities and powers spread across the land, not only the slaves, the free persons of colour but also the white communities and wealthy woman in particular.

Fourteen months after the death of her first husband Jacque, Ms Laveau began a relationship with a gentleman known as Louis Christopher Dominick Duminy de Glapion who was known as a hero who fought gallantly against the British in the defense of New Orleans. It was said that the Voodoo Queen of New Orleans had the power to elevate anyone into or out of the high political arena of city hall. Laveau spent much of her time helping the less fortunate as a healer and ministered to the condemned in the prisons, but she was also accused of causing multiple deaths through Voodoo. Especially the deaths of the governor of New Orleans. Those that were game spoke against her as a Witch, but she was too powerfully respected and too loved by the entire community.

Laveau continued her reign as Queen of Voodoo until the early 1870s, when she tired and handed over her reign to her daughter Marie Laveau II, who was wilder and freer than her mother with more daring rituals, until she had an accident and was drowned in 1897 whilst crossing the flooded Lake Pontchartrain.

Marie Catherine Laveau, the Voodoo Queen of New Orleans passed this life on June 15, 1881, three days after her death, the New Orleans Daily Picayune printed this article:

Death of Marie Laveau

"At 5 o'clock yesterday evening Marie Laveau was buried in her family tomb in St. Louis Cemetery No. 1. Her remains were followed to the grave by a large concourse of people, the most prominent and the humblest joining in paying their last respects to the dead.

Fifteen children were the result of her marriage. Only one of these is now alive. Capt. Glapion died greatly registered, on the 26th of June 1855. Five years afterwards, Marie Laveau became ill, and has been sick ever since, her indisposition becoming more pronounced and painful within the last two years.

Besides being unbelievably beautiful Marie also was incredibly wise. She was skilled in the practice of medicine and was acquainted with the valuable healing qualities of the indigenous herbs.

Besides being charitable, Marie was also very pious and took delight in strengthening the allegiance of souls to the church. She would sit with the condemned in their last moments and Endeavor to turn their last thoughts to Jesus. Whenever a prisoner excited her pity Marie would labor incessantly to obtain his pardon, or at least commutation of sentence, and she generally succeeded.

All in all, Marie Laveau was a most wonderful woman. Doing good for the sake of doing good alone, she obtained no reward, oft times meeting with prejudice and loathing, she was nevertheless content and did not lag in her work. She always had the cause of the people at heart and was with them in all things. During the late rebellion she proved her loyalty to the South at every opportunity and fully dispensed help to those who suffered in defense of the "lost cause." Her last days were spent surrounded by sacred pictures and other evidence of religion, and she died with a firm trust in heaven. While God's sunshine plays around the little tomb where her remains are buried, by the side of her second husband, and her sons and daughters, Marie Laveau name will not be forgotten in New Orleans."

On my visit several times to my friend and Witch Sister Velvet Reith, she took me to the tomb of Laveau, and showed me the correct way that Voudoun Priestesses enter the cemetery by walking in backwards stamping your feet three times and praying to the Archangels. And again, when leaving to do the same thing as to not take any spirits with you when you leave.

Marie Laveaus' Tomb in New Orleans Cemetery

Eliphas Levi
Magician, Occultist and Alchemist
February 10th, 1810 – May 31st, 1875

Portrait of Eliphas Levi

Born Alphonse Louis Constant on the 10th of February 1810 to a shoemaker in Paris, Eliphas Levi Zahed became one of Frances, if not Europe's top authors on the occult and Ceremonial Magic. As a young man he entered the seminary of St. Sulpice to study to become a Roman Catholic priest, but just prior to being Ordained he met and fell in love with a young lady and left the seminary to be married in 1836 to Marie-Noemi Cadiot (1882-1888). As a result of him trying to translate his name from Alphonse Louis into the Hebrew language, he ended up with his pseudonym name - Eliphas Levi.

Levi spent many years following along with his socialist friends, which included Henri-Francoise-Alphonse Esquiros and Gerard de nerval, a so-called Petits romantiques and also Theopjile Gautier.

During this period Levi had turned to radical socialism which was inspired by Felicite de Lamennais who the former leader and was the influential and well known Neo-Catholic movement who had broken away with Roma and the Vatican Church to propagate a Christian Socialism. During this time Levi published his first radical writing, La Bible de la Liberte (1841, The Bible of Liberty), which caused him many problems where he was also fined and sentenced to a period of eight months imprisonment.

Levi had many of his books published at this time and like many socialists he propagated socialism as "True Christianity" and denounced the Church as corruptors of the true original teachings of Jesus Christ. He eventually had many influential friends due to his writings next to Esquiros, he was also associated with well-known feminist Flora Trastan, and the eccentric socialistic mystic Simon Ganneau and Charlet Fauvety. Levu created many close toe's to the Fourierist Movement and in the 1940s also published their publications praising Fourierism as the True Christianity.

In December 1851, Napoleon III organized a coup that ended the Second Republic and gave rise to the Second Empire. It was here that Levi saw the emperor as the true defender of the people, and as the restorer of public order. He eventually became disillusioned with their rigid unbending dictatorship, and again was imprisoned in 1855 for publishing a polemical chanson against the emperor. With Constant's attitude toward the people as well with the Saint-Simonians, he had adopted the theocratical ideas of Joseph de Maistre in order to call for the establishment of a spiritual hierarchy and authority to be led by an elite class of priests, who were separate from the Catholic Church.

Levi eventually developed a desire and interest in Magic, and in a specific milieu that was marked by the confluence of socialistic and magnetistic ideas. Authors such as Henri Delaage (1825-1882), and Jean du Potet de Sennevoy who were propagating magnetitic, Magical and Kabbalistic notions as the very base of a superior form of socialism. Levi used this system of magnetism and Dream Magic to critique what he saw as the excesses of philosophical materialism.

Levi commenced in writing.
"*Histoire de la Magic*" (History of Magic) in 1860, and in 1861 he published a sequel to "*Dogme et Rituel, La clef des grands mysteres*" (Dogma of Ritual: The Key to the Great Mysteries).
After visiting London, he had further Magical works in 1861 as "*Fables et Symboles*" (Fables and Symbols), 1862,
"*Le Sorcier de Meudon*" (The Wizard of Meudon), an extended version of two previously published novels in 1847.
"*La Science des Esprits*" (The Science of Spirits) in 1865.
In 1868 he wrote "*Le Grand Arcane, ou L'occultisme Devoile*'", (The Grand Secret, or Occultism Unveiled).

Levi although exceedingly popular and well known whilst alive, it was not until his death that his Magic propagated through his form of Spiritualism, which became so popular and widespread throughout the entire world from the 1850s. Levi later in life digressed from Spiritualism and actually criticized it. He started to believe that only mental images and certain astral forces still existed and continued after one has died, that could be freely manipulated by a skilled Spiritualist or Magician. Levi was also famous for incorporating the tarot cards into his Magical workings and due to this the tarot became an important part of the Tools of the Western Magician and Witch alike, along with the millions of tarot readers, who actually do not even know the original meanings, symbolism and usage of the tarot as was created by Tehuti Thoth., but they have today in the 21st century become one of the most public tools of the Occult thanks to Levi.

Levi also deeply influenced the Magic and ceremonies of the Hermetic Order of the Golden Dawn, along with Aleister Crowley. Levi was also the first person to declare that the inverted Pentagram with its spirit point submerged into matter, was symbolic of spirit overruling the physical and the elements and was adopted by Christians and alike as a symbol of evil and dark magic. The Pentagram with its point aright was the true symbol of the Witch on the Path of Light, as it represented the Elements within Nature ruled by the Spirit within. Levi's ideas and works influenced so many occultists and Magicians including Madame Helena Blavatsky of the Theosophical Society, and through his courage and inspiration shall be remembered as one of the key figures of our world, as an Elder of the 20th century revival of Magic and the Occult.

Constant disappeared with the demise of the Second republic giving way to Eliphas Levi. A different narrative was independently developed by Arthur Edward Waite, who was less informed about Constant's life and his involvement in matters of the occult and Magic. Aleister Crowley was born the year that Levi died and claimed to be the reincarnation of Levi.

Eliphas Levi Books:
- *Transcendental Magic: Its Doctrine and Ritual*
- *The Doctrine and Ritual of High Magic: A New Translation*
- *The Kabbalistic and Occult Tarot of Eliphas Levi*
- *The History of Magic*
- *The Mysteries of the Qabalah: or Occult Agreement of the Two Testaments*
- *The Key of the Mysteries*
- *The Book of Splendors: The Inner Mysteries of the Qabalism*
- *Transcendental Magic*

George Pickingill
High Priest and Witch Elder
1816 – April 10th, 1909

Photograph of George Pickingill

George Pickingill was born in 1816 to Charles Pickingill and Susannah Cudner, a rural working-class family in Hockley. Pickingill eventually moved and grew up in the east English country of Essex in the small town of Canewdon. Pickingill became very secretive in his adult years, and many saw him as a Cunning Man, as he was well known already as a Folk Magician, but to the locals they knew him as a Witch, where he used his Magic and herbal remedies for anyone who sought out his medicines and cures. Many spoke of his great talent at finding lost property. When the price was right, he also placed curses and charms on people, depending on what they asked of him.

Pickingill was baptized into the Church of England on the 26th of May 1816, but only attended church as a child, as his path lead him elsewhere and he never entered a church again during his adult life. Pickingill was a farmer, and he eventually married Sarah Ann Bateman on the 18th of May 1856 in Gravesend, Kent. Together they returned back.

to his home in Essex and settled in the town of Canewdon and over the years had four children. They were happy until his wife took ill and died in 1887 at the young age of 31 through consumption.

Pickingills' notoriety was minimal in comparison to when a wider public attention in the early 1960s by the folklorist Eric Maple, as part of Eric's research into the beliefs of Folk Magic and Witchcraft in the 19th century Essex. Maple made it his mission to meet and interview as many of the locals to collect as many stories about Pickingill as he could. According to most Pickingill attracted many the inquisitive from near and far seeking his Magical and Healing help, especially his abilities to control animals, command spirits and imps to do his bidding, and also raise the power against other evil witches and hexes, he supposedly did not charge for these services to those who could not afford his treatments, but to those that could afford him he charged well to compensate his life.

Pickingill was the Clan Father of his Covens that were kept in secret and ran privately by him in Canewdon, supposedly along with eight covens across Britain. It was supposed to have been Pickingill who reformed and established a Traditional Witch Line by incorporating Danish and French Witchcraft from classical sources. Many believe that it was he who created the foundation for Gardnerian Wicca which emerged in the 1950s. Doreen Valiente and Lois Bourne criticized these claims, which we also rejected by certain historians such as Maple Hutton, Owen Davies and Aidan A. Kelly.

Pickingill called himself the Master of Witchcraft, and by the end of the 19th century Canewdon was called The Witch County. Pickingill was also known as the Horse Whisperer as he had power over and could control horses. There were many claims that he travelled extensively but these are false as he never had the financial means to do so, and in fact never travelled at all in his entire life. In his later years he relied on the government for assistance, and also the kind donations of friends and his Covenstead members.

According to the records, in Pickingill's last few weeks where he had become very ill, he was moved by the medical body to the infirmary against his will, where he declared that at his funeral, he would demonstrate one more Magical Marvel. As his body was being taken in a hearse to the cemetery grounds of the church the horses somehow stepped out of their harness shafts. Against his wishes he was still buried in the church grounds, whilst through time his abandoned house became dilapidated and eventually fell down. According to his death certificate, "George Pettingale" died on the 10th of April 1909 at the age of 103, and the cause of his death was "Senile decay" and "cardiac failure". Pickingill's death attracted national press where it was claimed that he was believed to be the oldest man in England who died at the age of 106.

Charles Godfrey Leland
Witch Elder and Stregheria Priest
August 15th, 1824 - March 20th, 1903

Portrait of Charles Godfrey Leland

Charles Godfrey Leland was born in Philadelphia on the 15th of August 1824. Leland was fascinated by English Gypsies and Italian Witchcraft (Stregheria) and became a famous folklorist who wrote several classic books on the subject. Throughout Leland's entire life, commencing when he was just a child, he was always intrigued and fascinated with folklore and Magic. Leland wrote "Etruscan Roman Remains", "Legends of Florence", "The Gypsies", "Gypsy Sorcery", and to me my favourite of his, "Aradia, Gospel of the Witches".

During the 19th century Leland did a lot of field studies and deep research throughout Italy that revealed to him and proved the existence of an ancient surviving tradition of Witches, with an old bloodline going back to ancient times. They were the Stregheria, the Blood Witches. Gardner, the Founder of Gardnerian Wicca, fifty years later incorporated many of his elements into his writings as Gardnerian

Wicca. Interestingly, Leland in chapter four of his book Gypsy Sorcery and Fortune Telling, which was published in 1891, makes the earliest connection between Wicca and modern Witchcraft, where he says:

"As for the English word witch, Anglo-Saxon Wicca, comes from a root implying wisdom..." Leland's footnote here reads: "Witch. Mediaeval English wicche, both masculine and feminine, a wizard, a witch. Anglo-Saxon wicca - masculine, wicce - feminine. Wicca is a corruption of witga, commonly used as a short form of witega, a prophet, seer, magician, or sorcerer. Anglo-Saxon witan, to see, allied to witan, to know..."

In 1906 the Charles Godfrey Leland biography, a two-volume set, was written by his niece Elizabeth Robins Pennell. Where she in the first chapter recounts his personal memoirs saying:

"In both the 'Memoirs' and the 'Memoranda' he tells how he was carried up to the garret by his old Dutch nurse, who was said to be a sorceress, and left there with a Bible, a key, and a knife on his breast, lighted candles, money, and a plate of salt at his head: rites that were to make luck doubly certain by helping him to rise in life and become a scholar and a wizard."

Pennell goes on to say that Leland's mother, claimed as an ancestress, married into "sorcery". Leland also writes in his memoirs: "my mother's opinion was that this was a very strong case of atavism, and that the mysterious ancestor had through the ages cropped out in me".

Sir James George Fraser
Occultist
January 1st, 1854 – May 7th, 1941

Portrait of Sir James George Fraser

James George Frazer was born on the 1st of January 1854 in Glasgow, Scotland to a Chemist, Daniel F. Frazer, and his mother Katherine Brown. Frazer loved school and attended the Springfield Academy and also Larchfield Academy in Helensburgh. Frazer loved knowledge and yearned for as much as he could get, especially when it involved the very truth of that knowledge. Fraser later as a young man became a student at the University of Glasgow, and also Trinity College-Cambridge where he graduated with honors in Classics. Fraser remained a Classics Fellow the rest of his life. After Trinity, due to his love of study and knowledge he continued his study and went on to study law at Middle Temple, although he never wanted to practice law, he just wanted to get a grasp on it and understand it. Fraser was elected four times to Trinity's Alpha Fellowship as he was associated with

Trinity College for the entirety of his life.

Fraser was knighted in 1914, and in honor of his esteemed works and knighthood in 1921, public lectureship in social anthropology commenced at the universities of Cambridge, Glasgow, Liverpool, and Oxford. Fraser was always commonly mentioned as an atheist due to his constant criticism of Christianity, especially Catholicism, which he disliked immensely and criticized his feelings strongly in his bestselling book and one of my favorites The Golden Bough. Fraser was far from an atheist, as he was an ambivalent believer in Neoplatonism and also Hermeticism.

Fraser was a private man personally where he dedicated his life to the pursuit of Truth and from this truth, myth and religion became his expertise. Although immensely knowledgeable and skilled, he hardly ever left the comfort of his home, except for minor trips to Italy or Greece. Although travel lacking, his skills of research from within the walls of his home, had an endless array of prime services of ancient texts and their history, he continually corresponded with genuine scholars with their expertise all over the world. It was Fraser who was the very first to describe the correlation between myths and rituals, with his vision of the annual sacrifice of the Year-King which had been born out of his studies.

Frasers immense and unbridled constant study of ancient cults, rituals, Magic along with the myths, gave him some of the best writings in his famous book The Golden Bough which includes many parallels in early Christianity, through his in-depth effort and findings, his teachings have continued into the 21st century with mythographers worldwide.

Frasers fascination constantly with the cycles of and within nature of birth, life, death and rebirth, aided him in believing that they were all divined in ALL myths of the ancient Pagan traditions, cultures and religions all over the world, which captivated and confused people worldwide. The Golden Bough has its critics like most books, but more so some saw it as anti-Catholic, classist, imperialist and also racist, including his beliefs that all European peasants, Aboriginal Australians, Native American Indians, and Africans all represented fossilized, early stages of cultural evolution. He passionately believed that all cultures passed through three divine stages, that they all moved from MAGIC, to RELIGION, and eventually to SCIENCE (The Magic of the future). Fraser openly and publicly believed his belief in Magic and Science being remarkably similar due to the fact that they both shared an emphasis on experimentation and practicality.

Fraser wholeheartedly believed in both Magic and Religion will persist and return, and that Magic would sometimes return as a new form of science, much like Alchemy, that it would undergo a revival in Early Modern Europe and change its name to Chemistry.

Sir James George Frazer OM FRS FRSE FBA, was a social anthropologist and folklorist who was influenced by mythology and comparative religions. He is considered by many to be one of the Founding Fathers of modern Anthropology. His famous book The Golden Bough (1890) documents in detail the similarities between Magickal and Religious beliefs around the entire world. By 1930 he became visually impaired and was nearly and totally blind. The beautiful part of his story is that both he and his wife, Lilly, died in Cambridge within just a few hours of each other. They are both buried at the ascension Parish Burial Ground in Cambridge England.

Frasers Books:
- *Totemism,* 1887
- *The Golden Bough: A Study in Magic and Religion,* 1890
- *Description of Greece,* 1897
- *Pausanias, and other Greek Sketches,* 1900
- *The Golden Bough, 2nd Edition,* 1900
- *Psyche's Task,* 1909
- *Totemism and Exogamy,* 1910
- *The Golden Bough, 3rd Edition,* 1906 (12 volumes)
- *Taboo and the Perils of the Soul,* 1911
- *The Belief in Immortality and the Worship of the Dead,* (3 volumes) 1913
- *Folk-Lore in the Old Testament,* 1918
- *The Library, by Apollodorus,* 2 volumes, 1921
- *The Worship of Nature,* 1926
- *The Gorgons Head and other Literary Pieces,* 1927
- *Man, God and Immortality,* 1927
- *Devil's Advocate,* 1928
- *Fasti, by Ovid* (translation 5 volumes), 1929
- *Myths of the Origin of Fire,* 1930
- *The Growth of Plato's Ideal Theory,* 1930
- *Garnered Sheaves,* 1931
- *Condorcet on the Progress of the Human Mind,* 1933
- *The Fear of the Dead in Primitive Religion,* 1933
- *Creation and evolution in Primitive Cosmogonies, and Other Places,* 1935.

Arthur E. Waite
Magician, Occultist, Freemason
October 2nd, 1857 – May 19th, 1942

Portrait of Arthur Edward Waite

Arthur Edward Waite was born on the 2nd of October 1857 in Brooklyn, New York, but sadly his father Captain Charles F. Waite died when he was still a young infant. After his father's passing the family, still grieving, returned back to Britain, the mother's homeland, where he remained for the remainder of his youth and young adult years. They were quite unfinancial, even though Waite's mother worked awfully hard for everything they had, she spent most of her money making sure that he had the best education at a small private school in North London. When he turned thirteen, he went to school at St. Charles College until his leaving to become a clerk where during this spare time, he wrote verses and poetry.

Waites mother converted into Catholicism in 1863, and it became taboo for him to be interested in the areas that he was attracted to such as the occult and any other forms of spirituality outside of the Roman Catholic faith. In 1874 Waites sister Frederika died suddenly and his attitude took a turn as he became more interested in the spiritual cycle of birth, life, death, and rebirth, especially the hereafter the place in between this world and the next. This magical and mystical psychic world lured him more and more into psychical research and the paranormal. Waites when only 21 started to visit the library of the British Museum where he read fanatically everything, he could get his hands on in all areas of the Occult, Supernatural and the Paranormal phenomena. Waite also discovered a book on the occult by author Eliphas Levi in 1881.

Waite went on to get married at 29 years of age to Ada Lakeman (Lucasta), they had a daughter, Sybil. Many years after his wife's death in 1924, Waite remarried to a Mary Broadbent Schofield. They spent most of their life close together, living near London where he became involved with many publishing houses and also edited a magazine, The Unknown World. Waite was more popularly known as A.E. Waite, especially as a poet, mystic and eventual author where he wrote extensively on the Occult and all Esoteric matters. Waite became famous more so for being the co-creator of the Rider-Waite Tarot Deck which I believe to be one of the truer versions of the original tarot and always recommend it to those interested and to my students. R.A. Gilbert as Waites biographer described him: "Waites name has survived because he was first to attempt a systematic study of the history of western occultism-viewed as a spiritual tradition rather than as aspects of proto-science or as the pathology of religion."

Waite throughout his life had a hunger for as much knowledge as he could gain, he constantly searched hard and long for his Truth, which eventually attracted him to and where he joined the Outer Order of the "Hermetic Order of the Golden Dawn" after he was introduced by E.W. Burridge, but after a couple of years Waite left the Order but re-joined again in 1896, but into a different branch of the Outer Order of the Golden Dawn. It was in 1899 that he entered the second Order of the Golden Dawn. Waite was still hungry for more and deeper insight and knowledge and so became a Freemason in 1901 and also entered the Societas Rosicriciana in Anglia in 1902. Waite still wanted more knowledge, and so decided to set up and found an independent and Rectified Order R.R. et A.C. but it was disbanded in 1914.

The constant feuding within the egos of the Golden Dawn were fueled by Waite and he departed the Order in 1914, but in July 1915 he formed the Fellowship of the Rosy Cross. At this time, there were only six branches left of the Golden Dawn, and it never fully recovered to the full extent that it was in the beginning of its creation. Even today in the 21st century the Golden Dawn has dwindled to just a few small Orders left in the world. Throughout Waites life he had a great foe, one namely Aleister Crowley, who always referred Waite as a "Villainous Arthwate" in his novel Moonchild and also mentioned him as "Dead Waite". Even in the short story of H.P. Lovecraft The Thing of the Doorstep was a character called Ephraim Waite, and according to Robert M. Price the character was based on Waite himself.

Waite was well received in most academic circles as a prolific writer on the occult including areas of divination, ceremonial magic, esotericism, Rosicrucianism, Freemasonry, the Kabbala and alchemy, he also translated and rewrote several important mystical and alchemical writings. His greatest work I believe was on the Holy Grail, influenced by his friendship with Arthur Machen.

The Rider-Waite-Smith tarot was notable for being the first tarot decks to illustrate all 78 tarot cards fully, instead of just the 22 major arcana.

It was the artwork of fellow Golden Dawn member Pamela Colman Smith who illustrated the cards for Waite, where the full deck was published in its entirety in 1909. (It is known that the inspiration for this deck was partly provided by the Sola-Busca Tarot from Northern Italy of 1491, which was the first and only Tarot deck published up to the time of Waites deck.)

A.E. Waites Books:

- *Israfel: Letters, Visions and Poems* 1886
- *The Mysteries of Magic: A Digest of the Writings of Eliphas Levi* 1886
- *Alchemists Through the Ages* 1888
- *Prince Starbeam* (Fantasy) 1889
- *The Occult Sciences: A Compendium of Transcendental Doctrine and Experiment.* 1891
- *The Hermetic Museum,* 1893

Dr. Margaret Alice Murray
Witch Friend
July 13th, 1863 – November 13th, 1963

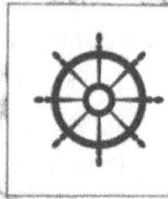

Margaret Murray Painting (Public Domain)

Margaret Alice Murray born 13th July 1863 to a wealthy English family, James, and Margaret Murray Snr, in Calcutta, Bengal Presidency, British India, which was a major military city. Murray lived with her extended family, her siblings, grandparents in an exceptionally large luxurious mansion where they also had 10 omars (servants) where three of them lived also in the house. The Murray family travelled quite extensively where they lived between India, Britain, and Germany. Murray studied to become a nurse in her late teens and also a social worker. When she completed her qualifications as a nurse and social worker she decided to move to London at the age of 30 in 1894, as she had an interest in all things Egyptian and wanted to become an Egyptologist (something at the time that only men did). Murray went on to study at the University College London (UCL), where she studied specifically Egyptology and also Coptic languages. It was here that a special friendship developed with the head of the department Sir William Flinders Petrie.

Petrie encouraged Murray in her early academic publications, and she was eventually appointed as Junior Professor in 1898. Murray went on to write many academic publications but her first research paper was titled The Descent of Property in the Early Periods of Egyptian History. Murray became so good at what she did that she started teaching courses on ancient Egyptian history, religion and also language, she also started to teach night classes at the British Museum and also the Manchester Museum.

Due to her growing acknowledgment and her growing up in India, her entire life was embellished with the Indian Culture, religion, and lifestyle as she had fond memories as a child, she also loved the incredible eclectic and diverse cultures and religions that all existed side by side in the one land. Although living amongst this diverse culture she was brought up with strong Christian education from her uncle John, who was a Vicar with the Church of England, and he had strong beliefs in the inferiority of all women, and this antagonized Murray with ideals that she totally rejected. Because of her rebellious nature and always in the search for Truth instead of someone just telling that this is the way, her intrigue into searching with archaeology and the very answers herself became imperative.

Murray's father retired and she decided to move back in with him as company and eventual carer until his passing in 1891.

Murray ended up joining Petrie in 1902-1903 in his excavations at Abydos (Egypt), where together they excavated continuously since 1899. Whilst they were excavating at Abydos, Murray uncovered "The Osirion", an ancient temple that was dedicated to the Egyptian God Osiris (Greek title and name) who was originally worshipped by his Egyptian name as Assur. This temple had been constructed by Pharaoh Set 1 during the period known as the New Kingdom. Murray was so particular about everything she wrote down about her findings, where she personally examined everything carefully, especially in the deciphering of all the inscriptions that were found. Murray later in 1908 who was the first woman to ever unwrap a mummy publicly, in particular this was Khnum-nakht from the Tomb of the Two Brothers.

Murrays archaeological finds and further excavations that were done at Abydos, Saqqara Cemetery, publicly recognized and acknowledged British Egyptomania as a widespread interest in everything that was Egyptian. Today Egyptian artifacts and artwork are the biggest selling business in the world. Murray's expertise in her fields became so academically accepted, that she went on to write several books on Egyptology that actually led her to become involved in the first wave of the feminist movement. It was here that she joined The Women's Social and Political Union, where she spent much of her time dedicated to fighting to improve women's status at UCL.

Due to the commencement of the First World War, Murray focused her attention and researched the awakened Witch-Cult hypothesis, the theory that the witch trials of Early Modern Christendom were nothing more than the attempt to extinguish the surviving pre-Christian, Pagan religions that were devotees of a Nature Goddess and the Horned God of

Nature. Murray was a significant influence on the revival of the old religious movement of Witchcraft that was reborn under the guise of Wicca in the New Age.

Murray underwent more excavations between 1921-1931 on sacred sites in Malta and also Menoprea, and it was here that she became interested in Folklorists. Around this same time, she was awarded an honorary doctorate in 1927 and appointed assistance Professor in 1928. Murray eventually retired from UCL in 1935. Her amazingly accurate work earned her recognition as an acclaimed archaeologist with the moniker of "The Grand old Woman of Egyptology". Murray also focused on Witchcraft and Wicca and many scholars also acclaimed her the title as the "Grandmother of Wicca" even though not being a Wiccan or a Witch herself but was always a friend to Witches and the like because of their truth throughout ancient history. Sadly, after her death, much of her hard work and accomplishments were overshadowed by Petrie.

Murrays' incredible foresight and research was widely accepted by Occultists and many Witches such as Dion Fortune, Ralph Shirley and also J. W. Brodie Innes. Murray spoke highly of her Witch-cult theory in her 1933 book The God of the Witches. She always described the "Old Religion" in a positive format and included many details of the origins and positive side of Witchcraft and Wicca and opened the coffers of knowledge to the world especially the Seekers of the Old Ways and started the R-Evolution of Wicca as the religion of the 20th Century.

In Murrays later years she was crippled with severe arthritis and was moved into a nursing home in North Finchley, North London, it was here that she was cared for by a retired couple of nurses, but due to the severity of her health was eventually moved to the Queen Victoria Memorial Hospital where she lived for another 18 months. To mark her 100th birthday on the 13th of July 1963 a large group of her friends, former students, and doctors gathered for a celebration, she actually was driven to two other special parties for her milestone 100th birthday. Dr Margaret Murray died on the 13th of November 1963, and her body was cremated.

Murray although not being a Witch herself, had through her research and openness opened up a blueprint for the contemporary Pagan religion of Wicca, and also believed that Witches wrote down all their rituals and spells in a special book, which became the famous "Book of Shadows" (Not her wording). Before Murrays publications there was no other writing or mention of the religion of Wicca in publication. She is the "Grandmother of Wicca", even though never actually attending a ritual ceremony. Hail and Farewell and thank you!

Margaret Murray's Books:
- *Guide to the Collection of Egyptian Antiquities,* 1903
- *The Osireion at Abydos,* 1904
- *Saqqara Mastabas Part I and Gurob,* 1905
- *Elementary Egyptian Grammar,* 1905

- *Index of the Names and Titles of the Old Kingdom,* 1908
- *The Tomb of the Two Brothers,* 1910
- *Elementary Coptic (Sahidic) Grammar,* 1911
- *Ancient Egyptian Legends,* 1913
- *The Witch Cult in Western Europe,* 1921
- *Excavations in Malta, Part I,* 1923
- *Excavations in Malta, Part II,* 1925
- *Excavations in Malta, Part III,* 1929
- *Egyptian Sculpture,* 1930
- *Egyptian Temples,* 1931
- *The God of the Witches,* 1931
- *Maltese Folktales,* 1932
- *A Coptic Reading Book, with Glossary, for the Use of Beginners,* 1933
- *Cambridge Excavations in Minorca, Sa Torreta,* 1934
- *Corpus of the Bronze Age Pottery of Malta,* 1934
- *Saqqara Mastabas Part II,* 1937
- *Cambridge Excavations in Minorca, Trapuco,* 1938
- *Petra, the Rock City of Edom,* 1939
- *Ancient Egyptian Religious Poetry,* 1949
- *The Splendor that was Egypt,* 1949
- *The Divine King of England,* 1954
- *My First Hundred Years,* 1963
- *The Genesis of Religion,* 1963

Aleister Crowley
Occultist and Magician
October 12th, 1875 – December 1st, 1947

Photograph of A Young Aleister Crowley

Aleister Crowley was born in 1875 to a wealthy Plymouth Brethren family in Warwickshire, UK. Crowley even as a child rejected all fundamental Christian attitudes, as he believed that there was so much more that was kept secret and from their congregations. Crowley started at a young age on his personal quest to find the truth within the Occult and was led into a world of eclectic esoteric paths and traditions. He always showed a high level of intelligence and questioned everything, but never got the answers that he wanted, as he was always veered into other directions except for the answers. He was highly intelligent and was schooled at Cambridge University, where he was also entered in 1895 for the Moral Science Tripos which studied philosophy. It was here that Crowley started being drawn into mountaineering and also to the other spectrum poetry, both these events took up most of his time.

It was around this time that many started to believe that he was recruited into the BIA (British Intelligence Agency) that it was suggested that he remained a British spy throughout the rest of his life due to his specialised interests in the occult.

The one thing I must say is that Crowley was not a witch, but he was particularly important to the changes and awareness of the occult world including Witchcraft and the very movement of everything occult and spiritually alternative as a whole. But he was a devout Occultist and a Magician as he was drawn to all forms of Magic especially Ceremonial Magic, in fact he loved anything that his grandiose manner could be taken to extreme showing the world his showman and evangelical character. Although his manner was quite grandiose, he was better known and acclaimed as the "wickedest man in the world", which he absolutely loved this title to the fullest. As a true Occultist he loved to experiment with absolutely anything and to him nothing was off limits, and I mean nothing due to his investigatory nature, as he had to experience and know everything from top to bottom as he believed to be the most knowledgeable man in the world meant that he had to know and experience everything that life had to offer. Crowley was an artist, poet, novelist, and loved to be with nature no more than climbing every mountain he saw, and he loved sexuality in all its extremes.

Crowley not liking established religions decided to form his own and founded the new religion known as Thelema, where he saw himself as its Prophet, and that he was entrusted with guiding mankind into what he termed the Aeon of Horus, which was supposedly to take place sometime during the 20th century. Crowley also became a prolific writer and wrote everything down as a full lengthy diary, he also published everything he could over the whole course of his 72 years on Earth.

Crowley met with likeminded Occultists in 1898 when he joined the esoteric group Hermetic Order of the Golden Dawn, and subsequently was trained as an apprentice by the inhouse Ceremonial Magicians, Samuel Liddell, MacGregor Mathers and also Allan Bennett. From here Crowley spent his life on a personal journey searching for and researching everything that he could and travelled extensively around the world searching for all his answers. The sad thing about Crowley is that he had a mouth to match his ego and could never keep secrets or oaths, as he spoke always openly and freely about everything, and bragged and embellished mist things in his life, and this was well-noted by all those round him.

Crowley met and fell in love with and then married Rose Edith Kelly in 1904, and for their honeymoon they went to Cairo, Egypt, where Crowley claimed that he was contacted by a spiritual entity of the sacred Law that was named Aiwass, who bequeathed unto him the sacred Book of Law, that eventually was to become the sacred text as the foundation for his religion Thelema. Within these sacred writings were announced as the start of the Aeon of Horus. These writings declared to all followers "DO WHAT THOU WILT!" and seek to align themselves with their innate True Will through the practice of Magick, spelt with a "K".

Crowley continued to travel extensively and then decided to return back to the UK where he started to attract much media attention and notoriety as an author. The co-founder of the Masonic Lodge George Cecil Jones came along in 1907 and together they propagated the religion. Spending a great deal of time together in Algeria, and in 1912 Crowley was Initiated into the German-based Ordo Templii Orientis (OTO), and eventually rose to become the head of the entire British Order which he then changed and reformed with his Thelemic beliefs. From here he established lodges in Britain, Australia and also North America.

During WW1 Crowley spent his entire time in the US, and this is where he brought out his creative side where he started painting and also started to campaign for the German war effort against Britain, later he revealed that he infiltrated the pro-German movement to assist British Intelligence Services.

It wasn't until 1920 (100 years ago) that he established and founded the Abbey of Thelema, which was a spiritual commune in Cefaku, Sicily where he along with many of his Seekers lived and cohabited together. Because of Crowley's notoriety and libertine lifestyle was convicted in 1923 and evicted from Italy forever, and spent the next twenty years between France, Germany, and Britain, all this time he continually promoted his religion of Thelema until his death in 1947.

Due to Crowley's very open sexual lifestyle, being a bi-sexual and an experimenter of every type of drug that was available, he was publicly denounced as a good man and all the press slammed him, claiming him to be "The Beast" and "The Wickedest man in the World", and by adding a little Christian mudslinging he was also accused of being a Satanist. Crowley was open about everything that he was both spiritually and sexually, and he was a very gifted man, one who had the courage to be himself and not afraid of what others thought of him, he followed his own desires and feelings and was open about everything in his life. Thelema still radiates his power as a Prophet even after his death, but a Satanist he never was. He did have a lot of downfalls but in his own way he was a very devoted and spiritual person who had a yearning for adventure and experimentation, as these were his callings.

Crowley's original writings from the Liber Al vel Legis were later adopted by Gerald Gardner, where he borrowed, altered and added a few witchy words here and there to make it more exciting for new Seekers who were none the wiser, and also for the readers of his books, especially where he added his flare to the rituals and ceremonies including Initiation rituals into his tradition of Gardnerian Wicca, it was Gardner that mixed everything up together; the Kabbala, Ceremonial and Ritual Magick, eastern and western Magic, Traditional Witchcraft and Paganism. For your own personal research please read Rodney Orpheus essay: "A New and Greater Pagan Cult: Gerald Gardner & Ordo Templii Orientis."

Crowley was also acquainted with L. Ronald Hubbard, the Founder of Scientology, and even Hubbard claimed that Crowley was a good and dear friend, but in one of his recordings could not even get his name correct, it was after this and a few failed businesses that Hubbard started his sci-fi religion Scientology.

Most of Crowley's writings had a serious side to them but he always seemed to add a little sense of humor to his stories, some of his comments are:

"One would go mad if one took the Bible seriously; but to take it seriously one must already be mad." — Liber ABA, Chapter XVI.

"May the New Year bring you courage to break your resolutions early! My own plan is to swear off every kind of virtue, so that I triumph even when I fall!" — Moonchild

"Theosophist: A person who talks about Yoga, and does no work." — Liber ABA, Glossary.

"Some men are born sodomites, some achieve sodomy, and some have sodomy thrust upon them…" — The Scented Garden of Abdullah the Satirist of Shiraz.

"[I adopt the phrase 'Holy Guardian Angel'] Because since all theories of the universe are absurd it is better to talk in the language of one which is patently absurd, so as to mortify the metaphysical man." — The Temple Of Solomon the King in The Equinox I, no. 1.

Crowley in his life set forth a torrent of waves that influenced the shaping of the Occult counterculture movement of the 1960s. He believed that there was so much more to explore, experience and understand, even in his study and efforts to make Eastern philosophy more acceptable to the West, it was this that launched the inspirations of many especially the birth of what we now call The New Age Movement.

For more in-depth exploration into Aleister Crowley read the biographies by:
- *Perdurabo: The Life of Aleister Crowley*, by Richard Kaczynski
- *Aleister Crowley: The Biography*, by Tobias Churton

Crowley was always attracted to and fascinated by anything that was taboo, and anything that shocked people generally he loved to test peoples delicately nurtured senses, he also loved to write about taboo subjects, and being a very open bi-sexual always used this to shock people. His most risqué' book that he published was called White Stains, which was written under the pen name of George Archibald Bishop. Many of these "R" rated books were seized by British customs when he entered back into Britain, which was only three years after the world-famous poet and author – Oscar Wild was imprisoned for his poetic allusion of homosexuality. But in the typical Crowley fashion he thought he was untouchable with his shock tactics and open promiscuity, where he loved to accentuate his sexual poetry, of which many would actually shock people of the 21st century due to their explicit nature. Crowley only had one true love and that was in a woman named Leah Hirsig where he wrote a piece that was inspired by her entitled "Leah Sublime".

Ian Fleming, who was to eventually become the future author and creator of the James Bond novels, was also a Navy Intelligence Officer, and knew Crowley quite well and had many discussions, and at the time wanted to use and feed misinformation to the Nazis through Rudolph Hess. Many also speculated that it was Crowley's handiwork that actually led to the capture of Hess. If you wish to know more about this spy, a good read is his book Secret Agent 666, by Richard Spence. John the Divine prophesized that Crowley was the Great Beast 666, and Crowley loved this title even though it was intended as a joke, but he took the label with respect and fun.

Crowley has always been the target of many accusations, especially since 1904, some true and many false, but because and through him we have seen unimaginable changes in the world. Whether you are aware of Crowley's Magickal workings or not, the fact is that he was the original Father who started the revolution of religious change, and through him many people with courage became aware of their own inherent divinity, and the divinity of every man, woman and child is a self-evident fact of life. Sadly, a few years later on the 1st of December 1947, Aleister Crowley took his last breath, letting all know that he will return!

Gerald B. Gardner
King of Gardnerian Wicca
Father of Modern Wicca & Witch Elder
June 13th, 1884 – February 12th, 1964

Gerald Gardner in Ceremony (Public Domain)

Gerald Brosseau Gardner was born on the 13th of June 1884 the second youngest of five children to a wealthy, upper middle-class family, his father William Robert Gardner and Mother Louise Burquelew Ennis who was also from a wealthy Stationary family, an American company called Joseph Gardner and Sons. The Gardner's within the next two years decided to go back to England in 1873 and settle in The Glen, in a large Victorian mansion in Blundell sands, Lancashire, which was an exclusive and wealthy part of Liverpool.

Gardner as a child suffered severely with asthma which continued throughout his entire life, but the severity was worse as a child. Gardner's nursemaid whose name was Com, was asked at the expense of the parents to take young Gardner overseas to a warmer climate to help his health with his asthma. Whilst continually travelled in warm climates, Gardner's parent realised how much it was helping his health and in the summer of 1888 Gardner with Com travelled via London to Niece, Southern France where they spent many years living well supported by his father around the Mediterranean. Later in 1891 they travelled to the Canary Islands where the young Gardner started to take a deep interest in all types of weaponry, especially in swords and daggers.

Due to his constant travel his schooling suffered and he was quite illiterate but he was smart enough to educate himself in reading and writing although under-average, but he taught himself by the many magazines that he read whilst travelling, although his grammar and spelling was quite atrocious, this never changed as he was quite a lazy student in this respect. He did eventually become highly influenced by a book that he read by Florence Marryat called There is no Death, this was about Spiritualism and started him on his quest and deep interest in the afterlife.

Eventually Gardner's nursemaid Com, married David Elkington in 1900, he was very financial as he was the owner of a large tea plantation in the British Colony of Ceylon. Gardener's parents agreed that he remain in Ceylon for his health with Com at the Ladbroke Estate in Maskeliva. Mr Elkington took Gardner under his wing and taught him everything he knew where he started to learn a trade as schooling was out of the question. They all lived together in a typical Bungalow in Kandy, which was not too far from another bungalow that was leased to the famous Occultists Charles Henry Barret and Aleister Crowley, which had just become vacant. It was in 1904 that Gardner decided to move into his own bungalow and commenced working in a rival tea company at the Non Pareil Estate.

This was the beginning of his attraction to hunting and his favourite pastime, as he spent most of his free time hunting, which was not just a passion but had become an obsession. Gardner started to also invest in antique and ancient weaponry especially if they were connected to Napoleon Bonaparte and also the Asian cultures. Gardner in 1907 returned back to Britain to visit his family and in his search and longing for the hunt and guns he joined the Legion of Frontiersmen, who were the militia that were formed to repel any threat of invasion from the Germans.

Gardner had many interests, but he was drawn to Freemasonry that eventually led to his Initiation in 1910, he became an apprentice Freemason into the Sphinx Lodge No. 107 in Colombo which was affiliated with the Irish Grand Lodge. This started his appetite for more knowledge especially more in-depth spiritual activities, it grew so strong that he made sacrifices so that he could attend the Masonic meetings where he had to arrange weekend leave, walk 15 miles to the nearest railway station in Haputale and then continue to catch the train to the city. It was his eagerness and determination that helped catapult him through the ranks very quickly and all within just a month into getting his 2nd and 3rd degree of Freemasonry. Gardner always wanted to know more as he got bored quite easily and always needed his attention to be activated in areas of intrigue. Shortly after he left the lodge which was around the same time his father sold his rubber plantation.

Gardner decided to move to Borneo again for his asthma as it was better suited in these tropical damp climates, but sadly he caught malaria. Gardner loved this place and the romance of the tropical rainforests, especially the people that he was drawn towards because of their gentleness, but the climate again was not suited for his health as it started to diminish again, and his bouts of asthma increased so he decided to move to Singapore which had a better drier climate. He was fascinated by their local spiritual and Magical beliefs especially in their ritual dagger which is called "The Kris", which is used both in ritual and fighting.

At this same time, he was offered an employment opportunity working for the Malay Government and was quickly promoted to the Principal Officer of Customs, a role that meant he was the official inspector of all the Rubber Companies of Malaysia and oversaw their regulation, laws, and sales in all its entirety. Gardner became particularly important as head, where he also monitored all the opium sales, which is where he became wealthier than he already was, due to taking many bribes offered his way, and these made him an absolute fortune.

Gardner's mother died in 1920, but he decided not to return for the funeral in Britain, but when his father became extremely ill with dementia in 1927 Gardner had to be by his side. It was here that he started to prepare for his father's loss, and at this time got heavily involved in the Spiritualist movement where he studied to become a medium (a Channel). It was here that he met Jack Bracelin, as well as a woman whom he eventually married, Dorothea Frances Rosedale (Donna), after their meeting they married only a month later on the 16th of August 1927. He became very content with his life and maintained his interest and involvement in Freemasonry by searching deeper and became drawn to his long time interest of Anthropology which took him on a further adventure onto his first Archaeological dig, at a place where there had been no archaeological excavations at all due to the law of the Sultan at the city of Johore Lama, which had to be done in secret due to the Sultan seeing archaeology as another form of being a graverobber and disrespectful to the dead.

Gardner unearthed tons of earth and found tombs, pottery and porcelain dating back to the Ming Dynasty. He went on to display a talent at finding and luckily having a display at the National Museum of Singapore titled "The Early History of Johore". This was another feather in his cap. After which he attended a conference at the King's College in London where he attended two lectures both on the Cult of the Mother Goddess, where he met and befriended Pagan archaeologist Alexander Keiller, who was acclaimed for his Avebury Excavations, and who actually encouraged Gardner to join in some of his digs at Hembury Hill in Devon.

Gardner's father died in 1935 and bequeathed to him Three thousand pounds, which added to his financial fortune with more independence and security. Although he loved Malaysia, both he and his wife discussed about returning permanently back to Britain, where they firstly decided to rent a fat in 1936 in London. Gardner's health again started to decline due to the climate and so upon visiting his doctor who suggested that he try nudism, which actually helped him quite a lot. Gardner did join a nudist camp at Fouracres near Bricket Wood in Herefordshire, where he felt comfortable and attended as often as he could, sometimes staying for long lengths of time. He also loved being around other free-thinking people and met with and made friends with a great deal of people who were actually associated with the Victoria & Albert British Museum and one who was also an Elder member of the Order of Woodcraft Chivalry, who was in fact a Pagan associated with Dionysianism, a Pagan religion. Gardner joined and later wrote for the Folk-Lore Society where he wrote in their journal "Folk-Lore".

Gardner became a member of the governing council in 1946 even though many of the members did not actually like nor trust him, as he always stated many academic claims but never had any verifications. One of his claims was that he had met with Old Dorothy Clutterbuck, which was not true as she was not of the Craft and was a true devout Cristian which showed when she died as she left her entire estate to the local church. Gardner's first actual meeting with a Pagan was at Spielplatz Nudist Colony where he befriended Ross Nichols, who introduced him to the Druid religion. It was Nichols and his devoutness to this faith for the entirety of his life where he eventually founded the "Order of Bards, Ovates and Druids". Gardner also befriended the Christian Mystic J.S.M. Ward, who was the proprietor of the Abbey Folk Park, which was Britain's oldest open-air museum. One of its main features was an old 16th century cottage that Ward had purchased and had it transported to his park, where it was exhibited as a Witches Cottage.

Gardner wanted this cottage so badly and so made a deal with Ward in exchange for some land that Gardner owned in Famagusta, Cyprus. So again, the cottage was dismantled and transported to Bricket Wood on Gardner's 5-acre lot. Gardner loved this little cottage and held certain ceremonies within it. Also furthering his interest in Esoteric Christianity, Gardner was ordained as a priest of the Ancient British Church, open to anyone who was monotheist. Gardner also joined the Ancient Druid Order, being so hungry for knowledge he also joined in 1946 the Society for Psychical Research.

Gardner was introduced by his good friend Arnold Crowther to Aleister Crowley, and they communicated a great deal, just prior to Crowley's death he Initiated Gardner and elevated him to the 4th Degree of the Order Templii Orientis (OTO) and was issued a legal charter decreeing that Gardner was able to admit new seekers into its Minerval degree. Gardner and his wife again toured the US, during which Crowley died, and Gardner considered himself as the new head of the OTO in Europe of which Lady Freda Harris accepted his appointment and position.

Although Gardner loved the OTO and Magick he was more drawn towards Witchcraft and took hold as he felt it his mission in life to spread its tradition as much as he was able but under the new title of Wicca. Gardner's first book of rituals and spells called Ye Bok of Ye Art Magical, which was later changed to The Book of Shadows, as he liked this name after reading the writings of Mir Bashir where he mentioned his book as the Book of Shadows, so it is Mir who was the original creator of the title The Book of Shadows and not Gardner. Gardner from the publishing of his book had Seekers contacting him and asking for Initiations which commenced between 1949 and 1950. Gardner also met with Cecil

Williamson who was eager to open his own Witchcraft Museum, and after much hard work the result was the "Folk-Lore Centre of Superstition and Witchcraft", which opened its doors to the public in Castletown on the Isle of Man in 1951.

Gardner and his wife together decided to move to the Isle of Man where he took up the position as the resident Witch. Although the museum has a lot of media attention was not a financial success, and it became a financial burden. The stress and the relationship between Gardner and Williamson became strained and faded quickly where Gardner after long negotiations brought out the museum from Williamson, who opened another museum in Britain as the "Museum of Witchcraft", where eventually due to problems in the community had the museum transported to Boscastle, Cornwall, which he ran until his death, and still exists today in the 21st century. Gardner had renamed his museum to the "Museum of Magic and Witchcraft".

Gardner started to communicate via correspondence with Doreen Valiente who eventually asked him for Initiation into his coven, although reluctant at first Gardner agreed to meet with her at the home of Edith Woodford-Grimes, and Valiente was Initiated by him on Midsummers Eve in 1953. Both Gardner and Valiente became very close and formed a special bond of trust, eventually Valiente went on to join the Bricket Wood Coven and due to Gardner's illiteracy helped to revise and improve his writings, particularly his Book of Shadows, which was atrocious, and she wanted to make it more presentable and also readable for the Seeker, so Valiente added her professionalism and her flare to make it what it has become today, with the majority of it being Valiente's work and poetry.

Valiente went on to become the Coven High Priestess due to her servitude and intellectual capabilities. But it was Gardner who knew how to attract and impress the media making Wicca quite a frenzy for the time. He made the growth and movement of Wicca grow way too fast with immense inquiries from all over the world due to the press. He created an awakening of the old soul and the Seeker of the Old Ways.

Gardener's official biography titled "Gerald Gardner: Witch" was published in 1960, that was written by his good friend Idries Shah who was a Sufi Mystic. But due to his own following did not use his name as the author but one of Gardner's High Priests, Jack Bracelin, as he was careful not to be associated with Witchcraft due to his involvement and commitment to Sufism. Gardner's wife died and he became unwell and unhappy, so his friends advised him to go on a trip, he travelled with Idries Shah and also Lois Bourne to Majorca to holiday with famous poet and friend Sir Robert Graves, author of The White Goddess which was in truth the stepping stone for the whole Wicca and Goddess movement along with Gardner's media attention and the spread of the Gardnerian Covens worldwide.

Sadly in 1963, Gardner alone, returning home from Lebanon on the ship The Scottish Prince on the 12th of February 1964 at the age of 79, suffered a fatal heart attack at the breakfast table. He was alone and was buried at the next port of call at Tunisia where the only person in attendance was the ship's captain. In Gardner's Will he had left everything he owned, his property, museum, rights of the covens, artefacts, even the copyright of his books to his then High Priestess, Monique Wilson. Sadly Wilson and her husband decided to sell off everything to the consortium of "Ripley's Believe it or Not", where they dismantled the museum and took the entire collection to America where it was displayed in two museums, before being sold off again in the 1980s. Gardner also bequeathed parts of his inheritance to Patricia Crowther, Doreen Valiente, Lois Bourne and Jack Bracelin, who inherited the "Fiveacres Nudist Club when he also took over Gardner's Coven as High Priest of the Bricket Wood Coven.

Plaque of Gerald B. Gardner

Many years after Gardner's death, Wiccan High Priestess Eleanor Bone visited North Africa in search of Gardner's grave, when discovered that the cemetery had been interred and was to be redeveloped. Bone raised enough money for his body to be moved to another cemetery in Tunis where it currently remains. In 2007, a new plaque was attached to his grave, describing him as the "Father of Modern Wicca, Beloved of the Great Goddess".

No matter what faults Gardner had, he was a giant in the spearhead of bringing the Wiccan movement out into the real world, he forged roads and pathways for everyone that followed in seeking the ways of the Old Religion, he started a whole tradition known as "Gardnerian Wicca" and now has instigated hundreds of covens worldwide, and also has many hive-offs from those original covens. He is the Father of Modern Wicca and shall be respected as such, "Long Live the King!"

Gardner's Books:
- *High Magic's Aid* – 1949
- *Witchcraft Today* – 1951
- *Meaning of Witchcraft* – 1959

- *The Gardnerian Book of Shadows – 2007*
- *Witchcraft Today and the Witchcraft Revival*
- *A Goddess Arrives*
- *Keris and Other Malay Weapons*
- *La Stregoneria Oggi – 1954*
- *Sacred Text of Wicca – 2011*
- *Witchcraft Revival*
- *From Man to Witch*
- *The 161 Laws of Wicca*

Dion Fortune
Magician & Occultist
December 6th, 1890 - 1946

Photograph of Dion Fortune

Dion Fortune was born Violet Mary Firth on the 6th of December 1890 in the village of bryn-y-Bia, in Liandudno, to her parent s who were followers of the Christian Science Religion. Her father who was a well-respected solicitor and her mother was a registered Christian Science Healer. Fortune was lucky in the fact that from an early age she claimed to have mystical and psychic abilities, she often had visions of Atlantis as early as four years of age, where she believed that they were of her past life memories as a Priestess of Atlantis in a former incarnation as the Priestess named Avenor.

Fortune always knowing of her social gifts as a medium even as early as being in her teens. She joined the Theosophical Society in 1906 for a short time and left due to rejecting their ideologies and association on Eastern thoughts due to Indian revolutions against the British rule. She was a very emotional person and sadly had a nervous breakdown just prior to WW1 which she believed was brought on due to being psychically attacked from a former client of hers. Fortune went on to study Psychology, especially attracted to the works of Dr. Carl Jung by her Professor Flugel who just so happened to also be a member of the Society of Psychical Research. Being so drawn to the works of Dr. Carl Jung where she loved his dual analogies which also involved spirituality, the occult, esoteric and parapsychological aspects of his system of the collective consciousness. Fortune actually rejected both techniques due to being unable to grasp the full range of the mind's capabilities.

It was during WW1 where Fortune worked in the Government agency on the development of proteins and supplements from soybeans, it was this inside information where she talked her parent into investing into soybeans as a business venture manufacturing and distributing soy products. Beyond their dreams this soy business grew beyond their expectations and made the family a small fortune. It was during these years that Fortune became deeper involved in her yearning to research at the deepest levels the Occult, and also her abilities as a Medium, Magic and psychology as these three became her main priorities where she decided to write and have published her first writings with the "Hermetic Order of the Golden Dawn" and also with the "Fraternity of the Inner Light".

Fortune also made herself available as a professional Medium to clients that sought out her abilities, and she went to great lengths to always explain to everyone that she "did not disturb the spirits of the dead but rather channeled their higher intelligence from a higher astral plane of existence". This explanation of hers was constant throughout all her writings so that no one was very confused by her dealings with the spirit world and Mediumship. She became a prolific writer for many magazines, newspapers, and books, and so she decided to create her own magazine titled "The Inner Light", which she edited from 1927 until 1940.

Fortune, due to being so immersed in Magic, was also fascinated by the ancient legends of Britain, especially of King Arthur, the Knights of the Round Table and of course Merlin the Magician, the sacred advisor to King Arthur. Fortune strongly adhered to her belief that these legends along with the famous Welsh poem "The Mabinogian", were true and existed as historical basis in British history at the countryside of Glastonbury in Somerset, where she established a retreat for the Fraternity of the Inner Light.

Fortune had a series of novels that were so detailed and had such sacred and in-depth information into these writings and that written between the lines were concealed messages to those enlightened enough to know fact from fiction, they incorporated aspects of Initiations at differing levels from Seeker, Neophyte, Initiate, Priesthood and High Priesthood, that would only be recognized by those knowledgeable enough or spiritually attuned, each book in procession was in fact an introduction to the ancient yet modern form of what was required through the stages of Initiation rituals at the 5 levels known as the Epagomenes "The Secrets of the Pentagram". These books in order were: The Sea Priestess, The Goat-Foot God, Demon Lover, Moon Magic, and the Winged Bull.

Fortune was not a Witch, but she was a true Magician and Occultist and spent most of her life involved in the Hermetic Order of the Golden Dawn, and it was during this Magical life that she adopted the phrase Deo Nun Fortuna, (by God and not by luck) as her official name Dion Fortune. She worked on many of her books from 1921 with Frederick Bligh Bond who was in the group of Arthurian enthusiasts known as the Watchers of Avalon. Fortune advanced through the degree's and eventually established her own lodge of the Golden Dawn in 1922 called the Christian Mystic Lodge of the Theosophical Society, because she believed that Christian Gospels were allegories. She also believed that Jesus (fortunes personal spiritual guide) was a prophet likened to Orpheus, Mithra, Tehuti Thoth and Melchizidek.

Fortune dedicated her last years to the Goddess Aset (Isis) as she saw in Isis just an older aspect of the Virgin Mary. She continued writing until 1939, when her health started to diminish. One famous act that Fortune did was to gather a group of people during WW2 to stop the Nazi's from bombing London and not to attack Britain. She did write and publish it as "The Magical Battle of Britain".

Dion Fortune died in 1946, just one week after being diagnosed with leukemia. Her Society of the Inner Light has continued, and her works have continued to inspire true occultists, Pagans, Witches, and all students of Magic.

Adrian Reinman
Clan Grandfather Elder
Clan of Boskednan & Black Forest Witches
July 18th, 1892 – June 6th, 1967

Adrian Reinman Berlin University

Adrian Reinman was born in Berlin on the 18th of July 1892 to farming parents Detlev Reinman and Olga Heist. Reinman came from a traditional family of Witches who came from the Black Forest but moved to Berlin for the education of their children. This Blood Witch family had three Covens that convened only once a month for any and all ritual workings that needed to be done.

Reinman at an early age showed so much interest in Witchcraft but due to his age was forbidden from learning or being involved by the Elders until he was old enough to understand and choose for himself. This was the law of the Blood Wicches of The Black Forest. He was taken aside by his father who was der Zauberer (Wizard, Magician, Conjurer or Sorcerer) and explained that in their tradition only women can be Zauberin (Witches, Sorceress, and Enchantress) which they complement each other and are also very different in their Magical elements. He was taught the art of Magic from the male line of his family and showed great talents at being able to tap into the spirit world. He drew close to Natural Medicines from an early age and so embarked on learning all he could about Herbalism, the Elements and Magical Medicine. He studied to become a doctor at Berlin University but did not complete his studies due to the war. He also became a member of an association of "der Zauberer and Zauberin", which he did not stay long as he believed it all seemed more theory and not as real as what he had been taught by his kin.

He travelled to the UK as a young adult to study and whilst in Cornwall he met his future wife Margaret DeLille Quinn, who had already a small Coven that was being run by her mother and father in Cornwall called The Clan of Boskednan. Adrian had to return back to Germany and so Margaret, and he packed up and moved to Hertzberg and connected with the family Clan. They went on to have 3 children and only their daughter Layla became interested in the family tradition of Witchcraft, where the others found others interests such as economics and mechanics.

Reinman met with a Dr. Frederick Santee from the US in the early 1940s and together they formed quite a friendship and bond due to their interest in the Pagan ways. Santee was initiated into the Black Forest Coven by Reinman and Quin but was also told that secrecy was their main law. Santee was gifted some notes and items that were traditional to the Black Forest, such as a Wand/Dagger that was made of Oak from the Dragon Tree in the Black Forest, and he was told to carve a personal symbol on it that was personal to himself. This coven never used daggers or swords, as they were not a part of nature, and were not seen as truly of the Craft. He was also given a small vial of oil, that had been added to by all those Elder before him and was to be used when he thought someone was of great benefit to the Witch community and a mentor, where during a ceremony their blood was added to the vial (3 drops).

Reinman was an academic in natural medicines and had an alternative store in Berlin, where he had to drive for several hours to get there and then came home to Hertzberg on the weekends. At the onset of WW2, they decided to move back to Margaret's hometown Boskednan in the UK in Cornwall. Where again they formed their Circle and worked privately as they always did. Reinman tried to open up a Herbal Store but it failed due to financial issues.

Reinman then set up his Natural Medical Practice Apotheker at his home and they turned the front of the home into a consultation room and a small shop with all his natural medicines and products. Margaret had her own room as she was excellent at Spellcraft and Tarot and Tealeaf Reading and together they earned enough money to support their family comfortably.

Reinman was diagnosed with bowel cancer in 1965 and died two years later. Which saw Margaret go into a state of depression, but her family lifted her out of that, and she decided to take the family and move to Australia to a warmer climate due to her health. They sold everything they had and boarded a ship to Fremantle, Western Australia in 1969 where they brought a beautiful small home in East Street, East Fremantle which was an influential suburb. Margaret continued to do her Spellcraft and Readings to make ends meet in Fremantle at her home, Layla became a model and travelled the world, and the two sons took on their careers one as an Economist and the other a mechanic.

The Coven of Boskednan continued through Margaret and Layla, and later with me when I joined them in the mid-70s. Reinman left a legacy in Margaret and their children with the continuance of the Clan of Boskednan Circles now being in 8 different countries, still private but strong.

Lady Margaret De Lille Quinn
Clan Grandmother Elder
Clan of Boskednan & Black Forest Witches
June 18th, 1894 - March 21st, 1995

Lady Margaret De Lille Quin and Lord Manannan

Lady Margaret De Lille Quinn was born in 1894 to her father William and mother Rosemary Quinn in the town of Boskednan in Cornwall, UK. They were a humble and private people who lived and worked in their family business which was farming.

Quinn married Adrian Reinman in 1915 who was from a bloodline of Traditional Witches of the Black Forest. They had three secret and closed Circles that met in the Black Forest for the occasional Celebrations and also the Family Circle just outside of Berlin and Hertzberg. They did not believe in Karma and also believed that only women could be true Witches (Zauberin), and men were (Zauberer) Sorcerer, Wizard, or Magician. They revered and followed the local Goddess Obby Oss Penglas who was the Goddess of horses, and sometimes Quinn would call her Clan the Sacred Clan of Horses, they also honored other Goddesses connect to the nature such as The Horned God or the Greenman. Reinman was also an academic and also interested in occult circles, being involved in the Order of Magicians and Sorcerers in Berlin. Together they ran their Family Clan and eventually had three children, Michael, Jonathon, and Layla.

When WW2 commenced in Germany the family headed back to the UK and went back to the family town of Boskednan in Cornwall. It was during this time that they formed again their Clan and brought in outsiders – Seekers as Quinn always called them and later, she called them Witchlings when they were serious students who were selected for their worth and genuineness.

I had heard that over the years, many other Witches who wanted to meet with Margaret, many she declined as she was a private person and did not trust many people. Sybil Leek contacted her for a meeting who Quinn thought sounded genuine and real, her introduction was through a former US Initiate of hers and Adrian's who was named Dr. Frederick Santee, that Quinn and Reinman Initiated in 1925 after they had met at the Berlin University. Quinn decided to meet with Sybil Leek at a hotel for a chat. She met with Sybil on three separate occasions, and began to trust in her, asking that she never disclosed their meetings nor herself. It was at the last meeting that they had met this time in Margaret's home, where she shared a few of her writings, and also explained that they did not have a formal Initiation for outsiders, and that it was more of a dedication and secrecy ritual.

In 1967 Margaret's husband Adrian died and she decided to move to Australia as the cold damp weather was taking its toll on her health. She arrived at the Fremantle Port in Western Australia with her daughter and sons and acquired a beautiful property in East Fremantle, which was at the time a very affluential suburb of the wealthy.

Both Michael and Layla enjoyed being in Australia, but their other brother Jonathon returned back to the UK and later died. This was now their home and Margaret needed to connect with her own kind, the Magical Witchy kind and searched for a working Coven in Western Australia. This was the Coven of Draconis a Traditional working Coven run by the High Priest known as David the 5th. In this closed Coven was a variety of members consisting of 2 well-known madams Dorrie Flatman and Shirley Finn, plus a lead singer in a top band.

It was in this Coven that I first met Margaret and Layla, and at once, we connected. Eventually becoming adopted by the Quinn family and becoming a very close member of their family and Clan Blood line through ritual. After David 5th's passing into the Summerland a few years later, we were invited to join with an Alexandrian Coven run by a High Priest named Simon Goodman and his High Priestess Michelin. Lady Margaret, Layla, Dorrie Flatman, and I all joined this new Alexandrian Coven.

Sadly, Michael, Margaret's son also died in early the 70s with cancer, and on 28th May 1982 Layla was killed in an automobile accident, all that was left was (Ma) Margaret and myself. We became remarkably close, and she taught me as much as she could before her passing on the Autumn Equinox on the 21st March 1995, when I was at a Festival celebration, and when I returned and found that she has passed into the Summerland. Lady Margaret always tried to attend many festivities but only during the warmer weather.

We stayed with The Alexandrian Coven for several years but due to politics we decided to leave and formed our own Coven/Clan (as Lady Margaret did not like the term Coven) with Margaret as the Elder High Priestess, myself as the High Priestess along with my High Priest Imhotep – Geoff Camm (Initiated by Alex and Maxine Sanders) and Layla, we again took on the family name and it too was called "The Clan of Boskednan" or sometimes the Penzance Clan of Boskednan. From this line there are dozens of Covens throughout Australia and the US which are from the line of Boskednan, even the Church of Wicca was under the banner of the Clan of Boskednan.

Photograph of Margaret, Brianna, Lord Manannan, Lady Tamara, Lady Neith

Ross "Nuinn" Nichols
Arch Druid Elder
1902 - 1975

Ross "Nuinn" Nichols

Ross Nichols was born in 1902 and known at an early age that his life was to be a Druid and not any Druid, where he took on the Magical name of Nuiin. Through his determination and devout interest in Druidism he went on to become the most famous and important influential Druid in the world, as he was one of the Founding fathers of modern-based Druid spirituality.

Nichols as a young man graduated in history from Cambridge University at the same time as Sir James Fraser was teaching at the University and also published his famous book The Golden Bough. Nichols adored the writings and works of well-known authors such as Fraser, Freud, Jung, T.S. Elliot, Sir Robert Graves and Jessie Weston amongst many others. Nichols had a hunger for such knowledge in the fields of mythology, psychology, Magic, and ancient religions. Nichols also became a journalist and began to teach journalism and social work throughout the Great depression, and eventually became a dedicated Socialist and noted Pacifist.

Nichols was a strict vegetarian, socialist, pacifist and also a naturist, where in the 1930s he joined Britain's first Naturist community "Spielplatz" (translated to playground) which was close to St. Albans in Herefordshire. Nichols was lucky enough to have worked continuously during the war, and also stayed at Spielplatz most weekends as during the week he was the principal of a private college (Jimmy's) which was well known for teaching Sir Winston Churchill. His weekends were his relaxing times at Spielplatz where he first met Gerald Gardner, and they hit it off straight away having mutual interests.

Nichols became the assistant editor in 1949 of "The Occult Observer", which was published by Michael Houghton of the Atlantis Bookshop, and it was Houghton who also published Gardner's High Magic's Aid in the very same year, but in his book Nichols wrote about Druidism for the first time, and his friend Mir Bashir wrote a story titled "The Book of Shadows", which was what inspired Gardner to borrow and adopt the title for the Wiccan term of their spiritual book of writings, of which now every respectful Witch has their version of the Book of Shadows in some way or form.

Nichols at the age of 50, with the help of occult specialists who happen to also be his friends, wrote a two-volume edition of Paul Christian's History and Practice of Magic. It was just after this that he helped Gardner to produce in 1954 his first book on Wicca titled Witchcraft Today. In that very same year Nichols decided to join the "Ancient Druid Order" that Gardner also happened to be a member many years prior. Nichols was dedicated for 10 years and eventually became its chairman and he also lectured on Druidism in London and also Dublin, at this same stage in his life he was working on a new book titled "The land of the White Bull- a Mythology for Britain", but sadly many of its pages were lost or stolen.

In 1963 Nichols was Ordained as the Archdeacon of the Isles in the Ancient Celtic Church. In the following year 1964 sadly both Gardner and the Chief Druid of the ADO died, and it was that event that set Nichols with a few other devout Druids for form and Found "The Order of Bards, Ovates and Druids".

Within the last 10 years of Nichols life, he succeeded to radically change the practices of modern Druidism, where he shifted its focus towards Celtic sources, and also introduced the observance of all eight festivals of the Pagan calendar into the Druid framework, he also introduced the Three Grades or Degrees of Bard, Ovate and Druid which were based on classical accounts. In Nichols last few years he wrote The Book of Druidry.

Nichols' legacy is yet to be fully appreciated, but the Order that he Founded and dedicated his life to has become the largest Druid organisation in the world with thousands of members worldwide. To know more in-depth detail into Ross Nichols life please read his biography "Journeys of the Soul: The Life & legacy of a Druid Chief" by Philip Carr-Gomm.

Dr. Frederick LaMotte "Merlin" Santee
Lord Merlin Witch Elder
September 17th, 1906 – April 11th, 1980

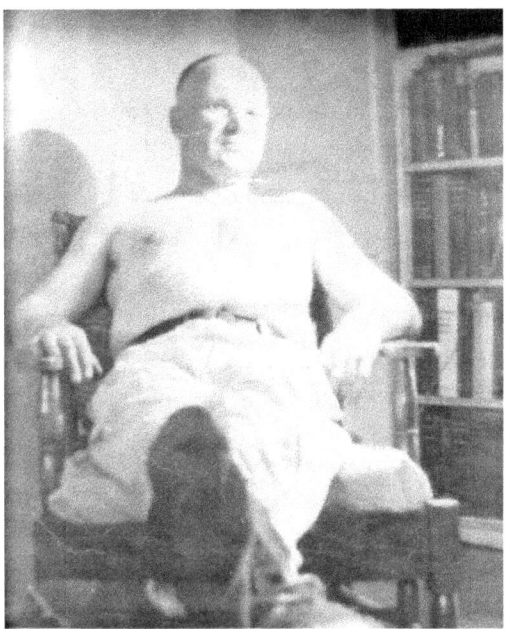

Photograph Courtesy of Catta Coven of Dr. Frederick Santee

Frederick LaMotte Santee was born on the 17th of September 1906 in Wapwallopen, Philadelphia. Born to Charles LaMotte Santee who held degrees as a doctor from LaFayette and Jefferson colleges, and his mother Verna Caroline Lloyd Santee. Santee's grandfather was a Civil War Surgeon who helped runaway slaves escape.

Santee from an incredibly early age showed the signs of a genius child and by the age of 3 could read both English and German. He also at a late stage learnt Latin fluently from his grandfather's grammar books. From the age of eight he was translating Caesar's Gallic Wars from Latin into English and back again to make sure his grammar was correct. Santee attended Wapwallopen High School and went on to Wilke-Barre High School for his final year. He also went on to Central High School in Philadelphia in Greek which took him onto Oxford University where he was the youngest to have graduated at the age of 22 and received the highest score in the whole of the US, in 1928 with an A.B. and then his M.A. in 1929. While he was in attendance at Oxford he joined "The Alpha et Omega Lodge of the Hermetic Order of the Golden Dawn" where he met with Aleister Crowley, H. P. Blavatsky, W. B. Yeats, Thomas Agee, Dion Fortune, A. E. Waite and also Israel Regardie.

Santee also joined the "Theosophical Society of England". Whilst at Oxford his main esoteric and occult influence was from his philosophy teacher, Professor Brabhart. He also travelled to and went to the University of Berlin between 1924-1925 but cut his studies down due to pending tensions in the country. It was hear that he met with a Blood Witch Coven and because of his massive interest in Witchcraft he was Dedicated into the Coven of The Black Forest in 1925, by the Clan Father Arnold Reinman and Clan Mother Margaret De Lille Quin where he was presented with a Wand/Athame made from the Dragon Tree (Oak) of the Black Forest and also a vial of Traditional oil and blood from several generations which was added to by others who dedicated their lives through Initiation at the highest level. Where he learnt as much as he could before travelling onto the Middle East where he met fellow adepts in the High Magic of Egypt.

Santee spent additional years in teaching positions at Harvard, Temple, Kenyon, John Hopkins, but held no tenure due to his socialist ideas. In 1928 on his return to the US he met with and married Edith Rundle from Allentown, and in 1930 had a daughter Ruth who died in 1938. In 1930 Santee was a "Sheldon Fellow" and Fellow at the "American Academy of Rome" for 3 years. Santee also joined the "Rosicrucian Society" and was Initiated into the "Illuminati". Santee graduated in 1938 from John Hopkin's University in Baltimore Maryland with his MD degree. From 1938-1941 he taught classical languages at Kenyon College Ohio. He opposed the US involvement in WW2 since he was an avowed Socialist. Santee divorced Edith in 1942 and married Betty Addis of Cumberland, also a MD. They adopted Tao and Betty died in 1966. Santee was drafted into the Navy and served in the South Pacific but never saw any action. Santee still interested in Witchcraft started collecting ancient books and built one of the world's largest esoteric, occult, spiritual and Witchcraft libraries with around 50,000 books.

Dr. Santee's Library

In 1956 Santee met Edna Jane Kishbaugh Williams who became his High Priestess and took on the name Lady Phoebe Athene Nimne (still as acting Elder HPs today), together they created one of the earliest covens in the US. Santee returned back to Wapwallopen to continue his medical practice, where his home and office were at the same address of 5 River Street, Wapwallopen.

Due to his massive collection of books, in 1970 he built a library to contain all the 50,000 books, this was next door to his medical center where he employed 2 nurses and 4 secretaries, and even had 2 librarians for his massive collection. He also wrote in a local newspaper column called "The Country Doctor" and Santee wrote a column called "The Witches Kettle". The locals always spoke highly of him as a gentle and kind compassionate man/doctor, but they all agreed he was a bit eccentric as he always treated the poor who could not afford to pay for his services, many times also paying for their surgeries if they needed and could not afford, so he paid out of his own pocket.

Santee rubbed shoulders with many of the occult and Witchcraft community, as he was also a scholar of the Faust novels and legend and also wrote his own Faustian story titled "The Devils Wager", which was set in modern times. He loved cats and due to his love of animals supported the Humane Society and money from his will was donated to them. He often went to New York and visited a bookstore called "The Magickal Childe", where he had met with Sybil leek and invited her to his established Covenstead. It was Lady Phoebe who encouraged him to be Initiated by her due to her notoriety and start a new Coven. This eventuated and he was Initiated by Sybil Leek in 1967 and received a charter from her, they named the Coven the "Coven of the Catta" named after their cat totem. This Coven still exists today with many offshoots who are dedicated to keeping this line going.

Sadly in 1979 someone broke into his library and stole some ancient texts and books, and to escape the law torched the place and destroyed nearly the entire library and much of their Covenstead tools, regalia and writings as well, this devastated Santee and also much of Lady Phoebe's personal Craft items were also destroyed, and losing his entire collection of rare books and artefacts was something he never got over as he saw the destruction of books as barbaric and pictured Hitler's burning of the books as sacrilegious.

Santee suffered a long battle with liver failure and on the 11th of April 1980 at the age of 72 he slowly slipped away into the Summerlands. His remains are buried at the Old River Church just north of Wapwallopen, Pa. His gravestone says: "I shall return when Spring's shadow trails".

Headstone of Dr. Frederick "Merlin" Santee

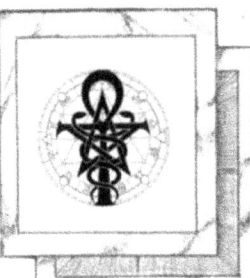

Israel (Regudy) Regardie
Magician, Freemason, Occultist
November 17th, 1907 – March 10th, 1985

Israel Regardie

Francis Israel Regardie born on the 17th November 1907 to father Barnet Regudy and mother Phoebe Perry, who were a hard working middle class family of Orthodox Jews that were immigrants from Zhitomir, Ukraine and now lived in the East End of London, their name changed from Regudy to Regardie due to clerical error, but in Regardies' younger years, the entire family decided to move to Washington DC in the United States. His parents were devout in their faith as Jews and believed that the Hebrew Talmudas stories were factual, and always urged young Regardie to study hard with an appointed Hebrew private tutor, which he saw as a waste of time and totally unnecessary due to his immense studies in the Holy Kabbalah later in life.

Regardie became very bored and defiant seeing all his tutoring and studies as a waste of time and not needed in his life's journey, all this mumbo jumbo was absurd nonsense, and his rebellious nature enhanced especially around his family where he accentuated his feelings and played up all the time. He rejected their faith which was bad enough to his parents but as his rebellion grew so too did his searching for the answers of his Truth and he became quite interested in Theosophy after he read Madame Blavatsky's book, and the Eastern religions such as Buddhism and Hinduism that also fascinated him, it was the Eastern philosophies that got him interested in Yoga.

Regardie being always creative and artistic in his talents, desired to become an artist, of which his parents allowed him to study at Philadelphia Art School, they saw it as nothing more than keeping his mind occupied in something that could be beneficial for him. Whilst he was studying at the library he came across the writings of Aleister Crowley, and so decided (although still noticeably young) to make contact and wrote Crowley a letter as an interested Seeker in the fields of the Occult. Crowley being as eccentric and as audacious as he was invited the young man to come and serve as his personal secretary, which also meant giving up his studies and moving from the US to Paris, France, this was in 1928.

Regardie being so rebellious and adventurous took up Crowley's opportunity, as he saw it as an opportunity to get away from his family and his studies, and join with and study under his new mentor Aleister Crowley, and so he went off to Paris and together they travelled to Britain, where Regardie wrote two books on the Holy Kabbalah: "A Garden of Pomegranates" and "The Tree of Life". Regardie was so intrigued by all areas of the Occult and decided he needed to learn more and so joined the Fraternity of Stella Matutina, which was an Order of Ceremonial Magicians that came from the defunct "Hermetic Order of the Golden Dawn". But again, due to his getting bored easy, he also became quite disenchanted here, as he found that it had a lack of organizational skills and the leadership was all over the place, he found it more of a men's club, so he left without explanation very abruptly.

Regardie thought that by studying Jungian Psychology it would help him with his search in the Occult, and also at the same time studied Christian Mysticism. He returned back to the US in 1937 and worried about the Golden Dawn system being lost or weakened due to its constant political bickering decided to publish the Stella Matutina, a book containing their rituals in a series of books between 1938 and 1940. This angered many of the members of the Order past and present, and he started to get threats from many Occultists from around the world as he had broken a most sacred vow, his Oath of Secrecy. Regardie continued on and brushed off the threats and also became interested in the Rosicrucians and joined the "Societas Rosicriciana in America".

It was around this time also that Regardie started to serve in the US Army during WW2 but only for a short stint, and upon his arrival back in the US decided to study again, and this time he gained a doctorate in Psychology, then relocated to Los Angeles in 1947, where Regardie set up a practice as a Chiropractor and Psychologist. Regardie still being accused by many as an oath-breaker, and hating the scrutiny decided during the 1950s that he would keep away from any and all Occult involvement and avoided the public eye, especially the media where he constantly refused media attention, and any interviews were non-existent. It was also a well-known fact that both he and Crowley experimented with many mind-altering drugs such as LSD, and as it was a public knowledge everyone wanted to know all about his involvement, especially the media.

Regardie went into retirement in 1981 and moved to Sedona, Arizona where he died of a heart attack four years later. Due to the immense fights between he and Crowley in later life, Regardie began editing many of Crowley's varied works for republication and among them were "Book Four", "Three Holy Books", "AHA", "The Vision and the Voice", "The World's Tragedy", "Magick Without Tears", and also a collection called "The Best of Crowley". In 1970 he republished the Entire Works of the Golden Dawn. He travelled during the year of 1983 where he visited Fiji, Australia and New Zealand, and when travelling on to Hawaii, loved it so much that he thought of moving there and retiring but Regardie passed away with a heart attack at a gathering of friends for a dinner party at a Sedona restaurant on the 10th March 1985 at the age of 77. His Will separated all his belongings to his nephew and his occult material to Hyatt who established the Israel Regardie Foundation.

Books by Israel Regardie:
- *Legend of Aleister Crowley*, 1930
- *The Tree of Life: An Illustrated Study in Magic*, 1931
- *A Garden of Pomegranates: Scrying on the Tree of Life*, 1932
- *The Middle Pillar: The Balancing Between Mind and Magic*, 1951
- *The Art of True Healing: The Unlimited Power of Prayer and Visualization*, 1964
- *The Art and Meaning Magic*, 1964
- *The Eye of the Triangle: An Interpretation of Aleister Crowley*, 1970
- *Philosopher's Stone*, 1970
- *How to Make and Use Talismans*, 1970
- *The Golden Dawn:* 1971
- *Practical Guide to Geomantic Divination*, 1972
- *Roll Away the Stone*, 1974
- *One Year Manual*, 1975
- *Ceremonial Magic*, 1980
- *The Regardie Tapes* 1982
- *Lazy Man's Guide to Relaxation*, 1983
- *What You Should Know About the Golden Dawn*, 1983
- *Teachers of Fulfilment*, 1983
- *The Complete Golden Dawn System of Magic*, 1984
- *Golden Dawn Audio, Volume II*, 1985
- *Golden Dawn Audios, Volume III*, 1985
- *Mysticism, Psychology and Oedipus*, 1986
- *Foundations of Practical Magic*, 1988
- *Healing Energy: Prayer and Relaxation*, 1989

- *Golden Dan Audios: The World of Enochian Magic*, 2001
- *The Golden Dawn Audio CDs: Volume 4*, 2001
- *My Rosicrucian Adventure,*
- *Gold: Israel Regardie's Lost Book of Alchemy*, 2015

Cecil Williamson
Wiccan Elder
September 18th, 1909 – December 9th, 1999

Cecil Williamson was born 18th September 1909 in Paignton, Devon, to his father who was a senior officer in the Royal Navy that was posted abroad. Williamson when only seven years of age encountered Witchcraft for the very first time, when he was on a visit to his uncle a local Vicar in North Bovey, Devon came across and viewed a local woman being beaten publicly due to be accused as being a Witch. Williamson automatically and without thinking of the consequences and being only a child went up to her and tried to defend her, and through this act of kindness befriended her. Williamson in 1921 attended the Malvery College boarding school, and was constantly bullied, but luckily received help and kindness from a woman who lived on the school campus, who was a Witch. She taught him how to become stronger and defend himself with Magic and use Spellcraft to protect himself. Williamson did his Spell and soon after the very bully broke his leg in a skiing accident, and actually stopped bullying him and others altogether. During most school holidays Williamson visited his grandmother in Dinard, France and her friend Mona McKenzie, who was a Medium and she taught him about divination.

Williamson after completing his schooling travelled to Rhodesia to grow tobacco, where his servant Zandonda taught him about African Magic. He returned back to Britain in 1930 and lived in London where he began a career as a production assistant on several film studios. His Occult interest started to peek, but he saw it only as a hobby. He started to collect occult objects and ended up becoming acquainted with Dr. Margaret Murray, Montague Summers and also Aleister Crowley. Williamson met and married Gwen Wilcox in 1933, a makeup artist and also the niece of the film director Herbert Wilcox. A big change occurred when he was hired by M16 to lead an investigation into Nazi's Occult interests, it was here at the same time that he Founded "The Witchcraft Research Centre", and in April of 1944 a news report reflected his area of expertise in claiming that Goebbels was going to harness fortune telling, astrology and necromancy to his propaganda

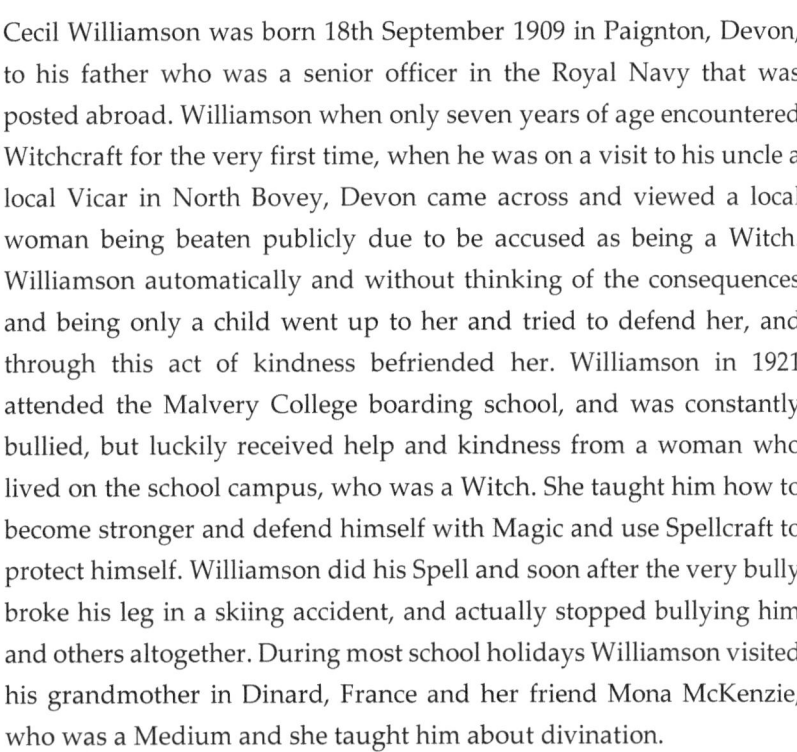

machine. After the war in 1946, Williamson met Gerald Gardner in the "Atlantis Bookshop", which was in London where he was giving a talk on Witchcraft.

The two had much in common especially their interest in the theory of the Pagan Witch Cult and they became close friends. A year later Williamson in 1947 tried to open a Witchcraft Museum in Stratford-on-Avon, but after lots of local opposition he had to change his plans. In 1948 he bought an old run-down windmill at Castletown on the Isle of Man and turned it into the "Folklore Centre of Supersticion and Witchcraft", it was officially opened in 1949 alongside an adjacent restaurant called the "Witches Kitchen". After discussions with Gardner employed him to be the resident witch at the museum, which had been renamed to the "Museum of Magic and Witchcraft" after the 1951 repeal of the 1735 Witchcraft Act.

Williamson and Gardner were good friends to start with, but both had differing views on how the museum should be run, and they started to argue and drift apart due to these differences, and Williamson desired to return back the England. So, in 1952 sold the museum to Gardner, selling many of the artifacts but kept quite a few for himself and took them to a new site in Windsor calling it the "Museum of Witchcraft". Gardner used his own larger artefact collection to fill the museum of the Isle of Man for the rest of his life. Williamson's museum remained open for only a year when he was forced to close it down due to lack of interest and support and also due to local opposition again. He again moved the museum in 1954 to Bourton-on-the-Water in Gloucestershire. Due to an arson attack the museum was heavily destroyed and so again moving the museum in 1960 to Boscastle in Cornwall, where it has grown and survives today in the 21st century.

Williamson was a British Screenwriter, editor, and film director, and also an influential Neopagan Witch and ran the Museum of Witchcraft. At midnight on the 31st of October in 1996, Williamson sold the museum to Graham King. He kept some of his special relics until his passing which were eventually bought by the museum from his trust. Cecil Williamson died on the 9th of December in 1999.

Eleanor Ray Bone – Lady Artemis
High Priestess-Witch Elder
December 15th, 1910 – September 21st, 2001

Eleanor Ray Bone

Eleanor Ray Bone born 15th December 1910, whose Initiated Craft name was Artemis, or more correctly after she became High Priestess, Lady Artemis. She has been one of the world's most influential Witches in the modern Neopagan religion of Wicca of the 20th century. Bone claimed to have been Initiated in 1941 by a couple of hereditary Witches in Cumbria, some say in Boskednan, but officially it was not until her meeting with Gerald Gardner where she was eventually Initiated into his Gardnerian Tradition of Wicca, and within time became a High Priestess of one of his Covens. Bone with her perfect gentle personality befriended many high-profile Wiccan figures including Jack 'Dafo' Bracelin, Patricia Crowther, Doreen Valiente and also Idries Shah (although he was not a Wiccan).

Bone became remarkably close friends to Gerald Gardner's Initiator "Dafo", where they both confided in each other a great deal and shared many an in-depth conversation concerning Craft matters and also Gardner. Bone also claimed that the New Forest Coven was a

Hereditary Coven that actually followed the old ways of the Hampshire region, and that they had traced their origins to the time of King William Rufus in the Norman era. Many have spoken of how she became the Mother of the Coven and in fact was regarded by many as the "Matriarch of Modern British Wicca". Bone also Founded many of her own Covens throughout the years and among them were the best known and most successful Covens in South London and Brighton in the 1960s.

Among Bone's own Initiatory Coven downline are Madge and Arthur Worthington, who together went on to Found the famous line of Wicca known as "The Whitecroft Line". With a strong ally in Patricia Crowther, they both together denounced Alex Sanders as a fraud as having invalid Initiations. Sanders's response and reaction to this public accusation made him decide to found his own tradition now known worldwide as "Alexandrian Wicca" which along with "Gardnerian Wicca" have thrived and grown throughout the world, with hundreds of covens globally, and many thousands of Initiates.

Sadly, the Mother of Gardnerian Wicca Eleanor Ray Bone respectfully titled and known as Lady Artemis, High Priestess Elder passed away on the 21st of September 2001, The Autumn Equinox (northern hemisphere).

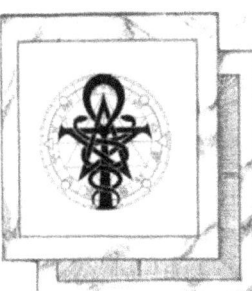

William G. Gray
Ceremonial Magician
March 25th, 1913 - 1992

William G. Gray

William G. Gray was born on the 25th of March 1913 in Harrow, Middlesex to his mother Christine Ash Gray who had an American Roman Catholic religious background. His mother had a great intrigue in Western Esotericism and started to associate with many occultists, as she believed herself to be the reincarnation of Marie-Noemi Cadiot (1832-1888) the wife of French Occultist Eliphas Levi (1810-1975). His father John McCammon Trew Gray was from a Low Church background and took little to no interest at all in the occult.

In 1914 when WW2 broke out and Britain allied itself with France, Gray's father went to war, and whilst there his mother sent young Gray to live with his elderly grandmother and Aunt Leila in Ramsgate. It was here that he started to really play up and became quite rebellious at any and all rules of the house, he disobeyed everything they asked of him, and this stressed them both out where his aunt fell ill. They did not cope with his carrying on and he was shipped off again, this time to his Uncle Will and Aunt Florence who were both active members of the Theosophical Society. They treated young Gray as a grown up and he felt more mature and so acted more mature, and he decided that he liked to be called Bill instead of William, he started an attraction in the occult and began learning more about its world.

When Gray was only 8, he attended the Forest Hill Primary School in London after the war had ended. Here he started to take his mother to Mass every Sunday at the local Roman Catholic Church, and amazingly he enjoyed, well the ritual side of it anyway, it was here that he decided that he wanted to become an Ordained priest when he was older. Again, Gray and his mother decided to move to Canada in Montreal, where she became terribly ill with severe bronchial infections and was hospitalized, this time Gray was shipped off again to another of his aunts, Aunt Leslie and Uncle Bruce, a wealthy stockbroker.

Gray like most young people lost interest in his childhood fantasy of becoming an Ordained Minister of the Catholic Church, and when his mother fully recovered, together they returned back to Britain and moved into a flat in Southampton. Gray's mother started working as a Professional fortune teller and Gray shared in his mother's interests in Western Esotericism, Metaphysics and also Psychology. Gray was continuously borrowing books from all the surrounding libraries and at the age of 14 he was determined to find himself a Magical Mentor that he could learn from.

On a visit to London to see his uncle, Gray decided to travel and visit the home of Dion Fortune, a noted Ceremonial Magician and leader of the Fraternity of the Inner Light. He arrived unannounced and knocked at her door, and she spoke to him briefly suggesting that he was too young and that they would not teach people under the age of 21 but wished him well in his endeavors for the future and closed the door.

Gray did continue on his endeavors and between 1913-1992, he became an English Ceremonial Magician, Hermetic Kabbalist and also an author, who published many books on Western Esotericism and the Occult. Gray went on to Found a Magical Order of his own known as "Sangreal Sodality". Gray met a lot of famous Occultists in his young years including Aleister Crowley, Victor Neuberg and Dion Fortune, as after their meeting he went on to become a dedicated student of Emile Napoleon Hauenstein. During WW2 Gray joined the army and served for many years. After the war he returned back home and befriended and did many rituals with many Occultists including Robert Cochrane, and also published several acclaimed books. Gray's Order is now an international trademarked spiritual brotherhood of the "Western Inner Tradition" that was Founded jointly by both William Gray and Jacobus G. Swart and had their official grand opening on the 19th of November 1980 in Johannesburg, South Africa. Gray now has temples set up in South and North America, Britain, Europe and Australia.

I was lucky enough to have had contact with Gray on several occasions through letters and have a few of his books signed by him as keepsakes for my collection of books, many autographed by the authors.

The term "Sangreal" is understood in this brotherhood to be "Sang" ("blood") and "Real" (authentic). The basic premise being the True Identity and Inner Values within each single human individual. The term sodality derives from a Latin root referring to a "Comradeship."

William "Bill" Gray died in 1992 at the age of 79, but his legacy still lives on in the Temples that he created around the world.

Stewart Farrar
High Priest-Witch Elder
June 28th, 1916 – February 7th, 2000

Stewart Farrar

Frank Stewart Farrar was born in the family home of 239 Winchester Road, Highams Park, Essex on the 28th of June 1916. Farrar although named Frank always went by his middle name by his family and friends as Stewart. The Farrar family were all well-educated of a middle class and of the Christian denomination known as Christian Scientists (Founded in 1886) which focused on the power of healing through faith rather than conventional medicine.

Farrar at the young age of 17 became a Socialist and later took a strong and dedicated stance and called himself a "Communist" as he rejected all forms of Christianity. Farrar studied journalism at the University College London in 1935, where he was eventually nominated and served as the president and editor of the "London Union Magazine". In 1937 Farrar ended his study and went to Germany

As an exchange student where he became fluent in the German language but hated right wing Nazism. Farrar returned back to Britain and immersed himself deeply in Communism and joined the "Communist Part of Great Britain" where he started to work for a communist tabloid called "The Daily Worker", where he met and fell in love with Jean Clarke.

When WW2 broke out against Germany in 1939, he immediately signed up and was hoping to be sent overseas to action, but instead was commissioned to be a combat trainer in Britain for the new recruits. After the world Farrar started to publish his exceptionally long list of books with his first book being The Snake of 99, which was a crime mystery novel, with success in this book he wrote another crime novel in 1961 Zero in the Gate. Farrar went on to write many novels which also followed by a romance novel Delphine, Be A Darling. This led him on a pat to writing movie scripts starting with Its All Ove Town and followed by Journey of a Lifetime, where he travelled to Petra and had many psychic and spiritual experiences, which changed his direction of focus. In 1968 Farrar won a "Writer's Guild Award" for his radio serial Watch the Wall My Darling which was based upon a Rudyard Kipling poem A Smugglers Song.

Farrar received an invitation to review a press screening of the film Legend of the Witches", which was attended by Alex and Maxine Sanders who were the Founders of the Alexandrian Tradition of Wicca and were also advisors for the movie. Farrar had always been skeptical of Magic and Witchcraft but was intrigued in meeting with the Sanders, he also requested a meeting after which he published the interview in a two-page spread. Alex Sanders was so impressed by his positive and honest article without adding all the added mumbo jumbo that many writers added for excitement, so Sanders contacted Farrar to thank him for the great article that he had done and so invited him to attend an Initiation ceremony, after which he was asked to write on their behalf his first non-fiction book What Witches Do (one of my favourite books that we use to call "The Witches Cookbook). It was from this book that Farrar's life changed drastically in a different direction than anticipated or could have ever imagined.

Farrar grew intrigued and became involved with the Sanders and commenced in studying his Outer Court training, and within a few months of being Initiated by the Sanders on the 21st of February 1970, was Ordained to the 2nd degree on the 17th of October 1970. Farrar then went on to Found his own Coven in South London with the young Witch at the time who was 34 years his junior that he had previously met at the Sanders Covenstead, it was this young Witch Janet Owen when eventually became his wife, and most importantly his first High Priestess.

Stewart and Janet Farrar decided to move to Ireland, where it is now estimated that three quarters of all the Covens in Ireland are hives from the Farrar's. It was around this time that they did a documentary by Neville Drury titled "The Occult Experience" which was based on Witches and Covens around the world. This documentary was filmed at their home

"Herne Cottage" in Kells, Country Meath, where they had a full working Coven. There is a beautiful quote from a letter from the Sanders about Farrar on the 8th of March 1976:

"Your letters give off good vibrations of work and happiness. I feel that all our growing pains concerning publicity and personalities of the Wicca, are beginning to bear fruit. A few of us in the midst of many are beginning to establish the foundation (I mean the building itself) on the raw materials, to get the foundation stone in place."

The Farrar's were later joined by Gavin Bone, where a 'polyfidelphous' relationship that was true and loving began, this was the beginning of a great triune in business, love and led them all together onto writing several more books and in 1999 the Farrar's received "The Aquarian Tabernacle Church" (ATC) Charter for Ireland, and were Ordained to the Third Level Clergy, which struct a chord at my heart as I too had become in 1992 the Charter for ATC in Australia was also lucky like them to be Ordained by Pete Pathfinder within the ATC.

Books by Stewart and Janet Farrar and Gavin Bone:

- *The Snake on 99*, 1958, Collins Press, London
- *Zero in the Gate*, 1961, Walker, NY
- *Death in the Wrong Bed*, 1963, Walker, NY
- *Delphine, Be a Darling* (as Laurie Stewart), 1963, Hurst & Blackett, London
- *What Witches Do: A Modern Coven Revealed*, 1971, Peter Davies, London
- *The Twelve Maidens*, 1973, Michael Joseph, London
- *The Serpent of Lilith* (as Margot Villiers), 1976, Arrow Books, London
- *The Dance of Blood*, 1977, Arrow Books, London
- *The Sword of Orley*, 1977, Michael Joseph, London
- *Omega*, 1980, Arrow Books, London
- *Forcible Entry*, 1986, Robert Hale, London
- *Blacklash*, 1988, Robert Hale, London
- *Witches' Dozen*, 1996, Godolphin House, New Bern, NC.

With Janet Farrar
The following are non-fiction books.

- *Eight Sabbats for Witches*, 1981, Robert Hale, London
- *The Witches' Way*, 1984, Robert Hale, London
- *The Witches' Goddess: The Feminine Principle of Divinity*, 1987, Robert Hale, London
- *The Life and Times of a Modern Witch*, 1987, Piatkus Books, London
- *The Witches' God: Lord of the Dance* , 1989, Robert Hale, London
- *Spells and How They Work*, 1990, Robert Hale, London
- *A Witches' Bible: The Complete Witches' Handbook* with Janet Farrar and Gavin Bone (re-issue of *The Witches' Way* and *Eight Sabbats for Witches*) Robert Hale, London

- *Pagan Path: The Wiccan Way of Life*, 1995, Phoenix Publishing
- *The Healing Craft: Healing Practices for Witches and Pagans*, 1999, Phoenix Publications Inc., Custer, WA
- *The Complete Dictionary of European Gods and Goddesses*, 2000, Capall Bann Publishers
- *Progressive Witchcraft*, 2004, New Pages Books

Rosaleen Norton
Witch, Magician Elder
October 2nd, 1917 – December 5th, 1979

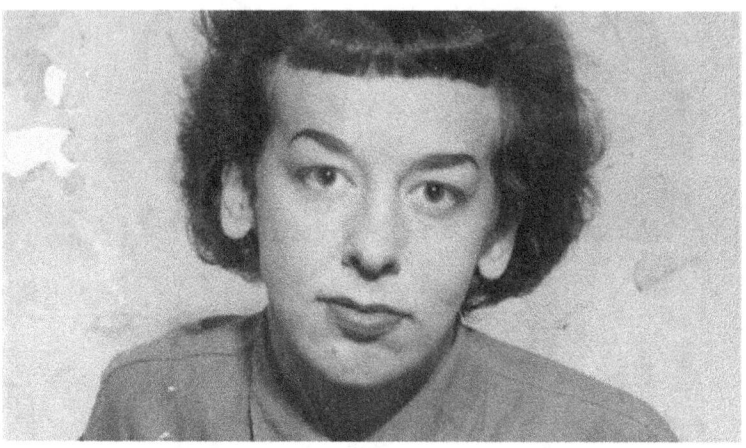

Rosaleen Norton

Rosaleen Miriam Norton born on the 2nd of October 1917 in Dunedin, New Zealand to English immigrants. Norton was one of three sibling sisters who were both ten years older. She was always an unusual looking child, and also played up to it claiming that she was born a Witch, and with the facial features to prove it. She would threaten to put spells on people if they upset her. When Norton was only eight years of age the family decided to move to Sydney, Australia for a better life due to lack of work where they lived, and they settled in a wealthy area called Lindfield in Wolseley Street.

Norton was never conventional in her mannerism and ideals, and disliked anyone especially adults who were authority figures, especially like her mother Beena, as they never connected as mother and daughter and clashed always which became quite physical sometimes. Beena, her mother, enrolled her at the local Church of England girls' school, where she thought it might quieten her and discipline her. But Norton's rebellious nature escalated where she aimed at getting into trouble as a game on a daily basis, she was so unruly that she eventually was expelled for being disruptive and continually drawing evil demonic forces and creatures. Norton's teachers feared that she was a corrupting influence on all the other students, who were intrigued and fascinated not only by her artwork but her antagonistic nature.

Norton was an angry young girl and despised anyone, and also targeted them if they pried into her life, especially as she put it "those obnoxious Christians". She disliked and distrusted everyone and decided that she did not want to live in the house again and so erected a tent in the back garden and moved her belongings into it and lived in the tent (her new home) for three years with "Horatio" her pet spider, along with her other pet cats, tortoises, toads and even a pet goat. Norton no matter what her dislikes, she was a brilliant artist even at an early age and showed a talent beyond her years. It was the one thing she loved above everything, and her parents allowed her to attend and study art at the East Sydney Technical College under the mentorship of her Arts teacher and sculptor Ralph Hoff, who always encouraged her unconventional and very occult oriented and sexual style creative nature of all her art. Hoff was the first person that she admired and trusted as he gave her free license to be herself and let her form of art flow freely. Following her studies she became a cadet writer with a local newspaper, Smith Weekly, and was given the chance to publish several of her horror stories in 1934 when she was only sixteen.

Norton became an illustrator, but due to her graphic portrayals were found to be too offensive and controversial and was fired from work. Not long after this her mother died, and Norton decided to move away from the family home and rented a room at the "Ship and Mermaid Inn" which was in a beautiful area that overlooked Circular Quay in Sydney. Norton always wanted more, and just wanted to be accepted for who she was and wanted her art to be appreciated. She was never content with what she was doing, and all her jobs never lasted long, whether she was a dishwasher, kitchen maid, waitress and even a toy designer, she also was a nude model for young aspiring artists.

Although Norton always claimed at being a Witch from very young, it was only now in later years that it really started to interest her, and so her search for Witchcraft and the Occult became an important past-time, she read every book she could get her hands on from Western Esoteric Traditions, Demonology, The Holy Kabbalah, Witchcraft and even alternative Nature Religions. She had a deep fixation and attraction towards the Greek God Pan, and so became a Pantheistic Neo-Pagan Witch although never being Initiated.

Norton lived most of her life in the Bohemian area of King's Cross in Sydney, which eventually led to her title and name as the "Witch of Kings Cross", where she did have a secret Coven that was entirely patriarchal and honored the Divine Masculine in Nature that she saw as Pan. Word of Norton became popular, and her fame brought tourists from all works of life to her, where they sought her out, usually in the same place sitting in her Bohemian dress code in a man's suit with tie and a long cigarette holder, always sitting on the pavement where she constantly did chalk paintings on the pavement of Kings Cross itself, with her paintings lined up behind her for sale. This became her place, and her cigarette holders and dress-style became her symbol of identity. She always saw the cigarette holder as a phallic symbol. She was also compared to the British artist Austin Osman Spare, who also depicted Pagan Gods, demons, and sexuality in his artwork.

Norton's artwork that she displayed on the pavement streets became controversial and many people complained to the council and the police seeing it as offensive to good Christian souls. As Neville Drury stated: "Norton's esoteric beliefs, cosmology and visionary art are all closely intertwined-and reflect her unique approach to the magical universe". Norton was always inspired by the Magic and mystery of the Night and fell in love with its dark Mystery.

Norton met and eventually married Beresford Lionel Conroy on the 14th of December 1940, and on their honeymoon, they hitchhiked up the north coast of Australia up to tropical Cairns in Queensland, but on their return trip back to Sydney Conroy enlisted as a Commando during WW2 and went off to war in New Guinea. When he returned, he realised that Norton had been forced to live in a stable during the entire war, Norton then demanded a divorce which was finalized in 1951. Norton went to live in The Rocks at a boarding house known as "Marangaroo" which was under the Sydney Harbour Bridge still a part of the Bohemian community, it was here that she flourished and so did her art. During this time, her art caught the eye of the famous poet Leon Batt, who described her: "an artist worthy of comparison with some of the best Continental, American and English contemporaries".

In 1949, Norton met with and became good friends and eventually lovers with Gavin Greenlees, they decided to hitchhike to Melbourne in search of a venue to hold a public Gallery for her art. They agreed and settled on a display at the University of Melbourne's "Rowden White Library", where a total of 46 of her best artworks were placed on display including "Timeless Worlds", "Merlin", Lucifer" and "The Initiate" were proudly hung on display for all the world to see. But the timing was very wrong as she was shut down by police only two days after her grand opening where they deemed her artwork as offensive and removed four of her paintings "Witches Sabbat", "Lucifer", Triumph" and "Individuation", as they were deemed obscene and offensive.

Norton was convicted and charged under the Police Offences Act of 1928, her lawyer fought for her and argued the case by quoting a previous case of a book that was published and accepted by the Australian censors titled "The History of Sexual Magic", was far more obscene than her paintings. Norton won the case and was awarded four pounds, four shillings, as compensation. Norton and Greenlees now lovers eventually moved back to Kings Cross, Sydney which was now classed as the Red-Light District (Brothels and Prostitutes) and was very Bohemian including poets, artists, the gay scene, depravity, crime, drugs, prostitution, eccentrics etc. Many of Norton's artworks were displayed at local cafes and hotels where she became quite famously a celebrity where even their home was turned into a gallery and became a main attraction for the media and tourists alike, where every room displayed her art, and it was her Bohemian Gallery that was filled with occult murals and above the main entrance over the door was a plaque that said:

"Welcome to the house of ghosts, goblins, werewolves, vampires, witches, wizards and poltergeists".

Norton was approached by a publisher who idolized her work and offered to publish her artworks in a limited-edition book in full colour that was titled "The Art of Rosaleen Norton", this was published in 1952 with a limited production of only 505 copies bound in red leather with gold embossed and high gloss pages of her art, but as it hit the market it was banned in New South Wales, Australia as obscene and also forbidden to enter the US. The law again had created a barrier for Norton and the legal system demanded that several of the images were to be blackened out due to the Obscenity Act. Glover (the publisher) was charged in court along with Norton.

Norton eventually divorced Greenlees, and not long after their divorce he was admitted to a Psyche Hospital in 1955 and in 1957, two years later he was diagnosed with schizophrenia. Norton maintained their friendship and visited him often until 1964 when he was released on a temporary leave of absence but suffered a schizophrenic attack where he tried to kill Norton with a kitchen knife, he was readmitted, and they never saw each other again. He was released from hospital four years after Norton's death in 1963.

The fact is that up until the 1950s in England when the Witchcraft Act of 1735 had been repealed, but it was still illegal in most parts of Australia with New South Wales being the first to have the Witchcraft Act repealed 1971. Much later in the other states up until the late 1980s when I fought the establishment to accept Witchcraft and associated acts and won in legal battles by establishing and legalizing Australia's first legal neo-Pagan Church "The Church of Wicca" 1989, and then later receiving my Charter after receiving my Third-Degree Ordination by Pete Pathfinder Davis and became the Arch Priestess of the Aquarian Tabernacle Church in 1991. Protecting Witches and Pagans to publicly follow their faith who were now protected by Governmental Charter.

Norton was always publicly declared that she was a Witch and sadly died from colon cancer in 1979 at the Sacred Heart Hospice for the Dying, in Darlinghurst, Sydney. She loved Pan her God and knew that at her deathbed he was their waiting for her and never lost faith in her Craft. Before she died, she is reported as saying: "I came into the world bravely, I'll go out bravely." A plaque has been placed on display at Darlinghurst dedicated to Norton as "The Witch of Kings Cross".

Upon Norton's death many of her paintings were owned by Don Deaton, a local pub owner who sold them at auction where a single collector Jack Parker purchased the entire collection for five thousand pounds. In 2019 I heard of some of her original books in red leather being sold but they are not genuine, they are copies created in the Philippines.

Books on Rosaleen Norton:
- *Pan's Daughter: The Strange World of Rosaleen Norton,* 1988, Neville Drury
- *The Witch of Kings Cross*, Neville Drury

- *Pan: The Life, Art and Sex-Magic of Rosaleen Norton* 2009
- *The Occult Visions of Rosaleen Norton*, 2000, The Ordo Templii Orientis
- *Thorn in the Flesh: A Grim-memoir,* Norton
- *The Art of Rosaleen Norton with poems by Gavin Greenlees*, 1952 and 1988.

Lady Olivia Melian Durdin-Robertson
High Priestess-Goddess Elder
April 13th, 1917 – November 14th, 2013

Photograph of Lady Olivia, Niamh, and Tamara Von Forslun

Olivia Melian Durdin-Robertson was born on the 13th of April 1917 in St. Marys Hospital in London. Olivia, a descendant of Richard Graves, cousin of author and Archaeologist Sir Robert Graves was also the granddaughter of Thomas Herbert Robertson, and her parents were good friends with W. B. Yeats. Robertson's family lived in Reigate, Surry until moving back into their family home, Huntington Castle in Ireland which they inherited from their grandmother who bequeathed it to them in her Will in 1925. Robertson was a student at Healthfield School, Ascot and also at the Grosvenor School of Modern Art.

Although Robertson was a pacifist, she decided with the outbreak of WW2 that she was going to serve in a capacity where she felt she could be of service, and that was as a V.A.D. Nurse in Bedfordshire in 1940. In 1942 she went to study at the University College of Dublin and went on to work at the Dublin Corporation until 1946, when she decided to publish the first of her books "St. Malachy's Court", which was followed by being awarded the "London Book Society's Choice Award" in 1948 for the book "The Golden Eye". Robertson went on to publish many more books in particular "The Dublin Phoenix" in 1956 which sold out on its first day of release. Although Huntington Castle was bequeathed to them by their grandmother at her death in 1921, they did not return to live in the castle until 1960, this was the family home and had been in the family since the 15th century.

Lady Olivia and Lord Lawrence Durdin-Robertson along with his wife Lady Pamela all moved back into the castle as their home. Due to their spirituality the Robertson family in 1963 decided to found "The Huntingdon Castle Centre for Meditation & Study", but it was not until 1976 when the biggest changes occurred when they legally Founded and created "The Fellowship of Isis" (FOI). Along with her busy schedule writing and having published more books, Robertson wrote her spiritual autobiography "The Call of Isis" in 1975 followed closely by the "Isis of Fellowship" which described how the FOI was formed and why. Excitingly I have copies of both books by Lady Olivia, and when she signed her books, she also did her artwork at the front of the book, they are cherished possessions of mine.

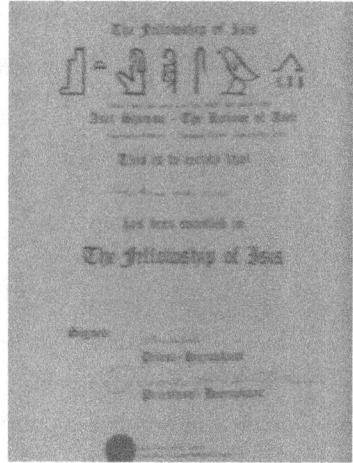

FOI Certificate 24th January 1978

I heard about this wonderful fellowship myself and decided to have written contact with them and was surprised when I received return letters and also a Certificate of membership to which everything Robertson did was added by her beautiful artwork. I became a dedicated member on 24th January 1978, eventually I went to Ireland to be Ordained a Priestess (21st June 1981) by Olivia and Lawrence along with two other ladies, one from England and the other from America. I later became a Lyceum of the FOI in Australia and loved my journey with them.

In 1993 "The World Parliament of Religions" invited Robertson to attend in Chicago, US where she represented the FOI and the world Goddess movement. One of the highest points in her life was when she had breakfast with His Holiness the Dalai Lama. It was in 2011 when they showed their respect at what she had achieved for the Goddess movement when a film was made of her life titled "Olivia, Priestess of Isis", it was also released on DVD in 2011.

Sadly, this great exciting and humorous lady died in Wexford on the 14th of November 2013, she had a private ceremony held in the FOI Temple which was organized by the Elders of the Fellowship of Isis, which is now one of the largest Goddess movements in the world in over 70 countries. For those interested just look up Fellowship of Isis in your country and you will be led to a FOI Centre.

Sybil Leek
High Priestess-Witch Elder
Lady Sybilla, Queen Mother
February 22nd, 1917 - October 26th, 1982

Sybil Leek

Sybil (Fawcett) Leek was born on the 22nd of February 1917 to a middle-class family in the small village of Normacot in Stoke-on-Trent, Staffordshire in Britain. Leek as a child was always quite adventurous and even as an adult this never changed, she learnt to grow up fast, and when she met her music teacher (who was many years her senior) they fell in love and married when she was only sixteen years of age, sadly as her first love, he died only two years later. This devastated Leek and she felt quite lost and confused with life in general, so she decided to return back home and live with her grandmother, but Leek became quite restless here as well, and was not sure what to do with her life. Leek moved out and in with a good friend to Lyndhurst in the New Forest where she became acquainted with the local gypsies.

Leek when she was only 20 years old, returned back home to be closer to her family, it was also near to the edge of the New Forest, Leek due to insurance from the death of her husband was in a good financial position where she leased three separate shops all at the same time in Ringwood, Somerset and Burley, they all became antique and second-hand shops and were situated around the New

Forest Village region. Leek eventually moved into one of the small houses set behind one of the shops and attached, this shop she called "Laeford's of Burley". She was always an outspoken person that spoke before she thought of the consequences, but she always said what was on her mind and never kept it a secret that she often said she was a self-described Witch, even though she had never actually been involved in a Coven or Witchcraft of any sort previously, she did not even know any Witches at the time.

Leek eventually became restless and was very dismayed at all the negative attention that she was getting from the locals, instead of positive acknowledgement as she believed people would draw to her honesty about being a Witch and her involvement. The media were cruel and started to call her a zealot or a fraud, but alas the media attention started to create a long line of tourists that were seeking her out, they came from near and far, they were not there for the business but for her involvement in Witchcraft, as they sought her help. Although many came from long distances, the locals rallied against her and she was targeted, and when her leases were up for renewal, the owners never renewed her leases, so she decided that nothing was of benefit here anymore and sold her businesses, packed up everything she had and moved to the United States of America.

Leek settled in the US in 1964 where she studied to become an Astrologer. From this her creativity began to flourish and grow and she began to put pen to paper and wrote her first book called A Shop in High Street, she was also doing many interviews around New York and through her book she was contacted by Hans Holzer, a parapsychologist who invited her to join with him on his investigations of psychic phenomena and hauntings. Together they made a great team and did in New York called "The Magickal Childe" many television and radio appearances and interviews. Eventually Leek decided to move across the country to Los Angeles where she met with Israel Regardie, who was an authority of Ceremonial and Ritual Magic and also the Holy Kabbalah.

Leek also met with Dr. Frederick Lamotte Santee in her favourite shop in New York called "The Magickal Childe", they formed such a great bond and friendship that he invited her to visit at his home and also to discuss his Initiation into a Traditional Blood Line of Witchcraft from Berlin in 1925 by Arnold Reinman (The Black Forest Coven) and Margaret De Lille Quinn (Clan of Boskednan, Cornwall). Later it was Dr. Santee's High Priestess Lady Phoebe that also talked him into being Initiated by Leek and forming a Charter from her Tradition and linking the Coven of Catta together. Leek was told about Reinman and Quin now living back in her family home in a county called Penzance and her Coven was called The Clan of Boskednan. Leek started to write to Quin, and when she went back to Britain asked to meet with her.

Leek and Quinn had met on three separate occasions discussing her Tradition of the Craft, they shared information and Quinn gave Leek some of her notes and had a dedication ceremony welcoming her into the Clan, she was presented with a Dragon Tooth, which was a combination of Wand and Athame carved from an old Oak tree from the Black Forest in Germany. This Oak tree still exists today and from its limbs are still made the ritual Daggers and also Sacred Altar Pentacles that are presented to Initiates or special guests, but never sold. Leek was also presented with a small vial of oil that had drops of blood from the line of every Elder who underwent a form of Ordination as responsible for the community, she was also asked by Quinn not to reveal anything about her, as she was a very private lady.

Leek was very stern in her beliefs and often argued and fought against modern contemporary Wiccans and Witches and she was in total disagreement about certain modern concepts of Wicca such as nudity and drugs etc. Leek's unusual way of teaching was quite different to any of the other Elders of the Craft as she never taught in groups but always one to one, and never taught the same thing, always swaying easily with her responses and answers. Even one of her students, Christine Jones admits that Leek "mixed truths with untruths liberally, causing great harm as she went".

Sybil Leek died of cancer Tuesday, 26 October 1982 at the Holmes Regional Medical Centre in Melbourne, FL.

Books by Sybil Leek:

- *Ancient Wisdom,*
- *The Jackdaw and the Witch,* 1966
- *Astrological Guide to Success*
- *Diary of a Witch,* 1968
- *Diary of a Witch Sybil Leek - Prentice-Hall,* 1968
- *Practical Candle Burning Rituals,* 1969
- *The Zodiac Cookbook,* 1969
- *Dreams-Your Magic Mirror*
- *What's New in Magic*
- *Phrenology,* 1970
- *Sybil leek's Curious Occult*
- *My Life in Astrology,* 1972
- *How to be Your Own Astrologer,* 1974
- *Vintage Cast Your on Spell,* 1975
- *Reincarnation, The Second Chance,* 1975
- *Sybil Leek's Astrological Guide*
- *Reincarnation*
- *The Complete Art of Witchcraft*
- *Driving Out the Devils,* 1977
- *The Story of Faith Healing*
- *Astrology and Love*
- *Zodiac of Love*
- *Ring of Magic Islands,*
- *Sybil Leek Book of Fortune Telling,* 1969
- *The Assassination Chain*
- *Telepathy: The Respectable Phenomenon*

- *Moon Signs Lunar Astrology, 1977*
- *Star Speak, Your Language from the Stars*

Lady Sheba
High Priestess-Witch Elder
July 18th, 1920 - March 2nd, 2002

Lady Sheba

Lady Sheba (her Craft name) born on July 18th, 1920, as Jessie Wicker Bell in the mountains of Kentucky, rose to becoming one of America's famed Witches and self-acclaimed "Witch Queen" during the 60s and 70s. In 1971 she was one of the first to write and have published her Book of Shadows. Sheba always bragged about her family line who were practicing Witches for seven generations, and through her bloodline had inherited her Magical and Psychic gifts. She grew up with her grandmother introducing her to Witchcraft and most importantly what was termed the little folk who lived in the local forest. Each evening at sunset she placed a small saucer of milk out for the little folk so that they would bring blessings to the household and all within. As Sheba grew older so too did her abilities grow and she believed that she had been granted the sacred "Hand of Power", she also stated that she had been Initiated as a Witch in the 1930s and spent her divided time between blood family and craft family, where she combined her own Celtic heritage with American Indian Magic.

When reading her books, I find that they are in line with the Gardnerian Tradition of Wicca and remarkably similar in many ways. Sheba had gained much notoriety from the media and many people seeking her out due to the new publication of her book "The Magick Grimoire" which is a collection of her personal spell book of spells and rituals, some she says were handed down through her family line. Her second book and the most well know and famous was her Book of Shadows, in 1971, through this publication she was accused of betraying the Wiccan movement but defended her decision with saying that she was directed by the Goddess to open up the knowledge to the world and the Seekers who wanted to know the truth.

Lady Sheba died and entered the Summerland's on the 2nd of March 2002.

Lord Lawrence Durdin-Robertson
Baron Riadh/Robertson of Strathloch
High Priest-F.O.I. Goddess Elder
May 6th, 1920 – August 4th, 1994

Photograph of Lord Lawrence in Isian Temple

Lawrence Alexander Durdin-Robertson was born on May 6, 1920, and was the 3rd of 4 siblings born to Manning and Nora Durdin-Robertson. He studied at St. Columba's College in Dublin and went on to serve in the Irish Army. During the war Robertson worked at the Admiralty Research Lab in Teddington, Middlesex.

When Robertson's father died in 1945, he inherited Clonegal Castle, but decided not to live in it until a few years later, this was due to the fact that he, being deeply religious, decided to enter the Seminary at the Wells Theological College and was Ordained an Anglican Priest in 1948. Just after his Ordination he met and fell in love with Pamela Barclay, and later in the very same year they were married. He was so proud of being a Priest and with his excitement he became the Rector of two churches: Aghold, Co. Wicklow from 1951 to 1952, and East Bilney, Norfolk from 1952-1957. It was during these later years that Robertson started losing faith within the Christian church and its system and his form of faith was making a major shift spiritually, where he was having revelations that God was Feminine, and decided to leave the Priesthood and the Church of England completely and to return back to his family home at Clonegal Castle.

Robertson had a deep insight and revelations of the Divine Feminine that awakened his searchings, and he ventured on a quest to find out more about the Divine Feminine and the Goddess Mysteries where his research took him within the confines of the Hebrew texts of the Bible, and it was these readings that changed his entire outlook of spirituality and religion, as he then started to realise that his Awakening and true Mission in life was for the Goddess in all her forms and names and in particular to the Goddess Isis.

Robertson discussed this with his family and together with his wife Pamela and sister Olivia, formed the "Huntington Castle Centre for Meditation and Study". Since Robertson's' awakening of the Goddess he began writing about the Goddess and all that she was revealing to him, and also received his vocation as the Priest of the Goddess Isis in 1972, together as a family they all formed "The Fellowship of Isis" (FOI) in 1976. It was in the year of 1978 that I first made contact with the FOI in my personal search for my own answers and became a member, and after a couple more years I decided to be Ordained as a Priestess of the FOI and travelled to Ireland and was Ordained at Clonegal Castle at the Summer Solstice in 1982 in the deep recess of their castle where the dungeon use to be, that was now dedicated to the Goddess Isis as Her Temple.

Robertson received his official ancestral title of Baron Ruadh (Robertson) of Strathloch. Robertson then entrusted in 1981 to the FOI, being held by trustees "Through Deed of Gift – The Temple of Isis" which is the basement level of the castle. I was one of the lucky ones to have met with Robertson and his family and respected him enormously for his truth and dedication in creating this whole Foundation and pathway for the world to find the Goddess. He was such a gentle and determined man and was one of my many mentors who assisted me in my Ordination into the FOI in the early 80s. Sadly we lost him when he ascended to spirit in the arms of Isis on the 4th of August 1994. To know more about Baron Lawrence Durdin-Robertson and his views on the Goddess please read many of his books, especially my favourite "Juno Covella-The perpetual Calendar of the Fellowship of Isis", which is used by FOI members worldwide.

Books By Lawrence Durdin-Robertson:

- *Juno Covella-Perpetual calendar of the Fellowship of Isis*
- *God the Mother*
- *Life in the Next World*
- *The Religion of the Goddess*
- *Guide to Clonegal Castle*
- *Women in Arts, Crafts and Professions*

Communion with the Goddess Series

- *The Vital Elements*
- *Initiation and the Mysteries*
- *Priestesses*
- *Idols, Images & Symbols of the Goddesses Egypt Part 1: Isis*
- *Idols, Images & Symbols of the Goddesses Egypt Part II:*
- *Idols, Images & Symbols of the Goddesses Egypt Part III:*
- *Idols, Images & Symbols of the Goddesses: India*
- *Idols, Images & Symbols of the Goddesses: South-East Asia & Tibet*
- *Idols, Images & Symbols of the Goddesses: China & Japan*

With others at Ordination with Olivia and Lawrence

Doreen "Lady Ameth" Valiente
Grand High Priestess-Witch Elder
January 4th, 1922 – September 1st, 1999

Born Doreen Edith Dominy on the 4th of January 1922 in Mitcham, South London to parents Harry and Edith. Valiente had a soft speaking and gentle English accent due to her moving around a lot as a child. She recalls her first Magical experience at the age of seven when she was playing as a Witch riding on a broomstick up and down the street, where others had their pushbikes, she had her broomstick as her mode of transport. Due to this strange behavior, her parents started to worry about her desires in the Magical realms and the Occult world.

As a teenager Valiente intensified her interest in Magic and in particular Witchcraft, when she started to learn and use Spellcraft to hex away the constant harassment of a local woman who was slandering and gossiping about her mother, so she made a Fif-fath (poppet) which is an act of Sympathetic Magic (the law of Like attracts like) which worked quickly as the woman was surrounded with a myriad of problems herself, including the constant swooping of a local blackbird. Like most teenagers, Valiente started to be very rebellious with any and all rules of the home and so she was shipped off to a Christian Convent School which was also a live-in girl boarding school. She absolutely hated this place and the severe strictness that was part of their rules, this made her very reluctant to attend any of the classes, but due to her only being 15 she had no say in the matter. Being so rebellious one day she had had enough and just woke up, packed her bag and walked straight out through the front gate, and decided she would not attend any school ever again.

Valiente did not like any authority figures at all, and due to her decision not to attend school again she got a job working in a factory, and this infuriated her parents. She went on to become a typist where her language skills became her best benefit. She found it very easy to pick up and learn languages quickly, and this helped her during WW2, but she never spoke openly about any involvement during the war, but in 1941 in the South of Wales, at the tender age of 19 she met and married Joanis Vlachopoulos, who was a merchant seaman of Greek descent and who was also 15 years her senior. But although the age difference worked for them, shortly after their marriage Joanis was lost at sea, presumed drowned, this was only 5 months after their wedding.

Three years later Valiente had met and fallen in love with a Spanish gentleman named Cosimiro Valiente, where they married and remained together for most of her life. Valiente was also treated as a Spanish National by the British authorities.

Valiente still very much interested and more so attracted in the Occult became a student of the Golden Dawn, after reading a magazine article on the "Museum of Witchcraft and Magic" on the Isle of Man, it was through this article Valiente decided to contact the curator Mr. Cecil Williamson, who passed her letter onto fellow director and the resident Witch, Gerald Gardner. Upon receiving Valente's letter, Gardner immediately replied, and they made an appointment to meet up at Dafo's house near Christchurch in September 1952. It was this auspicious meeting that was lucky for both Valiente and Gardner that formed the establishment of what we now know as the greatest modern Tradition of Witchcraft in the world called Gardnerian Wicca.

Valiente studied very hard as her hunger was immense and on Midsummer's Eve in 1952 whilst on a trip with Gardner to lend his Sword to the Arch Druid for his Solstice Ceremony, which was held at Stonehenge, and on the eve of the Solstice she was Initiated by Gardner and the day after participated in the Druid ceremony at Stonehenge, which became one of her fondest memories.

When they went back home, it was time for her to copy out Gardner's Book of Shadows, where she spotted not only a lot of errors but also a mixed set of writings from other authors such as Aleister Crowley and also quotes and poems from Rudyard Kipling, she addressed this to Gardner, and he got into a fit of rage and through the BoS at her saying "so you think you can do better?" It was this incredible statement that Valiente took Gardner's BoS, and totally reconstructed and rewrote a majority of it by adding her own personal flare giving it character and a flow that was acceptable and beautiful with her gifts of adding poetry that was appropriate, it was this that became the Gardnerian Book of Shadows that has now been adopted, added to and pulled apart by nearly every Wiccan and Witch alike throughout the 20th and 21st centuries to create their own personal BoS.

Valiente being eloquent as she was at speaking, focused on becoming the official teacher and mentor as the Gardnerian Spokesperson, where she also educated Gardner on dealing with the media as he wanted more and more media attention, it was in fact Valiente that dealt with the main dealings of all the inhouse training and workings of their Coven as she became eventually the Mother of the Coven and with her professional touch took the Craft and their Covens to the next level as the official Mentor and Mother of the Gardnerian Tradition of Wicca. But the workload became too much as she was not getting much support and assistance, and so decided to leave, and just prior to leaving she created a manuscript titled Proposed Rules for the Craft, which was written to help curb Gardner's excess dealings with the media and also hopefully quieten his outgoing loud nature, as he was always bragging and in this bragging he gave away and revealed many Craft secrets especially their Initiation rituals and its process etc.

Gardner never listened to Valiente even after many attempts to quieten down his rebellious and shock tactic nature, due to this Valiente left the Coven and they never worked again, but their friendship was restored much later. She never abandoned the Craft but instead founded her own new coven with a new High Priest as her working partner – Ned Grove. 1964 was a turbulent and hurtful year for Valiente as her mother died and so too did her mentor Gerald Gardner. With her constant searching she eventually met and was Initiated into a Traditional Witchcraft coven the Grove in Glastonbury. She was also later Initiated into the Coven of Atho.

The Craft movement grew beyond expectations especially with the awakening revival of everything spiritual including a new enthusiasm in Wicca, Paganism and Witchcraft. Sadly, Valente's devoted husband Casimiro died in 1972, where she once again tried to keep herself busy and came back into the limelight and she began again to write books on Wicca and Witchcraft. She also founded and established an organisation known as The Pagan Front, which the name later was changed to "The Pagan Federation", this organisation still continues strongly today in the 21st century and is there to help fight prejudice against Pagans from both the media and the public community at large.

Valiente did not like people that changed the truth to suit their ideas, she made it her mission to research everything carefully and clearly, especially when it had to do with the origins or history of Witchcraft, and especially her involvement was more committed in the 1980s. She downsized and moved into a flat in "Tyson Place" where she met Ron (Cookie) Cooke who became her partner for the rest of his life until his passing in 1997. The sadness was unbearable three husbands she had lost, and losing her greatest love Cookie was devastating to her, but she got back up again and became involved in the group called "The Centre for Pagan Studies" which was run by a Witch - John Belham-Payne and his wife Julie, together being tired of all the charlatans that were coming out of the woodworks and into public view with claims of everything back to their grandmothers. They all combined their forces together with initiative and sought to seek the truth about everything. This became pivotal in their workings and Valiente became the Patroness of the CFPS and also made John her final High Priest of her coven.

Valientes health started to decline with the onset of pancreatic cancer (which was the same cancer that took her mother). Her newfound Coveners and friends John and Julie were close with her till the end and hardly left her side. Valiente passed her personal Magical legacy to John on the promise that he remain trusted to her and knew what to do as the right thing with it. Valiente slipped away into the Summerland at 6.55am on the 1st of September 1999. John and Julie along with fellow Coveners officiated at her funeral, they later formed a charitable trust in her name to which her entire collection of artefacts, books, letters, photographs, documents, which were the lifelong collection of Doreen Valiente, and now left as a legacy in "The Doreen Valiente Foundation", which raised funds and approval for a blue plaque to commemorate Doreen's life and her achievements which was officially unveiled at Tyson Place, Brighton on Midsummer's Day, 2003, the 60th anniversary of her Initiation into the Craft by Gerald Gardner, the plaque reads:

"Doreen Valiente (1922 – 1999) – Poet, Author and Mother of Modern Witchcraft"

Doreen Valientes Books:
- *Where Witchcraft Lives,* 1962
- *An ABC of Witchcraft,* 1973
- *Natural Magic,* 1975
- *Witchcraft for Tomorrow,* 1978
- *The Rebirth of Witchcraft,* 1989
- *Charge of the Goddess,* 2000
- *Doreen Valiente – Witch,* 2016, The Centre for Pagan Studies

Monique "Lady Olwen" Wilson
Gardnerian Witch Queen
1923 – 1982

Born Monique Marie Mauricette Arnoux in Haiphong, North Vietnam in 1923 to loving French parents, with her father being a French naval officer who was stationed in the Haiphong seaport. Wilson as a young lady worked at the customs office for the British Government in Haiphong, which is where she first met Gerald Gardner. When WW2 broke out in 1939, she witnessed the brutal murder of her father at the hands of Communists in the streets of Hanoi. It was after this event that a string of events that made them run for their lives and become refugee's, they fled the country for fear of their lives like most and raced their way to the safety of Hong Kong, where they having harsh lives waited for the end of the war, the daily struggle of just surviving and getting enough food and supplies were very lacking.

At the end of WW2 and still being a refugee in Hong Kong, she met her future husband, Cambell Wilson, a Scotsman nicknamed "Scotty", who was an RAF commander who was stationed in Hong Kong. They became inseparable and in a few months they were publicly engaged and married not long after. Their loving relationship lasted, and they remained together until Scotty's retirement from the service in 1954, when they were still friends, decided to return back to Britain and settled in Perth, Scotland. It was three years later they had their daughter, Yvette.

Whilst living in Perth, Wilson started to grow an attraction to Witchcraft, which was firstly ignited with her first meeting of Gerald Gardner and his 1954 book Witchcraft Today, even though she was unaware that the very same author was the same man she used to call Uncle Gerald, that she had grown up with as a small child in Haiphong. Still unaware she decided to write to him at his Museum of Witchcraft & Magic, which was situated on the Isle of Man, she searched for more answers about Witchcraft. It was only when receiving a letter from Gardner that she realised that they were the one in the same, and it was here that they renewed their bonding friendship. Wilson was later Initiated by Gardner and Charles Clark in his Coven, and he gave her the Craft name Olwen. Wilson and her husband Scotty both became Initiated and were more involved in the Coven, and he eventually became her working High Priest, where he took the name Loic. Their daughter was also interested and was later also Initiated at a young age and given the name Morven.

It was in 1961 that Wilson's responsibility heightened when she asked for Ordination and Elevation to the 3rd Degree as a High Priestess, and she officially became the Mother and Lady of the Coven, known there forth as Lady Olwen, where she was guided by both Gardner and Clark, and decided to form her own Coven in Perth. Her bond with both Gardner and Clark always remained strong, and as good friends and fellow Coveners, and even respected each other as family where he always remained her Uncle Gerald.

Lady Olwen eventually became the official spokesperson for all of the Tradition of Gardnerian Wicca, due to her eloquence in the way she spoke in her strong and quiet refined manner which attracted media attention, and the publicity was never-ending. Lady Olwen's deep bond and close relationship with Gardner and all the many Gardnerian Covens was dubbed by the media as The Queen of Witches, this claim and title she loved and also sometimes embellished, but it was she with all her work that deserved this title.

It was the Wilsons along with Gerald Gardner that Initiated Raymond Buckland (author, mentor and Great Elder, now respected as the Father of American Witchcraft) along with his wife Rosemary into their tradition of Gardnerian Wicca. Sadly, it was only three months later that Gardner died at sea alone, where he bequeathed in his Will the majority of his estate to Wilson, including the "Museum of Witchcraft and Magic" at the Witches Mill in Castletown on the Isle of Man, along with his own street Cottage in Malew which contained just as many artefacts as was in the museum. In particular his vast array and collection of weaponry of swords and daggers that he collected from all over the world, also his ceremonial Tools and objects plus a room full of notebooks, papers and documents of great significance and important to the Craft as a whole and its legacy to the Pagan world.

The Wilsons decided to move into the Museum and decided to dedicate their time fully along with their own investments and money to market and promote the expansion and also redecorating the museum, they also purchased an attached restaurant called "The Witches Kitchen", with the hopes of making it all a viable business that would become a financial success for them. Wilson contacted all of the media outlets to promote the museum and focused on how to generate visitors and attention for the museum. Due to her notoriety in the public eye, she was attacked by Eleanor Bone outwardly and argumentatively using the media claimed title of the "Queen of Witches", as it was Bone who originally was given that title years before. Bone also opposed Alex Sanders for using the title of "King of Witches", as she saw only Gardner as the King, To me the truth is that they both deserved the title as they both worked hard and devoutly for the Craft in expanding the Wiccan movement and bringing out into the open beyond even their wildest dreams into a global Wiccan Tradition, Gardener was King of Gardnerian Wicca and Alex was King of Alexandrian Wicca.

Yes, both of them had their issues, and health problems with drinking, and eventually had many debts. The rumor mill started to move and change and grow and mudslinging always sticks whether true or not, it spreads like a virus that contaminates everyone to varying degrees. It's like the story of a drunk coming home from the local pub, when he returns back to the pub puffing and panting saying in a drunken state, "I saw a witch flying over the field", the next person has to make the story more his own and adds "He saw a gaggle of witches flying over the town". Exaggeration is the root of all evil, spreading gossip is one thing, but listening to it is just as bad. Wilson was attacked viciously but it was too late, she was devastated at the attacks, and it took its toll on her health with a nervous breakdown where she started to drink heavy.

Wilson had sacrificed much in her life due to being dedicated to the Craft, and worked tirelessly for the advancement of Wicca and the museum at great emotional and financial costs to her and her husband, but with her finances dwindling and nearly exhausted and with the lack of support from the Pagan community even her covens did not assist or help in keeping this venture alive and well, she did ask for help but none came. It was then due to mountable stress that her husband Scotty insisted they sell the Museum to the American organisation "Ripley's Believe it or Not" consortium. Regretfully they sold everything and moved to Torremolinos in Southern Spain where they bought a small café and practiced their faith privately and away from prying eyes and the media.

Sadly, due to the sale of the Museum and Gardner's legacy, the world's Pagan community were outraged as they saw his artefacts and writings that they believed belonged to the British National Heritage, they were slandered and attacked, constantly being accused of selling out. It was this final act that Wilson became an outcast of the Wiccan Community, but her legacy still thrives in a positive light in the US, through her positive connection and the Initiation and friendship of Raymond and Rosemary Buckland "The Buckland Museum of Witchcraft & Magic" in Cleveland, Ohio, which is owned and retained by Buckland's last High Priestess, Toni Rotonda. Maybe if the community supported the Wilsons and helped instead of attacking her, we would still have Gardner's artefacts in the museum.

Wilson has been and still is an important part of the Pagan and Wiccan history and is a significant figure, Raymond Buckland always praised her and defended her as his High Priestess, Lady Olwen, the Elder and true Queen of Gardnerian Wicca.

Sadly, Monique passed away in 1982, without the support of her community and not as a Queen, but as a mother and friend to many. Scotty, her devoted husband, lived until the 1990s in the USA, occasionally going to festivals and meeting with like-minded people but also distanced himself from the larger community. Yvette, their daughter avoids at every cost the Craft and its people due to the devastation and rumor mill that destroyed their family, she avoids at all costs any contact, discussion or even association about the Craft and her devoted and dedicated mother. None Greater, Lady Olwen, and thank you!

Francis X. King
Magician
January 10th, 1934 – November 8th, 1994

Francis X. King was born 10th January 1934 in England, not much is known of his early life, he became a famous occult writer and professional editor that wrote about tarot, divination, holistic medicine, sex magic, Witchcraft, and tantra. He became a member of the "Society of the Inner Light" which was a hive-off branch of the "Alpha et Omega", which was an off-shoot of the "Hermetic Order of the Golden Dawn".

In 1973, King broke his oath to the O.T.O. with his publication of The Secret Rituals of the O.T.O, which outraged the heads of the organization, especially the leader Grady McMurtry, because he revealed without consent the fraternity's secrets. He was accused of including documents which were believed to be a lot of nonsense, but it is believed that he was given the extra documents by Gerald Yorke.

King was an Elder as a Magician, and an author who publicly wrote about the taboo side of the Craft and opened up the doorway for a lot of people.

Books by Francis King:

- *Ritual Magic in England, 1887*, 1970.
- *The Rites of Modern Occult Magic,* 1971
- *Sexuality, Magic and Perversion,* 1971
- *Astral projection, Ritual Magic, and Alchemy,* 1972
- *The Secret Rituals of the O.T.O.,* 1973
- *Crowley on Christ,* 1974
- *Magic: The Western Tradition,* 1975
- *Satan and the Swastika,* 1976
- *Techniques of High Magic, (with Stephen Skinner),* 1976
- *The Magical World of Aleister Crowley,* 1977
- *Tantra: A practical Guide to its Teachings and Techniques.*
- *The Cosmic Influence,* 1976
- *Christopher Isherwood,* 1976
- *The Rebirth of Magic,* 1982

- *The Unexplained File Cult and Occult*, 1985
- *Tantra for Westerners: A practical Guide to the Way of Action*, 1986
- *Rudolph Steiner and Holistic medicine*, 1987
- *The Encyclopaedia of Fortune-Telling*, 1988
- *Tarot*, 1990
- *Witchcraft and Demonology*, 1991
- *Mind and Magic: An Illustrated Encyclopedia of the Mysterious and Unexplained*, 1991
- *The Flying Sorcerer: Being the Magical and Aeronautical Adventures of Francis Barrett*
- *Nostradamus: Prophecies Fulfilled and Predictions for the Millennium and Beyond*, 1993
- *The Complete Fortune Teller (with Paul Cooper)*, 1994
- *Encyclopedia of Mind, Magic, and Mysteries*, 1995
- *The Hamlyn Encyclopedia*, 1997
- *The Illustrated Encyclopedia of Fortune Telling*, 2001

Idries Shah
Occultist, Alchemist, Magician
June 16th, 1924 – November 23rd, 1996

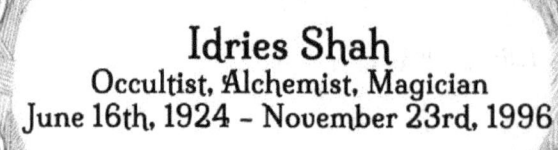

Idries Shah was born on the 16th of June 1924, in Simia, India to an Afghan-Indian father, Sirdir Ikbal Ali Shah who was a writer and diplomat, and his Scottish mother, Saira Elizabeth Luiza Shah. The family ancestral home was near the Paghman Gardens of Kabul, where his paternal grandfather was the Nawab of Sardhana in the North-Indian state of Uttar Pradesh, a hereditary title as Nobles that they had gained through thanks of the services to the British Government.

Shah at an early age along with his family moved from India to a suburb of London, Britain. He was so close to his father that he hardly ever left his side, in fact he was his father's little shadow. He accompanied his father on many of his business trips and also on social trips, always returning back home to Britain. Shah through his father's business travels met with many influential and prominent people of society including statesmen in both the East and the West. Shah from an incredibly young age was always fascinated by the variety and eclectic differences of the people that he met with, and at an early age showed that he was highly intelligent. Shah ended up having the contacts and a great deal of opportunities through his father in his international outlook, and later learned to use this to his advantage.

Shah, coming from a Sufi culture and religion, found that it heightened his spiritual appetite and also his senses. When WW2 commenced, the family decided to move from London to be safe to Oxford in 1940, this was to escape the constant bombing from Germany. He spent the following three years at the City of Oxford High School for boys. Even during his education, he still travelled, when possible, with his father as his personal assistant, and was made to return back to the UK when he was accused of allegations of misconduct. In 1958 he met and married the Parsi, Cynthia Kabraji, and together they had a daughter-Saira in 1964, followed by twins in 1966, a son Tahir and a daughter Safia.

Shah became deeply involved in Sufism and eventually became one of the world's greatest teachers of their particular Tradition and he decided to also become an author and share his experiences with over 36 books which covered many varied topics ranging from psychology and spirituality to cultural studies. His amazing views were changing and so were his writings, which started to change with his involvement centering on Magic and Witchcraft. He decided to found and create his own publishing house "The Octagon Press", and one of his first publishing's was Gerald Gardner's biography "Gerald Gardner, Witch", which he did not put his name to instead selected a fellow Wiccan as the author Jack Bracelin. Shah went on to found the "Institute for Cultural Research", this was a London based charity that devoted itself to the study of human behavior. In his writings Shah always presented Sufism as a universal form of wisdom that predated Islam, he always emphasized that it was not a stagnant religion, that it adopted and changed to suit the needs and times of mankind as it grew and changed.

Shah made contact with many Wiccans and Witches in London and by the 1950s and he ended up becoming Gerald Gardner's personal companion and secretary. Shah whilst with Gardner on a trip to Mallorca met with the famous poet and author Sir Robert Graves, where they all shared similar interests and all became the best of friends. Graves also took a supportive interest in Shah's writings and encouraged him to write books on Sufism. But he was not financial enough to do this and desperately needed the funds and so decided to sell off one of his plots of land that was once owned by Lord Frank Baden-Powel, who was the founder of the Boy Scouts movement, he sold it for 100,00 pounds, which was an astronomical amount for the time.

Shah went on to also found the "Society of Understanding Fundamental Ideas" (SUFI) in 1965, which later changed its name to the "Institute for Cultural Research" (CR). This was created to aid in stimulating the minds and intellects of his students, as it was about the debate sharing of ideas and views. Over the next few years, he spent most of his time promoting his publishing company Octagon Press, where he also published many of his own books as well, he also did a documentary called "The Dreamwalkers". Shah was not a Witch not even a Wiccan, but he was an important person who helped to open the minds of thousands of students into thinking for themselves, he got them to do the work and how to research everything before even asking questions or even (like so many) making uneducated and ignorant statements. Shah believed in the open mind and assisted many to search and look for their own Truth, and not to be sheep, and be told what to do or believe.

Shah before his death wanted to return for one more trip back to his homeland and so in the Spring of 1987 Shah suffered two massive successive heart attacks and was told he had only about eight percent of his heart function. Shah fought the odds against being told he did not have long to live and continued to work and produce many more books as his legacy over the next nine years. Idries Shah died in London at the age of 72 on the 23rd of November 1996 and was buried in Brookwood Cemetery. His obituary in The Daily Telegraph states that Idries Shah was a collaborator with Mujajideen in the Soviet-Afghan War, a Director of Studies for the Institute for Cultural Research and a Governor of the Royal Humane Society and the Royal Hospital and Home for Incurables. He was a long-time member of the Athenaeum Club, and at the time of his death Shah's book had sold over 15 million copies in a dozen languages worldwide and had been reviewed in a multitude of newspapers and journals.

Books by Idries Shah:
Magic

- *Oriental Magic*, 1956-2015
- *The Secret Lore of Magic*, 1957-2016

Sufism

- *The Sufis*, 1964-2014
- *Tales of the Dervishes*, 1967-2016
- *Caravan of Dreams*, 1968-2015
- *Reflections*, 1968-2015
- *The Way of the Sufi*, 1968-2015
- *The Book of the Book*, 1969-2016
- *Wisdom of the Idiots*, 1969-2015
- *The Dermis Probe*, 1970-2016
- *Thinkers of the East: Studies in Experientialism*, 1971-2016
- *The Magic Monastery*, 1972-2017
- *The Elephant in the Dark – Christianity, Islam and the Sufis*, 1974-2016
- *A Veiled Gazelle – Seeing How to See*, 1977
- *Neglected Aspects of Sufi Study*, 1977
- *Special Illumination: The Sufi Use of Humor*, 1977
- *A Perfumed Scorpion*, 1978
- *Learning How to Learn*, 1978
- *The Hundred Tales of Wisdom*, 1978
- *Evenings with Idries Shah*, 1981
- *Letters and Lectures of Idries Shah*, 1981
- *Observations*, 1982
- *Seeker After Truth*, 1982
- *Sufi Thought and Action*, 1990
- *The Commanding Self*, 1994
- *Knowing How to Know*, 1998

Headstone of Idries Shah

Vivienne Crowley
High Priestess-Witch Elder

Vivienne Crowley (not connected to Aleister Crowley) was one of the first Witches to bring not only the Alexandrian but also the Gardnerian Traditions of Modern Wicca to the forefront. Crowley was Initiated into the London Coven of Alex Sanders at the early age of eighteen, and later decided to join a Gardnerian Coven in the famous Whitecroft line which descended from Eleanor Bone.

Crowley in 1988 Founded the "Wicca Study Group" and also became the secretary of the "Pagan Federation" in the very same year. Crowley was a very influential Witch and Priestess in aiding the development of Wicca throughout the 20th and 21st century, also helping to bring together Alexandrians and Gardnerians through cross-initiation.

Professor Ronald Hutton described Crowley as "the closest thing that Britain possessed to an informal successor to Alex Sanders". Crowley was an Interfaith coordinator for the Federation, and also served as Britain's coordinator of the Pagan Chaplain Services for H.M. Prisons. Crowley in 1989 released her first book "Wicca: The Religion in the New Age," which to date has been one of the most valued and widespread books on Wicca.

Crowley did lecture on the Psychology of Religion at Kings College London, University of London as a Jungian Psychologist. Crowley holds a bachelor's degree and a Ph.D. in Psychology from the University of London. Crowley is also the adjunct professor at the Union Institute in Cincinnati, Ohio.

Books by Vivienne Crowley:
- *Wicca: The Old Religion in the New Age,* 1989 (revised and updated in 1996 as *Wicca: The Old Religion in the New Millennium*) Element Books Ltd.
- *Phoenix from the Flame: Pagan Spirituality in the Western World,* 1994 Thorsons Publishers (Reissue edition)
- *Principles of Paganism,* 1996, Thorsons Publishers (Reissue edition)

- *Principles of Wicca*, 1998, Thorsons
- *Principles of Jungian Spirituality: The Only Instruction You'll Ever Need*, 1998, Thorsons
- *Celtic Wisdom: Seasonal Festivals and Rituals*, 1998, Sterling Pub Co Inc
- *The Goddess Book of Days*, 2003, Vega Books

Rhiannon Ryall
West Country Wiccan Elder
January 5th, 1921

Rhiannon Ryall is the Magical name of English born Australian Witch, who achieved notoriety for her controversial claims regarding the existence of a Coven of Witches living in England's West Country during the 1940s, known as the Coven of Boskednan, although doubted in the early days it was found out that Boskednan was the Clan of Lady Margaret DeLille Quinn and Dr. Adrian Reinman, and that she was in fact an initiated member of this group. These facts are true and it was only in 1993 when the UK company Capall Bann published Ryall's "West Country Wicca: A Journal of the Old Religion", in which she states that as a child growing up along the borders between the English counties Cornwall, Devon and Somerset, she was Initiated into a local Witch Tradition that many of the people in the surrounding villages were actual members of. Ryall stated that they were old Traditional and pre-Gardnerian, she asserted that her family had been Witches, and as such she was not a hereditary witch, but at the age of sixteen, she like many other children of the same age were taken to the female "Elders of the Village" who taught them about the old traditions of the Craft.

Ryall always backed up her claims even when I met her in the 80s through my dear friend Lady Elizabeth Paterson, unbeknown to her that her mentor and Clan mother was also now living in Western Australia, Lady Margaret, and was invited to learn from her and so we formed a circle of woman (eight of us) and we were taught by Ryall and Lady Margaret a very different form of Witchcraft, she only called it Wicca because the word was more accepted than the word Witchcraft. Ryall taught about the connection to nature asserting always that her traditional followers worshipped the Divine Feminine, The Goddess, who was rightly known as "The Green Lady", and who was believed slept during the winter months, along with the Horned God "The Green Man", whom they referred to as "Old Horny".

Ryall always stated that Traditional Witchcraft Covens always met in secret and performed the "Drawing Down of the Moon" rite as part of their Traditional faith, as well as celebrating five Sabbats annually, Lady Day – 25th March, Summer Solstice – 21st June, Samhain – 31st October, and the Winter Solstice – 21st December. Ryall when describing the Covens practices, she stated that they all wore robes, typically they were earthy colours either brown or black and at festivals they wore green robes, they used a ceremonial cup, a knife, a wand and a dish of salt as their ritual tools. Ryall always said that they never wrote anything down, everything was actuated by the feel of the night, and there was no such thing as a Book of Shadows. As many are aware the term "Book of Shadows" was first used as a title of a book by Mir Bashir, as he always stated that that is where all the magic of the world existed, hidden in the shadows.

Ryall later embellished the notion that they were part of a large organization of Covens, but to me had stated several times that there were only 3 covens that she knew of, one in Cornwall, Australia and the US. Ryall had a great family here in Australia but sadly her son married and the couple both became heavily addicted to drugs, and they had a son which Ryall absolutely adored. Her son and wife neglected their son profusely and tried legally to have her grandson removed from them and into her custody, but the Court deemed they were worthy, and she lost the battle and also her family turned against her. But her grandson was still being neglected, and so Ryall decided to kidnap him and take him away from them to save him and left the state illegally and went to South Australia.

Ryall was eventually caught and arrested, she went to trial and lost the battle and went to prison as a kidnapper. She went to prison for several years, of which she had no contact again with her family, and she was devastated. Elizabeth and I went to visit her several times in prison, but even that was too hard for her. No matter what many people may say about her, she was a kind and gentle soul who cared about life and nature and her tradition, and no-one in this world to her was more special than her grandson, who she never saw again.

In later years, Ryall went on to write and publish a number of books on Wicca and Magic through Capall Bann.

Rhiannon Ryall's Books:

- *Celtic Lore and Druid Ritual*, 1994
- *Weaving the Magic: A Potpourri of Rituals, Chants, Dances, Webs, Cords, Runes, Talismans and Magical Information*, 1996
- *Teachings of the Wisewoman*, 2000

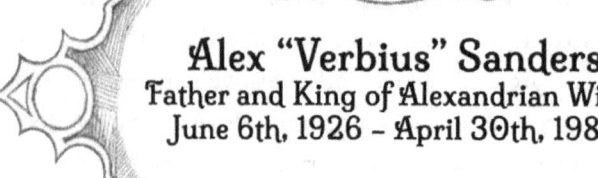

Alex "Verbius" Sanders
Father and King of Alexandrian Wicca
June 6th, 1926 – April 30th, 1988

Alex Sanders

Alex Sanders, born Orrell Alexander Carter at the family home in Birkenhead, Merseyside, England to his parents Margaret Bibby and Albert E Carter (a dance-hall entertainer). He was the first born and eldest of his 5 siblings: Joan 1928, Elizabeth 1929, Patricia 1933, John 1934 and David 1934. Later the family moved to Grape Street, Manchester and unofficially changed their name to Sanders.

Sanders was raised in a middle-class working family, growing up with his mother and grandmother who were both spiritual and were active with esoteric philosophies. At an early age he was attracted to the Spiritualist Church and was involved for many years as a practicing Medium prior to being lured to the more Magical side of Ceremonial Magick. At the end of WW2, he began working as an assistant in a pharmaceutical manufacturing laboratory in Manchester, where he met and fell in love with, and eventually married 19-year-old work colleague Doreen Strattin in 1948 at the age of 22 years old. He actually married under the name of Alexander O. Sanders, and they went on to have two children (Paul and Janice). The Sanders differed immensely with their religious views, and this saw their marriage solely deteriorating, and Doreen decided to leave Alex four years later, this made him incredibly angry and bitter where he made many threats to her as he was grief stricken at her decision, namely because she took away his children as well.

Sanders eventually started working at another pharmaceutical company, where he met a fellow colleague whom he befriended, who at the time did not realise that she was the mother to his new to be future wife Maxine, but Maxine's father despised Sanders as he saw Sanders as an atheist and refused his daughter to have anything to do with him, of course as a teenager she really listened, NOT! She snuck out with him all the time and they had a deep bond and infatuation with each other, she also came into his Coven, and they eventually were married even though she was so much his junior in age, but they connected well with each other no matter what their age difference.

Sanders suffered as a child with tuberculosis, and due his health issues went and lived with his grandmother (Mary Bibby) in the country fresh air, it was here that he first stated that he had been Initiated by her, the most famous version was in his biography "King of the Witches" by June Johns:

"One evening in 1933, when I was seven, I was sent round to my grandmother's house for tea. For some reason I did not knock at the door as I went in, and was confronted by my grandmother, naked, with her grey hair hanging down to her waist, standing in a circle drawn on the kitchen floor.

Regaining her composure, she told Sanders to step into the circle, take off his clothes, and put his head between his thighs. As he did so, she took a sickle-knife and nicked his scrotum, saying, "You are one of us now." (This was later revealed to be false, and Sanders was merely furthering his publicity) It was then that Sanders realised she was a witch. His Grandmother was a hereditary witch, a descendant of the Welsh chieftain Owain Glyndŵr, the last man (according to Sanders) to have called himself "King of the Witches"; supposedly his grandmother let him copy her Book of Shadows when he was nine and taught him the rites and magic of Witches. He was taught clairvoyance first by scrying in inky water, then in his grandmother's crystal. Sanders claimed that following the Blitz, and a few months before her death at age 74, Mrs Bibby conferred upon him second- and third-grade initiations, involving ritual sex."

Sanders had an evangelistic attitude and a charm that attracted many to him as he was very charming and many of his followers started to call him The King of Witches, of which he absolutely played up to and loved the title so much that he even believed it. Sanders due to his love of the limelight and the media opened up the Craft in such a manner to the world that along with Gardner they shared the credit of being both the Fathers of Modern Wicca, and they both need to be honored and respected as such no matter what their misgivings, as they brought the Craft into the limelight of the world in the 20th century when all odds were against them.

Patricia Crowther, Sanders first meeting of a Wiccan High Priestess of a Gardnerian Coven, tells the story very differently. As she kept all letters and claims that she received a letter from Sanders in 1961, where all he mentioned was that he had an affinity with the occult and had second sight as a medium. Sanders had an interview with Crowther in September 1962 and after their initial meeting convinced the "Manchester Evening News" to do an article on Wicca which was placed on the front page. This article went in several directions, and much of it not so positive as the side-effects made him lose his job, and also the estrangement from the Crowther's, who saw him as a troublesome upstart, and very impatient. After many attempts asking for Initiation the Crowther's agreed that he was not genuine in his search for Truth but only for knowledge and publicity.

Sanders eventually did get Initiated by a Priestess (Silvia) in 1963 that he had met who was Initiated by the Crowther's, and with whom he worked with for a while, he took on the Magical Craft name Verbius. He copied out his Book of Shadows (Gardnerian) from her which took him over 6 months to copy it out. Due to his mardigra attitude and personality, Silvia and all the others left the group and left Alex to continue as High Priest. His first coven was at his home address at 24 Egerton Road North, Chorlton-cum-Hardy in Manchester.

Sanders was a very believable person and was so good and colorful that he became a self-appointed High Priest of his own Coven, and eventually went on to Found (along with his wife Maxine) a whole new tradition of Wicca known as Alexandrian Wicca which has grown to be one of the largest Wiccan organizations in the world. Alexandrian Wicca is now in the US, Europe, UK, Australia, and New Zealand.

Sanders got more and more involved with the media and attracted all forms of media attention from newspapers, magazines, radio, and television appearances, also being in several documentaries. Sanders and Maxine eventually had two children, Maya Alexandria, and Victor Mikhael.

Sanders' status grew immensely due to constant attention from the media, and it created a ripple effect that brought him more and more contacts from all over the world, and with this more followers and eventually many Initiates. The length of training with Sanders was short and minimal to all extremes but by 1965 he claimed to have Initiated 1,623 Initiates in over 100 covens that he had at the time, with many covens becoming hive-offs from the original. His claim to fame as King of the Witches hit the hearts of many Seekers and attracted them to him. Sanders may have embellished many things but what was real was his commitment to the path of expanding the Alexandrian Tradition of Wicca worldwide, that made his title and crown fit earnestly. These followers are genuine in their pursuits, and still follow the laws and tradition of Alex Sanders and his covens are sincere and growing strong with a genuine sacredness and also a form of secrecy within their ranks, as I am too an Alexandrian High Priestess and Ordained as a Third Degree Alexandrian by one of his Initiated Priests Geoff "Imhotep" Camm, but it took me nearly six years to gain and earn this title.

Whenever anyone asked for elevation within his covens to the Priesthood, they usually went through a dual Initiation of a 2nd and 3rd degree Initiation ceremony at the same time. The problem I have with this is the act of Magical Sex with the acting High Priestess or High Priest, which to me has never belonged in Traditional Witchcraft. The act of sex between two Witches in the craft was important and safeguarded for hundreds of years in Traditional Covens, in bringing two covens or families together to keep them safe during any and all persecutions. As bringing two Covens together, kept the sacred vows of trust, by the joining of two families, but this was for Blood Witches.

Sanders was so fascinated by Magic that he was hungry for knowledge and so to get that knowledge joined several Magical Orders and Lodges starting from 1968 through to 1974 and maybe even more before his death, such as "The Knights Templar", "Order of St. Michael", "The Order of St. George" and the "Ordine Delta Luna". Sanders like Gardner was so hungry for knowledge and public attention that they both have incorporated many of these Magickal (spelt with a 'k' as taken from Magicians and Ceremonial Magick) practices into Wicca which became quite confusing, but it seemed to have worked well for them and many who follow their traditions. Sanders on several occasions tried to remove the media from attacking other Wiccans by putting himself in the firing line.

He always offered the media an alternative where he disclosed a sacred and ancient ritual, he once planned a ritual to raise the dead at a sacred site at Alderley Edge. The stage was set, and the place prepared with a bandage (mummy-like) figure lying on a large central stone altar, with one of Sanders Coveners posing as a doctor, to certify that the corpse was actually dead. He then commenced with the ritual with onlooking reporter and photographer, and the invocation to raise the dead (which was in fact a cake recipe spoken backwards) after which the corpse was meant to sit up. As this was happening the media, being so shocked, ran away and reported what they had seen and photographed, it made the headlines the very next morning. This then took Sanders to a higher level as a star of the media again.

Alexandrian Covens are traditionally Skyclad (naked), although Sanders, to stand out from the others, always wore a robe or a small loin cloth. Around this time Sanders met with Stewart Farrar at the World Premier Preview of "Legend of the Witches". This was beginning of a great relationship as their bond grew and Farrar's interest within the Craft also grew and he eventually also became Initiated and within the Covenstead met with Janet Owen who was to be his future wife and his High Priestess of their own Coven in 1970. Sanders and his wife Maxine separated in 1971, and he moved to Sussex whilst Maxine remained in London with the children, where she continued to run the Coven and teaching all those that enquired. Although separated they were always close and remained friends with a binding and trusting relationship.

In 1979 Sanders announced to the Wiccan and Witchcraft community that he wished "to make amends for some of the past hurts that I have given and many public stupidities I created for others of the Craft", and expressed his desire that the Wicca should someday put aside their differences and "unite in brotherly love before the face of the Lady and the Lord", allowing the Craft to become great again, not with solitary's that owe only partial allegiance but to whole working and dedicated Covens to the Craft and the whole world.

The King is Dead, Alex Sanders died and entered the Summerland on May Eve, Beltane, 1988 after suffering from lung cancer.

Madge Worthington
Gardnerian High Priestess & Elder
1926 – 2018

Madge Worthington

Madge Worthington born in 1926 and lifelong member of the Pagan Federation, of both Wiccan and Witchcraft traditions, she was a champion, a spiritual warrior that fought for the rights of Pagans and for the cause of the Old Religion. Madge commenced on her journey within the Craft in the 1960s when she was in her 40s. This was exactly what she wanted, a life-affirming religion that was never burdened with sin and guilt, as was that of the Judaic and Christian faiths. Worthington was a woman who was not scared to show that women can do anything that men can do, especially Thames yachtsmen who were mortified when she openly took part in their annual race and had won by a huge stretch against the men.

When the Wicca was infiltrated by the media and she was outed, Worthington stood her ground although she was ostracized by many that new her. Following this atrocity of her involved in Witchcraft she hosted the inaugural meeting of the Pagan Front, on May Day in

1971, at her riverside home. By April, Worthington had already started to have open discussion groups on Witchcraft and Wicca at a coffee house in London, which started to encourage its members to form similar groups in their own areas across the United Kingdom. These became the Pagan Federation moots.

Worthington's most important role was in the spreading of the Craft to suitable Seekers and Initiates. Along with Arthur, her husband, and High Priest, they together Initiated many suitable Witches and gave them the experience of working in a traditional coven so as to learn enough to hive off and form their own covens. Like Worthington's Initiator Rae Bone, she has always disliked the introduction of ceremonial magick in the craft as it changed much of the old ways. The Worthington's had many Initiates pass through the portals of their coven but when Arthur died in 1981, she withdrew gradually from active involvement in Witchcraft and started to live a quiet life as a Pagan Federation Honorary Member, still supporting her animal charities, with no high profile in the Pagan World.

Vivienne Crowley writes:

In 1974, Madge became my High Priestess.

"The initiation ended with the removal of the blindfold, and I found myself facing a true witch queen Madge, her grey flowing hair unbound, magnificent in a moon crown, a true representation of the Goddess. I had never known that older women could be so beautiful. The lessons of those early encounters with Madge and Arthur have stayed with me: their willingness to bring a young witch into their coven, the power of ritual learned rather than read, that age, wisdom, and dignity have their own beauty, and the power of chant and dance for making magic. Madge and Arthur through their willingness to embrace others became two of the most prolific initiators of their generation. I have no idea of the numbers of their descendants. It is certainly hundreds; it may be over a thousand. Both had physical children. Both too have spiritual children, grandchildren, great grandchildren, great, great, grandchildren – at least four generations of witches around the world – for their descendants are found across Britain and continental Europe, in Canada and the United States, and in many other countries too. They are a living tribute to the dedication to the Craft, to the Goddess and to the rebirth of Witchcraft of Madge and of her High Priest Arthur who went to the Summerland's many years ago."

Patricia "Lady Thelema" Crowther
High Priestess-Witch Elder
October 14th, 1927 -

Born Patricia Dawson on the 14th of October 1927 in Sheffield, England and married later in life to Arnold Crowther (1909-1974) who was a stage magician and good friend of Aleister Crowley. Crowther always was intrigued and drawn to Witchcraft and eventually was Initiated by Gerald Gardner in 1960, where he Initiated both Patricia and Arnold together, and later they became High Priestess and High Priest of their own Coven that they Founded in 1961, only one year after their Initiation where they called their Coven the Sheffield Coven.

Crowther right from the start has been a strong advocate with both the Wiccan and Witchcraft Traditions and promoted it as much as she deemed befitting through several media outlets, inclusive of many appropriate magazines that Crowther contributed to with ongoing articles, also publishing several books and journals. Crowther had a myriad of interviews on radio and television. The Crowther's together co-wrote and produced A Spell of Witchcraft which produced and broadcast on the BBC Radio Sheffield in six 20-minute programs. It was the first of its kind anywhere based on the Wiccan Religion and its varied activities. Doreen Valiente put it on: www.youtube.com/watch?v=NrUmzSKIyNA%7Cdate=December 2012.

Crowther, now more respectfully as the High Priestess and a 3rd Degree Initiate took on the name and mantle of Lady Thelema who has throughout her life done an immense amount of hard work and a genuine and positive promotion of the Wiccan religion in the UK, along with other high profile High Priestesses such as Doreen Valiente, Vivienne Crowley, Eleanor Bone and Lois Bourne, all of the foresaid are respected as the 'first mothers' of the Wiccan Religion and were public faces and figures for the Craft and their devout beliefs.

Lady Thelema, still lives with her husband, Ian in Sheffield, UK.

Books by Patricia Crowther:

- *The Witches Speak* (with Arnold Crowther), 1965, Athol Publications,
- *Witchcraft in Yorkshire*, 1973, Dalesman
- *Witch Blood (The Diary of a Witch High Priestess)*, 1974, House of Collectible
- *Lid off the Cauldron: A handbook for witches*, 1981, Muller
- *The Zodiac Experience*, 1992, Samuel Weiser Inc
- *The Secrets of Ancient Witchcraft with the Witches' Tarot*, 1992, Carol Publishing
- *Witches Were for Hanging*, 1992, Excalibur Press of London
- *One Witch's World*, 1998, Robert Hale, (published in America under the title *High Priestess*, Phoenix Publishing
- *From Stagecraft to Witchcraft: The Early years of a High Priestess*, 2002, Capall Bann
- *Covensense*, 2009, Robert Hale

Dolores Ashcroft Nowicki
High Priestess-Witch Elder
June 11th, 1929 -

Dolores Ashcroft Nowicki was born on the 11th of June 1929, she was raised in Jersey Island by her parents who were both 3rd degree Initiates as a High Priestess and High Priest, and amazingly her grandmother was a full-blood gypsy. A life that many today would kill for, growing up in such a Magical family that were dedicated to the world of Witchcraft and the sciences of the occult, which was the very norm for her family, as she grew up not knowing any different, even as a child Nowicki had "the sight" and foretold of many a futuristic event for her family and friends.

During WW2 Nowicki' family moved away from the big cities and went and lived in Wirrel Peninsula in the Northwest of Britain, where she spent much of her free time with the local gypsies who camped nearby, and it was through their gifts and Magical talents that aided in helping her to develop her natural abilities and psychic skills with a little gypsy Magic thrown in as well, even though she was a 3rd generation psychic and occult practitioner.

Nowicki has always spent most of her free time out in the woods and amongst the Magic of nature, and the mysteries that the forest made her aware of and helped her to open her awareness of and connection with the spirits and Magic of Nature. Growing up her first love was the Magic of Nature and her second love became fortune telling and especially she had a great insight within the Tarot Cards. When WW2 ended, the entire family decided to move back to Jersey, where when they settled, they opened up a private and secretive Occult Discussion group due to the restrictions of the Law that was still opposed to things along these lines. Nowicki also was a gifted and talented artist and was drawn into the Arts and studied at the "Royal Academy of Dramatic Art", after which she went on to study Opera at "Trinity College of Music in Cambridge". During which time she met and eventually married, which also put a hold on her studies, which sadly after making that sacrifice found that this marriage was not for her and they were divorced only three years later, where she took up her studies again where she left off and completed her studies with honors.

Nowicki also took up Fencing as a sporting interest, and due to her competitive nature, she became quite a professional and represented the Islands against France and Britain. She won many ribbons and trophies as a Champion, and at a Championship she met with her new husband Michael Nowicki who was also involved in Fencing. They lovingly married in 1957 and had two children Tamara and Carl, when they also decided to move back to the Channel Islands of Jersey, situated just off the coast of France, where even today they still live in their family home, older but still with all the love around them of their family and friends. Nowicki became more interested in the occult in the 1960s and joined the "Fraternity of the Inner Light," a Magickal Order Founded by international Occultist Dion Fortune. Whilst being an active member within this Order she became acquainted with Walter Ernest Butler, and also Gareth Knight, and did the Helios Course in practical Kabbalah, which went on to become the Foundation of the "Servants of the Inner Light," on the eve of Samhain 1976. When Butler retired, Nowicki became the Director of Studies of the SOL, a position through her retirement that she handed on to Steven Critchley in June 2018. Although Nowicki has retired from being the director she still continues her active involvement today.

Books by Patricia Crowther:

- *The Witches Speak* (with Arnold Crowther), 1965, Athol Publications
- *Witchcraft in Yorkshire*, 1973, Dalesman
- *Witch Blood (The Diary of a Witch High Priestess)*, 1974, House of Collectibles
- *Lid off the Cauldron: A handbook for Witches*, 1981, Muller
- *The Zodiac Experience*, 1992, Samuel Weiser Inc
- *The Secrets of Ancient Witchcraft with the Witches' Tarot*, 1992, Carol Publishing
- *Witches Were for Hanging*, 1992, Excalibur Press of London
- *One Witch's World*, 1998, Robert Hale (published in America under the title *High Priestess*, Phoenix Publishing)
- *From Stagecraft to Witchcraft: The Early years of a High Priestess*, 2002, Capall Bann
- *Covensense*, 2009, Robert Hale

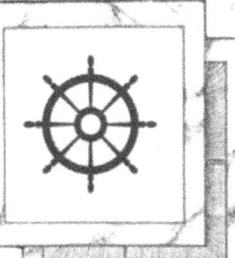

Carl Llewellyn Weschcke
The Father of The New Age - Llewellyn
Publisher
Wiccan High Priest Elder
September 10th, 1930 - November 7th, 2015

Photograph of Carl Llewellyn Weschcke at his Desk

Carl Llewellyn Weschcke was born on the 10th of August 1930. Carl was fundamental in getting the message of the Craft out there. He was a person who looked into the future and aimed at bringing the truth to everyone who wanted to either hear it or read about it. He is the owner, creator, and chairman of the world's largest metaphysical publisher; "Llewellyn Worldwide" and distributor in 1961. With thousands of books, CDs, Tarot and Oracle decks. He opened the doorways into the then forbidden worlds of the occult and played a Seminole role in the rise of Wicca and Neo-Paganism in the 1960s and 1970s and has been called "The Father of the New Age" for his public sponsorship and foresight of occult subjects. Weschcke was a hard worker and always inspired to share knowledge and interests outside the Judeo world.

He was an avid reader of books and loved all books and especially when they had a message to deliver, he saw it as his mission in life to bring this world of spirit and Magic to the world. He always wanted people to see the best they could be and achieve at every level especially aiming at their Higher Consciousness and the connection with the weblike harmony with the entire universe, no matter what one believed. He saw in books his way of delivering spiritual knowledge and the messages that it brings.

Llewellyn grew from a small mail-order publisher into a booming multi-million-dollar empire that sells hundreds of books around the world each and every day. I never had the pleasure of meeting such an incredible man but had heard from people that knew him like Raymond Buckland that he always listened, and in 85 years he accomplished more than he even dreamed, as a legacy for not only his family but for all those who had a voice and wanted to be heard. He made the world smaller by bringing everyone together in a harmonious web of sharing and caring, and touched with a bit of Magic.

Carl was Initiated in Lady Sheba's Coven, and throughout the rest of his life believed it to be the most powerful experience he had ever had. Carl eventually started with his own Coven called "Camelot Star of the North Coven" and was the High Priest at his temple in the basement of his Summit Avenue Mansion, where his Coveners met and practiced their Magic. Weschcke, although he published much, never published his own writings until he was at the tender age of 79. But from his extensive work during the Civil Rights Era, he assisted in organizing the "Council of American Witches" and drafted the "Thirteen Principles of Wiccan belief", that eventually were used in the "U.S. Army Chaplains Handbook". Weschcke also served as the 7th Past Grand Master Ordo Aurum Solis".

Llewellyn's books can be proudly and prominently displayed on the shelves of bookstores worldwide. Thankyou Mr. Carl Llewellyn Weschcke!

Carl Llewellyn Weschcke Books:

- *All About Auras*, Carl Weschcke & Joe H. Slate PHd.
- *All About Tea leaf reading*, Carl Weschcke & Joe H. Slate PHd.
- *Astral Projection for Psychic Empowerment*, Carl Weschcke & Joe H. Slate
- *Clairvoyance For Psychic Empowerment*, Carl Weschcke & Joe H. Slate
- *Communication With Spirit*, Carl Weschcke & Joe H. Slate
- *The Complete Magick Curriculum of the Secret order G.B.G.* , Carl Weschcke & Louis T. Culling
- *Doors To Past Lives & Future Lives*, Carl Weschcke & Joe H. Slate PHd.
- *Dream ESP: The Secret of Prophetic Causal Dreaming*, Carl Weschcke & Joe H. Slate PHd.
- *Growing Nuts in The North*, Carl Weschcke & Joe H. Slate PHd.
- *The Llewellyn Complete Book of Psychic Empowerment*, Carl Weschcke & Joe H. Slate PHd.
- *Moving Objects with Your Mind*, Carl Weschcke & Joe H. Slate PHd.
- *The New Science of the Paranormal*, Carl Weschcke & Joe H. Slate PHd.
- *Psychic Empowerment for Everyone*, Carl Weschcke & Joe H. Slate PHd.
- *Remembering Past Lives*, Carl Weschcke & Joe H. Slate PHd.

- *Self-Hypnosis For Success in Life*, Carl Weschcke & Joe H. Slate PHd.
- *Self-Empowerment and Your Subconscious Mind*, Carl Weschcke & Joe H. Slate
- *Self-Empowerment Through Self Hypnosis*, Carl Weschcke & Joe H. Slate
- *Vibratory Astral Projection & Clairvoyance CD Companion*, Carl Weschcke & Joe H. Slate

Leo Martello
Wiccan High Priest & Pagan Elder
September 26th, 1930 – June 20th, 2000

Leo Martello

Leo Martello was born on the 26th of September 1930 in Dudley, Massachusetts, and was raised on a small farm that was rented by his father who was an Italian immigrant Rocco Luigi Martello. After the economic turmoil of the Great depression, the Martello's were forced from their land and moved to Worcester, Massachusetts and then to Southbridge. It was here that Leo was baptized into the Roman Catholic Church, after which his parents soon divorced. Unable to care for him his father sent him to the Catholic boarding preparatory school attached to Assumption College, Worcester, which was run by "Augustinians of the Assumption". Martello spent six years at this school, and later described it as the unhappiest time of his life.

Martello studied graphology and from the age of 16 began making radio appearances as a graphologist, he also wrote stories for magazines. Martello experienced psychic interests as a child which lured him with the interest in Occultism. Martello as a teenager began also studying palmistry and the tarot with a local gypsy named Marta. Martello when he was 16 was told by his father that he had cousins in

New York City who wished to meet with him. So, he went to New York to meet with his cousins and was told that they were part of an ancient Tradition of Witchcraft from their Sicilian ancestors. Many believe that they had formed a Coven adopting Strega practices and so when he was 21, he was initiated into this family Coven.

Martello during the 50s stayed in New York where he worked as a graphologist and also as a hypnotist. He started to publish his books on the paranormal from the 1960s, and he publicly began identifying as a Wiccan in 1969 and stated that he was involved in a New York Coven. Martello who identified himself as a gay man, found that after the Stonewall Riots of 1969, involved himself in Gay Rights Activism, and became a member of the Gay Liberation Front (GLF). Martello left the GLF following an internal schism, he became a Founding member of the Gay Activist Alliance (GAA) and authored a regular column, "The Gay Witch", for its newspaper.

Martello in 1970 Founded the Witches Craft Associates (WICA) as a networking organisation for Wiccans, and under auspices organized a "Witch In" that took place in central park at Halloween in 1970, despite a great deal of opposition from the New York City Parks Department. Martello knew that to legally campaign for the civil rights of Wiccans, he Founded the "Witches Anti-Defamation League", which was later renamed the "Alternative Religions Education Network".

Martello visited the UK in 1973, to be Initiated into Gardnerian Wicca by the Gardnerian High Priestess Patricia Crowther. He continued practicing Wicca and fighting for gay rights well into the 1990s, when he retreated from public life, eventually succumbing to cancer in 2000. Not only was he a spokesperson for the Craft but also for the Gay community.

Books by Leo Martello:
- *Your Pen Personality*
- *It's in The Cards: The Atomic Age Approach to Card Reading*, Key Publications.
- *It's in the Stars: A Sensible Approach to and a Psychological Evaluation of Astrology in this "Age of Enlightenment"*, Key Publications.
- *How to Prevent Psychic Blackmail: The Philosophy of Psychoselfism*, S. Weiser.
- *Weird ways of Witchcraft*, HC Publishers
- *Hidden World of Hypnotism: Hoe to Hypnotize*, HC Publishers
- *Black Magic, Satanism, Voodoo*, Castle Books
- *Understanding the Tarot*, Castle Books
- *Witchcraft: The Old Religion*, Kensington Publishing
- *Reading the Tarot: Understanding the Cards of Destiny*, Perigee Trade.

Grandmother Elspeth Odbert
Priestess Elder & Storyteller
1930 -

Grandmother Elspeth

Grandmother Elspeth is a great-grandmother, environmentalist, healer, teacher, pastoral counsellor, and an irrepressible storyteller. Few of the cultural elders in America ever reach the status of "Living Legend" but 90-year-old Elspeth Odbert (better known as Grandmother Elspeth), just may be one. She has been enriching and strengthening the Neo Pagan movement for over 30 years. She consistently breaks through our isolating armor and bares us to the full light of, "Wake up! Take Charge of Your Life!" Her reputation for perceptive advice and earth-based "mountain wisdom" draws people to gather in her teaching circles. Outspoken and opinionated, Elspeth is an inspirational teacher and change agent, leading her listeners along an eco-spiritual path of personal and planetary transformation.

She and her husband Nybor were ordained, by the "Aquarian Tabernacle Church", in the late 90s. She is certified as a Shamanic Practitioner by the "Church of Earth Healing". As an honored Elder in the Neo-Pagan movement, she is a living example of the timeless truths that she teaches. She has published an illustrated storybook, "Gylantra's Journey", two spoken word CDs, "Out of the Forest" (a series of Trance Journeys.) and with the able assistance of her husband Nybor, Elspeth has created a storybook, "Gylantra's Legacy", this fully illustrated "fable for a possible future" presents their dream of what can be. Another place where Nybor and Elspeth are working together is with "Greensong" a not-for-profit organisation working toward sustainability and preparedness. Elspeth has also created (an audio book) and several T shirt designs. She is a gifted and experienced Tarot consultant and Spiritual Counsellor. I was gifted from her via Mama Vic, when I was a guest speaker at Circle Sanctuary's PSG Festival 2019, two pairs of her Amber bead necklaces which I shall treasure forever.

When Elspeth is not on the road, she is at home in West Virginia with Nybor and her two fur persons, Maggie, and Max.

Elspeth is a Certified Shamanic Practitioner, Master Gardener, author of:

- *The Challenge*
- *Out of the Forest*
- *Gylantra's Journey*
- *Greensong*

Frederic "Robert" Lamond
Witch Elder
1931 – 2020

Frederic Lamond

Frederic Lamond born 1931, who also goes under the Craft name "Robert" is a prominent English Wiccan and has worshipped Nature since he was 12 years of age when he lived in French Switzerland. Lamond was Initiated in February 1957 into the "Bricket Wood Coven" of Gardnerian Wicca in the presence of Gerald Gardner himself. Lamond is probably the longest continuously practicing Wiccan in the world. He had become involved in a number of Pagan organizations, including the "Fellowship of Isis", and the "Church of All Worlds", "Grey Council" and was active in the Interfaith movement between 1993, 1999 and 2004, where he attended "Parliaments of World Religions" in Chicago, South Africa, and Spain. He was also part of the first gathering of the "Elders of the Ancient Traditions and Cultures" in Mumbai-India in 2003. He has also written books on the subject of Wiccan Theology and History.

Books by Lamond

- The Divine Struggle, 1990
- Religion Without Beliefs: Essays in Pantheist Theology, Comparative Religion & Ethics, 1997
- Fifty Years of Wicca – Green Magic, 2004

Donata "Mama" Ahern
High Priestess & Shaman Elder
1932 -

Photograph of Donata Ahern

Ahern – (Chrysalis Heart Centre) born 1932. Ahern was raised a Roman Catholic and learned the love of ritual, which varied. Ahern left the Catholic Church because she needed to be responsible for her own conscience rather than accepting what she was told to believe. Ahern's true spiritual journey began when she was led to Raja Yoga, and then onto Buddhism. Ahern still practices Buddhist meditation, especially mindfulness.

It was still not enough for Ahern, so she began reading and seeking, and finally discovering the Goddess who was calling out to her. Over the next few years Ahern found and joined a Gardnerian Coven and through hard training eventually became a 3rd Degree, High Priestess and then decided to hive off to form her own Coven. Ahern approached Alexandrian Elders in Canada and was invited to study with them, eventually becoming a 3rd degree High Priestess of the Alexandrian Tradition. Aherns Coven now formally offers degrees in both Traditions, and they use Elements of both in their Circle. Ahern also led an online study group for Pagans for a few years as well.

Ahern had always had a calling of the Native American culture where it had spoken to her deeply from an early age as a child, especially the Medicine Wheel, which she studied what was available for a non-native at the time. It was around this time that Michael Harner published his ground-breaking book of Shamanism, which for Ahern, filled in her Wiccan practices. Ahern has now studied Shamanism with a teacher in "Alberto Villodos Tradition", and then later with a Harner teacher to learn healing methods.

Ahern earned a Master of Social Work, and then became a Certified Hypnotherapist, and further studied as a Past Life Regression Therapist. Ahern has a part-time practice as a Shamanic Counsellor and Past Life Regression Therapist. She is also a Druid in OBOD, and has served as a tutor to students in the Bardic and Ovate grades for several years where she has also served as a.o Ito.

Along Aherns journey she met with a Mayan High Priestess online and studied with her, and eventually was Initiated as a Priestess of the Maya Temple of the Deer, in Mexico a week after 9/11. Ahern discovered the Mayan Child's Count, a teaching form of the Medicine Wheel. She has been working regularly with the basic Plains Medicine Wheel and has now worked with the two Wheels until one day in meditation, one rose over the other to form one more complex Wheel.

Ahern then published a book, "The Medicine Wheel: Path of the Heart", which is her interpretation of the blending of the two wheels. This is when she decided to present workshops in 1990 at various festivals in the US and Canada. It was from here that she was asked to be a keynote speaker at a Druid Convention in Glasgow in 2005. Where she offered workshops locally, and for festivals at Brushwood (a Pagan campground near Buffo).

Along Ahern's journey she became a Dowser, and a Reiki Master. When Oberon Zell began the Grey School of Wizardry and Sages, Ahern became one of the first teachers, and later was honored to be asked to join the Grey Council. Ahern also contributed to one of Oberon's books.

Ahern now at the age of 87, still studies and offers a unique approach to her practice, utilising the complimentary healing modalities of Hypnotherapy, Past Life Regression, with the power of Shamanic Journeys and Ceremonies. Ahern still sees clients, offers workshops, and enjoys the blessings of her life. Also being a Peace Activist in the 70s, she now continually meditates on peace, justice with compassion, and for the healing of the whole of Mother Earth.

Aherns Books:
- *The Medicine Wheel: Path of the Heart*

Rev. Mother Laurie Cabot
High Priestess-Witch Elder
March 6th, 1933 -

Laurie Cabot showing me her Magick Board

Laurie Cabot was born Mercedes Elizabeth Kearsey on the 6th of March 1933. Cabot grew up in California and moved to New England as a teenager. Cabot's interest in the occult grew as a teenager when she developed deeper interest in all things occult, especially Witchcraft and she adored Boston and the Magic that it was filled with. Cabot as a teenager spent many hours sifting through the Boston Public Library researching everything she could find about Witchcraft.

In the 1950s Cabot worked as a dancer in a Boston nightclub called "The Latin Quarter", which was owned and ran by Lou Walters the father of television celebrity and journalist Barbara Walters. Cabot was asked to open and run Walter's Las Vegas Latin Quarter Nightclub, but due to being pulled in other directions with a greater interest Cabot declined and looked deeper into Witchcraft. Cabot is a Traditional old-school Witch, and she has always focused on the energies and powers of the science of Witchcraft, more than the spiritual/religious ideologies and concepts of the Craft. Cabot has always chosen to be different, whether it was her beliefs, strong character, or her dress style, where she always wore long black robes and dark make-up which separated her from the norm. Cabot raised both her daughters as Witches and Cabot is definitely a genuine Witch and a High Priestess of American Witchcraft, and one of the most high-profile Witches in the world. Cabot was one of the first people to make Witchcraft popular and accepted in the US. She also claims to be related to the prominent Boston Brahmin Cabot family.

Cabot went on to Found the "Cabot Tradition of the Science of Witchcraft" and also the "Witches league for Public Awareness" to be a defender of the civil rights of Witches everywhere. Cabot was officially declared by Governor Michael Dukis the title as the "Official Witch of Salem in Massachusetts" and presented with the key to the city in 1970, to honor her for her continued work with children with special needs. Cabot, although retired from public life and the many years running her Witchcraft shop "The Cat, The Crow, and the Crown" which was the first of its kind in Boston or Salem, opened in 1971, and quickly became a tourist destination for many. It eventually became the official Witchcraft shop, which sadly closed in early 2012 after 40 years. I was lucky to have met with Laurie Cabot on several occasions. Cabot will always remain a special part of Boston history and Witchcraft history as a great celebrity that many admire and love deeply. Cabot was always easy to give her time to any and all who needed it, she fell in love and married twice and divorced twice, but adore her two children Jodie Cabot (1963), and Penny Cabot (1965).

In 1970 the television sitcom "Bewitched" visited Salem for a series of episodes with much location filming and to this day there is a bronze statue of Bewitched riding on the crescent moon as a tourist attraction, which everyone seems to have a photo with, including myself. One of Cabot's great requests was from the Boston Red Sox Club and the Boston Radio Station which hired her, as a genuine Salem Witch to remove a curse that was cast on the team by an Arioles-employed Witchdoctor from Kenya, the Red Sox lost ten consecutive games until Cabot removed the hex prior to the May 13th game in Cleveland. Over Cabot's incredible years she has appeared uncountable times on Television and Radio shows as a guest, but her most high profile was on the "Oprah Winfrey Show" and the "Phil Donahue Show" in the late 1980s. Early this year (2020) Laurie Cabot celebrated her 87th birthday and is still going strong, doing rituals and readings always supported highly by her family and thousands of Witches around the world, especially her "Cabot Witches". Her daughter Penny is always by her side and acts as her go between for everything, and Cabot is presently co-writing her biography, so keep an eye out for that.

Books by Laurie Cabot:

- *The Power of the Witch: The Earth, the Moon, and the Magical Path to Enlightenment*, 1990
- *Love Magic* (with Tim Cowan), 1992
- *Celebrate the Earth: A Year of Holidays in the Pagan Tradition*, 1994
- *The Witch in Every Woman: Reawakening the Magical Nature of the Feminine to Heal, Protect, Create, and Empower*, 1997
- *Laurie Cabot's Book of Shadows* (with Penny Cabot and Christopher Penczak), 2015
- *Laurie Cabot's Book of Spells & Enchantments* (with Penny Cabot and Christopher Penczak),

Raymond "Robat" Buckland
Founder of Seax-Wica
Gardnerian High Priest-Witch Elder
August 31st, 1934 – September 27th, 2017

Photograph of Raymond Buckland

Raymond Buckland born the 31st of August 1934 in London to Eileen (English) and Stanley Buckland (Romany Gypsy). He was raised in the Anglican Church but developed an interest in alternative spirituality and all things Magical from around the age of twelve.

Upon the rise of World War II in 1939, the Buckland family moved to Nottingham, where he attended school and became involved with the drama department and became an amateur actor. Buckland went on to be educated at King's College School. He met and fell in love with his soon-to-be wife Rosemary Moss, and from 1957 to 1959 he served in the Royal Air Force. When this was finished, Buckland worked at a publishing company in London for four years, before he and his wife decided to emigrate to America in 1962, where they settled and lived on Long Island, New York. Whilst living in America, Buckland worked for British Airways.

On Buckland's downtime he started reading books by Margaret Murray "The Witch Cult in Western Europe" and Gerald Gardner's "Witchcraft Today". This gave him an insight into Witchcraft and Wicca and its religion. Buckland established contact with Gardner when he was running the "Witchcraft Museum" on the Isle of Man, and the two became friends, where after many long-distance phone calls, Gardner asked Buckland to be his spokesperson in America. Buckland also befriended Margaret St. Clair who was an author of the occult classic "Sign of the Labrys".

Buckland and his wife went on a trip to Scotland, where in Perth, they were Initiated into the Craft by High Priestess Monique Wilson (Lady Olwen). Gardner attended the ceremony as a guest and sadly died just after his Initiation where Buckland took the Magical name Robat. After the Buckland's returned home to America following their Initiation's and also bringing back a copy of the Gardnerian "Book of Shadows" with them. Buckland then formed the first Gardnerian Wicca Coven with a direct lineage of Initiation from Gardner. Nearly all fully Initiated Gardnerian Witches can trace their origins back to this Coven, which became the center for Neopaganism in America for about twenty years, this is why Buckland became the Father of American Gardnerian Wicca.

The Buckland's although being out there in the Craft world were trying to keep their identities secret as they were concerned with negative media attention and scrutiny, however a journalist Lisa Hoffman of the New York Times, without consent published a story about the Buckland's and their involvement in Witchcraft. Buckland decided then to do interviews and appeared on the Alan Burke Show which is when his neighbors found out that he was a Witch. Buckland, with his quirky and rebellious nature, decided to buy a hearse and drove around town slowly for all to see. Buckland and his wife decided to separate in 1973, where they both left their coven allowing someone else to run it on their behalf.

Like Gardner's English Museum, Buckland decided that he wanted to form America's first "Museum of Witchcraft and Magick", this was started in his own basement and was by appointment only, but his collection grew too vast, so he moved his museum to a 19th century house in Bay Shore. This was a good move as the museum received some media attention but not as much as he had wished, but there was a documentary produced about it. In 1973 Buckland moved his museum to Weirs Beach in New Hampshire, still not settled he again moved the Museum in 1978 to Virginia, but this time disbanding it and packed all the artefacts away in storage.

In 1974 Buckland founded his own tradition, Seax-Wica, based upon symbolism taken from Anglo-Saxon Paganism. He published in a book everything about the Foundation titled "The Tree: Complete Book of Saxon Witchcraft". He then began a correspondence course to teach people about Seax-Wica, which grew to having about one thousand members.

Buckland was married three times, to his first wife, Rosemary in 1955-1973. In 1974 he married Joan Helen Taylor, and his third wife he married in 1992, Tara, where they both moved to their farm home in North Central Ohio, where he continued to write his books and work as a Solitary Wiccan with his wife who was also Initiated. I was lucky enough to have met with Buckland on a few occasions, once in New Orleans at a festival, and kept in contact with him for many years, and because I ran the Church of Wicca, the main book I recommended was The Complete Book of Witchcraft, (Big Blue as we called it) by Buckland and it was he that dubbed me with the title of "The Witch of Oz" in the early 80s, and I asked him to send me some of his photos and autographs for our members, which he humbly did, and I received a whole folder of photos and autographs from him for his books. Upon our last meeting I presented to him some Aboriginal artefacts for his museum which belonged to a Kadaicha man, I also gave him more relics for the museum and some Aboriginal paintings, and some arrows/spears from Borneo.

In 2008, Buckland decided to entrust the Museum to my dear good friend Arch Priestess Rev. Velvet Reith of the Covenant of the Pentacle Wiccan Church (CPWC), having it based in New Orleans, Louisiana. After a period of neglect and mismanagement by another couple who managed this museum prior to Rev. Velvet who along with many of her members began to restore all the relics and items of the Museum and gradually put them on display. Sadly, not enough was done to establish its viewings and in 2015, due to Velvet being ill, and all the artefacts were turned back over to Buckland and a coven of his called the "Temple of Sacrifice" run by his present High Priestess Toni Rotonda. This collection has grown massively and had its home where it officially opened on the 29th of April 2017, where "The Buckland Museum of Witchcraft and Magick" was situated behind "A Separate Reality records" store in the Tremont, Cleveland area.

Buckland's ill health was on decline after suffering a bout of pneumonia and then a heart attack. He recovered, but later experienced more heart and lung problems in September 2017, which resulted his death on the 27th of September 2017, where I was informed from his Priestess of his Coven, Toni who also is the owner and custodian of the Buckland Museum. Buckland will never be forgotten for he is a pillar always of the temple of our community. Merry We Will Meet Again!

After much connection with Toni from the museum I was invited to the new premises of the Buckland Museum, which were grander and a better fit for the museum. Toni invited me to come and be a part of the Museum and do a meet and greet and help promote the museum as their first International Guest, which made me feel very special. The New "Buckland Museum of Witchcraft and Magic" is now at 2155 Broadview Road, Cleveland, Ohio. In Buckland's final years he explored a different avenue of interest and became a "stand-Up Comic" and after listening to his You Tube videos of it, he was very good at his newfound love especially being in his 80s.

Buckland published his first book, A Pocket Guide to the Supernatural. From here he wrote nearly one book every year until 2010 where he fixed his writing attention to fiction.

By 1973 he was earning enough income from his books to semi-retire and focus all his attention on the museum. I have bequeathed in my will many of my artefacts to go to the "Buckland Museum of Witchcraft and Magick", as I feel that if you have anything of importance and do not know what to do with it and it is related to the Craft then either donate it to the museum or offer it as loan object, this way no more of our history will be lost.

Books by Raymond Buckland:

- *A Pocket Guide to the Supernatural*, 1975, Ace Books, NY
- *Practical Candle burning Rituals*, 2000, Llewellyn Publications, MN
- *Witchcraft Ancient and Modern*, 1970, House of Collectibles, NY
- *Witchcraft From the Inside: Origins of the Fastest Growing Religious Movement in America*, 1995, Llewellyn Publications, MN
- *Pseudonym Tony Earl*, 1972), Warner Paperback Library, NY
- *Amazing Secrets of the Psychic World*, 1975, with Hereward Carrington Parker, Prentice Hall, NJ
- *The Tree: Complete Book of Saxon Witchcraft*, 2005, Samuel Weiser (Red Wheel/Weiser)
- *Here is the Occult*, 2009 House of Collectibles, NY
- *The Anatomy of the Occult*, 1977, Samuel Weiser, ME.
- *The Magick of Chant-O-Matics*, 1980, Parker/Prentice Hall, NJ
- *Practical Color Magick*, 1983, Llewellyn Publications, MN
- *Color Magick: Unleash Your Inner Powers* 2002, Llewellyn Publications, MN
- *Buckland's Complete Book of Witchcraft*, 2002, Llewellyn Publications, MN
- *Secrets of Gypsy Fortune Telling*, 1988, Llewellyn Publications, MN
- *The Buckland Gypsy Fortunetelling Deck*, 1989, Llewellyn Publications, MN
- *Secrets of Gypsy Love Magick*, 1990, Llewellyn Publications, MN
- *Secrets of Gypsy Dream Reading*, 1990, Llewellyn Publications, MN
- *Scottish Witchcraft: The History and Magick of the Picts*, 1991, Llewellyn Publications, MN
- *The Book of African Divination*, with Kathleen Binger, 1992, Inner Traditions, VT
- *Doors to Other Worlds*, 1993, Llewellyn Publications, MN
- *The Truth About Spirit Communication*, 1995, Llewellyn Publications, MN
- *The Committee* (novel), 1993, Llewellyn Publications, MN
- *Cardinal's Sin: Psychic Defenders Uncover Evil in the Vatican* (novel), 1996, Llewellyn Publications, MN
- *Ray Buckland's Magic Cauldron*, 1995, Galde Press, MN
- *Advanced Candle Magick: More Spells and Rituals for Every Purpose*, 1996, Llewellyn Publications, MN
- *Witchcraft: Yesterday and Today* (video), 1990, Llewellyn Publications, MN
- *Gypsy Witchcraft & Magic*, 1998, Llewellyn Publications, MN
- *Gypsy Dream Dictionary*, 1999, Llewellyn Publications, MN
- *Coin Divination*, 2000, Llewellyn Publications, MN
- *The Buckland Romani Tarot*, 2001, Llewellyn Publications, MN

- *Wicca for Life*, 2001, Citadel, NY
- *The Witch Book: The Encyclopedia of Witchcraft, Wicca, and Neo-paganism,* 2001, Visible Ink Press, NY
- *The Fortune-Telling Book,* 2003, Visible Ink Press, NY
- *Signs, Symbols & Omens: An Illustrated Guide to Magical & Spiritual Symbolism,* 2003, Llewellyn Publications, MN
- *Cards of Alchemy,* 2003, Llewellyn Publications, MN
- *Wicca For One,* 2004, Citadel, NY
- *Buckland's Book of Spirit Communications,* 2004, Llewellyn Publications, MN
- *The Spirit Book: The Encyclopedia of Clairvoyance, Channeling, and Spirit Communication,* 2005, Visible Ink Press, NY
- *Mediumship and Spirit Communication,* 2005, Buckland Books
- *Face to Face with God?,* 2006, Buckland Books
- *Ouija – "Yes! Yes!",* 2006, Doorway Publications
- *Death, Where is Thy Sting?,* 2006, Buckland Books
- *Dragons, Shamans & Spiritualists,* 2007, Buckland Books
- *Buckland's Doorway to Candle Magic,* 2007, Buckland Books
- *the Torque of Kernow* (novel), 2008, Galde Press/Buckland Books
- *The Weiser's Field Guide to Ghosts,* 2009, Red Wheel/Weiser
- *Buckland's Book of Gypsy Magic,* 2010, Red Wheel/Weiser

The Buckland Museum of Witchcraft and Magic
2155 Broadview Road, Cleveland, Ohio 44109. USA.
www.bucklandmuseum.org.

Nybor
Priest Elder
1936 -

Nybor is an internationally honored artist, as well as a healer, teacher, pastoral counsellor, spiritual theorist, self-taught ritual Magician, and a hermit at heart! Presently he is working on a theory of metaphysics, revealing a new way of looking at the relationship within and between the astral and physical worlds. His art has appeared on national logos, in Science Fiction and Pagan publications, and many paintings and portraits. In 2001 he completed a 3+ year project: "The Nybor Tarot Deck and Book", a divination system in keeping with our current culture. Nybor's current art project is a series of Goddess portraits: thirteen so far! Nybor's art may also be seen at NyborArt.com. Together, Nybor and Elspeth have created "Gylantra's Journey," a storybook to change minds and hearts. Also, they are both involved in "GreenSong", a non-profit organization of environmental awareness and personal preparedness.

In spite of his own reluctance, Nybor can be found at a few festivals each year. There he teaches, counsels and generally functions as an Elder. As such he is available to the Neo-Pagan movement as a resource. In between, he keeps the home base in West Virginia functioning, the fur persons happy, and a candle burning for Elspeth his loving partner wherever she is traveling!

Email at: nybor@mail.wvnet.edu

Jack L "Dafo" Bracelin
Wiccan High Priest Elder
- 1983

Jack L. Bracelin was a very influential figure in the early history of the Neopagan religion of Wicca, being Initiated in 1956 by Doreen Valiente as a member of the Bricket Wood Coven and eventually becoming a High Priest of Gardnerian Wicca. Prior to his involvement in the Craft, Bracelin had worked for the British Police in Palestine. Bracelin in 1959 met Idries Shah, the great Sufi and Occult writer at the Cosmo Restaurant in Swiss Cottage, North London. Shah was interested in Wicca, and it was Bracelin that introduced him to Gardner, where Shah wrote Gardner's first official biography, "Gerald Gardner: Witch", which was published by his company Octagon Press, in 1960. However, he used Bracelin's name as a pseudonym because he did not want to cause confusion amongst his Sufi students and friends as to his interest in a different tradition.

When Gardner died Bracelin was one of his beneficiaries of his estate, along with Monique Wilson and Patricia Crowther. Bracelin inherited enough of the naturist club that he eventually took it over. Bracelin due to disagreements in the Bricket Wood Coven decided to resign as coven High Priest, and soon left altogether. According to coven member Frederick Lamond, "he asked himself whether the Book of Shadows simplified Ceremonial Magick rituals expressed his own religious feelings, and concluded they did not". Bracelin married in 1966 in a ceremony held in a Roman Catholic Church, which many members of the Wicca felt he showed that he had turned his back on the craft. This was not so, as Bracelin continued to allow the coven to meet at the Witches' cottage, on the condition that they paid rent on the plot of land upon which it was situated.

In 1975, Bracelin tried to get them to pay for the nudist club's electricity as well, which the coven members were unwilling to do, and so they sold their plot to another nudist. Bracelin was a supporter of the hippie movement of the 1960s and 1970s, believing that it embodied the "life-affirming Goddess values" in its "true expression". Partially for this reason, he opened a disco in the West End of London, but it was a financial failure. In June 1976, Bracelin, by then in financial difficulties, was forced to sell the nudist club, though the new owners agreed to pay him a small pension.

Bracelin retired to live in Greece, and it was here that he died in 1983 of a heart attack.

Gardner's Witches Cottage

Rt. Rev. Pete Pathfinder Davis
Aquarian Tabernacle Church
High Priest-President Interfaith Council
- Witch Elder
August 14th, 1937 – October 31st, 2014

Photograph of Pete Pathfinder Davis in ATC Temple

Born Pete Claveloux Davis on the 14th of August 1937, in Jersey City to Catholic parents and well-known as Pete Pathfinder. He entered the Pagan life late in life and it was not until he was thirty-seven on the 14th of August 1974 that he became an Initiated Witch in the Dorpat Tradition. In 1976, he relocated to Index, Washington and worked in Law. In 1983 he was Initiated into the New Wiccan Church (Kingstone) tradition in Seattle, Washington. Davis, once established in Washington, began work on creating a sanctuary for local Pagans and Wiccans on his property which was beautiful alongside a flowing river set by steep snow-capped mountains. On Samhain (Halloween) 1979 he Founded the "Aquarian Tabernacle Church" (ATC), a Wiccan religious tradition.

By 1985, the ATC established a liturgy of Priests and Priestesses and also ATC's affiliated Churches around the world including here in Australia which I Chartered in 1991 as "Aquarian Tabernacle Church of Wicca-Australia". I was later ordained as a High Priestess of the ATC in 1996, by Pete Pathfinder. The ATC has centers in Australia, Ireland, England, Canada, and several throughout America. Their Sanctuary is beautiful and in 1985 created and erected a Circle of Standing Stones called "Moonstone Circle". Through all his hard work and constant work with governments the ATC received IRS 501c(3) exemption status, which was elevated to an umbrella status in 1991, which we also received in Australia. As an efficient and dedicated Arch Priest of the ATC, Davis also Founded "Panagyria Magazine", "Woolsten Steen Theological Seminary", "Spring Mysteries Festival", "Hecate's Sickle Festival", and "Spiral Scouts International". Davis advocated for Wicca and Paganism in its entirety as an expert witness, and was part of a successful group along with Selena Fox, who petitioned for ten years successfully for the Pentacle "Veterans Pentacle Quest" to be available as a symbol used on all US veterans headstones if they were Pagan or Wiccan. In 1985, Davis was retained by the Washington State Attorney General as an expert witness in Wicca for a civil rights case brought against by a Wiccan prisoner in federal court. In 1995, Davis was the first Wiccan elected as President of the Interfaith Council of Washington, where he served two terms.

I knew Pete well, who only ever showed his hospitality and friendship at every level. He was a great conversationalist, and his knowledge was something to truly admire. Sadly, Pete Pathfinder Davis passed away on October 31st, 2014, and prior to his death officially handed the reigns over of the ATC to the new Arch Priestess Belladonna Laveau, who has with her new motivations, ideas and youth taken the ATC to the next level world-wide.

The Aquarian Tabernacle Church Elders 1999

Marylyn "Motherbear" Scott
Goddess Elder
1937 –

Marylyn Motherbear Scott, fondly called the Poet Priestess, is a published author and Goddess-in-Chief of the "Magickal Cauldron", a non-profit educational and spiritual organisation. The Cauldron offers experiences of Magical practice and deep Initiation, Priesthood training and Ordination, conferences, and workshop events; its motto: "Personal Growth on the Ecstatic Edge". Motherbear, a Priestess in Her Own Rite, High Priestess of the Cauldron and of Eleusis, and the "Magickal Cauldron Mystery School", ordained in the "Fellowship of Isis", the "Temple of Isis", the "Temple of Ishtar", and is an Elder Priestess in the "Church of All Worlds".

The Cauldron is currently offering its Initiation Cycle, the Living Mysteries of Eleusis. Motherbear has been a Priestess of these Initiation rites for over 25 years. The Magickal Cauldron has brought these Rites, based on the Greek Rites and the Cult of Demeter, into deep resonance with those of ancient Greece.

Motherbear is Founder of the widely popular wisdom-sharing events, "Goddess Gather" and "Two-as-One, God and Goddess Gather Together". She has presided at the Church of All World's Wheel-of-the-Year events, at Ancient Ways presentations, Pantheacon, Bear River Sabbats, the Convocations of Isis; and at a special event that included the profound teachings of Elizabeth Kelley, Janet Seaforth, Lady Loreon, Oberon Zell, and additional Cauldron Priesthood. Birthing the True Self; Birthing the New Aeon — A Labor of Love, was a 12-hour ritual, presented at Isis Oasis on Winter Solstice on 12-12-12. She was a featured ritualist and poet at the Mendocino Goddess Festival in 2012; and for 7 years, at Burning Man's Temple of Ishtar, Women's Temple, Earth Tribe, and at Sacred Spaces where she created the Temple of the Red Root.

Marylyn "Motherbear" Scott has been a featured poet in the East Bay and in diverse NoCA's venues. She is published in "Circle Round" (by Anne Hill and Starhawk); in Beyond Absence: A Treasury of Poems, Quotations, And Readings on Death and Remembrance (by

Edward Searl), in Home Cooking by Oberon and Morning Glory Zell, in Green Egg and in Coreopsis. She has a poetry chapbook, Love's Journey, and a short fiction Dragonslayer's Daughter. Featured in Daughters of Aquarius: Women of the Sixties Counterculture, author Gretchen Lemke-Santagelo says, Marylyn Motherbear Scott is "a woman whose contributions altered the landscape [by bringing] natural childbirth and mothering, New Age spiritual beliefs, eco-feminism, holistic health and sustainable agriculture into the national discourse."

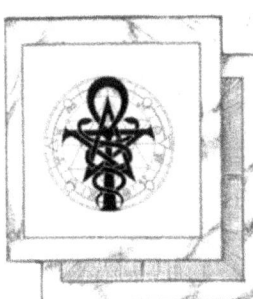
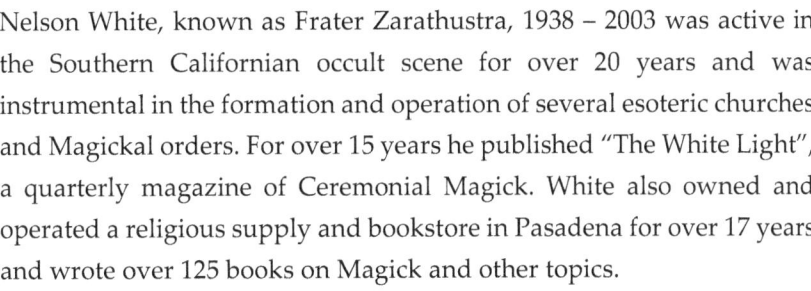

Nelson White
Frater Zarathustra
1938 – 2003

Nelson White, known as Frater Zarathustra, 1938 – 2003 was active in the Southern Californian occult scene for over 20 years and was instrumental in the formation and operation of several esoteric churches and Magickal orders. For over 15 years he published "The White Light", a quarterly magazine of Ceremonial Magick. White also owned and operated a religious supply and bookstore in Pasadena for over 17 years and wrote over 125 books on Magick and other topics.

Dr. White taught in a number of junior and senior high schools and was knighted by the "Alter Souveraner Templer Orden" based in Vienna, Austria. Retired from NASA's Ames Research center, he was a private pilot and ham radio operator, and sang in the Richmond Choir.

Dr. White died of a heart attack on August 23rd, 2003, just as the Grimoire for the Apprentice Wizard was being completed.

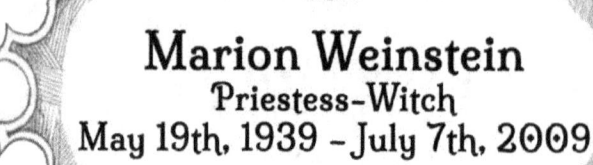

Marion Weinstein
Priestess-Witch
May 19th, 1939 – July 7th, 2009

Marion Weinstein was born on May 19th, 1939, in Queens, New York. Marion was raised in a Jewish family and began identifying with Witchcraft as a young girl and began a long dedication to the Goddess Diana, the Goddess of Witches, her one true deity that filled her life and her dreams. Marion graduated from Barnard College with a bachelor's degree in English literature, and also studied the Arts such as acting, dance, music, film, and voice.

Marion began practicing Witchcraft as a religion in the 1960s and founded the "Earth Magic Dianic Tradition". It was in 1969 that her career took off in radio, which combined her talents and her form of spirituality, called "Marion's Cauldron", on WBAI radio in New York City. Her show was the first Pagan show that ran on a weekly basis that reached out to the public with her views on Pagan spirituality and the Goddess Diana, this fabulously popular show lasted for 14 years.

Weinstein with modernization, she also started and became one of the first Pagans in the US to have a regular weekly Pagan internet show, and more recently, she entered the internet video world with a series of You Tube videos. In 1978, Marion wrote and had published her first book, "Positive Magic", and is still to this very day treasured by many Pagans, Wiccans and Witches as their practical guide to Pagan theory and practice. Marion also started on a career as a Stand-Up Comedian (who said witches weren't funny), this became part of her daily routine. Over Marion's life she wrote many books and many articles, made professional audio and video recordings, presented a variety of workshops, guided ceremonies, and was constantly in the media.

Marion's passion was also as an activist for world peace, religious freedom, and definitely Pagan rights. She hosted an annual Samhain Festival celebration on the Eve of Halloween for many years in New York City. Marion loved nature and ventured on her nature walks as often as she could get away. Marion networked from her family home near Atlantic Beach, Long Island, New York. It was from her home cum farmlet that she had many rescued animals caring for many cats and dogs in her garden that she adored, always feeding the local swans. Marion had a great sense of humor, a loving heart, and a brilliant mind, she was a giver and never a taker.

Weinstein was a life-long supporter of Selena Foxes "Circle Sanctuary" and "Lady Liberty League", and requested that after her death, that there would be a place of remembrance for her at "Circle Cemetery", the national Pagan Cemetery at Circle Sanctuary near Barneveld, Wisconsin.

Marion Weinstein was a High Priestess, author, radio host, comedian, teacher, and New York Witch. Marion sadly died on July 1st, 2009, after a battle with a long illness. Her family held a private memorial at Marion's family home on August 1st on Long Island, New York. The following day, her Coven members and very close friends also held a private memorial at a home in New York City's upper west side.

A public ceremony for Marion was held on Saturday, September 26th, at Battery Park in New York City as part of the Pagan Pride Day. Mama Donna Hennes and Margot Adler facilitated the ceremony. On Saturday morning, October 31st, 2009, Selena Fox and Circle Sanctuary Ministers assisted by Ministers-in-Training and other community members performed a memorial service for Marion as part of the Samhain Festival at Circle Sanctuary Nature Preserve in Wisconsin.

Tokens of remembrance from friends, family, and fans were interred in the cemetery as part of the memorial. A custom designed granite pentacle marker was placed there and dedicated. The cost of the marker was funded by donations from family, friends, and fans from across the USA.

Marion Weinstein's Books:

- *Earth Magic: A book of Shadows for Positive Witches*, 1978
- *Positive Magic: Occult Self-Help*, 1978
- *Magia, Ktora pomaga zyc*, 1978
- *Racewalking*, 1985
- *The Goddess Celebrates: An Anthology of Women's Rituals* with Diane Stein, Zsuzsanna E. Budapest, Jeannine Parvati Baker, Uzuri Amini, 1991
- *The Ancient Modern Witch*, 1993
- *Divination: Beyond Tea Leaves*, 1997
- *Personal Magic: The Role and the True Self*, 1997
- *Marion Weinstein's Handy Guide to Tarot Cards*, 2000
- *Positive Magic: A Toolkit for the Modern Witch*
- *How to Read Tarot Cards*, 2000
- *Positive Magic: Ancient Metaphysical Techniques for Modern Lives*
- *How to Use I Ching*, 2000
- *How to Use Words of Power*, 2000
- *Marion Weinstein's Handy Guide to the I Ching*, 2000
- *Magic for Peace*, 2007

- *Words of Power, Transform Your Life – The Art of Manifestation*, 2008
- *Magic For Peace: A Non-Sectarian Guide to Working Magic for Peace and Safety*, 2008

Michael York
Pagan Elder
September 15th, 1939 -

Michael York

Michael York was born on the 15th of September 1939. His first statement "Possibly reflecting an initial reluctance to engage in this world, my birth was breech/feet first, and my mother was 48 hours in labor with me. This occurred in the psychic catchment of Niagara Falls (Buffalo) and brought me into a strong matriarchal line that taught a deep appreciation of life as well as one concerning elves, goblins, leprechauns, and fairies".

York's childhood itself took place in New York City's suburbia and on the slopes of South Mountain. York's parents had chosen to move to New Jersey because of the Maplewood-South Orange school system, had been ranked the second best in the US. (Evanston, Illinois was the first, but for his mother it was too close to her in-laws). York retains the deepest gratitude to his parents for the education that he had received. Subsequently, this included attendance at Purdue University, New York University, UCLA, UC Berkeley – receiving a BA in English from the University of California in Santa Barbara, MA in International Relations from San Francisco State University, and PhD in Theology from King's College London. Eventually, he became

Professor of Cultural Astronomy and Astrology at Bath Spa University, England.

Much of his life has been one of vagabonding, and he has lived in Maplewood, New Jersey West Lafayette, Indiana Goleta, Los Angeles, Berkeley and San Francisco California, Amsterdam Netherlands, Provence France, Goulnacappy Ireland, London and Bath, United Kingdom, and Varanasi India. York's travels have been to and through Mexico, Scandinavia, the Low Countries, Germany, France, Great Britain, Ireland, Italy, Spain, Portugal, Greece, the former Yugoslavia, Switzerland, Austria, Hungary, Romania, Bulgaria, South Africa, Turkey, Morocco, Egypt, Pakistan, India, Bangladesh, Nepal, Thailand, China and Japan, and he is not finished yet.

York's Initiation and introduction to the otherworld were sponsored by Langston Bowen in 1960 in the fog-covered hills of a remote area in southern San Francisco. His pathway is primarily shamanic with a grounding in Greco-Roman mythology – extending into a search for Indo-European roots and understandings of the sacred. In San Francisco he co-organized the Strawberry Hill Coven in 1969. Their cycle of celebrations was held in Golden Gate Park including sky-clad dancing around bonfires and the use of flying ointment beneath a magical cloak of invisibility. During the 1970s, York was principally engaged in exploring the sacred geography of Europe. These studies were extended to the Indian subcontinent in the 1980s. From 'sacred fords' or tirthas, York has been privileged to commune with the Gods and the wonders of the otherworld on repeated occasions.

York's' doctoral dissertation was published as:
- *The Emerging Network: A Sociology of the New Age and Neo-pagan Movements*, 1995. The same year saw the publication of his magnum opus, *The Divine versus the Asurian: An Interpretation of Indo-European Cult and Myth*
- *The Roman Festival Calendar of Numa Pompilius*, 1986
- York's trilogy of *Pagan Theology: Paganism as a World Religion*
- *Pagan Ethics: Paganism as a World Religion*, 2016
- *Pagan Mysticism: Paganism as a World Religion*, 2019

At Bath Spa, he was allowed to establish an academic "Pagan Studies Programme". For the "Cherry Hill Seminary", the module teaching is "World Religions from a Pagan Perspective". Wendy Griffin and York served as the Co-Chairs for the "Pagan Studies Group" of the "American Academy of Religion" from 2005 to 2007.

Yorks' teachings aim to foster the cherishing and cultivation of the natural and co-natural through calendrical mindfulness. By celebrating the ancient holy days, he gambles with an enchantment-fused life. York succeeds or fails on that basis.

H. R. Giger
Occult Artist, Magician
February 5th, 1940 – May 12th, 2014

H. R. Giger

Hans Ruedi Giger born 5th February 1940 in Chur, the capital city of Graubünden, the largest and easternmost Swiss canton. His father, a pharmacist, viewed art as a "breadless profession" and strongly encouraged him to enter pharmacy. He eventually moved to Zurich in 1962, where he studied architecture and industrial design at the School of Applied Arts until 1970. Giger's first success was when the co-owner H.H. Kunz of Switzerland's first poster publishing company, printed and distributed Giger's first series of posters in 1969.

Giger was a Swiss painter, who was best known to his airbrush techniques with images of humans and machines that were absorbed together in a cold biochemical relationship like automated humans. Later in life he abandoned his airbrush work for working with pastels, markers, and inks. His design and artwork won him an Academy Award for the film Alien. In Switzerland there are two public bars that reflect his eccentricity, including with his interior designs, and his works of art are all on permanent display at the H.R. Giger Museum at

Gruyeres. His unusual style has been adopted and adapted to many forms of media, including record album covers, furniture and tattoos.

Giger's unusual technique and thematic execution were very influential. Where his influence was part of the special effects team that won an Academy Award for Best Achievement in Visual Effects for their design on the film Alien, which was inspired by his painting Necronom IV and also earned him an Oscar in 1980. Giger was admitted to the Science Fiction and Fantasy Hall of Fame in 2013. In 1998, Giger acquired the Château St. Germain in Gruyères, Switzerland, and it now houses the H.R. Giger Museum, a permanent repository of his work. Giger had a long-term relationship with a top Swiss actress Li Tobler until she committed suicide in 1975. It is Li's image that appears in most of his paintings and sculptures. He married Mia Bonzanigo in 1979, but sadly they divorced eighteen months later. He eventually met and remarried his second wife, Carmen Maria Scheifele Giger, who is presently the director of the H.R. Giger Museum. On the 12th of May 2014, Giger died in a hospital in Zurich after having suffered severe injuries in a fall.

Giger's Works:
- Dune (designs for unproduced Alejandro Jodorowsky adaptation of the Frank Herbert novel; the movie Dune was later made in an adaptation by David Lynch)[22]
- Alien (designed, among other things, the Alien creature, "The Derelict" and the "Space Jockey")[23]
- Aliens (credited for the creation of the creature only)
- Alien 3 (designed the dog-like Alien body shape, plus a number of unused concepts, many mentioned on the special features disc of Alien 3, despite not being credited in the movie theatre version)
- Alien Resurrection (credited for the creation of the creature only)
- Poltergeist II: The Other Side
- Killer Condom (creative consultant, set design)[24][25][26]
- Species (designed Sil, and the Ghost Train in a dream sequence)
- Batman Forever (designed radically different envisioning of the Batmobile; design was not used in the film)[27]
- Future-Kill (designed artwork for the movie poster)
- Tokyo: The Last Megalopolis (creature designs)[28]
- Prometheus (the film includes "The Derelict" spacecraft and the "Space Jockey" designs from the first Alien film, as well as a "Temple" design from the failed Jodorowsky Dune project and original extra-terrestrial murals created exclusively for Prometheus, based in conceptual art from Alien. Unlike Alien Resurrection, the Prometheus film credited H. R. Giger with the original designs).

Work for recording artists:
- Magma: Attahk
- Emerson, Lake & Palmer: Brain Salad Surgery

- Floh de Cologne: Mumien
- Steve Stevens' Atomic Playboys
- Deborah Harry, portraits for KooKoo album cover and videos "Backfired" and "Now I Know You Know"
- hide: Hide Your Face
- Carcass: Heartwork
- Danzig: Danzig III: How the Gods Kill
- Dead Kennedys' album Frankenchrist, Poster insert of Landscape XX (which led to an obscenity trial)
- Atrocity – Hallucinations
- Black Sun Productions
- Korn's Jonathan Davis commissioned Giger to design and sculpt a microphone stand, with the requirement that it be biomechanical, erotic, and movable. The contract allowed for five aluminum microphone stands to be made, but Davis purchased only two of the three to which he was entitled. The design of the microphone stand was later adapted to Giger's "Nubian Queen", transforming it into a fine art sculpture.
- Helped to design the first professional video clip of "Böhse Onkelz" called "Dunkler Ort" (dark location) from their album "Ein böses Märchen ... aus tausend finsteren Nächten", which was released in 2000.
- Ibanez Guitars released a series of H. R. Giger Signature Models with artwork on the body.
- Island: "Pictures"
- Triptykon: Eparistera Daimones
- Triptykon: Melana Chasmata

Lady Elizabeth "Ea" Paterson
High Priestess Traditional Witch Elder
1940-2022

Lady Elizabeth Paterson

Elizabeth "Patto" Paterson was a remarkable friend and woman, she was the mother of four children and then when she was 44 years of age fell pregnant with twins Michael and Renae, my Goddess Children. Elizabeth was a mentor to many and was well known and loved, even admired for her bush-style witchcraft. I first met her when she was working at "The Magic Circle" bookstore in Perth as a tarot reader and healer for David Mosley, also her working partner and High Priest. She was such a tiny lady but had an enormous heart. She loved the country and always lived in a rural setting.

Elizabeth is one of the most respected and highly held Priestesses to come out of Australia, she dedicated her entire life to the craft and her children. Elizabeth never wrote any books, or founded great legal bodies, but she was my backbone and assisted me with every venture that I went into, and if she were not in agreement, she would let me know. She had an amazing sense of humor and always laughed at everything in particular herself. Elizabeth supported the pagan community and between her and her High Priests lastly John, she initiated many welcoming Witches into the community. It was myself and my High Priest Geoff Camm that took her and David Mosley 3rd Degree assisted by all the High Priesthood of Perth in her rented two-story house in Perth Central. She was a true representation of the Goddess and an exceptional High Priestess that taught from the heart and soul, she never taught what most taught but instead everything was practical, as her Coveners worked with the raw energies of the living earth. She was my greatest friend for over 30 years, and I have always loved and respected her greatly for everything that she stands for. She is truly honored and missed.

Oberon Zell Ravenheart
High Priest – Magician – Witch Elder
November 30th, 1942 –

Photograph of Oberon Zell Ravenheart in Magician Regalia

Oberon Zell-Ravenheart (born Timothy Zell, November 30th, 1942, in St. Louis, Missouri; was formerly also known under the alias as Otter G'Zell). Oberon took a Bachelor of Arts degree in psychology from Westminster College in Fulton, Missouri in 1965 prior to briefly enrolling in a doctoral program in Clinical Psychology at Washington University in St. Louis. Oberon also received a Doctor of Divinity Degree from Life Science College in Rolling Meadows, Illinois (which is a defunct non-residential seminary analogous to the Universal Life Church) in 1967. In 1968, he completed a teaching certificate at Harris-Stowe State University.

Church of All Worlds:

Oberon along with R. Lance Christie Founded and formed the "Church of All Worlds" (CAW) on April 7th, 1962, by the ritual of 'sharing water'. This foundation ritual was practiced by a fictional church of the same name in Robert A. Heinlein's "Stranger in a Strange land". Oberon and Christie attributed their inspiration to Heinlein's novel. From the 1960s through to the late 1990s, Oberon served as the High Priest and Primate of the Church. He returned to lead the Church of All Worlds, Inc. in 2005 and currently serves as First Primate. He was the second to incorporate in Australia in the early 90s.

Green Egg Magazine:

Oberon as the original creator and editor of the Neopagan magazine "Green Egg" in 1968, Oberon was an early popularizer of the term "Neo-Pagan". When Green Egg began publishing as a spirit duplicated newsletter, Oberon used the term "Neo-Pagan" to describe the new religious pagan movement that he was helping to create. Green Egg later grew to be a semi-glossy magazine with international distribution and in an era prior to the Internet, its letters column provided a widely distributed public forum for discussion, networking, and contacts. From 1994 to late 2001, Green Egg was edited by Maerian Morris, a former High Priestess of the Church of All Worlds. Green Egg is currently published as an e-zine, edited by Ariel Monserrat.

Oberon is a Neo-Pagan writer, speaker, ecologist, and religious leader, also co-Founder of the Church of All Worlds, Green Egg, Ecosophical Research Association in 1977, and more. Oberon has never seen himself as a Witch but more so as a Wizard. Distinguishing his practice from the Wizards of fiction, Oberon used as with Aleister Crowley and many other writers the alternative spelling of the word Magick (with final 'k') and claimed his interest in ancient mythology and fairy tales helped create the Oberon of today. He became quite popular with his creation of goats on his farm where he trained the horns to form together in one singular twisted manner to form his Unicorns. One of their Unicorns, Lancelot, toured with the Ringling Bros, and Barnum and Bailey Circus. Also, along with his wife Morning-Glory Zell, created many numerous images of Pagan deities, which his family now runs "Mythic Images", a business through which their artwork is distributed.

Grey School of Wizardry:

Oberon is currently the headmaster of the "Grey School of Wizardry", which was incorporated on the 14th of March 2005 as a non-profit educational institution in the State of California. An online school which specializes in the teaching of a wide range of esoteric Magick. The "Grey School" was originally created by the Grey Council, a team of 24 practitioners, along with Oberon wrote the "Grimoire for the Apprentice Wizard" and later the "Companion for the Apprentice Wizard".

While initially conceived for ages 11–17, the school accepts adult students. The school comprises sixteen departments of study, various clubs and organizations, a forum area, a prefect/captain system, opportunities for awards and merits and a house/lodge system for adults and youths in which they can communicate directly with each other. Youth (under 18) students are sorted into four houses: Sylphs, Salamanders, Undines, and Gnomes. Adult (18+) students are sorted into four lodges: Society of the Four Winds, Order of the Dancing Flames, Coterie of the Flowing Waters, and Circle of the Standing Stones.

Oberon regularly presents workshops, lectures and ceremonies at Neopagan and New Age events, as well as at science fiction conventions and renaissance fairs. Oberon and Morning Glory Zell-Ravenheart lived in Sonoma County, California, where they were members of the Sonoma County Pagan Network. He is a frequent speaker at the organization's local activities and has contributed articles to its website.

I have just returned from the PSG Festival in Ohio where I met up with Oberon who also attended this gathering, and he seemed to be of fine health although he had a few scares with polyps that were cancerous, after having these removed and undergoing chemotherapy, he was designated ready to go walkabout (Australian Aboriginal term for wandering freely) and travel on his journey throughout the US to meet and greet his many adoring fans. We were also lucky to have him speak on our podcast show Spirit Talk Australia if you would like to listen to his wisdom.

Oberon and Morning Glory Zell in Oz

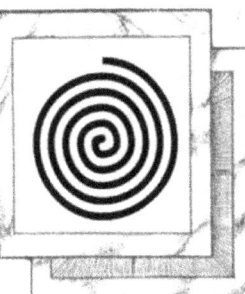

Nicki Scully
Shaman Elder
June 19th, 1943 -

Nicki Scully

Nicki Scully born 19th June 1943 in New York City, she is an American author, Shaman, Healer and Priestess, and occasionally a Witch. She was Ordained as a Priestess of Hathor by the late Lady Olivia Robertson, co-founder of the "Fellowship of Isis" at Clonegal Castle in Ireland. She has been visiting Egypt since 1978, when, as part of the rock band The Grateful Dead family. Scully travelled to Egypt for three nights of concerts in front of the Sphinx and the Pyramids, under a Full Moon, including a total eclipse the third night. Scully was smitten by Egypt, and returned three weeks later chasing the ineffable Magic and synchronicities that accompanied her first trip, and also to shop.

After three separate attempts that first year, she found herself in an emergency situation where medical help was required whilst sailing the Nile on a small felucca with friends including children, and they were hours away from help of any sort. Scully directed a small crystal that had been given to her by a Native American teacher, even though she did not fully understand what that meant. She soon realised that she could not fulfil her commitment whilst living amidst rock and roll royalty (her husband at the timer, Rock Scully, had been the original manager of the band and although he was then in a different position, they were sharing a home with Jerry Garcia and Scully was a "Gate-Keeper" of sorts during this difficult time.)

In January 1981, Scully packed up her children and moved to a friend's shack in Oregon where she spent six months looking for her own 'perfect place' when it occurred to her that with work, time and love, the shack and property could be exactly what she was looking for all along.

For the next 36 years Scully has held retreats and classes on the property, many of which were part of the Mystery School that was taught by herself and Normandi Ellis, a brilliant writer, poet, priestess who is fluent in hieroglyphics, having had to learn them to translate the Egyptian Book of the Dead (actually, The Egyptian Book of Coming into the Light), Awakening Osiris, and many other stellar books on Egypt.

Scully has since incorporated aspects of Egyptian Magic, lore and imagery into her shamanic work, her teachings, and writings. Scully specializes in spiritual tours to Egypt, Greece, Peru, and what she regards as other sacred power centers. Scully offers philanthropic projects through Sahalie Publishing Company, which was incorporated as a non-profit 5012©(3) Oregon corporation in 1977. One of its projects, the Animal Circus CD "And You Will Fly" featuring Scully, Roland Barker and Mark Hallert, which was created for children facing potentially terminal diseases, was produced with a grant from the Rex Foundation.

Around 1989 Scully created a corporation, Shamanic Journeys, Ltd., and has personally led more than 60 tours to Egypt before retiring her tour company in 2018. Scully has organized numerous tours for other teachers as they launch their careers. Her two daughters, Spirit Acacia and Sage, were gracious in putting up with her many travels whilst doing her best to support and raise them. Scully has lived with her husband, Mark Hallert since 1985 and they were married in 1990. They have an unusual relationship, filled with Magic that has resulted in a collaboration from which most of their teachings are born. Scully believes that mark is the true Shaman of the family, as he visions with all his senses, and she scribes his visions. Together they turn them into unique rituals, Shamanic Journeys, and ultimately most of all of Scully's presentations and books.

Fast forward to 2019, Scully is now 76 years young and in the process of retiring, although she still does mentoring, private sessions, and Anubis Oracle Readings, also teaches occasional classes, mostly via online video technology. Soon after asking her: "What did you learn from this lengthy career, after publishing eight plus books, and many tours, teaching and healing". Her answers are listed below:

1. Your children are your first priority. Raise them well and with love and they will be your first line of defense when you grow old and begin to slow down.
2. Greed will always bite you in the butt, as will arrogance.

3. Kindness is critical.
4. Stay curious. You are never too old to learn. Actually, she said that a healthy curiosity is a primary elixir of life, along with laughter, joy and love.
5. Avoid stress by learning and practicing those activities that will mitigate and alleviate the stress in your life.
6. Communicate with your friends and be there for them – and they will be there for you when you need them.
7. Always be willing to help others, yet be discerning, as they are all not yours to help.
8. Laughter and joy are the ultimate healers.
9. Magic is alive and well and miracles are always happening around you.
10. Observe the Moon and its phases and create ceremonies for the quarter and half quarter days when you can, but do not beat yourself up if you cannot.
11. And finally, attention is the coin of the realms; that's what you pay. Enjoy every precious minute of your life. It's fleeting.

"Nick Scully & Tribal Alchemy", a New Age/World music group, was featured at the Hog Farm's annual "Pig-Nic" in 1995, and as part of "The Celebration of the Psychedelic Sixties" in San Francisco, organized by Reg. E. Williams, author of "The Straight on the Haight" and founder of the "Straight Theatre". They produced one CD in 1997, entitled "Tribal Alchemy". Tribal Alchemy also performed at a number of music festivals, including Earth dances, Gaia Festivals, and Oregon County Fairs.

Nicki Scully Works:

- *Alchemical Healing: A Guide to Spiritual, Physical, and Transformational Medicine*, 2003, Bear & Co.
- *The Anubis Oracle: A Journey into the Shamanic Mysteries of Egypt. A book and card deck* with Linda Star Wolf, 2008, Bear & Co.
- *The Golden Cauldron: Shamanic Journeys on the Path of Wisdom* (Reissued with additions as *Power Animal Meditations*, 1991, Bear & Co.
- *Power Animal Meditations: Shamanic Journeys with Your Spirit Allies*, 2001, Bear & Co.
- *Shamanic Mysteries of Egypt: Awakening the Healing Power of the Heart* with Linda Star Wolf, 2007, Bear & Co. Contains the deeper initiations from *The Anubis Oracle*.
- *Planetary Healing, Spirit Medicine for Global Transformation* with Mark Hallert, 2011, Bear & Co. (Includes a journey CD narrated by Scully with music by Alexa MacDonald and Roland Barker)
- *The Union of Isis and Thoth* with Normandi Ellis, 2015, Bear & Co.
- *Sekhmet: Transformation in the Belly of the Goddess*, 2017, Bear & Co.
- *Women of Wisdom: Empowering the Dreams and Spirit of Women*, Kris Steinnes
- *A Call to Community: We Are All Relations* Brooke Medicine Eagle & Nicki Scully, 2008, Wise Woman Publishing, LLC

- *Heart of the Sun: An Athology in Exaltation of Sekhmet*, 2011, iUniverse
- *The Union of Isis and Thoth* with Normandi Ellis, 2015, Bear & Co

CDs & DVDs
- *Alchemical Healing: Experiences, Insights, and Empowerments* (DVD), 2005, Sacred Mysteries Productions
- *And You Will Fly!* with Roland Barker and Mark Hallert (CD for children) Sahalie Publishing Co.
- *Awakening the Cobra* with Roland Barker, Shamanic Journeys Ltd
- *Becoming an Oracle,* Seven CD Set, 2009, Sounds True
- *Journey for Healing* with Kuan Yin, Roland Barker & Jerry Garcia, Sahalie

Publishing Company & Shamanic Journeys
- *The Cauldron Journey of Rebirth with Tauaret*
- *Journey with Eagle and Elephant* with Roland Barker
- *Tribal Alchemy,* 1997, New Leaf Distributing Company

Audiocassettes
- *The Cauldron Teachings: The Eagle and the Elephant,* 1989
- *The Cauldron Journey for Healing* with Jerry Garcia, 1990, Cauldron
- *The Cauldron Journey for Rebirth,* 1994, Cauldron
- *The Cauldron of Thoth,* 1994, Cauldron
- *Journeys Into the Cauldron* (recorded live at the 1988 Starwood Festival), 1988, Association for Consciousness.

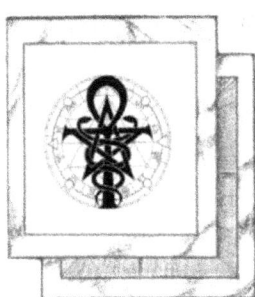

Richard Lance Christie
Magician & Pagan Elder
April 7th, 1944 – October 28th, 2010

Richard Lance Christie was born in Tulsa, Oklahoma to John Richard Christie and Dorothy May Hamilton. Christie entered Westminster College in 1961, where he met Oberon Zell. After reading R.A. Heinlein's science-fiction novel "Stranger in a Strange Land", the two of them shared water creating a water-brotherhood they called Atl (Aztec for Water). Christie married Penryn, and their daughter Michele was born 2nd December 1965. After graduation, Atl branched into two divisions: The Neo-Pagan "Church of All Worlds" (CAW), incorporated in 1968, and the "Atlan Foundation", which eventually became the "Association for the Tree of Life" (ATL), incorporated in 1986.

Christie remained director of ATL throughout his life. He earned a MA in Experimental Social Psychology from the University of California at Los Angeles (UCLA), where he met his soulmate, LaRue Crocker. LaRue earned her Ph.D from UCLA in Developmental Psychology, and they were married on 15th August 1975. Christie was a research associate to the UCLA Longitudinal Marijuana Study, a co-author of the "California Marijuana Initiative", and a regular contributor to "Green Egg Magazine".

In 1974 he was recruited by the New Mexico Health & Environment Department and spent the subsequent decade living in Santa Fe and working in N.M. state government, culminating his career as Chief of the Alcoholism Bureau. Christie and LaRue retired to Moab, Utah in 1985, where they were colleagues and partners in their unflagging commitment to the preservation of the natural environment. They lived life to the fullest for about 30 years until LaRue died from complications of Alzheimer's disease on 31st July 2008.

During Lance's erratic career he did psychoacoustical, altered states of consciousness and hallucinogenic research, designed and operated management information and computer systems, helped launch several Neo-Pagan and environmental organizations and served on their boards, designed, and built renewable energy systems, and managed behavioral health care systems.

In his later years Christie was a principal in the "Spine of the Continent" continental-scale environmental restoration initiative; the Relocalization Network initiative to relocalize community economies internationally; was principal author of the "Renewable Deal" which is the core of the Earth Restoration Portal on the Internet; worked as an organic crop, livestock, and processing inspector part time; and served in various appointed and elected local government positions in South-eastern Utah. With his unconquerable spirit, he survived pancreatic cancer for two years, allowing him to complete his book. Co-Founder, Council of Elders, Priest, and member of the Grey Council, he was a Polymath who co-founded Atl, The Church of All Worlds, Earth First, and the association for the Tree of Life.

He died at Samhain of 2010, leaving 80 unpublished proto-books and articles still in process.

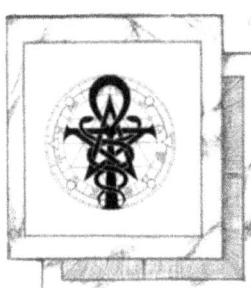
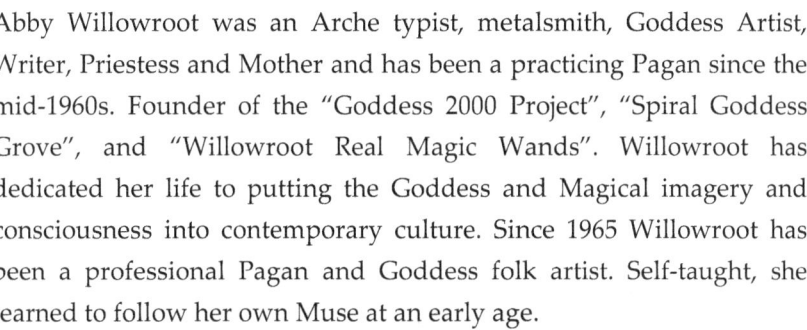

Abby Willowroot
Wizard and Pagan Elder
1945-August 4th 2018

Abby Willowroot was an Arche typist, metalsmith, Goddess Artist, Writer, Priestess and Mother and has been a practicing Pagan since the mid-1960s. Founder of the "Goddess 2000 Project", "Spiral Goddess Grove", and "Willowroot Real Magic Wands". Willowroot has dedicated her life to putting the Goddess and Magical imagery and consciousness into contemporary culture. Since 1965 Willowroot has been a professional Pagan and Goddess folk artist. Self-taught, she learned to follow her own Muse at an early age.

Willowroots art and writings have appeared in books, museum shows, WomanSpirit, SageWoman and Llewellyn publications. Nine pieces of Willow root's jewelry are in the permanent collections of the Smithsonian Institution. Willowroot lived and worked in Northern California and was Professor of Wizardry and Magickal Practices at the Grey School of Wizardry.

Rev. Paul Beyerl
High Priest-Witch Elder
September 2nd, 1945 – 30th December 2021

Rev. Paul Beyerl in Ritual

Rev. Paul V. Beyerl 16501 County 13 Houston, MN 55943 Author, Educator, Wiccan Priest, & Master Herbalist. Founder: of The Rowan Tree Church, (legal recognition since 1980) www.therowantreechurch.org. The Mystery School (teaching The Tradition of Lothloriën, established in 1981) The Unicorn Newsletter (published continually since 1977) The Hermit's Grove, a non-profit educational organization www.thehermitsgrove.org The Hermit's Lantern (a monthly journal published since August 1994) Master Herbalist Certification Program. Well-known throughout the neo-pagan and Wiccan world, Beyerl's columns and articles have appeared in many publications. A guest speaker at many of the early pagan gatherings, he has conducted seminars and workshops throughout the U.S. Rev. Paul began his life as a Wiccan living in Minnesota in the 1970s. His work as a teacher within herbal medicine and spiritual disciplines led to the founding of The School of Healing in the early 1980s in Minneapolis.

The Wiccan Tradition he created was incorporated as The Rowan Tree Church in 1979 and in 1980 he established The Mystery School as the means by which he could guide students into a profound mystical Tradition. During the 1970s and 1980s Beyerl appeared from New York to California as popular guest speaker, appearing as a guest presenter at the Harvest Moon Celebration in Los Angeles annually from 1986 through 1994. The Church began holding its annual retreats at Whitewater State Park, a beautiful setting in what is now known as the Driftless Area. In January 1990 he relocated to Dallas, Texas, expecting it to be temporary. After a year and a half, he was on to Los Angeles for a successful three years.

In 1993 as a guest speaker in Seattle he met Gerry. Rev. Gerry headed south that summer and assisted Rev. Paul during his final year in Los Angeles. The Holy Books of the Devas with artwork by Dianne Lorden, (my favourite little book). Painless Astrology and a revised edition of A Wiccan Bardo all emerged during this time. Rev. Paul offered most of his courses that year, usually to standing room only. In 1994 the Beyerls (Rev. Gerry adopted his partner's name) moved north to the suburban property Rev. Gerry owned. For the next 24 years his work was focused in the Pacific Northwest where he further developed The Rowan Tree Church and founded The Hermit's Grove. The Hermit's Grove also became the name for the 45,000 square foot botanical garden the Beyerls developed by hand, attracting many students and visitors. Beyerl further developed his work with incarcerated Wiccan offenders.

He spent ten years volunteering at Monroe Correctional Complex, four years as a staff Chaplain for the Wiccan population at Stafford Creek Correctional and made appearances at other facilities. Beyerl taught for several years at Bellevue Community College, Cascadia Community College, and began teaching a Seattle Central Community College where he offered an introductory program in herbal medicine for twenty years in several state prisons and taught at Seattle Central Community College for 20 years. With students from the very first class at Seattle Central he took his School of Healing work and created the Master Herbalist Program which remains strong today. After a long pause during which he focused upon creating the gardens, teaching, and putting more of his work into print, Beyerl resumed traveling to teach, now teaching in New Orleans and nearby, Hamilton, Canada, New York State and Portugal. In 2017 the Beyerls shocked many when the Board of Directors announced the selling of the Seattle suburban property. The equity from that 1.3-acre property allowed the purchase of an 11-acre property near Houston, Minnesota, in the Driftless Area, so-called because the last two glacial periods missed the corners of four states. The remaining Upper Midwest was enrolment by glacial drift. This area of the upper Mississippi Valley was first seen by Beyerl when he was four. It left its imprint upon him psychically and spiritually.

Beyerl first came into print as a young, emerging poet in New Dimensions: An Anthology of Modern Poetry, published by Idlewild Publishing Co. in 1967. Today he is best known for: The Master Book of Herbalism, a well-known book, having sold over 70,000 copies, considered an essential book by the metaphysically oriented herbalists. Beyerl has been teaching workshops and courses in various aspects of healing since 1976. Three of the four largest selling quarter sales for the book were in 2018 and 2019. The Master Book of Herbalism has become a true classic. The Master Book of Herbalism was the foundation for work which now includes A Compendium of Herbal Magick and an advanced program which leads to certification as a Master Herbalist. The Rowan Tree Church includes a diverse, North American membership. Lothloriën, a Wiccan Tradition, has been a landmark for many.

A Wiccan Bardo, Revisited describes this Tradition and Beyerl's view of ritual theology. A book speaking to the educated reader, it shows the integration of Eastern and Western metaphysical theology. The Church has its standing with the IRS. From its new central location, it is developing its programs of ritual, discussions, and meetings, now offering the ability for Members and students to spend time healing and growing. We have a research library for our students and Members which has more than 4,000 volumes. Rev. Gerry is developing the herbal and botanical gardens. The Unicorn newsletter, after 42 years, was merged with The Hermit's Lantern, 27 years old, and with The Rowan Tree News, thirty-some years old.

The Church, government recognized, offers a number of services: Sunday Circle discussion groups; ritual schedules; a 3,000 volume library & a 30 year-old periodical library; annual Retreats held at The Hermit's Grove (with every third year in Yellowstone National Park; The Unicorn, The Littlest Unicorn, and The Rowan Tree News. The Church, through The Mystery School provides intensive training for those who wish to pursue Ordination and training as teachers within The Tradition of Lothloriën. We have an average of 40-50 Members, many of whom live scattered throughout North America. Rev. Paul serves as the President of the Board of Directors. His other responsibilities include the legal work, bookkeeping, administrative work, and janitorial tasks. The Mystery School teaches our Wiccan Tradition but with a broad-based metaphysical curriculum reflecting Beyerl's experience. In many aspects it could be perceived as closer to the Tibetan concepts of training for the Priest/esshood than the Western Wiccan approach. It has a limited enrolment of students selected, literally, from throughout North America and Europe who share in a curriculum designed to work with the modern conventions of communication: post office boxes, computers, email, and cassette recorders.

The Mystery School appeals to those who have a long-term commitment to their Pathworking, an interest in a variety of metaphysical and religious disciplines, and a belief that there is much to learn through exploring other religions and paths. Beyerl continues to edit The Unicorn newsletter [believed to be the oldest Wiccan publication in North America]. Published eight times a year, The Unicorn is well-established in the neo-pagan market. Since its inception in 1977, The Unicorn has had a reputation for arriving on time, never having missed an issue. Appealing to the educated reader, it seeks provocative articles, book reviews and poetry. The Unicorn is admired by its readers for the quality of its visual appearance and the skill of its contributors.

In 1999 Rev. Paul took over the management of the Rowan Tree's Prisoner Outreach Program [POP]. Extending limited correspondence to prisoners through The Unicorn since the early 1980s, Beyerl guided The Rowan Tree Church into an accepting but educated approach to extending itself to prisoners. Over the years various methods were explored offering access to Church publications and, when adequate volunteers were available, correspondence and encouragement. Within two years the POP enrolment grew by 400%, offering a stamp barter for materials, requiring monthly progress reports and other options for prisoners wishing to study The Tradition of Lothloriën. In 2005 Rev. Paul began visiting the SOU prison at the Monroe Correctional Complex as a once a-month volunteer and visiting Stafford Creek Corrections Centre as a contract Wiccan Chaplain. He continued this into 2009CE, resigning due to a neurological leg condition making the drive hazardous to other drivers.

In addition to recognition as an herbalist and astrologer, Beyerl is known for his presentations on aspects of ritual, death and dying, ethics, alchemy, initiation, meditation, and visualization techniques, and for his performances of ritual which incorporate skills of theatre and music. Trained in classical music and the founder of The Unicorn Ensemble, a chamber quartet, of Minneapolis Beyerl is now retired from a ten-year career as a professional flutist. He has written songs and chants combining musical experience with poetic skills, performing upon a mountain dulcimer. 1990 concerts and workshops included Los Angeles, Minnesota, Atlanta, and New York State. 1991 included appearances in Cleveland and at the Brushwood Folklore Centre. 1992 included a successful musical/speaking tour of Baltimore, Philadelphia, Washington, D.C. and Wilmington, Delaware.

In the early 1980s, Beyerl's success as a teacher of herbalism, astrology and other metaphysical courses led to his founding The School of Healing in Minneapolis. The success of The Master Book of Herbalism and his skill as a teacher provided his students with access to a variety of metaphysical disciplines. Many of his former students have moved on to become reputable teachers. In 1989 Beyerl moved to Dallas as he began a circuitous journey which would return him to a northern climate. His work was completed in Texas, he moved to Los Angeles in 1991 where he taught classes three days a week, in addition to his administrative work with The Rowan Tree Church and the completion of two new books.

In 1994 the Beyerls returned to their roots, opening to a selected public their herbal gardens and a religious and educational center known as The Hermit's Grove in Kirkland (a Seattle suburb), a project begun over twenty years ago by Rev. Gerry on land known for its stone circle and gardens. Now living in Rose Hill, Beyerl teaches courses in herbal medicine, horticulture, and other studies at two Community Colleges and is the administrator of a Master Herbalist Program. The Hermit's Grove will continue to offer workshops and courses, serving students in the Seattle area and providing opportunities for the Beyerls' students from great distances as well. The Hermit's Lantern is the monthly publication of The Hermit's Grove.

Rev. Paul Beyerl Books:

- *A Book of Gem and Mineral Lore: Remedies, Magick and Folklore*, 2005, The Hermit's Grove,
- *A Compendium of Herbal Magick*, 1998, Phoenix Publishing Inc.
- *Andrius' Coloring Book of Numbers: A Book on the Mythology of Numbers*, 2009, The Hermit's Grove
- *A Wiccan Bardo: Initiation and Self-Transformation,* 1989, Prism Press, England; Unity Press, Australia
- *A Wiccan Bardo Revisited: Initiation and Self-Transformation,* 1999, The Hermit's Grove
- *On Death and Dying: There is Nothing Wrong with Being Compost,* 2015 The Hermit's Grove
- *Painless Astrology: A Simple and Fun Guide to Natal Chart Interpretation*, 1997, The Hermit's Grove
- *The Hatchling,* 2007, The Hermit's Grove
- *The Holy Books of the Devas: the secret mythologies of the herbal world* [4th edition], 1998, The Hermit's Grove
- *The Master Book of Herbalism*, 1984, Phoenix Publishing Inc.
- *The Symbols and Magick of Tarot*, 2005, The Hermit's Grove

For further information:

- 1-(833) HER MITS
- paul@thehermitsgrove.org.
- revpaul@TheRowanTreeChurch.org
- www.meetup.com/The-Hermits-Grove
- www.meetup.com/The-Rowan-Tree-Church
- www.en.wikipedia.org/wiki/Paul_Beyerl
- On facebook.com as Paul Beyerl also
- www.facebook.com/TheHermitsGrove
- www.facebook.com/pages/The-Rowan-Tree-Church.

Mama Donna Henes
Shaman and Witch Elder
September 19th, 1945 -

Mama Donna Henes

Donna Henes is a spiritual leader specializing in rituals and writings in support of personal and planetary transformation. She is an internationally renowned and acclaimed urban Shaman, contemporary ceremonialist, spiritual teacher, award winning author, popular speaker and workshop leader whose joyful celebrations of celestial events have introduced ancient traditional rituals and contemporary ceremonies to millions of people in more than 100 cities since 1972.

Henes composed the first and only satellite peace message orbiting in space. has performed a Purification Ritual for Obama's first inauguration, a Blessing of the Fleet for New York's Quadricentennial, and leads the annual "Greenwich Village Halloween Parade" with blessings. She has published five books, a CD, an acclaimed E-zine and writes for "The Huffington Post", "Beliefnet" and "UPI Religion and Spirituality Forum". A noted ritual expert, she serves as a ritual consultant for the television and film industry. Mama Donna, as she is affectionately called, maintains a ceremonial center, spirit shop, ritual practice and consultancy in Exotic Brooklyn, NY where she offers intuitive tarot readings, spiritual counselling and works with individuals, groups, institutions, Municipalities, and corporations to create meaningful ceremonies for every imaginable occasion.

- Unofficial Commissioner of Public Spirit of NYC – The New Yorker.
- "Henes is the real deal" – Time Out New York.
- "For 35 years, Henes has been putting city folk in touch with Mother Earth." – New York Times.
- "Part Performance artists, part witch, part social director for planet earth" – The Village Voice.
- "A-List exorcist!" – New York Post.
- "The Original Crystal-packing mama" – New York Press.

Donna Henes Books:

- *Celestially Auspicious Occasions: Seasons, Cycles and Celebrations*, 1996, Perigree-Putnam
- *Moon Watcher's Companion: Everything You Ever Wanted to Know About the Moon and More*, 2002, Monarch Press
- *The Queen of my Self: Stepping into Sovereignty in Midlife*, 2005, Monarch Press
- *Bless This House: Creating Sacred Space Where You Live, Work & Travel*, 2018, Ixia/Dover
- *Dressing Our Wounds in Warm Clothes*, 1982, Astro Artz
- *Reverence to Her: Mythology, The Matriarchy & Me* CD

Connect with her on Facebook:
www.facebook.com/MamaDonnaHenes
Follow her on X (formally Twitter):
www.x.com/queenmamadonna
Mama Donna's Tea Garden & Healing Haven
CityShaman@aol.com

Margot Adler
High Priestess-Witch Elder
April 16th, 1946 – July 28th, 2014

Margot Adler

Margot Susanna Adler was born April 16th, 1946, in Little Rock, Arkansas. Her well-known grandfather, Alfred Adler, was a noted Austrian Jewish psychotherapist, a collaborator with Sigmund Freud and the Founder of the school of 'Individual Psychology'. Margot received a Bachelor of Arts in political science from the University of California, Berkeley and also a master's degree from the Columbia University Graduate School of Journalism in New York in 1970. Margot was also a Neiman Fellow at Harvard University in 1982.

During the mid-1960s, Margot worked as a volunteer reporter for KPFA-FM, the Pacifica Radio station in Berkeley, California. After returning to New York City, she worked at its sister station, WBAI-FM, where in 1972, she created the talk show "Hour of the Wolf" (still on air as hosted by Jim Freund), and later another talk show, called "Unstuck in Time". Margot joined NPR in 1979 as a general assignment reporter, after spending a year as an NPR freelance reporter covering New York City, and subsequently working on a great many pieces, dealing with subjects as diverse as the death penalty, the Right to Die movement, the response to the war in Kosovo, computer gaming, the drug ecstasy, geek children and technology and even Pokémon. After 9/11, she focused much of her work on stories exploring the human factors in New York City, from the loss of loved ones, homes, and jobs, to work in the relief effort. She was the host of "Justice Talking" up until the show ceased production on July 3rd, 2008. She was a regular voice on "Morning Edition" and "All Things Considered". She was also co-producer of an award-winning radio drama, "War Day".

Margot was an American author, journalist, lecturer, Wiccan Priestess, and New York correspondent for National Public Radio (NPR). Margot authored her first book "Drawing Down the Moon" (1979), about Neo-Paganism which was revised in 2006. For many years it was the only introductory work about American Neo-Pagan communities. Adler was a Wiccan Priestess, an Elder in the "Covenant of the Goddess", and she also participated in the "Unitarian Universalist" faith community. I was lucky to have met her and found her a very gentle and powerfully direct person with a great deal of knowledge and concern for the Pagan movement. In early 2011, Margot was diagnosed with endometrial cancer, which metastasized over the following three years. Margot Adler died on July 28th, 2014, at the age of 68. She remained virtually symptom free until mid-2014. Margot was cared for in her final months by her son.

Margot Adler's Books:

- *Drawing Down the Moon: Witches, Druids, Goddess-Worshippers, and Other Pagans in America Today*, 1979
- *Heretic's Heart: A Journey Through Spirit and Revolution*, 1997, Beacon Press
- *Our Way to the Stars* with John Gliedman, 2000, Motorbooks Intl.
- *Out for Blood*, 2013, Kindle Single
- *Vampires Are Us*, 2014, Weiser Books

Maxine Sanders
Alexandrian Witch Queen and Elder
December 30th, 1946 -

Maxine Sanders

Arline Maxine Morris was born on the 30th of December 1946. Morris was raised a Roman Catholic and was educated at St. Joseph's Convent School in Manchester. In 1964, whilst still a student at Loreburn Secretarial College where she first met with Alex Sanders. They met through his friendship with her mother who worked where he worked, and Morris who had a range of esoteric and spiritual interests, but the accounts of her introduction to witchcraft vary, depending on who is telling the story. Maxine's memoir gives a quite different account, where she describes her experiences of Witchcraft as already been initiated at the age of 15 into a Magical lodge in rituals performed at Alderley Edge, Cheshire, England. Within the following year, she and at least one other person had been initiated and the coven was up and running. Maxine was quickly taken through the system of three degrees and by the age of 18, was already a third-degree High Priestess, although one source suggests that at that time her role was a somewhat passive one. It has been said that at Alex's Outer Court Lectures all Maxine had to do was sit there and look beautiful and represent the Goddess.

Maxine's early times as a Witch was not free from difficulties. In 1965, a midsummer festival was attended by a newspaper photographer, but unbeknown to some of those present, Maxine included. The report that was in the local newspaper published recognizable photographs of her and she was thus "outed" as a Witch without her permission. Maxine's unconventional spiritual path led to strife with her mother, who she eventually reconciled with prior to her death. Soon after Maxine's mother's death, members of her mother's neighborhood chased Maxine, throwing stones, and the windows of her mother's house were smashed. Sanders in Cheshire became a key figure in the development of modern Paganism, Witchcraft and Wicca especially Alexandrian Wicca, along with her late husband, "The King of the Witches" Alex Sanders, where she through marriage became the "Queen of Witches" under the new name of Maxine Sanders, and was the co-founder of the tradition known now as Alexandrian Wicca.

Maxine and Alex were handfasted at Alderley Edge in 1965 and continued to Initiate new Wiccans in Manchester. In 1967, they moved to London where they lived and practiced Wicca in a basement flat in Notting Hill Gate, attracting much publicity and initiating many would be Wiccans. At Beltane in 1968, the couple legally married in a civil ceremony in Kensington, London. Alex and Maxine had two children: Mya born in 1967, and Victor, born in 1972. Over the next years up until 1972, Maxine and Alex trained and initiated many new members of their coven, initially within a framework consistent with older traditions but incorporating more of the couple's own unique characteristics, preferences, and innovations. In 1971, Stewart Farrar, initiated by Maxine, gave their brand of Wicca the new name of "Alexandrian Wicca" partly honoring its leaders and also referencing the greatest city in the Hellenistic world and the library of Magical texts which it housed, the library of Alexandria.

In 1971, Alex and Maxine had acquired a second home outside of London in the village of Selmeston, Sussex. There Maxine became a 'fanatical gardener' while she and Alex set up a second coven and started to train people locally. Maxine, however, became concerned that the standards and expectations of training were not so high as they once were in London, and that there was an awkward atmosphere. The couple found the cost of running two homes too expensive, and they returned back to London in 1972. Maxine declared that she no longer wanted to bear the responsibilities that came with the title of "Witch Queen", and ritually destroyed her ritual robes and other items she had acquired. Shortly thereafter, Alex moved back to Sussex, and Maxine remained in London with her children.

Due to Alex and Maxine's openness about practicing Wicca from the early 1970s, media attention grew rapidly, where they appeared in a number of films, such as "Legend of the Witches (1970)", "Witchcraft '70' (1970)", "Secret Rites (1971)", and numerous documentaries. Not long after Maxine and Alex separated, Maxine remained in their London flat where she ran her own coven, "The Temple of the Mother", continuing to Initiate and train people in Alexandrian Wicca. Members of the Coven also trained in the art of healing and became well respected for it and other charitable works in the community.

Maxine remained in close contact with Alex until his death in 1988, and shortly before his death, he named Maxine as his next of kin. In 2000, Maxine moved to Snowdonia, Wales, until 2010, but returned to Abbey Road, Load. Today Maxine teaches in the Coven of the Stag King in London, which holds monthly meetings. She continues to travel, giving talks to those interested in the Craft especially the Wiccan path, she is truly the Queen of Alexandrian Wicca and an Elder of the Craft.

Maxine Sander's Books:

- *The Ecstatic Mother*, 1977
- *Maths through Language*, 1994
- *Maxine The Witch Queen*, 1976
- *Fire Child: The Life of Maxine Sanders "Witch Queen"*, 2013.

Rev. Dr. Jacqueline "Omi" Zaleski Mackenzie
President Elder of Summerland Monastery, Inc. Church of All Worlds.
1947 -

Rev. Dr. Jacqueline "Omi" Zaleski Mackenzie

Jacqueline Mackenzie was born in 1947, which is quite interesting as shortly after Mackenzie was born, her Polish father's psychic abilities lead him to the Roswell, New Mexico "Space Alien" landing site near their farm. He informed the US Air Force, as he was recently separated from active duty from them and informed them as to what he saw. They made him return to active duty and stay silent. When Mackenzie began to display reliable psychic insights, her father encouraged her.

Mackenzie's early religious training was from her father. He was raised a Roman Catholic but later converted to Lutheran after his son died at four days of age to his mother's Rh-Negative blood being incompatible with the second child or additional children. Therefore, Mackenzie was raised as an only child, who by the age of 8, had already moved house 23 times without any ties whatsoever to her siblings, cousins, long-term friendships, or even relatives. It never occurred to her that most children did not receive frequent physical beatings (pre-internet). Vacations or moves were outdoor camping experiences. Mackenzie's father taught her that nature was Divine. Religious activities were her constant for any social services. No matter where they were, she attended Sunday school; Brownies, Girl Scouts, Senior Scouts; summer church camp; church choirs; and catechetical classes.

At age 15, Mackenzie was raped, became pregnant (pre-Internet – she had no idea what even caused a pregnancy), and spent nearly a year in a Roman Catholic Nunnery, the nun's, and priest's hypocrisy, regarding noncelibate sexual activities, inside the facility, sickened her. Due to Mackenzie's age, her parents were allowed to adopt her son without her permission. "If you had delivered a girl, I'd have given her away," her heartless mother said the day Mackenzie gave birth in 1962.

At age 16, and on her own, Mackenzie joined the Unitarian Universalist Church (UU), that was in 1963. It was here that she thrived as a what was later called Neo-Paganism as she studied Renzi Zen Buddhism also in the 1970s in addition to UU (CUUPS when formed). In the late 1980s, Mackenzie began Northern European Shaman training. In 1987 and 1989, she was awarded a BS and MS in Business Systems Management as she wanted to do a good job running non-profit organizations. Meanwhile she was raising her only daughter who had suffered a heart attack at the young age of only 4.5 months; she also raised foster children.

When Mackenzie completed her Northern European Shaman training, she took the name Amaterasu Omi Kami – the Sun Goddess of Japan. Because: (1) she studied Zen (2) Her symbol is the Sun in the circle of the Mercury symbol – her Sun is two minutes from her Mercury in Aquarius. (3) "Omi" is Gaelic for Grandmother – Mackenzie adored being around children and now a faux grandmother called "Omi." In January of 1991, Mackenzie joined The Aquarian Tabernacle Church (ATC). Within three years of incorporating "The Church of Iron Oak, Inc. ATC", and "Summerland Corp, ATC" as churches, a four-year legal battle for the right to practice Wicca began: "The Church of Iron Oak, ATC vs The City of Palm Bay, Florida". Mackenzie was in the local paper, on the cover of Parade Magazine in the Miami Herald, in a newspaper in Europe, and on CNN. Her phone rang up to 75 times a day, usually with one or two death threats among the phone calls. Although they won, at the State Supreme Court level, the right to worship outdoors, Mackenzie lost her marriage, her job, her house, and her Covens.

Mackenzie for over 20 years as an ATC Elder, facilitated two incorporated ATC affiliates: "The Church of Iron Oak, Inc. ATC", & "Summerland Corp, ATC", in Palm Bay, FL. When Mackenzie left Florida in 1994, she united with CAW member "Don Mackenzie". Summerland Corp. became a Religious Order, and the name was changed to Summerland Monastery, Inc., ATC. In June of 1994, both CAW member Don Mackenzie and Jacqueline took a legal vow of poverty to Summerland Monastery, Inc., ATC (now located at Wind

Tree Ranch in Arizona as a foreign corporation). Additionally, Mackenzie became the corporate sole of "The Provence of Arizona and New Mexico, Inc. ATC"; it was incorporated in Arizona. Rt. Rev. Pete Davis taught this professional student a great deal and told her where to learn more about non-profit management.

From the fall of 1996 to May 2008, they lived and worked for Summerland Monastery, Inc. ATC, at Wind Tree Ranch, it was 1,227 acres of dry desert land off the power grid. They installed the first up/down Internet from a satellite in the State of Arizona. That land was the home of the religious order they managed and 14 eco-buildings plus a ritual partially underground Kiva 32' across. Don and Jacqueline were handfasted on the land on May 1, 1999; later, they are also legally married. Don already had the experiences of over a decade of living off the power grid in Hawaii and Belize. Jacqueline's father not only taught her that nature was Divine, but he also instilled fear in her that December 31, 1999, was going to be an international nightmare. With 28 years in the USAF working on the largest government computer and another 17 years as the last inspector for three NASA projects: Saturn, Apollo, & Shuttle, Mackenzie assumed her dad knew what he was talking about. Don, as a scientist, felt the same way. Therefore, before Y2K (December 31, 1999), they taught others various ways to build eco-friendly homes, live a self-sustainable lifestyle, connect spiritually to the planet, and set aside seeds and dried food for five years or more of living eco-connected lives. The Y2K issues near our home were shortly resolved. So, the Mackenzie's continued their spiritual growth and teaching others. They facilitated Summerland Monastery, Inc., ATC, and The Provence of Arizona and New Mexico, Inc. ATC, from Wind Tree Ranch.

During that time, the University of Arizona began a cohort of post-graduate work nearby; later, Mackenzie commuted to Tucson to study at the main campus. After the economy buckled in 2007, and she heard a lecture by Noble Prize Winner, John "Peck" Overpeck regarding climate change factors in Arizona, they decided to move to Central Mexico. Mackenzie had already been volunteering teaching disabled children there in the summers since 2005. They located in an indigenous village, built a library, rebuilt a burned-out home for a family, taught economically marginalized children, built another concrete ritual circle, and other projects common to a non-profit in service.

In May 2010, Mackenzie was awarded a Ph.D. in Special Education, Bilingual Education, and Sociocultural Studies from the University of Arizona. She assumed she would be hired and able to do more public service work with the income, but no one wanted a person her age. The following year, Mackenzie wrote a textbook: "Empowering Spanish Speakers", that won four national awards. Mackenzie released the book at the ATC Spring Mysteries in 2011.

Mackenzie feels that she had made two mistakes. She assumed the book would sell and make her able to do more public service work with the income; it never broke even. Mackenzie assumed ATC would be supportive of both the book and her diploma; but she was wrong on both assumptions. The new administrative parameters that were outlined for me by "Rt. Rev. Pete Davis" and his Arch Priestess, "Belladonna LaVeau", after she participated in her ordination the fall of 2012, caused her to choose to leave ATC. Fortunately, their Religious Order was accepted by CAW, an organisation far more in line with her eagerness to teach diverse students; their service to others continues. Mackenzie has since written 12 more books, but averages less than $10 a year in royalties, which is sad, so please support our authors. Don is a Purple Heart Awarded 100% Disabled Vietnam Veteran, every move they have made, the location was supposed to ease his service-connected health challenges. In September 2013, on the advice by seven Mexican doctors, they moved again.

Since relocating to Ecuador, South America, they have always been volunteering teachers and coordinating or attending rituals with various other Pagans. We just completed building an Eco-Hobbit House in an Eco-Village in S.E. Ecuador. The house is a classroom for a "stimulus for reawakening Gaia and reuniting Her children through tribal community" (a line from the CAW Mission Statement). As non-profit has been a CAW BoD member for about a year and received her CAW HPS Certificate dated May 1. 2019. From August 11 to September 9, 2019, Mackenzie will be hosting Oberon Zell Ravenheart at her home in S.E. Ecuador, South America, in an Eco-Village. They will be planning the 50+ year anniversary of CAW on an international level.

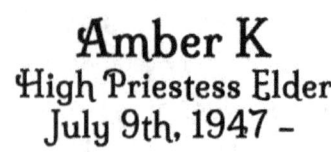

Amber K
High Priestess Elder
July 9th, 1947 –

Amber K

Amber K was born Kitty Randall on 9th July 1947 in Bronxville, New York. Amber grew up spending most of her childhood in Chicago. Her father was a Roman Catholic, and her mother was Episcopalian, and she attended each on alternate Sundays. After completing her formal education, Amber attended Colorado State University in Fort Collins and graduated in 1970 with a BSc. Degree in Social Sciences.

In 1978 Amber joined "The Temple of the Pagan Way" in Chicago and received her Initiation and Ordination with them. The Pagan Way was formed in the early 1970s in response to the high demand of people wishing to join established covens, and in this they provided an alternative to the intensive screening programs and year-and-a-day probationary periods required by traditional Alexandrian and Gardnerian covens. After joining and advancing through four of their five degrees, in 1980 Amber moved to Wisconsin with her then-partner Catelaine and was later Ordained a Wiccan High Priestess in a separate ritual.

Moving to Wisconsin, Amber worked first with the "Pool of Bast" and then with "New Earth Circle" before co-founding with Catelaine the "Coven of Our Lady of the Woods" in 1982. The coven thrived for a while in Wisconsin but is now located in Los Alamos, New Mexico, where it is incorporated as a church. Since then, a number of covens have hived off and evolved into the "Ladywood Tradition of Wicca". Ladywood covens are mainly Initiatory teaching covens and provide an eclectic mix of training drawn from various Pagan traditions, including the provisions of Wicca 101 courses. Covens celebrate the Esbats and Sabbats which are generally open in their efforts to educate the general public about the Craft. She has served as Publications Officer and National First Officer of the "Covenant of the Goddess" and taught in the Cella (priestess) training program of RCG, a national Dianic network.

Amber is an author of books about Magic, Wicca and Neopaganism, and a Third-Degree High Priestess of the Wiccan faith. She has worked with various Neopagan organizations such as Circle Sanctuary and the Reformed Congregation of the Goddess, and the Grey Council member of the online Grey School of Wizardry founded by Oberon Zell Ravenheart in 2004. She is the direct executor of Ardentane, a non-profit Wiccan and Pagan school and seminary in northern New Mexico.

Amber K Books:

- *True Magick: A Beginner's Guide*, 1991, Llewellyn Publications
- *Covencraft: Witchcraft for Three or More*, 1998, Llewellyn Publications
- *Pagan Kids' Activity Book*, 1998, Horned Owl Publishing
- *Preámbulo a la Magia*, 1999, Llewellyn Espanol
- *Candlemas: Feast of Flames*, 2001, Llewellyn Publications
- *Heart of Tarot: An Intuitive Approach*, 2002, Llewellyn Publications
- *RitualCraft: Creating Rites for Transformation and Celebration* with Azrael Arynn K, 2006, Llewellyn Publications

Rev. Robert Lee "Skip" Ellison
Druid & Wiccan Elder
1948 –

Robert Lee "Skip" Ellison is a Druid Priest and liturgist as well as an author in the fields of Druidry, Magic and divination. He was Initiated in a Celtic Traditional Wiccan Coven in 1982. He has been a member of the Druid organisation "Ár nDraíocht Féin" since 1990, serving on its Mother Grove since 1992. He served as ADF's Arch Druid (now Emeritus) and is Chief of its Magician's Guild. He was the Grove organizer for Muin Mound Grove, ADF (a Druid group that maintains a camping and ritual facility in Syracuse, New York by the same name) and became its second Senior Druid, a position he held since 1992. He has been a frequent speaker at Neo-Pagan events including Starwood Festival, Sirius Rising, and the Wellspring Gathering.

Ellison serves on the faculty of the Grey School of Wizardry as its instructor in Beast Mastery, Divination and Lore. He has created a Magical training system based on the trees of the forest and has authored four books on Druidry and divination. He is also a retired industrial electrician.

Robert Lee Ellison Books:

- *The Wheel of the Year at Muin Mound Grove ADF: A Cycle of Druid Rituals* (W/CD or cassette)
- *The Divine Liver — The Art and Science of Haruspicy as Practiced by the Etruscans and Romans* (W/42 card set)
- *The Druids' Alphabet: What Do We Know About the Oghams?*, 2003, Dubsar House
- *The Solitary Druid: Walking the Path of Wisdom and Spirit*, Citadel.

Zsuzsanna Budapest
High Priestess-Witch Elder
May 30th, 1948 –

Zsuzsanna Budapest

Zsuzsanna Emese Mokcsay born 30th January 1940 in Budapest, Hungary. Her mother, Masika Szilagyi was a medium and a practicing Witch, as well as a professional sculptress whose work reflected all themes associated with the Goddess and the Divine Feminine especially within Nature spirituality. In 1956, when the Hungarian Revolution broke out, she left Hungary as a political refugee. Zee (as she was well called) finished school in Innsbruck and graduated from a bilingual gymnasium. Zee also won a scholarship to the University of Vienna where she studied languages.

Zee immigrated to the United States in 1959, where she continued her studies at the University of Chicago, with ground-breaking originator of the art of improvisation, Viola Spolin, and the improvisational theatre group "The Second City". Zee married and had two sons, Laszlo, and Gabor, but eventually divorced after realizing that she was a lesbian and chose, in her own words, to avoid the "duality" between man and woman.

Zee eventually moved to Los Angeles from New York in 1970 and became an activist in the "Women's Liberation Movement". Zee was on the staff of the first 'Women's Centre' in the US and became the Founder and High Priestess of Susan B. Anthony Coven #1, the first feminist, women-only, witches coven, in 1971. Zee was responsible for the creation of an Anti-Rape Squad and the "Take Back the Night Movement" in Southern California and facilitated many of their street marches.

Zsuzsanna was an American author, activist, journalist, playwright, and songwriter who wrote about feminist spirituality and Dianic Wicca under the pen name Zsuzsanna Budapest or Z. Budapest. Her non-profit organisation featuring lectures, retreats and other events, led to a cable television show called 13th Heaven. She had an online autobiography entitled "Fly by Night" and wrote for the religion section of the San Francisco Examiner on subjects related to pagan religions. She is the composer of several songs including "We All Come from the Goddess".

The Witch Hunt:

In 1975, Zee was arrested for "fortune telling" at her candle and bookstore in Venice, California following a sting by an undercover policewoman Rosalie Kimberton, who received a tarot reading from her. Subsequently Zee was charged with violating a municipal by-law, Code 43.30, which explains that fortune telling was unlawful. Zee and her defence team described the event as "the first witch prosecuted since Salem", and the ongoing trial became a focus for much media and Pagan protesters. Zee was found guilty. Zee and her council set out to establish that Wicca, and specifically Dianic Wicca was a bona fide religion. The states Supreme Court reversed the guilty verdict as unconstitutional and in violation of the Freedom of Religion Act.

It was Zee with her constant fight of nine years of appeals on the grounds that reading of the tarot was an example of women's spirituality counselling women within the context of their religion. With pro-bono legal representation, she was acquitted, and the laws against "fortune telling" were struck from California law. Zsuzsanna wrote the words to the song "We All Come from The Goddess", that nearly every pagan, Wiccan and Witch constantly sings to this very day around the world.

Zsuzsanna Budapest Works:

- *The Feminist Book of Lights and Shadows*, 1975, Feminist Wicca, Luna Publications
- *The Holy Book of Women's Mysteries: Feminist Witchcraft, Goddess Rituals, Spellcasting and Other Womanly Arts*, 1989, Wingbow Press
- *The Grandmother of Time: A Woman's Book of Celebrations, Spells, and Sacred Objects for Every Month of the Year*, 1989, Harper One
- *Grandmother Moon: Lunar Magic in Our Lives—Spells, Rituals, Goddesses, Legends, and Emotions Under the Moon*, 1991, Harper San Francisco
- *Grandmother Moon*, 2011, Amazon CreateSpace

- *The Goddess in the Office: A Personal Energy Guide for the Spiritual Warrior at Work*, 1993, HarperOne
- *Goddess Gets to Work,* 2012, Amazon CreateSpace
- *The Goddess in the Bedroom: A Passionate Woman's Guide to Celebrating Sexuality Every Night of the Week*, 1995, Harper San Francisco
- *Summoning the Fates: A Woman's Guide to Destiny*, 1999, Three Rivers Press
- *Summoning the Fates: A Guide to Destiny and Sacred Transformation*, 2013, Amazon CreateSpace
- *Celestial Wisdom for Every Year of Your Life: Discover the Hidden Meaning of Your Age* with Diana Paxson, 2003, Weiser Books
- *Rasta Dogs*, 2003, Xlibris Corporation
- *Selene, the Most Famous Bull-Leaper on Earth*, 1976, Diana Press
- *Selene, the Most Famous Bull-Leaper on Earth*, 2011, Amazon CreateSpace
- *Z's Easy Tarot*, 2012, Amazon CreateSpace
- *My Dark Sordid Past as a Heterosexual*, 2014, Amazon CreateSpace

Morning Glory Zell Ravenheart
Church of All Worlds
High Priestess-Elder
May 27th, 1948 – May 13th, 2014

Photograph of Morning Glory Zell Ravenheart

Morning Glory Zell-Ravenheart was born Diana Moore on May 27th, 1948, in Long Beach, California. Also known as Morning Glory Ferns, Morning Glory Zell and Morning G'Zell. Morning Glory was raised as an only child in a strict Christian household by her Pentecostal mother, though she switched from attending a Methodist church to a Pentecostal church around the age 10-12. It was at the tender age of 14 that she broke from Christianity after arguing with her Methodist minister grandfather that animals had souls and also went to heaven like humans. She was strongly influenced by the Sybil Leek book, "Diary of a Witch", which she read during high school. At the age of 17, she began practicing Witchcraft and at the age of 20 she changed her name to Morning Glory because she did not care for the chastity requirement of followers of the Goddess, Diana.

Whilst enroute to join a commune near Eugene, Oregon in 1969, Morning Glory met a hitchhiker named Gary Ferns who joined her. The two were soon married, and the next year she gave birth to a daughter who she named Rainbow. As a mother she was known as Morning

Glory Ferns. Although Gary and Morning Glory conducted an open marriage, the union was broken when she met Timothy Zell after he gave the 1973 keynote speech at Gnosticon in Minnesota. Morning Glory divorced Gary and brought her daughter to St. Louis, Missouri, to live with Zell. Morning Glory and Zell married at the Gnosticon of Easter 1974, the well-attended ceremony performed by Arch Druid Isaac Bonawits and High Priestess Carolyn Clark. In St. Louis, Morning Glory studied and was made a Priestess of Zell's "Church of All Worlds". She helped him to edit the group's journal, "Green Egg". In 1976 the two began almost a decade of traveling, adventure, and living in various retreats and on a school bus they converted to a mobile home. They together Founded the "Ecosophical Research Association" in 1977 at Copeden Brith, a ranch in rural Mendocino County, California, northwest of Ukiah, to investigate arcane lore and legends of cryptids, such as bigfoot and mermaids. Their wandering years ended in 1985 when they took up permanent residence at Coeden Brith, initially for the purpose of raising "Unicorns" that they created from horn surgery on baby goats.

In 1979 Timothy Zell changed his first name to Otter, and for a short time the couple styled their surnames as G'Zell, a contraction of Glory Zell. In 1994 he again changed his name to Oberon, which has stuck up to this date. The ideal marriage for Morning Glory was an open one, where her relationship with Oberon developed into a polyamorous one made up of three people from 1984 to 1994, which included Diane Darling. When the trio ended, Oberon and Morning Glory bonded with others to make marriage of five sometimes even six. The group took the collective surname Zell-Ravenheart and lived in two large homes. Morning Glory's article of May 1990 "A Bouquet of Lovers", first published in "Green Egg", promoted the concept of a group marriage having more than two partners. The article is widely cited as the original source of the word "polyamory", although the word does not appear in the article-the hyphenated form "poly-amorous" does instead.

The "Green Egg" had been defunct since 1976, and Morning Glory along with Darling revived the "Green Egg" in 1988. Also, in 1990 Morning Glory established the business "Mythic Images" offering for sale reproductions of Goddess, God and mythology sculptures that were crafted by Oberon and herself. Morning Glory also ran lectures and loved to write. Morning Glory became a great respected pagan community leader, author, lecturer, and Priestess of the Church of All Worlds. She was an advocate of polyamory, where she credited the coining of the word. In 1999, they moved to Sonoma Country, California, where Oberon started the "Grey School of Wizardry", which as of 2014 is the world's only registered wizard academy. In 2005 Morning Glory went to hospital to treat broken bones which she suffered due to a fall. There, she learned that she had multiple myeloma. She received surgery, chemotherapy, and radiation treatments, and also entreated her friends to form a healing circle. She experienced a great increase in health in 2007, but she lapsed in taking her medications in late 2011, and the disease returned in early 2012. During the period of remission in August 2012 she was filmed for a documentary about polyamory for the "Destination America" television channel, the show call "Hidden in America", the segment titled "Polyamory in America".

Her devoted husband Oberon along with their long-term marriage partner Julie O'Ryan appeared together on screen to talk about their practice of polyamory. In reporting about the upcoming broadcast, Alan M of "Polyamory in the News" wrote that Morning Glory and Oberon, both battling cancer, looked "hale and hearty" in the preview available online. Morning Glory died at her home on May 13th, 2014, two weeks before her 66th birthday, after a long fight with cancer.

Morning Glory's Books:
- *Grimoire for the Apprentice Wizard*, with Oberon Zell-Ravenheart, et al., 2004, New Page Books
- *Creating Circles & Ceremonies: Rituals for All Seasons and Reasons*, with Oberon Zell-Ravenheart, 2006, New Page Books

Morning Glory as Queen of the Unicorns

Selena Fox
Church of All Worlds
High Priestess-Witch Elder
Circle Sanctuary
October 20th, 1949 -

Selena Fox with her Cauldron

Selena Fox was born on 20th October 1949 in Arlington, Virginia. Selena Fox is a Priestess, environmentalist, religious freedom activist, writer, author, teacher, podcaster, spiritual counselor, and psychotherapist with a BS in Psychology from the College of William & Mary in 1971. Also known as Rev. Selena Fox, she is senior minister and High Priestess of Circle Sanctuary, which has been serving Wiccan, Pagan, and other Nature religion practitioners worldwide since 1974.

Selena has been active in environmental education, ecological restoration, and Nature preservation for more than fifty years. She was among the Founders of Earth Day in 1970 and has continued to be active in organizing and speaking at Earth Day events ever since. She facilitates Ecopsychology and Eco spirituality workshops, ceremonies, and Nature communion experiences online and at conferences and festivals in the USA and other countries.

Selena is Founder and Executive Director of Circle Sanctuary Nature Preserve, a 200-acre Nature sanctuary and headquarters for Circle Sanctuary located near Barneveld, Wisconsin. Circle Sanctuary Nature Preserve includes the 20-acre Circle Cemetery, a national Pagan cemetery that is the first green cemetery in Wisconsin and one of the first green cemeteries in North America.

Selena has a B.S. cum laude in Psychology from the College of William and Mary (1971) and a M.S. in Counseling from the University of Wisconsin-Madison (1995). She does counseling, readings, and life coaching through zoom video conferencing and telephone consultations with clients of many places and backgrounds. She also does some dream interpretation sessions and Oracle card consultations in connection with some of her speaking travels. Selena travels widely presenting workshops and facilitating ceremonies at universities, wellness centers, sacred sites, conferences, festivals, and other venues. She also teaches at Circle Sanctuary events and online through podcasts and social media.

Selena's writings, chants, rituals, meditations, and photographs have been widely published in-print and on-line. She is the author of the online guide, Celebrating the Seasons.

Selena is author of the handbook, Goddess Communion Rituals and Meditations (Circle Publications, 1988). Her Master's of Science in Counseling research study, When Goddess is God, Pagans, Recovery, and Alcoholics Anonymous (UMI, 1995) was among the first to identify and examine the needs to assist others with addictions.

Selena's audio albums include Sacred Cave Ritual (1995, ceremony, with Pagan Spirit Gathering Community), Magical Journeys (1988, meditation), Circle Magic Songs (1976, music, with Jim Alan) and Songs for Pagan Folk (1977, music, with Jim Alan and others).

Selena is Founder of the Circle Craft tradition. This approach to spirituality emphasizes Nature communion and blends together transpersonal psychology, multicultural Shamanism, Nature mysticism, Hedge witchery, and Pagan folkways.

Selena is widely known for her Pagan civil rights and religious freedom work. She is Executive Director of the Lady Liberty League, a global Pagan rights network sponsored by Circle Sanctuary. Selena has been a Pagan spokesperson in the public media for more than forty years. She is active in local and global interfaith endeavors and has been among the Pagan Elders speaking at the Parliament of the World's Religions and other international interreligious conferences. Selena has done diversity consulting and training for federal and state agencies and other institutions as part of her work to enhance public understanding and respect for Paganism and Nature religions.

Selena was among the Pagan leaders that worked together to defeat anti-Wiccan federal legislation, including the attempt to remove tax exempt status from Wiccan churches (1985) and the attempt to prohibit the practice of the Wiccan religion by Wiccan soldiers at US military installations (1999). She was among the leaders of the decade long Veteran Pentacle

Quest which finally met with success in 2007 when the US Department of Veterans Affairs added the Pentacle on its list of emblems of belief that can be included on the grave markers it issues for deceased veterans.

Selena is active in chaplaincy networking and is the chaplaincy endorser for Circle Sanctuary. Selena provides spiritual care and support for Pagan individuals and groups in a variety of settings, including hospitals, hospices, birthing centers, prisons, universities, and military installations. In addition, over the years, Selena has been doing diversity consulting and training for federal and state agencies and other institutions as part of her work to enhance public understanding and respect for Paganism and Nature religions.

Contributions:
- *Encyclopedia of Women and Religion in North America*, Rosemary Skinner Keller and Rosemary Radford Ruether, ed., 2006, Indiana University Press.
- *Religions of the World*, J. Gordon Melton and Martin Baumann, ed., 2002, ABC-CLIO, Inc.
- *The Encyclopedia of Modern Witchcraft and Neo-Paganism*, Shelley Rabinovitch & James Lewis, ed., 2002, Citadel Press.
- *Circle Guide to Pagan Resources*, Editor, directory, 1979–present, Circle Publications.
- *Circle Magazine (formerly Circle Network News)*, Founding Editor, Advisor, 1978–present, Circle Publications.

Books, Articles and Recordings:
- *Celebrating the Seasons*. On-line guide with rituals, chants, articles - www.circlesanctuary.org/index.php/education/celebrating-the-seasons.html
- *Circle Magick Songs*, with Jim Alan, 1979, Circle Publications
- *Goddess Communion: Rituals and Meditations*, 1988, Circle Publications.
- *Planetary Healing Rituals: Meditations, Rituals & Prayers for a Healthier World*, 1991, Circle Sanctuary.

Recordings:
- *Circle Craft Podcasts* - recordings of weekly classes, meditations, & rituals on internet radio at circlepodcasts.org
- *Sacred Cave Ritual* with Selena Fox and Pagan Spirit Gathering Community, ritual with chanting & guided meditation, 1995
- *Magical Journeys* with Selena Fox, guided meditation, 1981
- *Songs of Pagan Folk* with Jim Alan, Selena Fox and Friends, songs, and chants, 1980
- *Circle Magick Music* with Jim Alan and Selena Fox, songs, and chants, 1976.

Selena at PSG Remembrance

Isaac Bonewits
Druid High Priest-Elder
October 1st, 1949 – August 12th, 2010

Isaac Bonewits

Phillip Emmons Isaac Bonewits was born October 1st, 1949, in Royal Oak, Michigan, as the fourth of five children. His parents were both Roman Catholics. Isaac spent most of his childhood in Ferndale, then he moved to San Clemente, California when he was 12 years of age, here he spent a short time in a Catholic high school before he returned back to public school to graduate from a year early. He enrolled at UC Berkeley in 1966, where he graduated in 1970 with a Bachelor of Arts in Magic, perhaps becoming the first and only person known to have ever received any kind of academic degree in Magic from an accredited university.

Bonewits had a busy life and was married five times. He first married Rusty Elliot from 1973 – 1976. His second wife was Selene Kumin Vega. Followed by Sally Eaton (1980 – 1985). His fourth wife was author Bedorah Lipp from 1988 – 1998. On July 23rd, 2004, he married in a formal handfasting ceremony to a former vice-president of the "Covenant of the Unitarian Universalist Pagans", Phaedra

Heyman Bonewits. Although he was not legally divorced from Lipp, their handfasting was not yet legal. Eventually the paperwork and legalities were done on the 31st of December 2007 which made them legally married.

Bonewits' only child was Arthur Shaffley Lipp-Bonewits, who was born to Deborah Lipp in 1990. In 1966 whilst enrolled at UC Berkeley, Bonewits joined the "Reformed Druids of North America", or RDNA. Bonewits was Ordained as a Neo-Druid Priest in 1969. During this period, the then 18-year-old Bonewits was recruited by the "Church of Satan" but left due to political and philosophical conflicts with Anton LaVey. During his stint at the "Church of Satan", Bonewits appeared in some scenes in the 1970 documentary "Satanis: The Devil's Mass". Bonewits in his article "My Satanic Adventure", asserts that the rituals in Satanis were staged for the movie at the behest of the filmmakers and were not authentic ceremonies.

Bonewits first book, Real Magic, was published in 1972. Between 1973 and 1975 Bonewits was employed as editor of Gnostica Magazine in Minnesota (published by Llewellyn Publications), established an offshoot group of the RDNA called the "Schismatic Druids of North America", and helped Found a group called "Hasidic Druids of North America" (despite his life-long status as a gentile). He also Founded the short-lived "Aquarian Anti-Defamation League" (AADL), and early Pagan civil rights group. In 1976, Bonewits moved back to Berkeley and re-joined his original grove there, now part of the "New Reformed Druids of North America", he was later elected Archdruid of the Berkeley Grove.

Bonewits published a number of books on the subject of Neopaganism and Magic. He was also a public speaker, liturgist, singer and songwriter, and Founded the Druidic organisation "Ár nDraíocht Féin" in 1983 and became incorporated in 1990. Bonewits has been heavily involved in Occultism and Paganism since the 1960s.

Bonewits' hunger for knowledge and involvement was in many areas with occult, and mystical organizations such as "Ordo Templi Orientis", Gardnerian Wicca, and the "New Reformed Orthodox Order of the Golden Dawn" (a Wiccan organisation not to be confused with the Hermetic Order of the Golden Dawn) as well as a few others. He was a regular presenter and speaker at Neopagan conferences and festivals all over the US, as well as attending gaming conventions in the Bay area, where he constantly promoted his book Authentic Thaumaturgy to gamers as a way of organizing "Dungeons and Dragons" games and to give credence and background to games of "Magic: The Gathering". He made the organization's first public announcement in 1984 and began the membership sign-up at the first WinterStar Symposium in 1984. Since that time, ADF has developed into one of the world's largest forms of contemporary Druidism practiced as a religion.

Although illness curtailed many of his activities and travels for a time, he remained Archdruid of ADF until 1996. In that year, he resigned from the position of Archdruid but retained the lifelong title of ADF Archdruid Emeritus.

In 1990, Bonewits was diagnosed with Esinophilia-myalgia syndrome. The illness was a factor in his eventual resignation and retirement from the position of Archdruid of the ADF. On October 25th, 2009, Bonewits was diagnosed with a rare form of colon cancer, for which he underwent treatment, but eventually passed away in his home surrounded by loved ones on August 12th, 2010.

He also:

- Pioneered the modern usage of the terms "theology," "Paleo-Paganism," "Meso-Paganism," and numerous other retronyms.
- Possibly coined the term "Pagan Reconstructionism," though the communities in question would later diverge from his initial meaning.
- Founded Ar nDraiocht Fein, which was incorporated in 1990 in the state of Delaware as a U.S. 501(c)3 non-profit organization.
- Developed the Advanced Bonewits Cult Danger Evaluation Frame (ABCDEF).
- Coined the phrase "Never Again the Burning."
- Critiqued the Burning Times / Old Religion Murray thesis (in Bonewits's Essential Guide to Witchcraft and Wicca).

Isaac Bonewits Books:
- *Real Magic: An Introductory Treatise on the Basic Principles of Yellow Magic,* 1972, 1979, 1989, Weiser Books
- *The Druid Chronicles (Evolved)* with Selene Kumin Vega, Rusty Elliot, and Arlynde d'Loughlan, 1976, Drunemeton Press, 2005, Drynemetum Press
- *Authentic Thaumaturgy* with others, 1978, 1998, Steve Jackson Games
- *Rites of Worship: A Neopagan Approach,* 2003, Earth Religions Press
- *Witchcraft: A Concise Guide or Which Witch Is Which?,* 2003, Earth Religions Press
- *The Pagan Man: Priests, Warriors, Hunters, and Drummers,* 2005, Citadel
- *Bonewits's Essential Guide to Witchcraft and Wicca,* 2006, Citadel
- *Bonewits's Essential Guide to Druidism,* 2006, Citadel
- *Real Energy: Systems, Spirits, And Substances to Heal, Change, And Grow,* with Phaedra Bonewits, 2007, New Leaf
- *Neopagan Rites: A Guide to Creating Public Rituals that Work,* 2007, Llewellyn

Andras Corban Arthen
Pagan Elder
1949 -

Andras Corban Arthen

Andras Corban-Arthen is the founder and spiritual director of the "Earth Spirit Community". Andras has taught and lectured publicly about the Pagan traditions throughout the US and overseas since the 1970s. Andras has also been featured in quite a few books as well as news media. He currently serves as Vice-Chair of the Board of Trustees of the "Parliament of the World's Religions", the oldest and largest interreligious organization. He was chosen to represent the Pagan Traditions at the United Nations Interfaith Conference on Religion and Prejudice in 1991 and has been a featured presenter at the Parliaments of the World's Religions held in Chicago, Barcelona, Melbourne, and Salt Lake City, as well as the Ecuentro Mundial Interreligioso and the Dialogo Cultural Universal in Mexico.

More recently, he spoke at the Religions of the Earth Conference, and at the concurrent People's Climate March in New York City. Andras also serves as president of the European Congress of Ethnic Religions, headquartered in Vilnius, Lithuania, and sits on the advisory board of the Ecospirituality Foundation, a United Nations Consultative NGO based in Torino, Italy. Originally from Galiza, Spain, he now lives with his extended family in Glenwood, a 135-acre Pagan Sanctuary and nature preserve in the Berkshire Highlands of Western Massachusetts.

Carol Garr
Wiccan Elder
December 27th, 1949 –

Carol Garr

Carol Garr has been openly Wicca for over 25 years, and was instrumental in educating the public in Tucson, Arizona of the truth about her Path. It all started with 7 years as coordinator of the Tucson Area Wiccan (now Wiccan/Pagan) Network (TAWN), which sponsored her entry-level race car at a red-neck NASCAR track with a Pentagram on the side. Involvement in the Arizona "Department of Corrections" followed in the capacity of Corrections Religious Advisory Committee since 1998. Chair of that Committee 2012-2015 and 2017-2019, and prior to this was the Secretary for several years. A visiting Priestess in the Arizona prison system since 1998. The 501-c-3 non-profit "Mother Earth Ministries", of which Gar is co-Founder, President and visiting Priestess, was born from the latter activity.

Volunteer of the Year at Tucson Prison Complex 2008. Religious volunteer with the Federal Bureau of Prison since 2009, 3-time presenter at their Life Enhancement Program, and subject matter presenter on Wicca for the Professional Chaplaincy Training course. Garr holds a BA from the University of Arizona in Social Psychology.

She was also the High Priestess of "Silver Midnight Coven" (2000-2010), co-Priestess of "Rainbow Circle" (1992-1995).

Books by Carol Garr with Ashleen O-Gaea.
- *Enchantment Encumbered: The Study and Practice of Wicca in Restricted Environments*, Carol Garr & Asheleen O-Gaea

Janet Farrar
High Priestess-Witch Elder
June 24th, 1950 -

Photograph of Janet Farrar & Gavin Bone

Janet Farrar (nee) Janet Owen was born on the 24th of June 1950 in Clacton. Her family of mixed English, Irish and Welsh descent, were members of the Church of England. She attended the Leyton Manor School, and the Royal Wanstead girls' high school. After high school, Janet worked as a model and receptionist.

Janet was initiated into Alexandrian Wicca by Founder's Alex and Maxine Sanders. She met them in 1970 through a mutual friend who had become interested in exploring Wicca. Janet accompanied her friend to keep the friend 'out of this weird cult', but instead was so interested that she joined the Sanders coven, and would go on to become, in the words of Knowles, one of England's most eminent and respected modern-day Witches. In the coven she met with Stewart Farrar, who eventually became her future husband and co-author.

Both Janet and Stewart Farrar were both elevated and Ordained to the second degree in Sydenham by the Sanders on the 17th of October 1970, and they then received their third degree of elevation to that of the High Priesthood in their flat on the 24th of April 1971. Both events are well documented and recorded by Stewart Farrar down to the smallest detail in his diaries.

The Farrar's began running their own coven in 1971, before their third-degree initiation ceremony. They were handfasted in 1972 and legally married in 1975. Janet left the coven in 1972 to explore the Kabala with a ceremonial magic lodge but returned the same year. In 1976 the Farrar's moved to Ireland to get away from the busy life of London. They lived in County Mayo and County Wexford, finally settling in "Herne Cottage" in Kells, County Meath.

Both Farrar's went on to publish many books on the Wiccan religion and on coven practices. Janet Farrar continued to model and appeared in the illustrations of multiple early books about Wicca, including the cover of the paperback version of Margot Adler's 1979 "Drawing Down the Moon". Farrar posed for many of the photographs in their 1981 "Eight Sabbats for Witches", which included material the authors claimed to be from the Alexandrian tradition's "Book of Shadows". The Farrars, with the support of Doreen Valiente, argued in the book that though the publishing of this material broke their oath of secrecy, it was justified by the need to correct misinformation.

Farrar indicates that some of the rituals contained in their books were actually written by them, and that left the Alexandrian tradition after the book's research was complete. The couple co-authored four more books on Wicca. Janet's post Alexandrian practice has been referred to as "Reformed Alexandrian".

They eventually were joined by Gavin Bone in 1993, with whom they entered into a 'polyfidelitous' relationship. The three of them would co-author two more books, "The Healing Craft" and "The Pagan Path", and investigation into many varieties of neopaganism. Stewart Farrar died in February 2000 after a brief illness. Janet and Gavin married in a handfasting in May 2001, and then legally married in Northern Ireland (Part of Ulster) in March 2014.

After Stewart's death, Janet and Gavin continued to author books, and have given many lectures on Wicca in the United States, Australia, New Zealand, South Africa, Italy and in Britain. The title of their 2004 book, "Progressive Witchcraft", is the description that the couple prefers for their current religious practice. This was later re-released in 2013 as a new edition called "Inner Mysteries". Their current area of work is in trance-prophecy, trance-possession and ecstatic ritual and they are currently working on a major book on the subject which they hope to release with Acorn Guild Publishing. They are also Founders of the "Alliance of Progressive Covens", which includes linked groups and covens in the United States, Ireland and Italy.

Farrar and Bone both became ordained as third level clergy with the "Aquarian Tabernacle Church" in Ireland. They also Founded the "Tempio di Callaighe" in Italy. Farrar when at home in Ireland also works as a professional Tarot Reader, whilst Gavin works as a natural Empathic Spiritual Healer. Both specialize in trance-prophecy and possession work.

Since Initiation into the Alexandrian Craft with Stewart, both Janet and Gavin have been given honorary Initiations into several other traditions, including Italian Strega, and also

Lesotho Sangoma (traditional healers) of South Africa. Farrar is a British teacher, and author on books of Wicca and Neopaganism. Along with her two husbands Stewart Farrar and Gavin Bone, she has published 'some of the most influential books on modern Witchcraft to date. According to George Knowles, 'some seventy five percent of all Wiccans both in the Republic and Northern Ireland can trace their roots back to the Farrar's.

Farrar and Bone both tour regularly doing intensive workshops in the US, Europe, Australia, New Zealand, and South Africa. They believe strongly in the idea of Witchcraft being both progressive and dynamic in nature, while remaining a clergy to those dedicated to serving the Gods and Goddess. They are responsible for setting up several progressive covens in the US, UK and Europe.

Janet Farrar's Books:

Farrar has co-authored a number of books about Wicca and Neopaganism.

With Stewart Farrar

- *Eight Sabbats for Witches*, 1981
- *A Witches Bible Volume I & II*, 1981
- *The Witches' Way*, 1984
- *The Witches' Goddess: The Feminine Principle of Divinity*, 1987
- *The Witches' God: Lord of the Dance*, 1989
- *Spells and How they Work*, 1990
- *A Witches' Bible: The Complete Witches' Handbook (re-issue of The Witches' Way and Eight Sabbats for Witches)* 1996

With Stewart Farrar and Gavin Bone

- *The Pagan Path*, 1995
- *The Healing Craft: Healing Practices for Witches and Pagans*, 1999
- *The Complete Dictionary of European Gods and Goddesses*, 2001

With Virginia Russell

- *The Magical History of the Horse*, 1992

With Gavin Bone

- *Progressive Witchcraft: Spirituality, Mysteries, and Training in Modern Wicca*, 2004
- *The Inner Mysteries: Progressive Witchcraft and Connection with the Divine*, 2013
- *The Pagan Path*
- *The Healing Craft, The Dictionary of European Gods and Goddesses, their Mysteries*
- *Lifting the Veil*

Janet Farrar & Gavin Bone

H.E. Rev. Patrick McCollum
Interfaith Elder
April 11th, 1950 -

Patrick McCollum

Reverend Patrick McCollum was born on the 11th of April 1950, he became a designer and jeweler, with his work being sold by retailers such as Fred Segal, Henry Bendels, Billy Martins, the Forum Shops at Caesars Palace, Boogies Diner and Barney's of New York. Some of his works have been commissioned by the British Royal Family and the White House.

H.E. Rev. Patrick McCollum was ordained in 1971 and has served as president of "Our Lady of the Wells Church", a California Non-Profit Religious Corporation. He is a member of the Advisory Committee of the Peace Service Center in Katmandu, Nepal, and has sat on the National Advisory Council of American's United for the Separation of Church and State for nearly two decades. In 2008, Reverend McCollum served as an Advisor to the United States Commission on Civil Rights on a special report to Congress and the President of the United States, outlining problems and solutions to religious discrimination in U.S. prisons.

In 2002 McCollum became the executive director of the National Correctional Chaplaincy Directors Association, and since 2004 also serves as the chaplaincy liaison for the American Academy of Religion.

He has served as the National Prison Chaplaincy Affairs Coordinator for the Lady Liberty League since 2001 and has served as the International Interfaith Ambassador for Circle Sanctuary since 2010. From 2005–2013 McCollum served as director of chaplaincy for Cherry Hill Seminary. He has also served as co-founder and co-facilitator of the G-Card program for the American Academy of Religion. McCollum served on the Executive Council of the American Correctional Chaplains Association, and as the Minority Faith Issues chair.

On February 5, 2008, Rev. McCollum testified before the U.S. Commission on Civil Rights, and his remarks were widely quoted in the Commission's report entitled "Enforcing Religious Freedom in Prison". McCollum met and befriended Jane Goodall, the protector of the gorilla population in Gombi, Africa at the 2004 Parliament of the World's Religions in Barcelona. Together they formed an alliance for ecological peace that now includes Goodall, H. H. Puja Swami Chidanand Saraswati, Vandana Shiva, and H. H. Amrta Suryananda Maha Rája.

In 2010 Rev. Patrick McCollum attended the first World Forum of Spiritual Culture in Astana, Kazakhstan. The event drew spiritual luminaries from across the world. During the Forum, McCollum addressed the Kazakhstan Parliament on the subject of "World Peace and Creating a New Narrative for Humanity." McCollum was invited by the Board of Directors for the Association for Global New Thought (AGENT) to join the Dalai Lama's International Peace Council and the Association for Global New Thought as a core group leader to help facilitate a world event in Rome, Italy, called Awakened World 2012. The event was attended by many political, religious and human rights leaders in the world.

On October 14, 2015, Rev. Patrick McCollum was elected as vice president of Children of the Earth (COE), a United Nations Non-Governmental Organisation (NGO) founded in 2001 by its president, Nina Meyerhof. COE is a non-profit organisation that "educates and mentors youth leaders around the world by inspiring and uniting them, through personal and social transformation, to create a peaceful and sustainable world." McCollum received the Mahatma Gandhi Award at the Capitol Building in Washington D.C. in 2010 for the advancement of religious pluralism, and the Ralph Bunche International Peace Award in March 2016 during the UN Conference on the Status of Women. The McCollum Foundation is dedicated to creating a better world. Their Mission is to create world peace on a universal scale through promoting a meta-narrative which establishes everyone and everything as equally sacred and essential, all sentient and non-sentient beings; family, and all needs, dreams and desires being met by empowering individuals and organizations to live this narrative.

One of the main aims of the Foundation is to empower youth across the world to become compassionate and pluralistic leaders of the future. They want to teach the children that they can live a life that will leave the world a better place than when they came into it. They are achieving this through education programs that allow the youth to understand their role in respecting people's faith and honoring the Earth by recognising that everyone has value, everyone is serving a purpose, everyone supports the whole, and each one of us is a critical piece of the overall puzzle. The McCollum Foundation also has a new project titled "Empowering Indigenous Peoples Project", 2019.

John "Apollonius" Opsopaus
Neo-Pagan Elder
August 4th, 1950 -

John "Apollonius" Opsopaus

John "Apollonius" Opsopaus' involvement in Neopaganism and Magic goes back to his "tweens" in the early 1960s when he was reading world mythology and collecting Magical folklore from old books and transcribing them into a Book of Shadows, which he made from tea-stained paper and bound in leather and birch bark. Magic was just one of his esoteric interests, which included hypnosis and parapsychology, and he corresponded about some of his experiments with pioneer parapsychologist J. B. Rhine, who encouraged the young researcher. He also began using self-hypnosis and practicing ESP to improve his psychic abilities. In high school Opsopaus became interested in space and time and found his way to Ouspensky's Tertium Organum, which introduced him to Gurdjieff's Fourth Way. This is also when he began to study Crowley. These studies opened his mind to new ways of thinking.

In college in the late 60s Opsopaus conducted rituals with Magical groups around campus (mostly Golden-Dawn oriented). They also discovered an out-of-the-way corner of the university library, which was stocked with occult books bequeathed by an alumna in the 1920s. Among other books, they found an old hardbound edition of the classic Mathers' translation of The Sacred Magic of Abramelon the Mage. They immediately entered into the Abramelon working, in so far as possible while still attending classes.

In graduate school Opsopaus realised that he had much more in common with the ancient Greeks than with contemporary people, and he began learning ancient Greek. A few years later he encountered Druids and other Neopagans but realised that he felt more at home with the Greek Gods than with any other pantheon. Over the years he has had a number of patron deities, including Athena, Apollo (from whom he takes his Neopagan name, "Apollonius"), Aphrodite, Dionysus, Hekate, Hermes, and Persephone. At different times in his life different Gods have stepped to the fore and guided him.

In the 1980s and 90s, practical material on ancient Greek and Roman religious ritual and Magical practice were scarce, worshippers of Greek and Roman Gods often had to settle for "Wicca in togas." Therefore, Opsopaus started researching scholarly literature so that he could construct modern religious and Magical rituals based on ancient practices. This illustrates the approach he advocates first, understand what our spiritual and Magical predecessors did so successfully for so many centuries, and then make necessary changes to suit contemporary times. In recent years, his focus has been on Pythagoreanism and Neoplatonism as a philosophical framework for Hellanismos and theurgical spiritual practices.

Followers of the Greek and Roman traditions have always been a minority among Neopagans, and especially in pre-Internet days it was difficult to find others for group rituals and study. Therefore, in the early '90s Opsopaus founded the Omphalos, a networking group for Graeco-Roman Pagans of all varieties. At first it operated through snail mail and email and was listed in the Circle Guide to Pagan Groups for many years. Then in 1995 the Omphalos established an Internet presence (which is still online: omphalos.org), becoming one of the first online resources for Graeco-Roman Neopagans.

Opsopaus has been involved in the Magical and Neopagan communities online since the 1980s, and his Biblioteca Arcana website (omphalos.org/BA) has won numerous awards and has been featured in several Internet guides. His fiction (hymns, poetry, and prose) and nonfiction (rituals, translations, divination systems, essays) have been published in various Magical and Neopagan magazines and anthologies (over 50 publications). Many of his rituals and writings are in the Biblioteca Arcana section of The Omphalos website. Since his teens, Opsopaus had practiced various methods of divination as a means of spiritual guidance, including the I Ching, tarot, and runes. He was disappointed, however, that techniques of rune interpretation seemed to be largely a modern invention, but he discovered that there are well-documented systems of dice and alphabet divination from the ancient Greek world, which he translated around 1994. They have been popular among

Hellenists and other Neopagans, and several commercial versions have been produced. He recently published The Oracles of Apollo: Practical Ancient Divination (Llewellyn, 2017), which teaches the ancient Alphabet Oracle and Oracle of the Seven Sages.

In the 1990s Opsopaus was working on a project applying authentic Pythagorean numerology, alchemy, and Jungian psychology to tarot interpretation. Eventually he put all his interpretations on the web along with descriptions of a Pythagorean Tarot deck (omphalos.org/BA/PT). Opsopaus created a physical deck for his own use, but people kept requesting a copy; therefore, he published his Pythagorean Tarot deck and the definitive Guide to the Pythagorean Tarot (Llewellyn, 2001).

In the early 1990s Opsopaus was a Third Circle member of the Church of All Worlds (CAW) and Coordinator of its Scholars Guild. He has also been Arkhon of the Hellenic Kin of ADF (A Druid Fellowship) and a member of Hellenion, PEN (Pagan Educational Network), OTO (Ordo Templi Orientis), and other organizations. He was listed under "Who's Who in the Wiccan Community" in Gerina Dunwich's Wicca Source Book (Citadel, 1996). Opsopaus has been a member of the Grey Council and has been a professor in the Grey School of Wizardry since it opened in 2005; he was its first Dean of Ceremonial Magick and first Dean of Mathemagicks. Opsopaus believes that workshops are often the best way to teach esoteric topics, which are imperfectly expressed in writing. Therefore, he does regular workshops on Hellenistic Paganism, Pythagoreanism, theurgy, Magic, divination, and related topics at festivals and other gatherings, such as local Pagan Pride celebrations and PantheaCon.

Website: www.opsopaus.com and www.omphalos.org

Kat Tigner
Elder High Priestess
November 24th, 1950 -

Kat Tigner with Raymond Buckland

Kat Tigner was born Beverly Tigner, on the 24th of November 1950. As a child, Kat was introduced to the occult by her grandmother Hazel and an aunt who sought answers from Ouija boards, fortune tellers and tarot cards. Both women knew the power of these tools and lived their lives according to what they predicted. Today, Kat is a gifted psychic, mental medium and tarot intuitive who has spent years developing her skills with divination tools including tarot cards, crystals, pendulums, and spirit boards.

Tigner's solitary training began over 5 decades ago when she started reading and collecting books on the occult. Her library contains over 1500 titles, many of which are out of print, rare editions or personally signed by the authors. One day she plans to add these to the other printed materials already displayed at Buckland Museum of Witchcraft and Magick in Cleveland, Ohio.

If asked what Tigner believes are her greatest accomplishments in the Wiccan movement, she will undoubtedly say teaching others. She likes to stay in the shadows, but for nearly two decades has been a close friend to one of the movement's greatest teachers, Raymond Buckland and she has been instrumental in preserving his legacy through the Buckland Museum of Witchcraft and Magic. As a solitary practitioner, Tigner began making and using her own candles for spells and rituals. Candles that are infused with magical properties proved to have greater results. Kat was one of the first to sell magical candles online when she started www.BlackKatKandles.com in 1998. As her sales grew, she began supplying many Wiccan shops, including one owned by a witch named Laurie Cabot in Salem, Massachusetts.

A Sagittarian and fire woman, Tigner is naturally drawn to candle magic. She has decided to pursue authoring her own book with her favourite candle magic spells and is currently working on publishing Black Kat's Kandle Magic. With so many books on the subject already on the market, Kat was unsure if, yet another book was needed. Encouraged by her friend and mentor, Raymond Buckland assured her there is always a need for another perspective on magic.

In 2000, Tigner took her candle business to the next level and opened a brick-and-mortar shop called The Cat & the Cauldron, in Columbus, Ohio. She did not realise when she opened this shop that doors to the occult would open as well.

No longer a solitary, Tigner was initiated into the Gardnerian tradition by her new friend, mentor and Wiccan author Raymond Buckland. Together they did many classes, séances and psychic fairs and expos. During the séance, Kat channeled Sybil Leek. Sybil expressed concern about being overlooked as a Wiccan leader. It was up to Kat to see a book was written about her before the last of her generation crossed over. Due to her efforts this is stated in a book by Sybil's student and friend, Christine Jones which was published in 2010. Kat has conducted many séances, both public and private, where she has achieved communication with the spirits and delivered messages to their loved ones. Those who attended will attest to her gift.

In a dream, Tigner received the 33-page mandate, and 5 chamber pyramid system of a new order called Isiac Wicca. She immediately shared this information with Ray Buckland and the Temple of Sacrifice was conceived. Since 2005 Kat, a 3rd degree Arch Priestess with Ray acting as her Arch Priest, have trained and ordained new Wiccan leaders who will carry on the great work of the Craft's elders. Tigner is especially proud of the work of two of her students and Ordained Priestesses; Toni Rotonda and Patti Wigginton.

Toni Rotonda is the legacy holder and custodian of the Buckland Museum of Witchcraft and Magic and explains the importance of the museum's Founder and its many artifacts. Rotonda also lectures at colleges around Ohio and is the officiating High Priestess of Kat's coven, the Temple of Sacrifice. Patti has authored several books on Wicca and Magic, and travels around the country doing lectures and classes at Pagan festivals and shops.

Tigner a dedicated teacher of Wicca, and the fundamentals of witchcraft and the magical arts, is an Elder High Priestess, spiritual advisor and licensed Wiccan minister in Ohio where she lives with her family and two black cats. As one of the last High Priestesses of Raymond Buckland, the Father of American Wicca, she holds steadfast his legacy with honor and respect along with his last official working High Priestess – Toni Rotonda, who has been passed his legacy as Custodian of the Buckland Museum of Witchcraft & Magic.

Buckland Priestesses

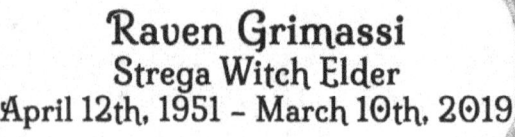

Raven Grimassi
Strega Witch Elder
April 12th, 1951 – March 10th, 2019

Raven Grimassi

Raven Grimassi was born Gary Charles Erbe on the 12th of April 1951. Grimassi became involved in Wicca in 1969 where he created and founded his own system of Wicca known as the "Arcadian Tradition" ten years later, also publishing it in print in 1981. Grimassi was the co-director and Elder of the Ash, Birch and Willow Tradition. In 1994 Llewellyn Publications accepted his manuscript for Ways of the Strega, which was reprinted the following year as Italian Witchcraft: The Religion of Southern Europe.

Grimassi claimed to have belonged to a 'family tradition' of religious Witchcraft which has opened him up to criticism, and lately revealed as incorrect by Professor Magliocco, as she points out that Grimassi never claims to be producing exactly what was practiced by Italian immigrants in North America , he admitted Italian-American immigrants 'have adapted a few traditional modern Wiccan elements into their ways'. After personally meeting with Grimassi, Professor Magliocco writes in her letter to the "Pomegranate Readers Forum": "I had the pleasure of meeting Raven Grimassi during the summer of 2001, unfortunately after the final draft of my article had already been submitted to the Pom. He was very gracious and helpful to me. From information he revealed during our interview, I can say with reasonable certainty that I believe him to have been initiated into a domestic tradition of folk magic and healing such as I describe in my article."

Grimassi won "Book of the Year" and "First Place-Spirituality Book" from the Coalition of Visionary retailers in 1998 for his book The Wiccan Mysteries, and his book the Encyclopedia of Wicca & Witchcraft was also awarded "Best Non-Fiction". His publisher Weiser Books produced the author's biography Horns of Honor.

Grimassi was an Italian-American author of over 20 books and is a Pagan scholar with over 40 years of research and study in the genre of Wicca, Stregheria, Witchcraft and Neo-Paganism always under his pen name of "Raven Grimassi" he presented this material as a Neo-Pagan version through his books. Grimassi was a practitioner for over 45 years and sadly died on the 10th of March 2019.

Raven Grimassi's Books:

- *The Book of the Holy Strega*, 1981
- *The Book of Ways Volumes I and II*, 1981
- *Ways of the Strega*, 1994, reprinted as *Italian Witchcraft: The Old Religion of Southern Europe*, 1995
- *Hereditary Witchcraft: Secrets of the Old Religion*, 1999. Llewellyn Publications
- *The Encyclopedia of Wicca and Witchcraft*, 2000, Llewellyn Publications
- *Beltane: Springtime Rituals, Lore and Celebration*, 2001, Llewellyn Publications
- *Hereditary Witchcraft*, 2001, Llewellyn Publications
- *Wiccan Magick*, 2002. Llewellyn Publications
- *The Wiccan Mysteries*. 2002, Llewellyn Publications
- *The Witches' Craft: The Roots of Witchcraft & Magical Transformation*, 2002, Llewellyn Publications
- *Spirit of the Witch: Religion & Spirituality in Contemporary Witchcraft*, 2003, Llewellyn Publications
- *The Witch's Familiar: Spiritual Partnership for Successful Magic*, 2003, Llewellyn Publications
- *Witchcraft: A Mystery Tradition*, 2004, Llewellyn Publications
- *Well Worn Path: Divination Kit,* with Taylor Stephanie, 2005
- *Hidden Path: Divination Kit,* with Taylor Stephanie, 2007
- *Crafting Wiccan Traditions*, 2008, Llewellyn Publications

- *The Cauldron of Memory: Retrieving Ancestral Knowledge & Wisdom, 2009,* Llewellyn Publications
- *Old World Witchcraft: Ancient Ways for Modern Days, 2011,* Weiser Books
- *Grimoire of the Thorn-Blooded Witch, 2014* Weiser Books
- *Communing with the Ancestors, 2016,* Weiser Books

Starhawk
Priestess, Witch and Goddess Elder
June 17th, 1951 -

Starhawk in her Garden Hat

Starhawk born Miriam Simos on June 17, 1951, in Saint Paul, Minnesota to her mother, Bertha Claire Goldfarb Simos (professor of social work at UCLA), and her father Jack Simos who died when she was only 5 years old. Both her parents were the children of Jewish immigrants from Russia. Starhawk later in high school, became best friends with fellow feminist Christina Hoff Sommers.

Starhawk received a BA in Fine Arts from UCLA. In 1973, whilst she was a graduate student in film there, she won the Samuel Goldwyn Writing Award for her novel A Weight of Gold, a story about Venice, California, where she then lived. She received an MA in Psychology, with a concentration in feminist therapy, from Antioch University West in 1982.

Following her years at UCLA, after a failed attempt to become a fiction writer in New York City, Starhawk returned back to California. She became active in the Neopagan community in the San Francisco Bay Area, and trained with Victor Anderson, Founder of the "Feri Tradition of Witchcraft", and also with Zsuzsanna Budapest, a feminist separatist involved in Dianic Wicca. Her claim to fame was in the writing of her book, The Spiral Dance, on the Goddess religion, which she finished in 1977 but was unable to publish it at first. Feminist religious scholar Carol P. Christ included an article on witchcraft and the Goddess movement in the anthology Womanspirit Rising in 1979. Christ put Starhawk in touch with an editor at Harper & Row, who eventually published the book.

First published in 1979, The Spiral Dance: A Rebirth of the Ancient Religion of the Great Goddess became a best-selling book about Neo-Pagan beliefs and practices. A 10th anniversary edition was published in 1989, followed by a 20th anniversary edition in 1999. The Spiral Dance has become a classic resource on Wicca and modern Witchcraft, spiritual feminism, the Goddess movement, and ecofeminism. The work is distinguished by its visionary mysticism, "Broad philosophy of harmony with nature", and ecstatic consciousness.

Starhawk believes that the Earth is a living entity, and that faith-based activism can reconnect oneself to basic human needs. She posts core religious values of community and self-sacrifice as important to eco-pagan movements, as well as the broader environmental justice movement. Starhawk advocates combining social justice with a nature-based spirituality that begins with spending time in the natural world, saying that doing so "can open up your understanding on deeper and more subtle levels where the natural world will speak to you". Starhawk's activism is deeply rooted in an anti-war philosophy, as she believes that war teaches one to see people culturally different than themselves as inhuman and dangerous. Starhawk has written extensively on activism, including advice for activist organizers, examinations of white privilege within radical communities, and calls for an intersectionality of fighting oppression that includes spirituality, eco-consciousness, and sexual and gender liberation.

Starhawk's feminist writings have been used to analyze the differences between mainstream rhetoric and feminist rhetoric, particularly in relation to her motive of writing rhetoric as revealing immanent truths rather than being utilized for persuasion. This latter purpose of mainstream rhetoric is viewed by Starhawk as adhering to patriarchal logic, and her vision of 'empowered action' – which involves rejecting the tenets of the oppressive system and then openly challenging them – attempts to transform persuasive mainstream rhetoric to immanent feminist rhetoric.

In 1979, partly to commemorate the publication of The Spiral Dance, Starhawk and her friends staged a public celebration on the Neopagan holiday of Samhain (Halloween) incorporating an actual spiral dance. This group became the "Reclaiming Collective", and their annual Spiral Dance ritual now draws hundreds of participants from all over the country. Starhawk continues to work with Reclaiming, a tradition of Witchcraft that she co-founded. This now international organisation offers classes, workshops, camps, and public rituals in earth-based spirituality, with the goal to 'unify spirit and politics'.

Starhawk also works internationally as a trainer in nonviolence and direct action, and as an activist within the peace movement, women's movement, environmental movement and anti-globalization movement. She travels and teaches widely in North America, Europe, and the Middle East, giving lectures and workshops. Starhawk was instrumental in the decision by the Unitarian Universalist Association to include earth-centered traditions among their sources of faith. She had numerous workshops for and was an active member of the Covenant of Unitarian Universalist Pagans (CUUPS), and interest group of Unitarians honoring Goddess-based, earth-centered, tribal and pagan spiritual paths.

Starhawk is an American author, writer, teacher and activist. She is well known as a theorist of feminist Neopaganism and ecofeminism. She is a columnist for Beliefnet.com and for "On Faith", the Newsweek/Washington Post online forum on religion. Starhawk's book The Spiral Dance (1979) was one of the main reasons behind the Goddess Movement. In 2012, she was listed in Watkins' Mind Body Spirit Magazine as one of the 100 Most Spiritually influential Living People.

Starhawk's Works:

Starhawk is an author, activist, permaculture designer and teacher, who has a prominent voice in modern earth-based spirituality and ecofeminism. She has written a number of books and has also contributed works in other media. Her works have appeared in translation in Spanish, French, German, Danish, Dutch, Italian, Portuguese, Polish, Czech, Greek, Japanese, and Burmese. She is also author or co-author of 13 books, including the most famous of them all The Spiral Dance: A rebirth of the Ancient Religion of the Great Goddess and the ecotopian novel The Fifth Thing, and its sequel City of Refuge. Starhawk's most recent non-fiction book is The Empowerment Manual: A Guide for Collaborative Groups, on group dynamics, power, conflict, and communications.

Starhawk Founded Earth Activist Training teaching permaculture design grounded in spirituality and with a focus on activism, the tools of ritual, and the skills of activism.

Non-fiction:

- *The Spiral Dance: A Rebirth of the Ancient Religion of the Great Goddess*, 1979, 1989, 1999
- *Dreaming the Dark: Magic, Sex, and Politics*, 1982, 1988, 1997
- *Truth or Dare: Encounters with Power, Authority, and Mystery*, 1988
- *Webs of Power: Notes from the Global Uprising*, 2003
- *The Earth Path: Grounding Your Spirit in the Rhythms of Nature*, 2004
- *The Empowerment Manual: A Guide for Collaborative Groups*, 2011

As co-author:

- *The Pagan Book of Living and Dying: Practical Rituals, Prayers, Blessings, and Meditations on Crossing Over* with M. Macha Nightmare and the Reclaiming Collective, 1997
- *Circle Round: Raising Children in the Goddess Tradition with Anne Hill and Diane Baker*, 1998
- *The Twelve Wild Swans: A Journey into Magic, Healing, and Action* with Hilary Valentine, 2000

Fiction:

- *The Fifth Sacred Thing*, 1993
- *Walking to Mercury*, 1997, (prequel to The Fifth Sacred Thing)
- *The Last Wild Witch*, 2009, (children's book)
- *City of Refuge*, 2015, (sequel to The Fifth Sacred Thing)

Other media:
Starhawk has contributed to films:

- *Signs Out of Time: The Story of Archaeologist Marija Gimbutas*
- *Goddess Remembered*
- *The Burning Times*
- *Full Circle*
- *Permaculture: The Growing Edge*, 2010
- *United Natures*, 2013, directed by Peter Charles Downey

She participated in the Reclaiming CDs Chants: Ritual Music and recorded the guided meditation Way to the Well. On YouTube Starhawk speaks on spirituality and activism at UUA. She also wrote the call-to-action for the women's peace organization Code Pink.

Starhawk in Ritual

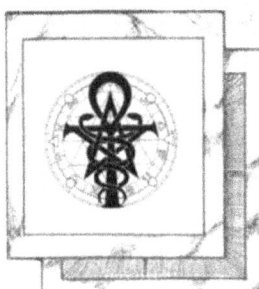

Donald Michael Kraig
Ceremonial Magician & Witch Elder
March 28th, 1951 – March 17th, 2014

Donald Michael Kraig was born March 28, 1951 – March 17, 2014. Kraig graduated from UCLA with a degree in philosophy and studied public speaking and music at other colleges and universities. He was initiated into "Aridian Witchcraft" by author Raven Grimassi, and into American "Traditionalist Witchcraft" by Scott Cunningham.

After a decade of personal study and practice of the occult, he taught courses in Southern California and at Neo-Pagan festivals and events on topics including Qabalah, Tarot, Magick, the Lovecraft Mythos, Psychic Development and Tantra, and was an Initiated Tantric who ran a lodge of AMOOKOS, an east-west tantric occult group.

Kraig was a member of several spiritual and Magical groups. He was a professional musician, as an organist, synthesist, keyboard player, theremin player, and singer. He taught computer skills at the University of Southern California and was a member of Hollywood's Magicians club The Magic Castle. He was awarded the honor of Certified Tarot Grand Master by the Associated Readers of Tarot. He was an editor of Fate Magazine. Kraig signed to Llewellyn Publications (now Llewellyn Worldwide), publisher or co-publisher of his main books, articles, and tapes; he was editor for The Llewellyn Journal in 2001 and for Llewellyn's New Worlds in 2003.

He received training and certification as a clinical hypnotherapist by the American Board of Hypnotherapy (ABH), the National Guild of Hypnotists (NGH), and the Association for Integrative Psychology (AIP). He was also certified as a hypnosis instructor by the ABH and as a master practitioner of Neuro-Linguistic Programming (NLP) by the AIP.

Media Appearances:

Kraig was a guest on Coast-to-Coast AM with George Noory, Personal Life Media, The Deviant Minds Salon, Pagans Tonight! on BlogTalk Radio, Right Where You Are Sitting Now, and Occultists Radio. Kraig published several books, including his 1988 introduction to ceremonial magic, Modern Magick. He was also an editor for Fate Magazine and for his main publisher Llewellyn Worldwide.

Kraig died March 17, 2014, after battling pancreatic cancer.

Donald Kraig Books:

- *Modern Magick: Eleven Lessons in the High Magickal Arts,* 1988, Llewellyn Publications, (republished in 2010 re-subtitled: *12 Lessons in the High Magickal Arts.*)
- *Magical Diary,* 1990, Llewellyn Publications
- *The Truth About Evocation of Spirits,* 1994, Llewellyn Publications
- *Modern Sex Magick: Secrets of Erotic Spirituality,* 1998, Llewellyn Publications
- *The Truth About Psychic Powers,* 1999, Llewellyn Publications
- *Tarot and Magic,* 2002, Llewellyn Publications
- *Graeco-Egyptian Magick* with Tony Mierzwicki, preface by Donald Michael Kraig, 2006, Megalithica Books
- *The Encyclopedia of Magic and Alchemy,* with Rosemary Ellen Guiley, foreword by Donald Michael Kraig, 2006, Checkmark Books
- *The Resurrection Murders,* 2009, Galde Press
- *Modern Tantra,* 2015, Llewellyn Publication

Simon Goodman
Alexandrian High Priest
September 16th, 1952 - 1991

Simon Goodman, born Ian Watts, on the 16th of September 1951, started his attraction to witchcraft while he was still at high school in the 1960s. Many believe Simon to have studied with the Sussex coven, but this was not so as he had no initial contact with craft people until he started, his own form of witchcraft with Faye Cubbin known as Lady Helen as there were no official covens or public covens in the Perth area that he knew of. He with Lady Helen decided to place an ad to attract members, this they did with a great response. Two of them being Malcolm (Mithrandir) and Marie (Tanith), who were professional fire-eaters. It did not end well between Helen and Simon as they parted ways. Through this Helen Initiated Malcolm and asked that he took over the coven within 6 weeks, and he became the official High Priest, calling their circle the "Coven of Lothlorien".

Simon now living in a set of apartments on the 10th floor in Guildford had met up with a lady named Michelin who eventually became his High Priestess in the 70s who was also a schoolteacher. They called their Coven the "Coven of the Acorn". Simon had correspondence with Alex and Maxine Sanders of England and eventually went to visit them and Maxine initiated Simon 1st and 2nd degree, of which later Betty Britton ordained him to the 3rd degree as a High Priest. Simon received photocopied works of Alex Sanders and brought them back to Australia to teach his Coveners through an Outer Court. I was one of those students who had to copy out the BoS line for line, word for word and dot for dot, and if we got anything wrong they would lean over our shoulders and point out the mistake and then proceed to tear it up and demand that you start again.

Simon like other covens in Perth were invited to be a part of a documentary titled "Supernatural Influences", this is where he first saw and heard of myself and my friend Astra who were also in another local Traditional Witchcraft Coven and were also involved in the documentary, and he asked my friend Terri Willisee who was the Director of the Documentary for an introduction to meet with us, but we refused at first. As we were part of a Traditional Coven in the foothills of Perth with our mentor David the 5th.

Simon through his contacts overseas eventually formed connections with Alexandrian, Gardnerian and Traditional Covens. Simons first coven was called "The Coven of the Acorn", where he gave each Initiate an acorn necklet on their Initiation. And I was one of those Initiate's initiated by Lady Michelin and Simon in 1976 at the tender age of 18. I came into Simon's coven with a few other members of my Traditional Coven after the passing of our High Priest, David 5th. There was myself, Margaret De Lille Quinn, Layla Quinn, (both Hereditary Witches from Cornwall, Clan of Boskednan,) and Dorrie Flatman, who were all Initiated prior to joining his Coven, but we all still went through his Outer Court as this tradition was called Alexandrian and was quite different. I never saw Simon as a Wiccan or a Witch but always saw him as an occultist or a Magician due to his quirky nature. As he was intrigued with unusual things especially drugs, but he never took them himself, instead they were tested on others that he knew, especially a young teenage boy in his Coven. Simon was extremely strict and disciplinarian and did not settle for any rules being broken at all. Simon's coven disbanded due to politics, and this is where he renamed his new coven, Covanentus Quercus, in the late 70s early 80s.

He was a very undiplomatic man, I did not like Simon very much towards the end because of an act he did within the Coven where he ceremonially in front of the whole Coven formally banished Tony Love (Tristan) a priest of his Coven because he worked with Layla and myself outside of the Coven, he called a meeting and then in front of everyone cut up Tristan's Singulum and burned his BoS that he hand copied from Simons BoS (Sanders), this was quite cruel to me and to others so we left the Coven after this act, never to return. He always spoke down about other people and their Covens, and created a nasty file on many Crafters called the "Cockroach Files" where he had something bad to say about everyone, and I mean everyone.

Setting aside all this I must say that he was a great teacher and knew how to teach people in Australia. Simon eventually, moved from Western Australia and started up working covens in Victoria, Canberra, South Australia and even New Zealand. He was a great teacher and taught well but was not one to share his affections randomly. Simon was very scholarly and also had a flare for creativity. Simon in his later years left a great legacy for those to follow with his ways. But on the morning of the Vernal Equinox in 1991, Simon left this world.

Goodman's High Priestess Lady Michelin eventually became in her elder years the Elder of my Covens and was introduced to them in a ceremonial Festival at "The Rock" where we always met for large gatherings.

Ellen Evert Hopman
Druidess Elder
July 31st, 1952 -

Ellen Evert Hopman

Ellen Evert Hopman born 31st July 1952 in Salzburg, Austria. Hopman's mother was an artist and keenly interested in the ancient Celts. As a child, Hopman heard her mother speak with awe and reverence about the archeological digs that were going on in the Salzburg area. She assumed everyone knew about these things and did not think much more about it. Hopman was raised by atheist parents, and began doing Zen Meditation at the age of 13, after reading Zen Flesh, Zen Bones by Paul Reps. In college she became a Transcendental Meditation Initiate and also studied Tai Chi and Kundalini Yoga (with Yogi Bhajan in Los Angeles). Hopman eventually lived in a Sufi Ashram for eight years and was a disciple of Guru Bawa Muhayadeen from Sri Lanka. Later, as an Art History student in Italy she stumbled into a Franciscan community in Assisi where she lived for a short time. She has also studied with Native American Elders for over thirty years.

Hopman first realised she was a Pagan on the Winter Solstice in 1978. When driving down the road with her then husband who was listening to a hockey game, she heard the announcer casually remark that "today is the day of the Winter Solstice". She had a sudden overwhelming urge to do something but had no idea what. She begged her husband to stop the car, which he finally did, but just kept listening.

to the hockey game. Hopkin bolted into a forest on the side of the highway, having no notion of what to do. She finally stopped when she came to a clear stream, rimmed by ice. The sun was shining on the water as she cupped her hands into the golden liquid, anointed herself with the water and finally felt satisfied.

It was a few years later when Hopman was taking the case of an herbal client that she first heard the word "Druid". The client mentioned that she met Pagans before but was not impressed until she met a Druid (Isaac Bonawits as it happens) at a festival. The moment Hopman heard the word Druid, she felt as if a harp string had been plucked in her soul. It was an immediate recognition of the power of that word. It was around the same time that Hopman heard traditional Celtic music on the radio and was immediately hooked. She went on to become a Ceili dancer, in the Irish Tradition.

Hopman graduated Summa Cum Laude from Temple University, Philadelphia, PA with a BS in Art Education, and received a master's degree in Mental Health Counselling from the University of Massachusetts (Amherst) in 1990. She trained in Herbalism primarily with William Le Sassier in New York in 1983, at the Findhorn Foundation in Scotland under Barbara D'Arcy Thompson, and received professional training at the National Centre for Homeopathy.

Hopman joined the modern Druidic organisation Ar nDraiocht Fein in 1984, which had around thirty members at the time. By 1986 Hopman was an Initiate and had received her Second Circle Initiation from Isaac Bonawits at a PSG Festival, that same week, at the same festival, Hopman and five other ADF members got together and began talking about how they wished there was a group dedicated solely to Celtic Druidism, not the Indo-European version espoused by ADF. The group crafted a list of concerns, number 1-12…95 (in a tongue in cheek reference to Martin Luther's 95 thesis) and taped the document to Isaac's van door. Then they went on to Found the Henge of Keltria Druid Order. She is a co-founder and former co-Chief of The Order of Whiteoak (Ord na Darach Gile), a Reconstructionist Druid organisation. She held the position of vice president of the Henge of Keltria, an international Druid Fellowship, for nine years. She has been on the staff of Keltria: Journal of Druidism and Celtic Magick and has been a contributing author to many New Age and Pagan journals.

Eventually, Hopman wanted deeper Celtic Reconstructionist Druidism, and she was also concerned by events uncovered in the Druid community – that there were convicted pedophiles and embezzlers who still claimed the title "Druid". She found that shocking and offensive, so she started a Yahoo group called White Oak in 1996, specifically to discuss these developments. She gave it that name in consultation with the trees in her front yard, she lives in an oak forest and the trees told her to call it that. She found out years later that the largest White Oak on the east coast of the USA was 20 minutes from her house!

She pulled together many of the most prominent Druids of the time to discuss "What is a Druid" and "What a Druid is not". After a year of hashing out the basics, a book list, Druid tools, training requirements, basic rituals and so forth, a new Order was born on the Winter

Solstice when twelve list members self-initiated and formed The Order of White Oak www.whiteoakdruids.org. Hopman was co-Chief (with Craig Melia, an English Druid) there for five years. As often happens in Pagan groups and in religious societies of all denominations, members began to complain about how Hopman was handling aspects of the Order, so she started delegating tasks to other members. But as they claimed each job for themselves, they immediately dropped the ball. Things came to a head when a male officer misbehaved with a female student and Hopman called him out. A row ensued and Hopman, now in her 60s, finally felt the need to start her own group. Coincidentally, at the same time an arsonist decided to torch the six-hundred-year-old White Oak that was just twenty minutes from Hopman's house.

Hopman is now the founder and Archdruid of Tribe of the Oak www.tribeoftheoak.com with members and Initiates in the USA, Ireland, and South Africa. She wonders why it took her so long to claim leadership and is incredibly grateful for the good will, dedication and scholarship found in her Celtic Reconstructionist Druid tribe. Hopman lives and works in an oak forest in western Massachusetts, USA, where her two cats supervise her writing career. She was the founder of The New England Druid Summit, a yearly gathering of Druids in New England. In 2009 she presented a paper on Celtic Cosmology at the International Centre for Cultural Studies (ICCS) Conference on Spirituality in Indigenous Cultural and Religious Traditions. Hopman a professional member of the American Herbalist's Guild, Hopman teaches Herbalism and Druidism in the US and in Europe.

Hopman has appeared on several radio and television programs including National Public Radio's Vox Pop and the Gary Null Show in New York City, and just recently on our own Spirit Talk Australia Podcast. She was also featured in a segment of the series Living the Wiccan Life produced by The Witch School. She presented a weekly "herb report" for WRSI radio in Greenfield, MA, and was featured in a documentary about Druids on A&E Television's The Unexplained (Sacred Societies, February 1999). Hopman is the author of several books and videos on Herbcraft and Druid wisdom. To listen to Ellen speak we have her at an interview on Spirit Talk Australia vlog.

Ellen Evert Hopman Books:

- *Tree Medicine, Tree Magic*, Illustrated by Diana Green, 1992, Phoenix Publishing, Seattle, WA
- *A Druid's Herbal for the Sacred Earth Year*, 1994, Destiny Books
- *People of the Earth: The New Pagans Speak Out*, with Lawrence Bond, 1995, Inner Traditions
- *Walking the World in Wonder: A Children's Herbal*, with Steven Foster, photographer, 2000, Healing Arts Press
- *Being a Pagan: Druids, Wiccans, and Witches Today*, with Lawrence Bond, (Revision of *People of the Earth: The New Pagans Speak Out*), 2001, Destiny Books
- *Priestess of the Forest: A Druid Journey*, 2008, Llewellyn Publications

- *A Druids Herbal of Sacred Tree Medicine*, 2008, Inner Traditions International.
- *The Druid Isle*, 2010, Lewellyn.
- *Making Kitchen Medicines –A Practical Guide*, 2010, Dreamz-Work Productions, LLC
- *Scottish Herbs and Fairy Lore*, 2011, Pendraig Publishing
- *Priestess of the Fire Temple– A Druid's Tale*, 2012, Llewellyn.
- *The Secret Medicines of Your Kitchen*, 2012, mPowr Publishing, London
- *A Legacy of Druids – Conversations with Druid leaders of Britain, the USA and Canada, Past and present*, 2016
- *Secret Medicines from Your Garden: Plants for Healing, Spirituality, and Magic*, 2016, Healing Arts Press
- *The Real Witches of New England: History, Lore, and Modern Practice*, 2018, Destiny Books
- *Tree Medicine Tree Magic: 2nd Edition*, 2018, Pendraig Publishing.
- *The Sacred Herbs of Samhain*, 2019, Destiny Books
- *The Sacred Herbs of Beltaine – Magical Healing and Edible Plants to Celebrate Spring*, 2020, Destiny Books.

Video's:

- *Gifts from the Healing Earth: Volume I*, Sawmill River Productions
- *Gifts from the Healing Earth: Volume II*, Sawmill River Productions
- *Pagans: The Wheel of the Sacred Year*, Sawmill River Productions
- *Celtic Cosmology*, 2009, Sawmill River Productions.

Find them on her website www.elleneverthopman.com

Morgana Sythova
April 15th, 1952 -

Morgana on Women's Stones in Moscow

Morgana, born in Holyhead, on the Isle of Anglesey, Wales but grew up in Lancashire - region known, among other things, for Pendle Hill and the Lancashire Witch trials, as her parents were stationed at a Royal Air Force Base. Morgana's life was further complicated when it was discovered that she was born with CHD – Congenital Hip Dysplasia/Dislocation when she was only 2 ½ years old when a doctor who was studying Orthopedics noticed that there was something seriously wrong with her hips. She was sent off to hospital and was hospitalized for two and a half years, mostly in quarantine. Due to the family not being financial, she only received a visit from her mother once every fortnight.

In 1974, after graduating from Teacher Training College, Morgana moved to the Netherlands, looking for work and adventure. There she met Merlin, a young Dutch fellow, who was studying Psychology at the local University (Utrecht). They discovered their common interest.

in spirituality. They were both particularly interested in Paganism and other religions that enable women to directly participate in religious rites on par with men. They were looking for a philosophy that leaves room for Magic, thus offering a deeper meaning to human existence, a certain sense of mystery.

In 1977, Morgana embarked on a spiritual journey to India. She was probably one of the last of the hippie generation to follow the famous "hippie trail". It was a journey by bus through Greece to India, via Istanbul, Turkey, Iran, Afghanistan, and Pakistan. She also visited Nepal and Sri Lanka. When her mystical and enchanting "Indian journey" ended, Morgana returned to the Netherlands. Flying back from Delhi to Kabul, she witnessed the Soviet troops in Afghanistan. Hers was the last train to the "land of hippies ". War and destruction forever closed that path shortly after.

On her return to the Netherlands Morgana met up again with Merlin – who had, in between times, met with Initiates of the Alexandrian tradition of Wicca, the modern Magical tradition of Witchcraft with European Pagan roots. They heard of Wicca before, but never met any actual practitioners of this religion. After talking with them, Morgana and Merlin did not continue with them. In modern Wicca it is most important to feel some instinctive, intuitive push inside – a "feeling in the stomach", so to speak, a "gut feeling", and have people "click" together. It is necessary to feel this elusive "click" for people to work well together in the circle. If the "click" is not there, it certainly does not mean that you have met bad people, but simply that you probably should not be with them in a Magic Circle.

After their experience with Alexandrians, Morgana and Merlin started to look at other opportunities to learn more about Wicca and pagan Witchcraft and found Marian Green's Natural Magic correspondence course. This course left a strong impression on Morgana and Merlin. Silver Circle's "earthy" and very natural philosophy in many ways resembles Marian's approach to Witchcraft and paganism. Marian was not initiated into British Traditional Wicca and her practice is exclusively solitary to this day. Over time, they became acquainted with Marian personally and they remain good friends. They still meet regularly when Morgana visits England.

Around the same time, Morgana and Merlin learned of another correspondence course, the one offered by Dolores Ashcroft – Nowicki, a British esoteric and occult practitioner, author of many popular books on Magick, working in the Western Hermetical tradition. She is the Director of Studies in Servants of the Light, a modern British esoteric order founded by W.E. Butler in 1965. Both W.E. Butler and Dolores were involved with the Fraternity of the Inner Light, an offshoot of the famous Order of the Golden Dawn vie Alpha et Omega, initially founded by Dion Fortune in 1922. Accordingly, Servants of the Light system is also causally related to the teachings of the Order of the Golden Dawn.

At a later point in time, Morgana and Merlin met Dolores personally and became friends. They corresponded throughout the years, learning Magic and occult philosophy from this great matron of modern occultism. Dolores' teachings had a strong influence on Merlin and Morgana's Magical practice.

Life never stands still. The European economy was going through another round of rough times. You can call it a coincidence, or, as Carl Jung would have said, synchronicity, but Morgana lost her job, and her landlord terminated the rent on her room. In such dire circumstances, our young people did not allow themselves to be discouraged. They simply loaded all their belongings into the car and hit the road! They went on a grand road trip to England. It was very much in the spirit of the times. Along with visiting relatives and the usual sightseeing, they made sure to pay homage to sacred Pagan sites. In addition, there are many places like that in England!

They also visited the oldest and most famous occult bookstore in London (and the entire western world) – "The Atlantis Bookshop". Merlin picked up a newsletter there featuring a call for new members from a coven in Brighton. No phone number, just an address. Morgana and Merlin felt they had nothing to lose, and they paid a visit to Brighton on the last leg of their grand tour of England. This is how Morgana described their fateful encounter:

"There one late afternoon I knocked on the door of an old Victorian house. The door opened and a man – the splitting image of Gerald Gardner, stood before us. However, he just looked at us and closed the door! A minute later the door re-opened and he said: "I have to pick up my wife, would you like to come!" Therefore, 2 seconds later we were in a car with a complete stranger heading for the center of Brighton. We met a woman - in her late 30s early 40s. she looked at us and said "aha…". Later she told us that they had been expecting us! We joined them for dinner and talked and talked. Who were we? What were we looking for? Why were they? We met them once more before leaving back to Holland."

Excerpt from Morgana's interview with ACTION magazine, by Christopher Blackwell, 2009.

Back home in the Netherlands, about 3 weeks later, the phone rang, and they heard: "Would you like to be initiated?"

The coven in Brighton was descended from Eleanor Bone (1911-2001), one of several High Priestesses, who worked directly with Gerald Gardner. Eleanor's first experience in witchcraft came from a traditional coven in Cumbria. Truly little is known about that coven's practices, although Eleanor did mention that they were very much unlike what Gerald Gardner was practicing. Eleanor said that during the Second World War, she was called into service and performed her duties in Cumbria, where she stayed in the house of an elderly couple. They took the young lady under their wing, so to speak. One evening they were having tea, and she said something about her beliefs in reincarnation and the fact that animals have souls too. In return, her hosts shared that they are some of the last practitioners of the ancient art of Witchcraft and invited her to participate in their rituals.

After reading Gerald Gardner's book "Witchcraft Today" in 1959, Eleanor wrote him a letter describing her experiences in the Cumbrian coven. She also expressed a wish to meet other witches, the ones Gardner mentioned in his book. Shortly afterwards they met in person. Gardner introduced her to the members of the Bricket Wood coven, and she was initiated in 1960. Eleanor's experience in the hereditary Cumbrian coven and her undeniable talent enabled her to quickly become the High Priestess of her own Gardnerian coven in Tooting Bec, London. It should be added that Gerald made Eleanor promise not to mention the Initiation she had undergone in the family tradition in 1941.

This coven was responsible for producing some of the best witches in England. One pair of her students – Madge and Arthur Worthington – established the very respected and vibrant Whitecroft line of the Gardnerian tradition in the UK. Prudence Jones, author of "History of Pagan Europe" and Vivienne Crowley, author of numerous works, including the extremely popular book "Wicca: The Old Religion in the New Age" also descend from Eleanor via Madge & Arthur.

Eleanor was an amazing woman. She combined her down-to-earth wisdom with ecstatic sacraments of ancient mysteries. In ordinary life, she ran a nursing home, helping people in their twilight years live out their lives with dignity and respect. She supported the living and comforted the dying. And at full moon she called up her coven to worship the Old Gods and do magic. Eleanor was a good teacher, and her coven was always an excellent place for learning. She did not shy away from the attention of the press either, generously agreeing to participate in several TV shows and documentaries in the 1960s, giving interviews to newspapers and magazines. She was featured on the front cover of Life magazine in 1964.

In the 80s and 90s Eleanor kept her life away from the prying eyes of the national press. She retired and moved back to Cumbria, effectively retiring from directly leading covens as well. However, she remained available to her students on the phone, and was gracious with guests. In later years, her health deteriorated, her husband Bill died, and Eleanor herself started feeling the pull of the Other World. Predicting the date of her death during a teleconference at Occulture (an Occult Festival), Eleanor Bone, the Grand Matron of Gardnerian tradition, died a month later, exactly twelve years ago, at the Autumn Equinox in 2001. She was in the 91st year of her life. Many of her students still love her dearly, and pass on stories about her to their students, thus keeping memories of her life and work alive.

Eleanor considered Wicca, first and foremost, to be the religion of nature, closely related to the earth. She paid special attention to healing and doing magic to help coven members and others, ease the burdens and mundane worries. Sometimes, she held healing rites for residents of her nursing home, upon receiving such a request from a suffering soul. Eleanor sympathized with the ideals of the Pagan Federation, although she personally never participated in this organization. Eleanor Bone's legacy lives on among many of the priests and priestesses, whose lines of initiation descend from her. This is also true of the Silver Circle.

The Brighton couple hived from Eleanor and passed on the Gardnerian tradition to Morgana and Merlin in 1979. They frequently travelled to Brighton to participate in rituals and training sessions. Back in those days airfare was still awfully expensive, so travelling from the Netherlands to England was not for the faint of heart. In the following year, Morgana and Merlin launched their quarterly magazine "Wiccan Rede". It was the first

Wiccan magazine in the Netherlands. Most articles were written by Morgana and Merlin themselves, and the articles were in English. Soon they began translating articles into Dutch.

In those days, there was almost no Wiccan literature in Dutch and Wiccan Rede articles were extremely popular. Readers would often write letters to the editors, wanting to learn more about Wicca, asking how they can become part of the tradition. Some readers wanted to meet them in person. Through Wiccan Rede Morgana and Merlin were getting to know quite a few people and if they felt that special "click" we mentioned before, they would consider taking them in as students. Slowly a so-called "Outer Court" group formed around Morgana and Merlin, which later grew into the first Gardnerian coven in the Netherlands.

Gradually, initiates gained enough experience, by working the rites and going through the appropriate initiations. At a later date, some initiates hived and established their own covens. These daughter covens often maintain a close relationship with their "upline" initiators. Thus, a true "network" of covens was formed around the parent group, with Silver Circle growing from a networking organisation to a true fully-fledged separate line of the Gardnerian tradition. This line is now known as the Silver Circle line in the Benelux whilst worldwide it is referred to as the Andred / Silver Circle line. Andred refers to the area (and Goddess) of the original English coven. **

Silver Circle covens are still quite close. From time to time, Silver Circle initiates come and celebrate their anniversaries together. A summer picnic in Panbos over time turned into a traditional annual gathering of Silver Circle. Morgana and Merlin's students are involved in the production of Wiccan Rede. Their first initiate is now the magazine's editor. With the advent of digital technology and the spread of Internet technology, Silver Circle also gained its online presence with the silvercircle.org site and the discussion forum there, uniting all Silver Circle initiates and seekers into a single community. Merlin was the techno-wizard behind all of that.

On January 3, 2012, at the height of his strength and potential Merlin stepped into the "other world". We miss him dearly.

Previous issues of Wiccan Rede, starting from 1984, can be found at archive.silvercircle.org. Recently, Wiccan Rede moved entirely to an online format, available free of charge. Silver Circle has never been an exclusively Dutch organization. Merlin, Morgana, and their "downline" also had British, American, Belgian, Canadian, German, Hungarian, Polish, Spanish and Russian initiates. The unification of Europe into a single union contributed to the strengthening of ties between various Continental nations. Modern technology such as the Internet, affordable air flights, superfast trains, allowed seekers and teachers to find each other.

Silver Circle practice was always securely within the strictest definition of the Gardnerian tradition. It successfully retained the quiet, simple, "earthy" Witchcraft, which Eleanor passed to Silver Circle through the coven in Brighton. Due to Morgana and Merlin's close relationship with Marian Green, her down-to-earth, "green" rustic witchcraft flavors also organically made their way into Silver Circle's practice. When Morgana and Merlin started to practice the tradition in the Netherlands, they quickly realized that the flow of forces and spirits of the land in this country were different from those in Britain. They listened to the feel of the land, experimented with the flow of power, and worked on integrating some of the local folk customs into their witch practice. Therefore, Silver Circle obtains its unique Dutch flavour. That is how Morgana and Merlin were able to help the foreign British religion of Wicca take root in the Dutch soil. After all, the only way for a tradition to survive is to become rooted in the local soil, otherwise it will never last beyond its original founders and carriers. This is and was always true everywhere, in all religious traditions of the world.

The Netherlands is a small country, stretching along the shores of the North Sea. The water and the sea are always there, always close to the people. The sea is a man's best friend, a source of wealth, the means of communication and transportation. It is the bosom of the Great Mother, and at the same time, a rival, eroding the coasts, a destroyer of dikes, a killer through storms and floods. Here we see a primordial aspect of a chthonic Mother Goddess, who gives life and may bring death. The entire country lies at or below sea level; a complex system of dikes keeps the sea from repossessing the land. The Dutch have a saying: "God created the earth, and the Dutch created Holland." In ancient times, the "Lowlands" were inhabited by various tribes speaking Celtic and Germanic languages. The Romans called this region Lower Germany (Germania Inferior). The Romans also founded the first cities in this country (Utrecht). Historians found references to the ancient local goddess Nerthis, whose chariot was ceremonially bathed in the sea and was taken around the countryside during an annual procession.

This land had been forcibly baptized during the Frankish rule in the 9th century CE, and for quite some time local folks retained their pagan customs, alongside the official Christian faith. In the 16th century, most Dutch people moved away from the Catholic Church and became Protestant. During the decades of religious wars of the 16 – 17th centuries, the Dutch have learned to appreciate the value of patience, tolerance, and non-interference in the personal space of others. That is why, in spite of the general conservatism and Christian beliefs of most Dutch folks, they are quite tolerant to Wicca and Paganism.

Silver Circle is a good example of how Wicca may become an integral part of a diverse tapestry of various religious paths in a non-English-speaking country, an example of how a vibrant and active community may be created through love and labors of dedicated people. It is also an excellent example of how the Gardnerian tradition can take root in a foreign soil, while not just simply preserving its core and essence, but also increasing the tradition's treasury. Silver Circle, therefore, remains within even the most stringent definition of the Gardnerian tradition, recognized by Gardnerian initiates all over the world.

Silver Circle's relationship with other pagan religions and Wiccan traditions is also worth mentioning. The Alexandrian tradition also came to the Netherlands in 1979 or so. Alexandrian and Gardnerian covens have grown beside each other, and, thanks to wisdom, tact and diplomacy on both sides, witches from both traditions seem to be getting along quite well.

It was not easy, and both sides had to learn the fine art of compromise, so that traditions remain friendly with each other, with a share of mutual respect. Community leaders worked hard to nip any "witch wars" in the bud. They were also instrumental in creating the "Witch cafes/heksen cafes" which are monthly informal moots for seekers, throughout the Netherlands and Belgium. When PFI was being formed in the Netherlands, Morgana offered Lady Bara, one of the leaders of the local Alexandrian community to join her as a co-national coordinator of PFI Netherlands. In fact, Morgana performs many other duties in PFI, both on the national (Dutch) and international level. To this day Lady Bara organizes regular workshops and the lovely PFI International Conference in Lunteren.

Silver Circle is a living and growing network. New seekers come looking for tradition all the time. Morgana and many others continue to work hard to ensure that Silver Circle is open to seekers including those from other countries. Morgana still runs introductory correspondence courses in English. In order to join the course, the applicant must send her a letter of introduction, explaining why they want to take the course and describing some of their own experiences. This course is not designed to teach the Gardnerian tradition, of course, because it is impossible to train Gardnerian without being initiated first. Nevertheless, this course is valuable to seekers, because it enables them to evaluate whether the Gardnerian path is right for them and helps them acquire the knowledge base and skills any modern witch needs these days.

This path requires a great deal of patience, willpower, the ability to motivate oneself, and the ability to learn independently. This path is not for everyone. However, this is how Traditional Wicca usually spreads into different countries. Either the initiates move to another country and bring the Tradition with them, or folks living in other countries travel or immigrate to a country, where Wicca already exists, try to learn as much as they can there and then continue their training though written correspondence and rare personal meetings. This is how Raymond Buckland trained with Monique and Scotty Wilson, Morgana and Merlin – with a coven in Brighton, Jim Baker in the London coven of Alex and Maxine Sanders. Roy Dymond was initiated in New York and moved back home to Canada. Janet and Stewart Farrar trained in England and then immigrated to Ireland. There are many more examples, of course.

These days, a well-developed network of modern information technology, such as Skype, email, and social networks, allows people to communicate with each other over long distances free of charge. Foreign seekers can easily find Silver Circle websites, Wiccan Rede Online and back issues. Seekers can always chat with Morgana and her friends at PFI – Pagan Federation International – forum. Seekers can attend one of several PFI national conferences; many Traditional Wicca initiates visit these conferences, as well as local pagan pub moots. There will always be representatives of Silver Circle at the annual PFI international conference in The Netherlands.

Silver Circle is keeping the old traditions alive and strives to keep up with the changing times. Learn what it means to be a Tradition in the 21st century. Europe and the whole world are getting smaller all the time. What was difficult to imagine in the 1980s, like Gardnerians in the Soviet Union, is now a reality. It is a new world out there!

How Silver Circle started:

- "Beyond the Broomstick – a conversation with Morgana Sythove
- www.silvercircle.org
- www.paganfederation.org
- www.forum.paganfederation.org
- www.wiccanrede.org
- Spain: www.silvercircle.es
- Russia: www.silvercircle.ru
- Germany: www.silvercirclegermany.de
- and many Facebook pages… Silver Circle, Wiccan Rede Online and PFI.

Professor Jack Montgomery
Shaman
1953 -

Jack Montgomery

Originally from South Carolina, Jack was born in 1953 in Columbia, South Carolina. He was raised United Methodist but left the church at age 15 over segregation of the races during worship. His family though Christian, practiced elements of folk religions which he later came to learn stemmed from his maternal great-grandfather who was a Powwow Doctor who specialized in healing animals through sacred touch. Jack was raised not to fear, but to accept the presence of spirits, dream interpretation and spiritual visions.

Jack earned his B.A. from the University of South Carolina in 1976 with a major in Religious Studies and Psychology and a minor in Anthropology. Jack earned his Master of Library Science at the University of Maryland–College Park in 1987. First, as a law librarian Jack worked in academic law libraries in Virginia, Ohio, and Missouri. In 1998, he made the transition to the general academic library and to Western Kentucky University in 1998 where he is now a Professor/Collection Services Coordinator.

As a spiritual person, Jack has been involved with traditional American Shamanism since 1974 as a folklorist and practitioner of

Powwow and Hoodoo shamanic traditions. He received training in Hoodoo from James E. McTeer, 1903-1979, and others and learned Powwow/Braucherei from Hexenmeister, Lee Raus Gandee, 1917-1998 who wrote Strange Experience: The Secrets of a Hexenmeister. Their student/teacher relationship lasted from 1973-1977.

Jack went on to meet and learn from other Powwow doctors in Pennsylvania and mountain magic from an Appalachian granny woman in south central Virginia. His own practice has led him to speak since 1976 at events in Tennessee, Ohio, Missouri, Illinois, Georgia, North and South Carolina and even at institutions like Harvard University and as far afield as Pescara, Italy. He has written numerous articles for spiritual magazines and his book, American Shamans: Journeys with Traditional Healers, was published March 2008 by BUSCA Press. The book is still selling well in the U.S., U.K., and Europe and as far away as Japan and South Africa. Jack discovered modern paganism in 1991 through the CUUPS group and has been going to gatherings like PCCO, PSG and PUF ever since.

Jack also began studying guitar at age thirteen and played his first professional gig in 1967. He sings and plays guitar, harmonica, and Appalachian dulcimer. Musically, he is interested in pagan, Celtic and traditional folk music. He writes his own songs and poetry. Just recently in 2020 he was a guest our very own Spirit Talk Australia Podcast show hosted by Renata & Anne.

Jack Montgomery Works:
Book:

- *American Shamans: Journeys with Traditional Healers*, 2008, BUSCA Press

CD's:

- *Onward to Avalon*
- *Everywhere I Look*
- *Tradition with a Twist*
- *Watersprite*

Professor Ronald Hutton
Pagan Elder
December 19th, 1953 -

Ronald Hutton

Ronald Hutton born 19th December 1953 in Octacamund, India to a British Colonial family, and is of part Russian and British ancestry. When his family arrived in Britain, he attended Ilford County High School, and started to have a deepening interest in archaeology, and joined the committee of the local archaeological group and took part in excavations from 1965 through to 1976, including such sites as Pilsdon Pen Hill Fort, Ascott-under-Wychwood Long Barrow, Hen Domen Castle, and a Temple in Malta. Between 1966 and 1969 he visited nearly every prehistoric chambered tomb that survived in Britain and Wales and wrote a guide to them.

Despite his great love of archaeology, he decided to study history at university, believing that he had more aptitude for it. He then won a scholarship to study at Pembroke College Cambridge, where he continued with his interest in archaeology along with history. In 1975 he took on a course run by the university archaeologist Glyn Daniel, and expert on the Neolithic. From Cambridge he went on to study at Oxford University where he gained a Doctorate, and he took up a fellowship at Magdalen College.

Hutton became an English historian who specialised in Early Modern Britain, British Folklore, Pre-Christian Religion, and Contemporary Paganism. He is a professor in the vary subject at the University of Bristol. Hutton has written 14 books and has appeared on British television and radio, and is a Commissioner of English

Heritage. He went on to become a Reader in history at the University of Bristol in 1981. He wrote three books on the subject "The Royalist War Effort", "The Restoration" (1985), and "Charles the Second" (1990). During the 1990s he wrote books about historical paganism, folklore and contemporary Paganism in Britain; The Pagan Religions of the Ancient British Isles (1991), The Rise and Fall of Merry England (1994), The Stations of the Sun (1996), and The Triumph of the Moon (1999), the latter of which would become praised as a seminal text in the discipline of Pagan Studies. In the following 10 years he wrote on other topics, writing a book about Siberian Shamanism in the western imagination, Shamans (2011), a collection of essays on folklore and Paganism, Witches, Druids and King Arthur (2003), and then two books on the role of the Druids in the British imagination, The Druids (2007) and Blood and Mistletoe (2009).

Many Pagans embraced his work, with the prominent Wiccan Elder Frederic Lamond referring to it as "an authority on the history of Gardnerian Wicca". Public criticism came from the practicing Wiccan Jani Farrell-Roberts, who took part in a published debate with Hutton in "The Cauldron Magazine" in 2003. Hutton dismissed Margaret Murray's theories about the Witch-Cult using Norman Cohn's theories, which she believed to be heavily flawed.

Ronald Hutton Books:

- *The Royalist War 1642-1646*, 1982, Routledge London
- *The Restoration: 1658-1660*, 1985, Clarendon
- *Charles the Second, King of England, Scotland & Ireland*, 1989, Clarendon
- *The British Republic 1649-1660*, 1990, Palgrave MacMillan
- *The Pagan Religion of the Ancient British Isles: Their Nature & Legacy*, 1991, Blackwell
- *The Rise and Fall of Merry England-The Ritual Year 1400-1700*, 1994, Oxford University
- *The Stations of the Sun*, 1996, Oxford University
- *The Triumph of the Moon*, 1999, Oxford University
- *Shamans: Siberian Spirituality*, 2001, Hambleton & London
- *Witches, Druids and King Arthur*, 2003, Hambledon
- *Debates in Stuart History*, 2004, Palgrave MacMillan
- *The Druids: A History*, 2007
- *Blood and Mistletoe*, 2009
- *A brief History of Britain 1485-1660*, 2011
- *Pagan Britain*, 2013
- *The Witch*, 2017

Pete Cropley
Wiccan High Priest & Elder
1953 –

Peter Cropley

Peter Cropley was born in Reading UK in 1953, and he was not expected to live the night as he was very prem and was immediately baptized as a Roman Catholic to ensure that if he died, he would be going to a good place.

Fortunately for him, a prem specialist doctor from America had just set up a special medical unit and Peter survived to grow up to be the person he has become today. Pete's parents were in the Royal Air Force and thus they travelled all through Britain, Scotland and even overseas to Cyprus. Therefore, his childhood involved a lot of movement and different cultures, in Scotland Peter was confirmed by the Bishop of Scotland in St Andrews Cathedral this was to be a start to becoming a good Roman Catholic and at this time he was also an altar boy. He comments and says he still lays a particularly good altar.

Peter at the age of 10 years of age, came to Australia with his family as a 10 Pound Pom luckily his father being a qualified electrician which was a required trade, Australia was happy for the whole family to emigrate with citizenship for the princely sum of £10. Peter, having gone through schooling, started an apprenticeship and following his father's footsteps also became an electrician. After a few years, Peter became a lecturer at TAFE teaching electrical, electronics and computing.

How did this affect his Magical journey, firstly Peter had become a Baptist and met a lovely lady and married her in the Baptist Church. After some years they discovered the Pentecostal church with its baptism of the spirit, and this appealed to both of them, and they became very strong Pentecostals speaking in tongues and laying on of hands for healing. Pete and his wife Cecily (also a Wiccan High Priestess) still do this because they believe that the gift is from the creator not necessarily one religion.

Pete's children were brought up in the Pentecostal church and he also became a lay pastor looking after our young married couples. This led to much inner conflict, as the church evolved into a mega-church where the direction of the teaching was focused on guilt and unworthiness instead of a person's personal journey involving life, love and happiness. Pete became quite disillusioned with the church direction and teachings and eventually they left this church. They then moved into a period of emptiness' not being involved in a church at all, with nothing to worry about, but this period only lasted about six months.

Pete met a lady called Fiona who introduced him to a Wiccan High Priestess Lady Fern, she lent him a book titled Moon Magic by Dion Fortune. Pete read this book and was immediately captivated by the idea of a Great Goddess. He came back to Lady Fern, and she lent him a second book titled the Sea Priestess also by Dion Fortune. Pete started to become interested and confronted Lady Fern stating his interest in this direction and enquired how he could learn more and participate. Lady Fern took him through her Outer Court training, which started him on his Magickal journey onto the Path of the Goddess, something that was quite different than what he followed in his past but was awakening to its teachings as his form of Truth.

After about six months Pete had to tell his wife Cecily that he was about to be Initiated as a Witch, of which this caused quite some discussion and also intrigued Cecily, Pete's wife with the result that she also was Initiated within a short period of time. This great step of change and direction begun their journey into the Wiccan world of Witchcraft as was practiced in Perth, Western Australia.

There were a number of teaching covens in Perth which resulted in a large community of pagans that would occasionally meet to celebrate the major festivals of the year. Pete and his family moved to join a second coven that allowed them to study and experience more in-depth and resulted in both Pete and Cesily progressing to becoming an Ordained Priest and Priestess of the second-degree. After a further period of time and learning they were Initiated and Ordained as High Priest and High Priestess by one of our most senior respected Elder High Priestesses in Perth.

As a High Priest Pete and Cesily started their own teaching coven called "The Temple" in Perth 22 years ago. The temple is responsible for the training of a large number of interested persons who have become Initiated Witches, some also second-degree Priests and Priestesses, where some, who also had the calling became High Priests and High Priestesses, At this time we have hived off from our coven four High Priestesses and One High Priest.

Pete's teaching focuses on celebrating the major festivals starting with Candlemas, Beltane, Lammas and Samhain. He went on to say: "The year begins with energizing and fertilizing the hopes aims and aspirations of the coven at Candlemas. Beltane allows us to fire up and take the group between the flames to allow focused energy to empower the seeds of Candlemas. Lammas, we expect to be able to present on the altar the fruits of our labors and to acknowledge the work that has occurred up to this time. Before Samhain we do a talismanic ritual usually to the planet Jupiter that focuses on prosperity and health this talisman is then kept on our persons to enable us to declare that by the work of our hands and the power of our minds, we will be prosperous and healthy for the forthcoming year."

Pete sees within his coven that they celebrate all the Wiccan festivals and as well as the Lesser Festivals, the Equinoxes and Solstices. They also study Magick along the lines of the Golden Dawn principles. They have an extensive library covering many eclectic areas of western Magickal traditions as well as Egyptian, Enochian, Golden Dawn, and the teachings of the Farrar's. One of the most important attitudes that Pete adopts and teaches is the ability to feel gratitude and acknowledge that each and every day. On his way to his work vehicle, he stops at his outdoor Temple which has a beautiful statue of the Goddess, and I thank Her for the day whether hard or easy, Pete is grateful for the opportunity to work and experience. At the end of his day when he arrives home and gives thanks for the Goddess and the God with whom he has shared.

Pete believes that the principle of gratitude is such an important Magickal constant, it colours and emphasizes the quality of his days. The Temple has a teaching session every week in which the new people can come into a training regime that allows them to progress through all levels of Wicca. Often Initiates will access the library and follow streams of study that allow them to progress in a number of magical ways.

A Typical Year for Pete:

A typical year is organized around a weekly teaching schedule as well as celebrating all festivals related to his Magickal Path. In addition, they focus on healing rituals and techniques and are often called upon to help people in need. Also, we are called upon to cleanse people, their homes and offices where significant activity has been experienced by the people and they wish a more settling calm and removal of negative energies. Sometimes, the entity or entities that have affected these people can be strong and Pete believes we have to be stronger in the authority given to us as Wiccan Priests and Priestess and our relationship to the higher powers.

Pete says there are many levels of cleansing that can be practiced, and we are required to know and to teach our people how to apply this power to the circumstances. Pete goes on to say, "We are different in one aspect only, we do not charge money for any of our services this is because I believe that once money enters into a coven or outsiders that wish to pay for cleansing and healing services that detracts from our religious path which is serving The Great Goddess."

Pete, as a Wiccan High Priest, is also recognized as a Wiccan Elder within the Australian context of the Wiccan Priesthood. I myself have worked many times with Pete and Ces's Coven whether in their circles or mine. I included them in my book as they have a great deal of respect from me for the commitment to the Craft and the ability to not gossip. They are genuine dedicated Wiccans and work diligently within the Pagan and Wiccan Community in Australia. Pete associates with a number of High Priests and High Priestesses around Australia and have been involved for a number of years in attending and organizing the Australian Wiccan Conference. This conference allows Wiccans and Pagans to freely meet and discuss issues and directions within our cultures as well as to celebrate with a well-planned festival and a great feast. This type of approach allows for strong communication and support for our religious persuasion within Australia with links to the rest of the world.

Pete sees his future as a Priest of the Great Goddess. He will continue to teach within the coven structure as well as using the Internet like his own educational videos on teaching from the Temple from his own website and also You Tube. Pete relates to people that whether we go to work in the mundane world or if we are in ritual, we are always the Priest or the Priestess foremostly and must relate our standards in all that we do. Pete believes that it is not only the words of our mouth but also the actions and attitudes that we take that proclaim that we are of the Priesthood.

Pete, now at the age of 66, looks forward to more teachings, more sharing, and more enjoyment on the Wiccan path with its Magickal overtones into the future. Pete is truly a dedicated Priest and servant of the Goddess as a Wiccan High Priest Elder.

Pete & Cesily Cropley welcoming at the 2010 AWC

Jesse "Wolf" Hardin
Shaman & Pagan Elder
1954 -

Jesse "Wolf" Hardin

Jesse "Wolf" Hardin was born in 1954 and began his career as a writer and author as a young runaway from military school in the 1960s, where he published short stories and poetry in alternative periodicals including Win, The Guardian, and Communities.

Hardin for the first thirty years wrote on subjects dear to him about wild and free nature and personal growth, responsibility and activism in self-help, alternative spirituality and ecology-oriented publications as Mother Earth News, The Trumpeter, Green Egg, Sowell Review, Sentient Times, Creations, New Thought Journal, Hight County News, Magickal Blend and Natural Beauty & Health.

Hardin's coining of the word Rewilding (under the pen name Lone Wolf Circles in 1986) and his writing son personal as well as ecological rewilding are considered seminal to the budding Neo primitivist and Wildcrafting communities. Hardin is also the Founder of the "Anima" nature-informed teachings and practice, as well as a great artist, poet, musician, historian, and wilderness restorationist. Hardin has written 9 books and had published over 500 articles on personal growth, natural history, deep ecology, spirituality and nature, alternative healing, poetry, wildcraft, American history, and the legends of the Wild West.

Hardin lives and teaches at "Anima Sanctuary" which is located in the mountainous wildlands of Southwest New Mexico.

Hardin's work forms a body of nature-informed insights and lessons that can be utilized by people of any religious or philosophical persuasion to deepen, enliven, enrich and empower their lives. His work has been praised by a number of writers and thinkers from Edward Abbey to Terry Tempest Williams, Roderick Nash, Jerry Mander, Joanna Macy, Oberon Zell-Ravenheart, Gary Snyder and Ralph Metzner. Edward Abbey, a friend and supporter of Hardin's until his death, mentions him in his novel Hayduke Lives! Terry Tempest Williams writes that in 2000, Hardin founded the Animá teachings (www.animacenter.org), a self-described "empowering set of nature-based insights and practices" detailed in his self-published books The Way of Anima and Home: Reinhabiting Self, Recovering Sense of Place. Most recently he has authored detailed lesson materials for the Animá Shaman Path and Medicine Woman Correspondence Courses, and an illustrated children's book I'm A Medicine Woman, Too!

Hardin teaches Animá Correspondence Courses online, as well as presenting workshops on Earth Path Shamanism. He resides at and co-directs the Animá Center, a wildlife sanctuary and wilderness restoration project in New Mexico's Gila National Forest, where he and his partners Kiva Rose and Loba host workshops, vision quests, Medicine Woman Tradition student internships and wilderness retreats.

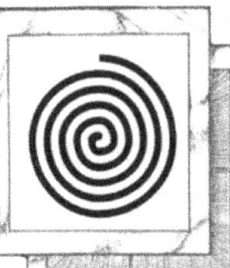

Sallie Anne Glassman
Manbo Asogwe – Priestess of Vodou
1954 -

Sallie Anne Glassman

Sallie Ann Glassman was born in 1954 of Jewish-Ukrainian heritage. An alumna of the New Orleans Art Institute, Ms. Glassman is an award-winning artist whose work has been exhibited in one-woman and group shows that have received significant critical reviews in local newspapers and international art magazines. She is represented in New Orleans with on-going exhibitions of her paintings and assemblage art Altars at Barrister's gallery and The New Orleans Healing Center. She has created numerous Altar installations as well as a permanent Altar installation for the Louisiana State Cultural Museum in Baton Rouge. She had the first one-woman show at Barrister's Gallery in post-Katrina New Orleans.

Ms. Glassman was the founder of The New Orleans Hope and Heritage Project, whose vision was to help rebuild New Orleans after Hurricane Katrina, person to person, neighborhood by neighborhood, and to reinvent what community means to the citizens of the city. Hope and Heritage morphed into The Sunday

Salon, which produced three projects: 17 Cultural videos (currently located at www.neworleanshealingcenter.org), a committee to advise the City Council on a sustainable energy policy, and The New Orleans Healing Center, of which Sallie Ann is co-founder and co-chairman of the Board of Directors. She is the founder of The Annual Anba Dlo Halloween Festival, The Day of the Dead/Fet Gede and the New Orleans Sacred Music Festival, all at the New Orleans Healing Center.

Ms. Glassman has been practicing Vodou in New Orleans since 1976. She is the owner of the Island of Salvation Botanica, a store and gallery specializing in Voudoun religious supply, medicinal and magical herbs, and Haitian and local artworks. She travelled to Haiti in November 1995 to undergo the week-long Couche initiation. During the initiation, Ms. Glassman was ordained as Manbo Asogwe, or Priestess of Vodou, and is one of the few white Americans to have been ordained via the traditional Haitian initiation.

Sallie Anne in Ritual

Rev. Velvet Reith
High Priestess - Witch Elder
November 15th, 1954 - January 4th, 2017

Velvet Reith

Velvet Reith was born on November 15th, 1954. Velvet was born in New Orleans to parents John and Dorothy West. She was a dear friend and sister, who showed me more about grace and giving than most. Although we were far apart, we kept in constant contact, my last connection with her was when she was planning a large world holiday and was thinking of visiting me in Australia, which was exciting. But this was not to be so, I had heard after an announcement that the Wiccan High Priestess Velvet Reith had died in her home surrounded by her loving and devoted husband Gil and her children and close friends.

Like many in Louisiana, she had a Catholic upbringing but, growing up in New Orleans, she was also exposed to magic and various forms of Witchcraft. Her father was also reportedly a very spiritual man, who did not turn away from non-conventional or non-Catholic ideas. Velvet began practicing Wicca in high school. In 1968, she enrolled in the newly established public "Grace King" all-girls school in Metairie, where she met a group of friends who were all interested in Wicca and Witchcraft. Velvet loved her first little touch with Magic and Witchcraft and loved this her first pagan group, as all the girls shared the common interest of being victims of child abuse and pedophilia. As a result of her traumas, they formed the "Crescent City Swamp Witches". This group of young women stayed lifelong friends and practicing Pagan colleagues, they were sisters of the spirit.

Although Velvet's introduction to witchcraft came at an early age, it would be another 20 years before she took her place as a leader in the Louisiana Pagan Community. After leaving high school, Velvet attended the Charity School of Nursing at Delgado Community College. She owned a bar for some time with her mother, Dorothy. And after several failed marriages and the birth of her four children, she eventually moved into a successful career as the director of counselling at "Causeway Medical Suite", an abortion clinic in Metairie. In that work Velvet became an outspoken local activist in support of a woman's right to choose. She was even interviewed for and quoted in a 1997 Simon and Schuster's publication: The Abortion Resource Handbook. It was also around this time that she met the love of her love and married Gilbert Reith, which began a beautiful journey and marriage that lasted the rest of her life with Gil for 25 years.

Velvet's work in community service was taking off, Velvet also began to step out as a leader in the Pagan community. She was fondly known as the "Swamp Witch". In 1994, she co-Founded "The Covenant of the Pentacle Wiccan Church" (CPWC), which became affiliated with the Aquarian Tabernacle Church based in Washington state, which is where I eventually met with this remarkable lady. CPWC performed both public and private rituals as well as legal weddings, hospital and prison chaplaincy, and interfaith services. The group eventually operated teaching circles in Baton Rouge, Lafayette, and Shreveport, and hosted a food bank. CPWC members followed Velvet's lead in being continually active and public in community support.

In 1996, through CPWC, Velvet began a successful Pagan Prison Ministry Service, through which ordained ministers of her group could enter the state prison system to help Pagan inmates. In the 2008 Times-Picayune interview, she explained "One day, the Goddess thumped me on the head and told me to start a prison ministry." CPWC's program was reportedly the only Wicca/Pagan based prison ministry service in the state. Velvet first spent over a year working with only the Allen Correction Centre in Kinder. Then, she added five more prisons to her program, including the Louisiana State Penitentiary in Angola. By 2003, CPWC's Pagan Ministry had grown in size to support federal facilities as well, and she began teaching other Pagan chaplains about the work.

Velvet was happiest when she was working on something that benefited others, she had a passion for humanity and believed that people could be their own salvation if they worked together. Velvet was often seen volunteering at soup kitchens, in homeless shelters, and offered all her services to those in need. She would often give a homeless person her last few dollars to give them a little comfort or just to put food in their bellies. She often took them home and showered them, fed them, and sometimes, if possible, helped them to find a job. Velvet helped many behind the scenes. In 2000, Velvet received a commendation by the Mayor of New Orleans for her work in the community.

Then in August 2005, Hurricane Katrina hit. New Orleans and the region was devasted, but that did not stop Velvet who also lost her home, she went straight out to work. After evacuating herself and her family, she pledged to help rebuild. Christopher Penczak first met Velvet during this time. He said, "Velvet was a force of nature in her community work, going above and beyond and not letting anything get in her way".

Velvet asked me to come to New Orleans and attend their Spring Festival to help raise funds for the New Orleans Appeal, she offered to pay for my trip, but I donated my money and time to her cause, along with many others of the pagan community such as Penczak, authors Dorothy Morrison and M/R. Sellers, Sally Anne Glassman. Velvet helped to organize relief efforts toward the rebuilding of the area, including the Pagan community. Through these efforts, Morrison said that they ended up raising $10,000, all of which was sent to Velvet who 'bought chain saws, heaters, cases of water, food and other supplies, and doled them out to those in need.' Morrison added, "it was quite a job, but she managed it."

Velvet's donation to community service and family did not end when the clean-up efforts were over. In 2007, Velvet published "My First Little Workbook of Wicca". Originally creating the book for her own grandchildren, Velvet decided to self-publish it so others could benefit. Then in 2009, she was appointed by Raymond Buckland, as the curator of the Buckland Museum. Raymond was a family friend and looked to her to help him re-establish his museum which was in disarray due to the previous curators taking advantage of Buckland's good deeds. For several years, Velvet carried his memorabilia to Pagan events, showcasing the various pieces and sharing Wiccan history.

However, her dream of a New Orleans based Buckland Museum was not to be. As it was at this time that Velvet began to show signs and developed in 2008 of the debilitating rare disease called Picks Disease, where she was forced to retire from public life, but not before she made a significant mark on the world around her. Over the next few years her condition worsened. It was not until 2014 that Velvet was actually given the official diagnosis of Pick's Disease, which as defined by WebMD, is a kind of dementia similar to Alzheimer's but far less common. It affects parts of the brain that controls emotions, behavior, personality, and language. Eventually the illness took control, and she had to be placed in a nursing home to receive the proper care. In October 2016, Velvet was given two weeks to live. Her family brought her home on hospice.

On January 4th, 2017, Velvet died surrounded by her immediate family. At the exact moment of her passing, the group performed a special ritual. It was led by her spiritual advisor Charlotte Pipes. Her children, husband, and sisters all participated.

Since announcement came of her passing, friends and colleagues have been sharing memories:

Author Christopher Penczak, a colleague and friend, recalls, "My last visit with her and some friends was at the New Orleans airport. She could not meet any other time during our visit, so she got up at an ungodly hour to have breakfast with us at the airport before we left. Even at dawn she was funny, smart, and inspiring. I will miss her."

Local witch Cairelle Perilloux, fondly remembers Velvet as an inspiration for her own work, calling her a tough lady but very generous. Perilloux recalls, "She took me to brunch, and I told her about my plan for the Witches' Ball and she was incredibly supportive and handed me a $100 bill and said, 'I believe in you and your vision. Get it going.' She was a great motivator."

Dorothy Morrison, a long-time family friend, said, "The Velvet I knew, though, was not only my friend, but the sister I wasn't granted at birth. We shared secrets and laughter and tears. We shared praline cheesecake, frozen Irish coffee, long walks through the French Quarter while singing, 'I Know What It Means to Miss New Orleans,' and never hugged goodbye without saying, 'I love you more than biscuits and gravy.' She was, without a doubt, one of my most cherished blessings, and I will miss her sorely."

Tamara Von Forslun said: "Of all the people met in the United States Velvet was the kindest, warmest and most caring person she had ever met, she was one in a million and shall be missed by all those that new her, and those that never had the good fortune to look into her eyes and know how much she cared about humanity. I love you sis. Merry we will Meet Again!"

Her son said, "I once told my mom, if I had to use an object to describe her it would be a piece of slate. Initially, she did not understand or like that answer. Then I explained. Slate is sedimentary. It is the culmination of many things that creates something stronger. Slate can be marked up and covered in anything and will always wipe clean. Mom was loved by many. I will miss her every day."

Although her life was cut short, Velvet Reith lived it to the fullest. As Morrison best said, she "was many things to many people." Velvet was a High Priestess, a magical practitioner, a teacher and lecturer, an activist, a prison chaplain, a dear friend, mother and wife. Her legacy is held steady by the many people she touched over the years, and it is entrenched in the vibrancy and growth of the New Orleans Pagan community.

That legacy will live on in the very spirit of community service and the devotion to family, both of which were at the heart of Velvet Reith's life.

"Now I lay me down to rest.
I know today I did my best.
Into the God and Goddess's care I'll be.
With the guardians watching over me."
    – Rev. Velvet Reith, My First Little Workbook of Wicca
What is remembered, lives.

Velvet Reith at the Tomb of Marie LaVeau

Phyllis Curott
Witch Elder
February 8th, 1954 -

Phillis Curott

A true spiritual pioneer, Phyllis Curott is one of America's first public Witches, an activist attorney, and author of 4 internationally best-selling books published in 14 languages; her YouTube series What is Wicca? has over 2,000,000 views, helping to introduce the world to Witchcraft and the Goddess. An outspoken advocate in the courts and media, she handled or consulted on ground-breaking cases securing the legal rights of Witches, including child custody, legally binding marriages, pentacles on military graves, gatherings in public places, wearing pentacles in schools and workplaces, religious holidays in schools and workplaces, religious assembly, organisation, expression and free speech.

In 2014 Phyllis was inducted into the esteemed Martin Luther King Jr. Collegium of Clergy and Scholars. She has also been honored by Jane Magazine as one of the Ten Gutsiest Women of the Year and received the One Spirit Seminary's 2018 Service to Humanity Award. TIME magazine published her IDEAS column, on the responsibility of the world's faiths to uphold the dignity and human rights of women, as one of America's "leading voices," and New York Magazine described her teaching as the culture's "next big idea."

Phyllis is the Vice Chair Emerita of the Parliament of the World's Religions and its first Wiccan Trustee. She is the creator of the historic 2015 Inaugural Women's Assembly and drafter of the Declaration for the Dignity and Human Rights of Women adopted by the 2015 Parliament. She was the Wiccan representative to the Harvard University Religious Pluralism Project's Consultation on Religious Discrimination and Accommodation, as well as the Wiccan representative to the Religions for the Earth Conference at Union Theological Seminary.

In the late 1970s Phyllis was a young social justice lawyer fighting organized crime in trade unions when a series of magical experiences and a profound sign from the Goddess, which tale she recounts in her internationally best-selling memoir, Book of Shadows, led her to a hidden coven of Witches in New York City. She began working with them and in 1981 Phyllis was initiated into the Mother Grove of the Minoan Sisterhood, a neo-Gardnerian Tradition with lineage through Ray Buckland to Gerald Gardner. She was simultaneously working with the now famous Brooklyn Group, the first drumming circle to practice the core shamanism of Dr. Michael Harner. Phyllis quickly discovered the 5,500-year-old shamanic roots of being a Wicce.

An early innovator, Phyllis intertwined ancient shamanic techniques with the modern revival of Witchcraft and founded the Temple of Ara in the early 1980s, America's first and oldest shamanic Wiccan tradition. For the last 20 years, she has cultivated a rapidly growing community in Italy which is expanding internationally through her online course, Awaken the Witch Within, for Hay House, and her webinars, Office Hours.

Quoting Noam Chomsky, if you're teaching the same thing now as you were five years ago either your field is dead or you are, Phyllis is a constantly questioning and questing priestess. In addition to the cultivation of Witchcraft's shamanic roots, her other notable contributions have been the deconstruction of patriarchal and Abrahamic remnants in the contemporary revivals of Witchcraft and critiquing notions of mechanical and manipulative magic, postures of commanding, controlling and using natural elements and spirits, and most notably, the fallacies of Threefold Law and Wiccan Rede. She offers a new foundation for Pagan and universal ethics called the First Principles rooted in the revealed wisdom of Nature as divine embodiment and has postulated new definitions and methods of magic, reconstructing common practices as methods of revelation and communion.

After a hiatus from the public limelight and a pilgrimage with the Green Man, Phyllis returned to writing, lecturing, and teaching internationally on the environmental crisis as a reflection of our spiritual crisis and the spiritual wisdom of Mother Earth as the key to the future of Life. Urging that the world needs its Witches, she is advocating for new levels of activism. Her current teaching offers a form of universal Witchcraft because just as you don't have to be Buddhist to meditate or Hindu to practice yoga, you don't have to be a Witch, or Wiccan, to benefit from its essential spiritual wisdom and practices.

Phyllis is First Officer Emerita of the Covenant of the Goddess and was responsible for spearheading the organization's notable presence at the first modern Parliament of the World's Religions in 1993, where Paganism was said to have "come out" on the global interfaith stage. She has continued to be active in the Interfaith movement and the Parliament. She also serves on the Advisory Board of Cherry Hill Seminary, the first Pagan seminary. Active in helping to make Witchcraft, Wicca and Paganism visible, acceptable and influential in mainstream culture, Curott speaks at universities, churches, organizations and conferences and has been widely profiled in the international media for almost 40 years.

Phyllis received her B.A. in philosophy from Brown University and her Juris Doctor from New York University Law School. She is currently creating The Witches Wisdom Tarot, a visionary deck with Hedgewitch and artist Danielle Barlow, September 2020, Hay House. She has begun her next book on the First Principles and her next memoir on her journeys with the Green Man.

Website: phylliscurott.com

Facebook: www.facebook.com/phylliscurott

Instagram: www.instagram.com/phylliscurott/

Awaken the Witch Within: www.hayhouseu.com/awaken-the-witch-within-online-course-hhu

Phyllis Curott Books:

- *Book of Shadows, A Modern Woman's Journey into the Wisdom of Witchcraft and the Magic of the Goddess, 20th Anniversary Edition,* 2019, Fourth Rune Books, New York
- *Book of Shadows, First Edition, Hard Cover,* 1998, Broadway Books/ Random House, New York
- *Witch Crafting: A Spiritual Guide to Making Magic,* 2001, Broadway Books/Random House, New York
- *The Love Spell: An Erotic Memoir of Spiritual Awakening,* 2005, Gotham/Penguin New York
- *WICCA Made Easy: Awakening the Divine Magic Within You,* 2018, Hay House UK, London
- *Awaken the Witch Within Online Course,* 2019. Hay House   www.hayhouseu.com/awaken-the-witch-within-online-course-hhu
- *The Witches' Wisdom Tarot with artist Danielle Barlow,* 2020, Hay House.

Phyllis Curott and Other Elders

Sam Webster
Mage Elder
1954 -

Sam Webster

Sam Webster, PhD, M.Div., Mage, hails from the Bay Area and has taught Magick publicly since 1984. He graduated from Starr King School for the Ministry at the Graduate Theological Union in Berkeley in 1993 and earned his doctorate at the University of Bristol, UK, studying Pagan history under Prof. Ronald Hutton. He is an Adept of the Golden Dawn, a cofounder of the Chthonic-Ouranian Templar order, and an initiate of Wiccan, Druidic, Buddhist, Hindu and Masonic traditions. His work has been published in journals such as Green Egg and Gnosis, and 2010 saw his first book "Tantric Thelema", establishing the publishing house Concrescent Press (www.Concrescent.net).

He was a member of Magical Acts Ritual Theatre and a founder of the Crescent Hellions, a Northern CA public ritual collective with Tara Webster, Laurie Lovekraft, Sharon Knight, and Winter.

In 2001 he founded the Open-Source Order of the Golden Dawn (http://OSOGD.org), which closed its doors in 2019 after initiating and raising adepts. Sam serves the Pagan community as a priest of Hermes (http://DigitalHerm.com).

Sam Webster was born in 1954 and like many who work magick, early on he discovered Tahuti, the ibis-headed Scribe God of the ancient Egyptians. Access to the Deva Loca, the Realm of the Gods, for him was almost reflexive due to his Pentecostal experience. He led Webster through much of the first decade of his study, exposing him to fundamental Magickal and illuminative experiences, including a full-blown theophany. Tehuti helped him with his hieroglyphic studies at the University of Chicago, gave Webster insights into Egyptian religious culture, and generally guided his way.

But while Webster was in seminary Tehuti 'told' him one day that Tehuti was too austere for the people that he was preparing himself to serve. So, He introduced Webster to Hermes.

Ever since then in the early 90s Hermes has been Webster's patron of art, teaching and guidance. Webster did not have much fortune with teachers. Most humans have something to teach him, in fact he has never found anyone who does not, but none have taken him on as a student. That intensive relationship has not manifested in his life. But Hermes took him in hand and in the way that only a Deity can He has slowly helped him to see and understand his experience. Webster bows in homage to his teacher.

As the community is maturing and they are rebuilding the Via Deorum, "the Way of the Gods", re-establishing the cults and priesthoods of the Old Gods, individuals will have to take on the task, or better, the duty of creating and maintaining those ways. Shortly after being introduced to Hermes, Webster discovered in Karl Kerenyi's book Hermes, Guide of Souls, that He was traditionally made offerings at the Dark of the Moon. So, on the mantlepiece of his tiny married student housing apartment he set up a stone and put out some fig newtons for Him. That was at the Dark Moon in January 1992. Ever since, and to the best of his knowledge without fail, Webster has been performing this rite, or rather the rite this practice evolved into.

Webster's spiritual life has been fortunate. Raised in a highly observant Catholic family, he had a solid inculcation in ritual sensibility. Even as a child he knew he had a calling to the priesthood. As it turned out, just not the Christian one. Webster's brother gave him a copy of Ram Dass' Be Here Now at age 12, beginning his long practice of inner yoga. He also brought home the Pentecostal infection. This was a critical part of my development. Ecstatic worship, shaped by Catholic ritual and dogma, authorized by Church and parents, it showed him the power and Divine presence that came when a community could invoke intensively. Weekly prayer meetings and the Life in the Spirit Seminar led to Baptism in the Holy Spirit and the manifestation of some of the gifts of the Spirit outlined in 1 Corinthians 12:8-10. Besides some interesting energy work amongst the Pentecostals, the more important phenomenon that shaped his spiritual growth was the profound and overwhelming experience of possession.

It came in a rather classic manner. In a prayer meeting when Webster was about 16 years old, during praise and after long rounds of song and prayer, then heat, light, and fantastic pressure enveloped his body, he could feel it entering him though the back of his neck. Words, "I love you, my children, I love you," were forced from his lips. It was Yahweh, and not the last time He made him speak. At many meetings thereafter He would come upon him, words would pour out of his mouth, and he had only the recollection that he had spoken. It was well received by the leaders and other authorities present, including his parents, but over time, he believes it wore on him. Webster began having dissociative experiences and certain inner conflicts brewed in the depths of his psyche. Eventually he did not want to be at the meetings. Webster felt alienated from the others there. His parents had become strangers, like pod people had taken away the harsh but rational people and had left these religiously obsessed manikins.

Later Webster would come to understand that Yahweh had dragged his soul into the Deva Loca in order to use his body as a mouthpiece. Unfortunately for Him, Webster already knew of other Gods. His paternal Grandmother had insisted that all the children were to read about the Classical Gods of Greece and Rome. Be Here Now had a two-page spread of Kali that him opened mind recognized as an expression of Divinity at least as true and holy as Jesus on the Cross. Later he recovered the memory, at best an approximation, where he had been dragged into a column of light in a space of infinite dark punctuated by many other columns of light. This column was Yahweh's and while He was using his body, he had a chance to look around. Since Webster was not entirely enthralled by Him, he saw the other Gods in Their columns of light. He feels they also saw him.

Once Webster had liberated himself from his family and the Christian religion, at first by the simple expedient of going to college, he found his way home to Paganism, and thereafter the Gods found him. As mentioned above, eventually he was introduced to Hermes, and since then he has been in His service, and has served our community in His name.

Sam Webster Works:

- *The Spell of Ra-Hoor-Khuit in Mezlim,* Beltane, 1990.
- *The House of Khabs in Mezlim,* Samhain, 1991.
- *Working Polytheism in Gnosis #28,* Spring 1993.
- *Structural Implications in the Sepherot in The Golden Dawn Journal, Book 2-- Qabalah: Theory and Magic.* Chic Cicero & Sandra Tabatha Cicero (eds.), 1994, Llewellyn Publications.
- *Pagan Dharma in Gnosis #39,* Spring, 1996.
- *Why I call Myself Pagan,* Reclaiming Quarterly, 1999.
- *Pagan Dharma 2,* PanGaea, 1999.
- *Tantric Thelema,* with Sam Webster, 2010, Concrescent Press

- *More than Human in Speculation, Heresy, and Gnosis in Contemporary Philosophy of Religion (Reframing Continental Philosophy of Religion)*. Joshua Ramey and Matthew S. Haar Farris, eds, Rli, 2016
- *The Principia of Theurgia or the Higher Magic in Commentaries on the Golden Dawn Flying Rolls. The Golden Dawn Community*, 2013, Kerubim Press
- *Offerings in Iamblichian Theurgy in Ritual Offerings: Feeding Your Spirits-Empowering Your Magic*. Aaron Leitch, ed., 2014, Nephilim Press
- *Iamblichus method of creating Theurgic Sacrifice in Platonic Pathways: Selected Papers from the Fourteenth Annual Conference of the International Society for Neoplatonic Studies*. John F Finamore and Danielle A. Layne eds., 2018, Prometheus Trust
- *A Practice Rooted in a Theophany of Thoth in A Silver Sun and Inky Clouds: A Devotional for Djehuty and Set*. Ashley Kent, Tatiana Matveeva eds., 2018, Bibliotheca Alexandrina

Dorothy Morrison
High Priestess-Witch
May 6th, 1955 -

Dorothy Morrison

Dorothy Morrison born May 6, 1955, in Columbus, Texas to a law enforcement officer and his wife, Morrison's maternal lineage includes William the Conqueror, Robert the Bruce of Scotland, a Kentucky Governor, the first Poet Laureate of Texas, and a charter member of the Texas Rangers. Raised Catholic, she attended parochial school and, at one time, even entertained the idea of becoming a nun. This was, of course, a short-lived plan. When the Pope decided that birth control – regardless of reason – was a heinous crime against humanity, she simply could not support his reasoning and begged her parents to allow her to attend a public high school. Her parents conceded to her desire, and she graduated from Columbus High School in 1973. It was at this point that her mother introduced her to the Tarot. Morrison then moved to Houston, where she was introduced to Wicca.

Eventually, Morrison moved to California – where she furthered her studies in Wicca – and from there to Missouri. While in Missouri, she discovered archery, and during her second year on the circuit, held three state championship titles. During that time, her writing career began to bud. In addition to writing for journals and quarterlies such as: The Crone Chronicles, Circle Network News, and numerous other Pagan publications; she joined the staff of several bow hunting magazines.

Morrison is an author and teacher in the fields of Magic, Wicca and Neopaganism. She is a Third-Degree Wiccan High Priestess and Elder of the Georgian Tradition and Founded the "Coven of the Crystal Garden" in 1986. Dorothy is a member of the Coven of the Raven, and as an Initiate study the "RavenMyst Circle" Tradition. Morrison has taught students in eight states and also in Australia. But since her true focus has always been on magic and its application to everyday living, she now considers herself to be nothing more than a Witch – a title that she not only embraces but wears proudly.

Morrison is an expert archer, a former staff writer for several bow-hunting magazines, and winner of three State Championship titles Arkansas, Tennessee, and Illinois. Morrison is a constant advocate for the protection and proper care of both wildlife and domestic animals. She has also been an administrator for the Humane Society for several years. Though initially an unexpected hardship, this allowed Morrison to pursue her writing career full time.

Dorothy is a member of the Pagan Poets Society and a charter member of M.A.G.I.C., a magical writers and artists organisation. Her work has been published in many journals and magazines, including Circle Network News, Sage Woman, and Crone Chronicles. Morrison presently lives near New Orleans with her husband Mark and their black Lab, Dixie. Morrison is the proprietress of "Wicked Witch Studios" – an online store specializing in handcrafted items designed for Witches of discriminating taste – and the creator of the effective but easy to use Hexology and Wicked Witch Mojo occult lines. Dorothy continues to travel with her book meet and greets, and give lectures, talks and workshops on Paganism.

I was lucky to have met Dorothy Morrison at the NOLA Festival to help Velvet Reith with her mission to help with the catastrophe after Cyclone Katrina. Along with many others we feel we helped enough to make a difference in New Orleans if only a little.

Dorothy Morrison's Works:

- *Bud, Blossom & Leaf: The Magical Herb Gardener's Handbook*, 2001, Llewellyn Publications
- *The Craft: A Witch's Book of Shadows*, 2001, Llewellyn Publications
- *The Craft Companion: A Witch's Journal*, 2001, Llewellyn Publications
- *Dancing the Goddess Incarnate: Living the Magic of Maiden, Mother & Crone*, with Kristin Madden, 2006, Llewellyn Publications

- *Enchantments of the Heart: A Magical Guide to Finding the Love of Your Life*, 2002, Career Books
- *Everyday Magic: Spells & Rituals for Modern Living*, 2002, Llewellyn Publications
- *Everyday Moon Magic: Spells & Rituals for Abundant Living*, 2004, Llewellyn Publications
- *Everyday Sun Magic: Spells & Rituals for Radiant Living*, 2005, Llewellyn Publications
- *Everyday Tarot Magic: Meditation & Spells*, 2003, Llewellyn Publications
- *In Praise of the Crone*, 1999, Llewellyn Publications
- *Magical Needlework*, 2002, Llewellyn Publications
- *Yule: A Celebration of Light and Warmth*, 2000, Llewellyn Publications
- *Whimsical Tarot Deck/Book Set with Book*, 2000, U.S. Games Systems

Tamara Von Forslun
Tribe of the Crow – Clan of Boskednan
High Priestess – Witch Elder
November 23rd, 1956 –

Tamara Von Forslun

Tamara Von Forslun, born in Victoria Park, Perth, Western Australia on the 23rd of November 1956. Dubbed by Raymond Buckland in the early 80s as The Witch of Oz has been involved in the Craft and teaching Wicca and Witchcraft for over 50 years, she is considered one of the world's respected Wiccan Elders and is the Founder and Creator of Australia's first legal Neo-Pagan Church "The Church of Wicca" (Australia 1989), Clan of Boskednan Elder (1978), Priestess of the Fellowship of Isis (1981), and the Arch Priestess of the Aquarian Tabernacle Church in Australia (1991). Also accepted as Elder of the Grey Council (2020).

Tamara then at the age of 14 met a gentleman at the "Mediterranean Restaurant" in Subiaco, where she worked, his name was David, and he had a Coven in the foothills of Perth called the Coven of Draconis and invited her to attend. She did attend their Festivities and found it was exactly what she was looking for; also, the people were exceptionally friendly and helpful in her endeavors. Tamara remained and was Initiated into this Coven on the 26th of June 1970 by David the Fifth who was the High Priest, and his High Priestess was Lady

Margaret deLille Quinn who was a Blood Wicche or better known as a Hereditary Wicche originally from Penzance, Boskednan in Cornwall who had met and married an academic named Adrian Reinman and they moved to Berlin, (his home) then Hertzberg in Germany. When the onset of WW2 came about, they went back to her home in Boskednan, Cornwall. When Quinn's husband died, she decided to move to Fremantle, Australia.

Von Forslun, being 14 years old, was Initiated into this Coven on the 26th of June 1971. After a couple of years of being with this Coven, David the 5th got terribly ill and eventually passed into the Summerland's. Von Forslun was then in a documentary (Supernatural Influences) with her best friend and fellow Witch Astra, as they were both professional dancers. They did the documentary and were approached by an Alexandrian High Priest named Simon Goodman (Ian Watts), of which they met with him and were invited to attend his circle, of which Von Forslun accepted, but Astra declined due to the fact she did not like him at all. So again, Von Forslun met with the fellow Coveners especially their High Priestess, Michelin. Von Forslun absolutely loved this Lady and respected her immensely as a Wiccan Mother figure. Coming across from her original coven (The Coven of Draconis) she came with fellow Coveners Margaret De Lille Quin and daughter Layla and Dorrie Flatman.

Lady Margaret De Lille Quin

Von Forslun was Initiated into the Coven of the Acorn on the 18th of September 1973 at the age of 17 years of age, (which later changed its name to Quercus Covenantus) and started on her training as an Alexandrian Witch. But after several years and due to politics and the non-disclosure of many questions that were asked but never answered Von Forslun along with a few other Wiccans decided to started up their own Coven (actually re-awakening the old one) with her High Priest, Imhotep (who Initiated by Maxine and Alex Sanders to the level of 3rd was degree) in Victoria Park, three doors down from the Freemasons Lodge. It was small but a happily working group. Von Forslun then purchased her first property in Mundijong, a small farm that was perfect for her lifestyle and her Coven to grow and learn. Both Imhotep and Tamara worked together for many years until it became too far a distance for Imhotep to travel due to his ill health. They did continue working together with Lady Elizabeth and David Mosley as a higher group of four, for about nine years working on High

Magick, separate from their individual covens. Von Forslun under her Magical name of Avena became a member of the Fellowship of Isis in 1978 and was later also Ordained a High Priestess at the Fellowship of Isis at Clonegal Castle in Ireland by Lady Olivia and Lord Lawrence Durden-Robertson in 1981. It was also around this time that she met with Rhiannon Ryall (priestess and author) who trained her in West Green Witchcraft.

Von Forslun started working alone without a High Priest and after a lot of money, legal endeavors, and many years of fighting the establishment and trying to legalize Wicca as a religion in Australia, eventually founded and had legalized at a federal level, Australia's first legal Neo-Pagan Church, "The Church of Wicca" in 1989. This was a great transition as it meant that Witches could not be prosecuted in Australia anymore, as it was still illegal in certain parts of Australia especially Queensland and Western Australia up until the 80s and if you were a Tarot reader you were also targeted under the Fraud Act.

Through Von Forslun's ambitions to make it recognized both federally, and by local authorities she endeavored to have more and more contact with the media due to the help of her friend Terry Willesee, of the Willesee media family. Where she did several documentaries, and hundreds of interviews on TV shows such as "The Midday Show", "The Ray Martin Show", "Mike Willesee Show", and several more, and at least 3 interviews a week on radio. Through this media connection she had contacts Australia wide and met up with fellow High Priestesses from other states who wanted to be a part of the Church of Wicca and the Tribe of the Crow, and so several Churches were set up in Queensland with Lady Brianna; New South Wales with Lady Mara; Victoria with Lady Mystl and in Western Australia eventually many High Priests and High Priestesses who hived off and formed their own individual covens from her Clan of Boskednan from the line of Quinn of Penzance. Lady Elizabeth, Lord Ariston, Lord Richardt, Lady Sharadon, Lady Tree, Lord Pilgrim, Lord Petrus, Lady Kundra, Lord Sylvanus, Lady Jade, Lord Palin, many dozens of Ordained Priests and Priestesses, and hundreds of Initiated Witches and Seekers.

Von Forslun also became the first and only legal Wiccan Marriage Celebrant in Australia and was always travelling interstate marrying Wiccan couples and also non-Wiccan couples who just loved her ceremony. Also, Von Forslun reached out and was Ordained 3rd Degree by Pete Pathfinder of the ATC and became Arch Priestess of The Aquarian Tabernacle Church (ATC) Australia. From 1991 she became a Chaplain at prisons and hospitals around Australia and would venture to those who asked for her services, where she also did Correspondence Courses for inmates Australia wide that wanted to study Wicca. She became quite recognizable as an award-winning marriage celebrant and officiated at hundreds of weddings and just as many funerals. Von Forslun was also an Advocate for the Protection of all wildlife and also the natural flora. She became a financial supporter of "Make a Wish Foundation", "Malcolm Sargent Cancer Fund for Children" and an avid supporter for "Sea Shepherd".

Being a Naturopath and Professional Herbalist, Von Forslun had a successful two-story Wiccan, Herbal and New Age store in Fremantle, Western Australia, called "The Alchemist" which was also the largest organic herbal store in Australia. With all alternative medicines, Wiccan products and much, much more. Von Forslun also hosted for Fiona Horne on 2 occasions with the publishing of her first two books at her shop, which was the largest gathering Fiona had. Von Forslun funded and supported financially The Church of Wicca through its complete life cycle, by running many training nights such as Outer Courts, Festivals and also had published a quarterly magazine called "Spirit Earth Magazine" which was distributed Nationally and became quite popular, and within a couple of years had a distribution of over 12,000. Through lack of support with the magazine she eventually sold it to "Insight Magazine" and continued writing for them for a few years.

Von Forslun due to being not so disciplined in meditation sought out a Buddhist Retreat and started learning meditation at a deeper level by a Buddhist monk named Saddhatessa (Derek Crowther). It was through Saddhatessa that Von Forslun met His Holiness the Dalai Lama, and they became acquaintances and kept in touch where Von Forslun and her personal Clan of Boskednan worked to assist with his visits in Australia, especially in security and finances. The Dalai Lama befriended Von Forslun by gifting to her his meditation prayer beads which were made of amber beads and jade carved images, and His Holiness nicknamed her "The Vicar of Wicca".

In a ceremony after her sister Layla was killed in an accident on the 28th of May 1982, Lady Margaret DeLille Quin officially adopted Tamara as her daughter and heir to the line of Boskednan. Sadly, her mentor and spiritual grandmother passed away in 2002, as she had no more need for the physical and just wanted to be with her daughter Layla. Merry We will Meet Again Ma! Von Forslun was always involved in environmental issues and held some of the biggest Pagan gatherings in Australia for "World Peace", "Peace on Earth Day", "Earth Alignment Day", "The Rites of Spring Festival", "Pagans in the Park", "The Witches Ball". Von Forslun was a great supporter of Greenpeace, Sea Shepherd, and was a contributor to the new ship the "Steve Irwin", as well as supported His Holiness on his visits to Australia for over 11 years and was dubbed by him "The Vicar of Wicca".

Due to politics and deceitful people trying to bring down Von Forslun, she eventually sold her shop in Fremantle in 2000 and stepped down from the Church of Wicca handing it over to Lady Amaris, her High Priestess in 2009. She felt that her legacy was in safe hands and with new blood and would flourish and bring newer connections to modern Wicca and those that were in search of the Goddess and God and the mysteries that Wicca teaches. But alas, it was also too much for her and she closed down the Church of Wicca in 2012 and went back to the old ways of having just a small suburban coven in a backyard. Lady Amaris had her reasons.

Von Forslun is still actively the Elder High Priestess of the Tribe of the 9 Maidens – Clan of Boskednan worldwide. Von Forslun through her myriad travels worldwide has learnt from the likes of Lady Margaret, her spiritual grandmother; David the 5th, a traditional Witch; Lady Elizabeth a Traditional Bush Witch; Rhiannon Ryall a Village and Green Witch; Imhotep and Simon Goodman as Alexandrian Witches; Pete Pathfinder a Gardnerian Witch and Founder of the ATC; Velvet Reith a Voudoun Priestess; His Holiness the Dalai Lama; Ariston her High Priest that taught her so very much about going within; Jubabe a Shaman from South America; and most importantly her mother Valma who was a Love Goddess and loved everyone and everything.

Von Forslun's series of books disclose everything that she has ever learnt at great depth during her awfully long and hard life. Along the way all that she has learnt, she has passed on freely to those who would listen and learn. Her classes, teachings, Outer Courts, Facilitations at Universities around the world, and open festivals were teaching the truth about Witchcraft. Von Forslun now at the end of her earthly cycle as a teacher reveals all she has ever learnt as a student of Magic, Witchcraft, Shamanism, Wicca, Tarot and Herbal Medicine in her books. If you wish to know all about Tamara's life, read her autobiography titled "The Magic Circle of My Life - Tamara Von Forslun, The Witch of Oz" autobiography.

At The Entrance to My Magic Circle

Tamara Von Forslun – Witch of Oz Books & Decks:

- *Complete Teachings of Wicca for the Seeker*, Twisted Souls Press
- *The Witches Coven – Tools & Activities*, Balboa Press
- *Tarot Mysteries of Thoth – Initiation & Inner Alchemy*, Balboa Press
- *The Little Witchling*, Bella Donna
- *Pagan and Witch Elders of the World – Past & Present*
- *The Divine Feminine – Goddess of 10,000 Names*
- *Oracles of the Divine Feminine – Goddesses of the World (50 Oracle Card Boxset with 125-page booklet)* www.tamaravonforslun.com

www.facebook.com/spirittalkaustralia

www.witchofoz.com

Scott Cunningham
High Priest-Witch Elder
June 27th, 1956 – March 28th, 1993

Scott Cunningham

Scott Douglas Cunningham was born on June 27th, 1956, in Royal Oak, Michigan, USA. Cunningham was the second son of Chester Grant Cunningham and Rose Marie Wilhoit Cunningham, his siblings were Greg and younger sister Christine. Due to his mother's ill health and with the advice of her doctors they moved the family to warmer climate to San Diego, California in the Autumn of 1959.

Cunningham lived in San Diego all of his life, and later with his wife Rose Marie owned and operated a small shop in Spring Valley called "Mystic Moon". With the passing of his wife Cunningham lost interest and gave up the shop to focus on his own health and also his ability to write. Cunningham had studied creative writing at the San Diego University, where he enrolled in 1978, and only after two years he had published more works than several of his professors, and so decided to drop out of Uni to write full-time. Cunningham during this time had a roommate, who was the Magical author named Donald Michael Kraig who often socialized with Witchcraft author Raymond Buckland, who was also at that time living in San Diego.

Cunningham started training in 1980 under the guidance of Raven Grimassi and remained as a 1st degree Witch until 1982, when he decided to leave the tradition to pursue Witchcraft as a Solitary practitioner. Cunningham practiced basic Wicca, and worshipped alone, and through his book series for solitaries described several instances in which he worshipped with friends and teachers alike. Cunningham also believed that Wicca being a closed and secretive Tradition up until the 1950s should become more open to newcomers. He was also drawn to Hawaiian Huna and a range of new movements and concepts that highly influenced and added to his personal Pagan spirituality.

Cunningham became the first new Age Witch by adding snippets from all his eclectic interests, as he was an expert in herbalism, of which he had a substantial herb garden that he cared for as his Goddess aspect within Nature. His deep connection with Nature brought him closer to the Divine Feminine and as an author of several books on Wicca and other alternative religious subjects. His work Wicca: A Guide for the Solitary Practitioner, is one of the most successful books ever published. Now as a good and close friend to Raymond Buckland and also being a member of the "Serpent Stone Family", where he also received his 3rd Degree Initiation in that Coven.

Cunningham was diagnosed with Lymphoma, which he successfully fought and overcame, but in 1990 whilst on a speaking tour in Massachusetts, he suddenly became ill and was diagnosed with cryptococcal meningitis. Cunningham suffered from several related infections and died on March 28, 1993, at the early age of only 36.

Scott Cunningham's Works:

- *Shadow of Love,* 1980 (fiction)
- *Magical Herbalism: The Secret Craft of the Wise,* 1982
- *Earth Power: Techniques of Natural Magic,* 1983
- *Cunningham's Encyclopedia of Magical Herbs,* 1985
- *The Magical Household: Spells and Rituals for the Home* with David Harrington, 1987
- *Cunningham's Encyclopedia of Crystal, Gem, and Metal Magic,* 1987
- *The Truth About Witchcraft Today,* 1988
- *Wicca: A Guide for the Solitary Practitioner,* 1988
- *The Complete Book of Incense, Oils & Brews,* 1989
- *Magical Aromatherapy: The Power of Scent,* 1989
- *Earth, Air, Fire, and Water: More Techniques of Natural Magic,* 1991
- *The Magic in Food,* 1991
- *Cunningham's Encyclopedia of Wicca in the Kitchen,* 1993
- *Divination For Beginners,* 1993
- *Living Wicca: A Further Guide for the Solitary Practitioner,* 1993
- *Spell Crafts: Creating Magical Objects* with David Harrington, 1993
- *The Truth About Herb Magic,* 1993
- *The Truth About Witchcraft,* 1994

- *Hawaiian Magic and Spirituality*, 1995
- *Pocket Guide to Fortune Telling*, 1997
- *Dreaming the Divine: Techniques for Sacred Sleep*, 1999
- *Cunningham's Book of Shadows: The Path of An American Traditionalist*, 2009 (A rediscovered manuscript written by Cunningham in the late 1970s or early 1980s)

Silver Ravenwolf
High Priestess-Witch Elder
September 11th, 1956 -

Silver Ravenwolf

Born Jenine Trayer – Silver Ravenwolf was born on the 11th of September 1956 and was raised in Pennsylvania. From an early age had visions of angels and a deep fascination with Tarot Cards and all tools of divining. Ravenwolf in 1991 received her 1st Degree Initiation from Bried Foxsong of "Sacred Hart" and is on the rolls of the International Red Garters, where she took the name Silver Ravenwolf. Ravenwolf also went 2nd and 3rd Degree in the "Temple of Hecate Triskele of the Caledonii Tradition". In June 1996 Ravenwolf was Initiated into the "Serpent Stone Family" Coven in North Carolina, and since also was Ordained as a High Priestess within that Coven as was Scott Cunningham.

Ravenwolf's hearthstone Coven is known as "Coven of the Omega Wolf". She is the leader of the "Black Forest Circle and Seminary", an organisation containing 38 clans and covens spanning the United States and Canada. Ravenwolf has appeared as a lecturer and workshop facilitator at events in the Neo-Pagan community. She has been active in Wiccan anti-discrimination issues. She is also a Powwower, having adopted the Pennsylvania Dutch practice in a Neo-Pagan context. Ravenwolf is the author of over 17 books on Wicca and Paganism in general and as busy as she is Ravenwolf is the mother of four beautiful children. She has also written several novels. Currently her books have been translated in Czech, Spanish, Italian, German, Russian, Hungarian, Dutch, and Portuguese. She is the director of the "Wiccan/Pagan Press Alliance Midnight Drive".

Silver Ravenwolf's Works:

- *American Folk Magick: Charms, Spells & Herbals*, 1999, Llewellyn Publications
- *Angels: Companions in Magick*, 2002, Llewellyn Publications
- *Halloween: Spells, Recipes & Customs*, 1999, Llewellyn Publications
- *HedgeWitch: Spells, Crafts & Rituals for Natural Magick*, 2008, Llewellyn Publications
- *Hex Craft: Dutch Country Pow-wow Magick*, 1997, Llewellyn Publications
- *Journey of Souls: Case Studies of Life Between Lives* by Michael Newton (introduction by Silver Ravenwolf), 2002, Llewellyn Publications
- *Mindlight: Secrets of Energy, Magick & Manifestation*, 2006, Llewellyn Publications
- *Silver's Spells for Abundance*, 2004, Llewellyn Publications
- *Silver's Spells for Love*, 2001, Llewellyn Publications
- *Silver's Spells for Protection*, 2000, Llewellyn Publications
- *TeenWitch!: Wicca for a New Generation*, 1998, Llewellyn Publications
- *To Light a Sacred Flame: Practical Witchcraft for the Millennium*, 2002, Llewellyn Publications
- *To Ride a Silver Broomstick: New Generation Witchcraft*, 2002, Llewellyn Publications
- *To Stir a Magick Cauldron: A Witch's Guide to Casting and Conjuring*, 2005, Llewellyn Publications
- *Solitary Witch: The Ultimate Book of Shadows for the New Generation*, 2003, Llewellyn Publications
- *Witches Runes: Insights from the Old European Magickal Traditions (Cards)* with Nigel Jackson, 2002, Llewellyn Publications
- *A Witch's Notebook: Lessons in Witchcraft*, 2005, Llewellyn Publications

Edain McCoy
Witch and Author
1957 – March 22nd, 2019

Edain McCoy became a self-initiated Witch in 1981 and has been an active part of the Pagan community since her formal Initiation into a large San Antonio coven in 1983. Edain has researched alternative spiritualities since her teens when she was first introduced to the Kabbalah (Jewish Mysticism). Since that time, she has studied a variety of Magickal paths including Celtic, Appalachian Folk Magic, and Curanderism (a Mexican-American fold tradition). Today Edain is part of the Wittan Irish Pagan Tradition, where she is a Priestess of Brighid and an Elder.

Edain is an alumnus of the University of Texas with a BA in history, she is affiliated with several professional writer's organization's and occasionally presents workshops on Magical topics or works individually with students who wish to study Witchcraft.

Edain was formerly a woodwind player for the Lynchburg (VA) Symphony Orchestra with claims that both the infamous feuding McCoy family of Kentucky and Sir Roger Williams, the seventeenth century religious dissenter, as branches of her ethnically diverse family tree. In Edain's "real life" Edain worked as a licensed stockbroker until her passing on the 22nd of March 2019.

Edain Books:

- *Celtic Women's Spirituality*, 2015, Llewellyn
- *A Witches Moon: A Collection of Lunar Magick & Rituals*, 2012
- *If You Want to be a Witch*, 2004
- *Advanced Witchcraft*, 2004
- *Sabbats: A Witch's Approach to Living the Old Ways*, 2002, Llewellyn
- *Celtic Myth and Magick*, 2002
- *A Witches Guide to Faery Folk: How to Work with the Elemental World*, 2002, Llewellyn
- *Astral Projection for Beginners*, 1999
- *In a Graveyard at Midnight: Folk Magic and Wisdom from the Heart of Appalachia*, 1995

- *Ostara: Customs, Spells & Rituals for the Rites of Spring*, 2002
- *Advanced Witchcraft: Go Deeper, Reach Further, Fly Higher*, 2004
- *The Healing Power of Faery: Working with Elementals & nature Spirits to Soothe the Body and Soul*, 2008, Llewellyn
- *Mountain Magick: Folk Wisdom from the Heart of Appalachia*, 1997, Llewellyn.
- *Astral Projection for Beginners: Six Techniques for Travelling to Other Realms*, 2012.
- *Making Magick: For Wiccans and Pagans*, 2002
- *If You Want to Be a Witch: A practical Introduction to the Craft*, 2013
- *The Witches Coven*, 2003
- *Bewitchments: Love Magick for Modern Romance*, 2000
- *Witta: An Irish Pagan Tradition*, 1993, Llewellyn
- *How to do Automatic Writing*, 2002, Llewellyn
- *Entering the Summerland*, 1996
- *Inside a Witches Coven*, 2003, Llewellyn
- *Past Life & Karmic Tarot*, 2004
- *Enchantments: 200 Spells for Bath & Beauty Enhancement*, 2001
- *Lady of the Night: Llewellyn*, 1990
- *Spellworking for Covens: Magick for Two*, 2002
- *Magick and Rituals of the Moon*, 2001

Melissa "Rose" Anderson
High Priestess and Witch Elder
1959 -

Melissa Anderson

Director of "Circle of Ancient Sisters, Inc." (Established and Founded 1978) a Khemetic Magic Tradition, Author of 3 books, BA in Psychology and an associate's in business and finance (Colorado State University). Cultural Anthropology (Panteion University, Athens, Greece). Currently Anderson is involved with "The Grand Command Union", "Fellowship of Isis", "Mother of Dynio Mwyn", "Welsh Traditional Witchcraft", Arch Priestess "Hemet Netjeri Ma'at", Head of "Houses of Kemet International Kemetic Faith", member of the "Egyptian Masonic Order of the Ancient and Primitive Rites of Memphis and Misraim", and advisor to several others. Former State Director of Intercultural Exchange Students under guidance of the "US Department of Education, Bureau of Cultural Affairs:" Founder of the Witches Brew Magazine, The Cauldron Radio, The International Pagan Music Association (Pagan Music Award) and several orders stemming from the "Houses of Kemet".

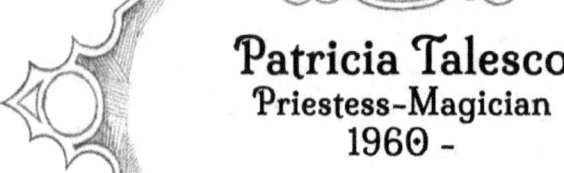

Patricia Talesco
Priestess-Magician
1960 -

Patricia "Trish" Telesco was born in 1960. What an amazing lady who I had the privilege to meet at the NOLA Festival in New Orleans run by Velvet Reith. Telesco began her Wiccan education and Initiation on her own, but later received Initiation in the Stregha tradition of Italy. She is a trustee for the "Universal Federation of Pagans", and member of the "Authors Guild", a member of the "Society for Creative Anachronism" and a professional member of the "Wiccan-Pagan Press Alliance".

Telesco is an American author, herbalist, poet, lecturer, Wiccan Priestess and Folk Magician, who has amazingly written more than 60 books on a variety of subjects ranging from self-help and cookbooks to magic, folklore and global religion. Articles by Telesco have appeared in several mainstream publications such as Cosmo, Women's World and Cats magazine, and in such Neo-Pagan publications such as Circle Network News and popular websites such as The Witches Voice.

Telesco has appeared on several television segments including "Sightings" and "National Geographic Today" and "Solstice Celebrations". She has also appeared at major events in the New Age and Neopagan Communities such as Starwood Festival and Pagan Spirit Gathering. Telesco also runs a small mail-order business called "Hourglass Creations", and lives with her husband and three sons in Western New York. At one stage her husband was looked at transferring with his work to Melbourne, Australia but that didn't eventuate.

Patricia Telesco Books:

- *Cat Magic: Mews, Myths, and Mystery*, 1999, Destiny Books
- *A Charmed Life*, 2000, New Page Books
- *The Cyber Spellbook: Magick in the Virtual World*, 2000, New Page Books
- *An Enchanted Life: An Adept's Guide to Masterful Magick*, 2001, New Page Books

- *A Floral Grimoire: Plant Charms, Spells, Recipes, and Rituals*, 2001, Citadel
- *Futuretelling: A Complete Guide to Divination*, 1998, Crossing Press
- *Ghosts, Spirits and Hauntings*, 1999, Crossing Press
- *Goddess in My Pocket: Simple Spells, Charms, Potions, and Chants to Get You Everything You Want*, 1998, Harper San Francisco
- *Healer's Handbook: A Holistic Guide to Wellness in the New Age*, 1997, Weiser Books
- *The Herbal Arts: A Handbook of Gardening, Recipes, Healing, Crafts, and Spirituality*, 1998, Citadel
- *How To Be a Wicked Witch: Good Spells, Charms, Potions and Notions for Bad Days*, 2000, Fireside
- *The Kitchen Witch Companion: Simple and Sublime Culinary Magic*, 2005, Citadel
- *Kitchen Witch's Guide to Brews and Potions*, 2005, New Page Books
- *Labyrinth Walking: Patterns of Power*, 2001, Citadel
- *The Language of Dreams*, 1997, Crossing Press
- *A Little Book of Love Magic*, 1999, Crossing Press
- *A Little Book of Mirror Magic: Meditations, Myths, Spells*, 2003, Crossing Press
- *The Magick of Folk Wisdom*, 2000, Book Sales
- *Mastering Candle Magick*, 2003, New Page Books
- *Mirror, Mirror: Reflections of the Sacred Self*, 1999, Book World
- *Money Magick: How to Use Magick to Gain Prosperity*, 2001, New Page Books
- *Seasons of the Sun: Celebrations from the World's Spiritual Traditions*, 1996, Atrium Publishers Group
- *Shaman in a 9 to 5 World*, 2000, The Crossing Press
- *Spinning Spells, Weaving Wonders: Modern Magic for Everyday Life*, 1996, Crossing
- *The Teen Book of Shadows: Star Signs, Spells, Potions, and Powers* ,2004, Citadel
- *365 Goddess: A Daily Guide to the Magic and Inspiration of the Goddess*, 1998, Harper One
- *A Victorian Grimoire: Romance - Enchantment – Magic*, 2002, Llewellyn Publications
- *The Wiccan Web: Surfing the Magic on the Internet*, 2001, Citadel
- *Wishing Well: Empowering Your Hopes and Dreams*, 1997, Crossing Press
- *A Witch's Beverages and Brews*, 2000, Career Press
- *The Witch's Book of Wisdom*, 2003, Citadel
- *Your Book of Shadows: How to Write Your Own Magickal Spells*, 2000, Citadel

Rev. "Mama Vic" Wright
Clan of Boskednan Elder and High Priestess
9th July 1961 -

Rev. "Mama" Vic Wright

Rev. "Mama Vic" Vic Wright of Circle Sanctuary has served the Pagan community for most of her life. Discovering earth-based traditions and the Goddess at an incredibly young age. In high school Vic was often sought out by friends and classmates who she helped understand and navigate the world around them using some unique methods. Vic received BAs in Music, Psychology and Christian studies, where she combined these skills to create a safe loving space that drew children and adults alike.

"Mama Vic" as she is called has spent the last 40 plus years ministering to youth and adults providing judgement free, education, compassion, and assistance. She helps others celebrate themselves. To truly look at who they are and be thankful for all the good while learning from the challenges in their lives without being defined by them. She is always there with a kind word or a well-placed kick in the butt. Mama Vic uses a variety of different tools in teaching about the Pagan Path.

Pathfinding exercises to retrain behavior that is negative or harmful such as self-worth, self-image, self-respect, self-belief, self-independence, or self-reliance. Mama Vic also helps with Family mediation to help everyone get on the same page is another of her respected tools. By far the most different tool she uses is role playing games. Anything from chess which builds problem solving, thinking ahead, and critical thinking to name a few. Magic, the Gathering which teaches those who play about the Elements - earth, air, fire, water, Spirit, ancestors, healing, thinking about the consequences of their choices before they act. Mama Vic teaches them how to learn to respond instead of reacting.

Mama Vic also uses AD&D to help them create a character that represents them. Sometimes it's exactly like them and other times the exact opposite or somewhere in between. She encourages them to work through their issues using game play. If they are mad at the world, then act it out in the game, learn coping skills they need in a game, where the consequences are not life-changing or debilitating so they learn coping skills whilst playing a game. Mama Vic teaches and guides them how to start working on it until they figure it all out before acting on it in the "real world".

Vic currently resides in Kentucky; however, she spends much of her time traveling to pagan festivals and fairs spreading love, acceptance and Magick wherever she goes.

I first met Mama Vic at a PSG festival, where she approached me in wheelchair to the authors booth and where she bought my books. After chatting with her for a while, I knew that she was a special lady. She spent her entire Pagan life caring or and guiding others, mostly children. She invited me to her marquee, which I might add was huge, it was divided up into sections with the front selling crystals and pagan items, the back for fellowship and living, and then to the side was a marquee set up with long tables and chairs with over 20 children and young adults, with a myriad of games for them to play. Unlike many pagans that focus on teaching and training adults, Mama Vic dedicated her life to the guidance of children and young adults on their personal journeys. Mama Vic is a Goddess sent Priestess that the entire community needs, as she supports families, and all that need her services. She is a true servant of the Goddess and to the entire Pagan and Wiccan community. Spending much of her life in a wheelchair, she still soldiers on with her lifetime partner and wife, always in service to the community.

Talyn Songdog
Wizard & Pagan Elder
1963 -

Talyn Songdog born in 1963 was introduced to the field of Wizardry by a high school science teacher, Talyn refined his philosophies and magickal skills in a variety of working groups, especially including DragonTree Grove, Church of All Worlds, Phoenix Festivals, Clan Ravenmyst, and apprenticeships to Sir Tarl Mapt, Morning Glory Zell-Ravenheart, and Lady Ravenweed. Moving from a background of Eclectic Celtic Wiccan studies to progressively more shamanic approaches, most of his experience is from doing rather than studying. Also following a Warrior path, Talyn has worked as a Guardian protector of the neo-Pagan community at many festivals across the United States. In keeping with his Trickster path, he is also known for maintaining an aura of mirth, especially when things appear to be most dire.

Gavin Bone
High Priest-Witch Elder
January 19th, 1964 -

Photograph of Gavin Bone

Gavin Bone, born on the 19th of January, was brought up in Portsmouth, Hempshire. His mother regularly visited mediums and tarot readers, which was a major influence in his interest in the occult and Witchcraft. He attended several conferences and events in Portsmouth on the unexplained, which made him become more interested in everything from UFOs to the Surrey Puma, Ghosts, and the Bermuda Triangle.

Bone pursued his career in the British Army but was unable to go into a regular service and served in 219 Wessex General Hospital RAMC (V) instead where he trained as regular nurse. He eventually left because of his political beliefs. He became involved with groups such as Greenpeace from 1981 and also became interested in Wicca during this same period, having previously explored Buddhism, Hinduism, and Taoism. He also started to train as a spiritual healer, after he had attended "The Joseph Carey Spiritualist Centre". He practiced solitary from 1982 before finding his first magical group in 1985 working from the "Fifth Dimension Occult" store in Eastney, Portsmouth. His group was eclectic and included earth healing practices as well as High Magic. It was from this group that the first coven he joined emerged, which was based off "Buckland's Seax Wicca". He was later Initiated into a Gardnerian based tradition.

Following his attendance to Link-Up 89 (September 1989) in Groby, Leicester, Gavin became involved in Pagan Link as a contact and facilitator for Portsmouth, and his wife Tania Andrade. They regularly held moots in Portsmouth, in the Milton area, and from this a small coven naturally developed of no specific tradition. He later became a contact for the Pagan Federation as it expanded its contact network. He and his wife also became part of Clan Bran, which is a clan of eclectic practitioners. It was based on Abbots Bromley Leicestershire before it moved to the Republic of Ireland.

Being trained as a registered nurse, and also studying complimentary healing techniques such as reflexology. He eventually was initiated into Buckland's Seax Wicca, and was involved in the revival of British/Anglo-Saxon traditional shamanism in the late 1980s through a web site called Pagan Link. He is currently developing the theory that Wicca may have some roots in tribal shamanistic healing traditions, as opposed to medieval ritual magic.

Bone first met Janet Farrar and Stewart Farrar in 1989 at a Pagan camp at Groby, near Leicester, where they became friends. He accompanied them on a tour to the United States in 1992, and after their return he moved to Ireland and became business partners. He joined the Farrar's as part of a "polyfidelitous" relationship, and they continued their personal and professional relationship since Stewart's death on the 7th of February 2000. He has co-authored many books with the Farrar's, and he is the production manager for their videos. He also set up their website in 1996, which has become the "Pagan Information Network", a contact network for Pagans across the Republic and Northern Ireland, for which Bone and Janet Farrar are the primary coordinators.

Bone and Janet Farrar are currently active members in the "Aquarian Tabernacle Church of Ireland" and have links with several covens in the United States, Australia, New Zealand, and Europe. They ran a progressive coven in Ireland call "Coven Na Callaighe" until early 2009 which was part of "Teampall Na Callaighe". Janet and Gavin handfasted in Ireland, May 2001. They have since legally married in March 2014.

Bone is an English author, and lecturer in the fields of Magic, Witchcraft, Wicca and Neo-Paganism, and an organizer in the Neo-Pagan community. At home in Ireland whilst Janet Farrar is a professional Tarot Reader, Bone works as a natural empathic Spiritual Healer. Both have specialised in trance-prophecy and possession work.

Since being Initiated into Alexandrian Craft both Bone and Farrar have developed their own unique brand of Witchcraft and both have been given honorary initiations into several other traditions, including Italian Strega, and Lesotho Sangoma (tradition healers) of South Africa. In 1999 both Bone and Farrar became Ordained as third Clergy with the Aquarian

Tabernacle Church in Ireland. They also Founded the Tempio di Callaighe in Italy. Gavin also works as an Adjunct Professor in the US based Woolston-Steen Seminary teaching Progressive Witchcraft and Runic studies.

Both Bone and Farrar tour regularly doing intensive workshops in the US, Europe, Australia, New Zealand and South Africa. They believe strongly in the idea of Witchcraft being both progressive and dynamic in nature, while remaining a clergy to those dedicated to servicing the Gods and Goddesses. They are responsible for setting up progressive covens in the US, UK, and Europe.

Gavin Bone's Works:

- *The Pagan Path*, 1999, Phoenix Publishing
- *The Healing Craft*, 1999, Phoenix Publishing
- *The Complete Dictionary of European Gods and Goddesses*, 2001, Holmes Pub Group LLC
- *Progressive Witchcraft* with Janet Farrar, 2004, New Page Books
- *The Inner Mysteries: Progressive Witchcraft & Connection to the Divine* with Janet Farrar, 2012
- *Lifting the Veil: A Witches Guide to Trance* with Janet Farrar, 2016

Lady Belladonna LeVeau
Arch Priestess of the Aquarian Tabernacle Church
August 18th, 1965 -

Arch Priestess Bella Donna Leveau

Lady Belladonna LeVeau, born August 18th, 1965, known as Mama Bella by those closest to her, is the Arch Priestess of the Aquarian Tabernacle Church. One of the world's largest organized Wiccan churches. The ATC membership is world-wide with organized churches in 7 countries. The church was founded in 1979 by Pete "Pathfinder" Davis, who appointed Belladonna as his successor and the Matriarch of the Organisation. Laveau was initiated into the craft in 1988 by an Englishman named Paul DeMartin, a descendant of Janet Farrar's Gardnerian line. Bella formed the WISE Tradition in 1999 and was appointed Arch Priestess in 2012. Laveau leads a ministry that is based on love. She puts heart into everything and creates a tradition where all magical beings are encouraged to embrace their divinity. Lady Laveau inculcates an atmosphere of love and safety within the Mother Church Monastery, where she lives with her husband, and Archpriest, Dusty Dionne. She strives to ensure people feel welcomed into a large family, encouraged to be their best, and are given opportunities to serve and shine.

Born August 18, 1965, to young parents, Bella was the first grandchild to two families. She spent the bulk of her pre-school years with her grandmothers "Mother Gennie" and "Mother Fae" where in their homes was much magic and fun. There was a raised stone circle in the front yard with a cauldron in the center that her and her grandmother would dance around on beautiful days. It was here where her father tried to turn her eyes green with magic and her grandfather used home remedies to cure common ailments. Laveau spent many long days playing dress up with her Great Grandmother and would enjoy statues of Buddha while she played the piano to a record player of Merle Haggard, Dolly Parton, and other classic music. During these early years, she felt like a princess.

Her parents converted to Mormonism around the age of 6. Going to church and the presence of God was comforting. But tragedy struck her family one Christmas Eve, when after all the presents were unwrapped and the family had gone to bed, the house caught on fire. Thanks to the family's St. Bernard dog that pulled her father out of bed by his ankle, all the family members made it out alive. However, everything they owned was lost in the fire. Things changed after that. Her mother had a second child, and the dream of a family farm caused her family to move away from her grandparents into "the country". It was an exceedingly difficult life change for a child who had been the center of attention for two sets of doting grandparents. Fortunately, their care had instilled confidence and a sense of personal worth that carried the young girl through many life trials.

Moving from the city of Atlanta to a family farm, Bella found a quick love for animals and the outdoors, but daily chores were hard. Laveau took care of her brother, while her two self-employed parents worked many hours away from home. This created a sense of duty and responsibility at an incredibly young age. Bella was responsible for cooking and cleaning, when she was so young she needed to stand in a chair to stir the pot and wash the dishes. But she had to do it, so she found a way. She developed critical thinking skills and learned how to be a self-sufficient problem solver in her elementary school years. Bella helped care for the farm animals, hunting dogs, and a 5-acre vegetable garden during these early years. Missing her grandparents and the comfort of family, she was unable to appreciate the romantic farm life.

Called to the path at a young age, Leveau always remembers the ability to talk to God and ask spirits for guidance. It was not until the age of 12 when she was caught making the wind blow in the backyard to help complete a household task, that her father told her that not everyone could summon the wind, and she should not let people know she could do that. Growing up in a Mormon household, the faith that God was always working magic in your life was an atmosphere that Bella appreciated. As She matured into a teenager, the burden of chores and raising her brother began to weigh on her. As she made mistakes with her brother, the guilt of the Mormon theology burdened her soul. She had a troubled childhood, where she managed to excel despite many problems in her home life. Growing up a Mormon girl in the 70s was an oppressive place for a headstrong teenager that had been doing the work of adults most of her life. She struggled for power in the family and had a difficult time respecting parents that had little skills in dealing with a very capable and intelligent, empathic, psychic witch child.

Leveau always a strong rule follower, could not find a way to apply the principles of Mormonism in a way that made her life work. In her early 20s, newly married, and struggling with her beliefs, she had a powerful moment in church where a visiting dignitary told her that there was more information about God and the church didn't have it. His speech was meant to encourage people to read their scriptures, but it led Leveau to look for God in other places.

As Laveau called out in prayer, the Goddess called Belladonna Leveau into service and presented her initiating High Priest and the world of Paganism. Bella received her formal training in a store called The Mysts of Avalon in Dallas, Texas in the late 80s. Trained Gardnerian by a Kabbalist, she learned the Art every day, as she volunteered her services in her High Priest's bookstore. Each day was filled with new opportunities to learn magic. Her teacher, Paul, played games with her and taught her how to tell if someone was a witch, and to what degree of study they had been initiated by reading their aura. She learned to see chakras, and connected her empathy with the original source, which as a child had been confusing and sometimes overwhelming, learning to use it as a psychic skill in healing and spiritual counselling. She learned the tarot, spellcasting, astrology, and formal ritual presentation.

The path led Leveau back to Georgia, where she had three children and got serious about a job, buying a home, and raising a family. After a short military career, she started her own business as a mortgage processor and began working out of her home after her children had an unsatisfactory episode at a local day-care. Self-employment was a phenomenally successful avenue for her, as she enjoyed being at home with her children. As the mortgage industry crashed in the early 2000s Laveau looked for a different income. This is where she returned to her magical skills learned from her teacher and became a professional spiritual counsellor.

Immersed in the craft every day and being a stay-at-home mom allowed Leveau to sink deeper into her spiritual practice. While she had always been close to spirit, having time for daily practice allowed the Goddess to speak to her, and gave her the time to listen. Leveau communed with the Great Mother each day and heard Her ask her to "Bring Her into the Light". In 1999, Bella received a powerful vision from the Goddess Cerridwen that she was ready to do the work she had been prepared to do and was told to start her own coven. As the High Priestess of Covenant of WISE, the Great Mother lead Leveau down the spiral path to service, putting several powerful teachers in her life at important times. Pete "Pathfinder" Davis, being one of the most important and influential of those teachers, took Leveau under his wing and trained her for 10 years to be the second, supernal leader of the ATC.

In Leaveau's early work history, she transcribed dictation, giving her the ability to type 100 words per minute. She began transcribing the messages that she was channeling from the Great Mother, and in 2004 published a compilation of these manuscripts which when put together became a curriculum for teaching magic upon the spiral path. 2004 was a powerful year of change. Bella took her published book on a festival tour, which included a trip to Washington to meet the powerful and charismatic Pete Davis and attend the Spring Mysteries Festival.

Spring Mysteries was particularly important to Leveau because she was a Priestess of the 4 Goddesses of the Mysteries: Aphrodite, Demeter, Persephone and Hekate. Leveau was trained on the subject and had personal gnosis which she had gleaned from holding the seasonal festivals of Eleusis on the East Coast. She looked forward to comparing what the ATC did against her own work. She was so impacted by her experiences at Spring Mysteries and by Pete Davis himself, that she committed to affiliate with the ATC. Pete Pathfinder took Leveau as a student of church government, religious law and policy, leadership, taxes, and non-profit organisation structure. For 10 years they had weekly meetings. In 2009, Bella began spending more and more time on the West Coast learning to run the church, until she eventually moved permanently in 2012, the year she was elevated to replace Pete Pathfinder Davis as Arch Priestess and Matriarch of the Church.

2004 was also the year Leveau went to Pagan Spirit Gathering for the first time, and met the young and charming Dusty Dionne, with whom she immediately fell in love. Their life became a whirlwind of magic together. With a focused magical partner at her side, Bella began to travel the festival circuit on the east coast while teaching and vending. A woman of many talents, Leveau was a Henna and Tattoo Artist, while Dusty sold her books and merchandise. In between festival season Leveau built a Spiritual Counselling Clientele that allowed her to travel and serve the Goddess in the greater community.

Leveau is a devoted mother and arranged a lifestyle where she was able to stay home with her children, take them traveling to pagan festivals all over the US, sometimes choosing home-schooling to enjoy the life experiences offered to a full time, self-employed High Priestess. Leveau's three children enjoyed growing up second generation pagans, learning camping, drumming, fire-spinning, belly dancing, and magic as a way of life. Leveau is a teacher and her love of teaching shows in her pet project, Woolston-Steen Theological Seminary (WSTS). Also known as WiccanSeminary.EDU, it is Wicca's only state recognized college degree-granting body. Leveau originally founded her own college, WISE Seminary, which is how Pathfinder discovered her in 2004. Leveau became Dean in 2009 following the footsteps of Deborah Hudson, who founded the school. WISE Seminary, Leveau's college that she created and was running on the east coast, merged with Woolston-Steen Theological Seminary, and brought forth a truly transformational Wiccan College experience. Wiccan Seminary focuses on teaching the sacred sciences that Spirituality is founded upon mythology, astrology, symbolism, cosmology, etc.

Laveau has authored Awakening Spirit, Accelerated Wicca, Between the Worlds and soon-to-be-released Channeling Divinity. These books are all texts for the seminary and revolve around a spiral based curriculum, which uses the "Wheel of WISE" as a scientific baseline for the school's training. They keep all the magical students energetically attuned and grounded to a common prevalent energy: the Earth. Laveau's books share her fresh look at Wicca from an astrological point of view, which leans heavily on metaphysical, magical principles, and comparative theology.

Leveau oversees the facilitation and production of two iconic pagan festivals each year, Spring Mysteries and Hekate Sickle. Spring Mysteries, which has happened every Easter weekend since 1985, is where the modern-established Eleusinian Priesthood hosts the ancient mysteries of the Great Mother Demeter and Her Holy Daughter Persephone. Each year pilgrims from around the world make the journey to New Eleusis to participate in the modern-day Rites of Eleusis. Hekate Sickle is a Samhain Festival, which explores different Gods, Pantheons, and mysteries each year, based on modern day revelation and guidance from the All Mother, Hekate. Leveau is an Oracle, and truly a Vessel of the Goddess. She has a strong connection with the Gods and believes that the ATC is the Goddess's church. She believes that modern day revelation and close guidance from Spirit is important for leadership in a religious organisation. Prayers before and after meetings and classes are common. Spirit, by whatever name you call it, is invoked at Leveau's events.

Among Leveau's accomplishments as a leader, she has brought the only state recognized degree-granting college in Wicca into its second decade of existence. WSTS is reviewed by the state of Washington every two years and has consistently met the state's requirements. The Mother Church is currently working with other schools of witchcraft to be able to have their work accredited to college standards, and for Wiccans to be able to have their work credited across traditions.

When Pete Pathfinder Davis died in 2014, the church experienced dark times as everyone grieved for their beloved spiritual leader. There were many thoughts about who should be appointed the next leader of the church, and not everyone agreed that it should be Leveau. It caused a split that hurt the church financially and spiritually. There were thefts of property and money, which left the church crippled financially and weakened. But Leveau asked the Goddess to call to Her people. She rallied the remaining members and poured love all over the situation, until the church blossomed into a new incarnation.

Today it's a little different in feel and flavour. Pathfinder's focus was more business-oriented and worship-based. He built the church as an administrator and legal eagle, confronting civil rights violations and gaining legal recognition as a minority religion. Leveau's focus is more heart centred. She is focused on teaching magic and witchcraft, while building a loving, welcoming, spiritual, family-safe, world-wide, congregation that serves the Gods together. It is not better, or worse, it's just what the church needs today in the 21st century.

In the interest of making the world a better place, and teaching the value of service, Leveau has opened the doors to charity organizations that promote the kind of planet Pagans wish to live upon. Pagan Earth Alliance and Save the Seeds Foundation are two important organizations that help serve the Great Mother's mission of saving the planet. Seeds of Persephone is another group that is part of the Beehive Coven – ATC in Louisiana that is working to build awareness about seed value and pollinators. The Pagan Gardner is a new YouTube show where High Priest Terry Riley shares magical gardening with the world. Terry was inspired by the World Love Tour, where Leveau and Dusty took Demeter and Her Hierophant on the road and taught Pagans everywhere the importance of gardening and supporting yourself.

Leveau is a beacon of welcoming strength to new beginners of Wicca. In a world where there are too many options, she makes learning witchcraft easy, inclusive and fun. She makes beginners feel as important to the cycle of service as Elder hands. Around her everyone is divine, encouraged to find their talents and value, and allowed to experience and appreciate the comfort of the Gods. Bringing the knowledge that the Gods know you and care about you drives her to continue the work, day in and day out. Leveau found herself alone and contemplative for long periods of time as a child. This instilled in her a compassion for those who feel lost, lonely, and forgotten. Bella lives by the philosophy that every person is an incarnated deity, and she shines her lights on people's values, so they can see for themselves their worth and importance to the world. She has taken the ATC to the next level, and I am sure that Pete Pathfinder (the founder) would be elated at what she has done.

Christopher A. LaFond
Pagan & Druid
1966 -

Christopher LaFond

Christopher LaFond born in 1966, is a Druid from Eastern Massachusetts and is a member and on-line moderator of the "Order of the White Oak". Once upon a time, in a galaxy far, far away, he spent three years in a Roman Catholic seminary, but was born again as a Pagan while living and teaching music in Ecuador, South America. To this day, he has a special focus on interfaith work among Pagans and Christians and was a performer and translator at the "Parliament of the World's Religions" in Barcelona in 2004. He plays the Celtic harp and sings and performs with Mother Tongue, Earth Spirit's ritual performance ensemble.

Chris specializes in Classical/Medieval/Renaissance Astrology and has lectured at local and international astrology conventions. He works full-time as a professor of Spanish at Boston College, and also weekly as a psychic and astrologer on Cape Cod. In addition, Chris is a perpetual student of languages and linguistics, and is a hobbyist beekeeper.

www.lafond.us

Peter Brabyn
Church of All Worlds Australia
Elder
1967 -

Rev. Peter Brabyn

Church of All Worlds Australia Inc., Priest, Treasurer, Past Secretary, Social Media Moderator, Web Wizard, Event Organizer, Scholars Guild.

Rev. Peter Brabyn lives in Queensland, Australia. He holds two academic degrees in education, is currently studying an engineering degree specializing in electronics, and holds several lesser qualifications. He is the head of his department teaching electronics to future electronics technicians and designers. He is the founding minister of the first Interfaith Church in Australia, an adult educator, a parent of an adult son (now in L.A.), ex-military, Australian, and more.

Brabyn born to non-practicing Christians of different denominations, could not find a religion that 'fit' for many years. In his 20s he began 'seeking God' but was dissatisfied with what organized religion had to offer. His first memory of 'doing magic' was related to a primary school romance.

Brabyn describes himself as an autodidactic polymath. He is often studying informally across a wide range of subjects including physics, chemistry, theology, neuroplasticity, quantum entanglement, psychology, mathematics, engineering, philosophy, history, and mythology. He holds qualifications in almost none of these.

Brabyn has journeyed through and studied many beliefs from the ancient to the modern. This has provided him with an in-depth understanding of human belief and a substantial understanding of many specific belief systems. Despite this journey he feels he cannot adequately define the thing that many people call God however his belief in the divine source they are relating to is unwavering. Brabyn's journey through earth-based beliefs has seen him become an active member of several Pagan, and interfaith groups. He continues to be actively involved with Church of All Worlds Australia.

In 2005, Brabyn had a divine revelation and felt called to serve deity. Even with what he believes to be direct contact with 'God' he still feels he cannot define who or what deity is. In 2007 Peter co-founded what would become the Interfaith Church of Australia.

Peter considers himself agnostic. While his specific beliefs are monotheistic, he has used many deities as a focus to the source. He also considers himself a pantheist and a pluralist; however, his personal belief is always open to refinement through experiential understanding. He joined the Church of All Worlds Australia in 2009 and was ordained in 2017.

For more information about the Church of All Worlds Australia, please see www.caw.org.au.

Utu Witchdoctor
Witch and Witchdoctor Elder
26th July 1968 -

Utu Witchdoctor

Witchdoctor Utu; Author of "Conjuring Harriet 'Mama Moses' Tubman and the Spirits of the Underground Railroad" founder of the Dragon Ritual Drummers, Niagara Voodoo Shrine, Niagara Pagan Men's Circle and member of the New Orleans Voodoo Spiritual Temple.

Utu was born in Scotland and raised in Canada and was exposed to many different spiritual paths as a youth travelling with his mother, who had an interest in South American indigenous cultures. They spent time abroad in the Colombian Andes living with the mountain tribes who were descendants of the Inca.

Despite his mother's flare for the exotic, Utu was raised by a traditional Scottish family with most of his kin still living in Scotland. Utu's father was a drummer in traditional Highland Scottish marching bands, and Utu was part of that world, raised in that band and taught to be a part of it. Utu's family were spiritualists on one side, with superstitions, tea leaf reading and spirit boards being commonplace to his mother in her childhood. Both sides of his family being traditional Scots also having a deep reverence for those before them; their ancestors, they feed them, remember them, and recognise them when they visit them from the hereafter.

The unique combination of spirituality in Utu's young life made his entrance into modern Witchcraft a comfortable one. Utu was initiated into Witchcraft by Lady Rebecca in St. Catharine's Ontario Canada, in 1994. Lady Rebecca had moved to Ontario from Texas, and she basically started the Niagara Pagan Community from the store she opened, The Ancient Earth.

Since 1999 Utu has been a very active member and presenter in both Canada and the United States, living in the Niagara Region on the border has him positioned well and both his communities on either side of that border exchange and attend each other's events all the time, the same is said for the Pagan communities on the border of Detroit and Windsor Ontario.

In 1996 UTU started the Niagara Pagan Men's Circle, which occurs once a month and has since 1996, with men from various paths and practices from both Canada and the U.S. attending as well as men who are straight, gay, and bi. This circle doesn't often focus on masculine Magick but more as a place for them to do ritual together, bond, foster trust, and help set the standard for the men's candor in the greater Pagan community, something he thinks is greatly lacking in our Neo-Pagan communities still. The pagan drum troupe Dragon Ritual Drummers was formed out of the men's circle, and they have become popular performers at Pagan and conjure festivals, events and conferences across North America. This has enabled Utu and drum colleagues to also present rituals and ceremonies and like their shows are meant to focus on unity and build common bridges between traditions and communities, Something we could all benefit from in this era.

In the year 2000 Utu began to serve Priestess Miriam Chimani of the New Orleans Voodoo Spiritual Temple. Miriam has been a tremendous inspiration to him, her unique work and tradition crosses spiritual lines as well as ones of colour and race. As a celebrated woman of colour, Miriam and her work is inclusive and inviting, her Temple flock is a veritable rainbow of colours and cultures, a true representation of their sacred Earth. From 2000 on Utu was not only serving the New Orleans Voodoo Spiritual Temple when possible, but as a proficient drummer starting from his days in youth, was being invited to drum at Ifa and Vodou ceremonies, and in particular began to be immersed in the Ontario Nigerian community centred out of Toronto, where he was mentored by Prince Bamidele Bajowa while he was living there before returning to be the Chief of Osoro. This was also the era when he was Initiated as a Witchdoctor, something completely different from traditional Yoruba religion but still an African lineage. This era in the early 2000s is also when Utu began the work that in many ways has come to define who he is today.

Utu lives in St. Catharine's Ontario, where the famed Harriet "Mama Moses" Tubman brought her particular track of the Underground Railroad to its end. Harriet Tubman lived in St. Catharine's for many years, and it was the base of operations during her years as the Underground Railroad conductor, wanted dead or alive. Between Utu's status in African

Traditional Religions as well as modern Witchcraft, being born in Scotland and raised on the Canadian/American border, it was the perfect storm for him to delve into a tangible spirit world that houses Underground Railroad heroes and figures that when living were black, white, rich, poor, Canadian and American, Christian and other, all of whom were united in the fight against the slave state and tyranny of human bondage.

Since 2004, with travels again being enabled by the Dragon Ritual Drummers, they were also sharing and facilitating ceremonies to celebrate and illuminate the Spirits of the Underground Railroad, the legacy of their town. This work has focused on not only the history and sacred deeds of the those who made the Underground Railroad what it was, but also shedding light on the ignored aspects of the spiritual and Magical practices of those that were on the trails to freedom as well as helping maintain them. Spiritualism conjure and Voodoo were as much an integral part of the Underground Railroad as the Quaker faith and other Christian offshoots, but academia ignores it all relegating it to superstition and ghost stories. Utu spent a great deal of time with Underground Railroad freedom seeker descendants, clergy and historians who have been a great support in his work and collaborate with him often.

The Underground Railroad spirit world is one that fosters the work needed in our modern times to again unite people from two countries, many colours, and spiritual paths to work together towards change. These modern times in North America are trying ones, with racial and economic division being some of the most challenging in years. Utu has found that the Spirits of the Underground Railroad along with the elevated spirit of Harriet Tubman are sacred inspirations towards the work we can strive for among our spiritual communities. If we cannot unite as spiritual workers, Witches, Pagans and Conjurers then it is not a very positive prognosis for the future.

Utu Witchdoctor in Ritual

Christian Day
Warlock Elder
December 25th, 1969 -

Christian Day

Christian Day born 25th December 1969 is a modern-day Warlock living in the Crescent City of New Orleans, Louisiana and is co-host of HexFest with his husband, Brian Cain. A practitioner of the ancient arts of Witchcraft—a spiritual path devoted to old world folk magic, healing, and veneration of the dead, Christian owns two occult shops in Salem, Massachusetts: HEX: Old World Witchery, dedicated to the practices of Witchcraft, Hoodoo, and Conjure, and OMEN, a psychic parlor and Witchcraft emporium which features a staff of gifted psychic readers. In 2012, he also opened a Hex shop in New Orleans, where he now lives.

Each October, Christian hosts Festival of the Dead, an annual event series in Salem that includes such popular events as the Official Salem Witches' Halloween Ball, an Annual Psychic Fair and Witchcraft Expo, and an authentic séance. Among his many media appearances, Christian has been featured on The Travel Channel's Ghost Adventures, Showtime, TLC, MSNBC, Biography, Dish Network and in The Chicago Tribune, The Wall Street Journal, The Boston Globe, The Boston Herald, CNN.com, USAToday.com and, of course, The Salem News.

Christian Day Book:

- *The Witches' Book of the Dead*

Other Events:

- Hexfest Festival – www.Hexfest.com
- Omen Store – www.OmenSalem.com
- Hex Store – www.HexWitch.com
- Festival of the Dead – www.FestivalOfTheDead.com

Christian & Brian at Salem Witches Ball

Kristoffer Hughes
Chief Druid of Anglesey
1971 -

Kristoffer Hughes was born in 1971 in the Mountains of Snowdonia to a Welsh family. He is a writer, actor, scholar, and teacher. He is Founder and chief of Angelsey Druid Order in 1999. Also, he is a 13th Mount Haemus Scholar of the order he has trained with and have published several books about paganism. Hughes has written a lot in association with many websites such as Hedge Witch Cooks and now he is currently writing for Llewellyn Worldwide. He lives in the district of Bodorgan on the Island of Anglesey in a small cottage overlooking the sea with his partner and cat. He is known for practicing a special kind of Druidry which is inspired by Swyn (Welsh Magical Craft).

The path of paganism is carved by his interest in folk magical traditions and Welsh Magic. With Anglesey Druid Order he practices and teaches mytho-centric and Swyn inspired Druidry. Kristoffer has released his main works with Llewellyn Worldwide. He imparts his teachings in the field of Celtic Mystery Traditions. He has trained with the "Order of Ovate, Bards and Druids" and now he is its scholar and teaches them. Kristoffer travels extensively throughout the United Kingdom, United States, Australia and Europe to give talks on magic and Celtic Traditions in various seminars and workshops. He has been a workshop leader with his quirky and humor, a frequent speaker and a writer at various camps, events and conferences. For Welsh television, Hughes works as an occasional actor and part time for Her majesty's Coroner. Anglesey is considered to be a sacred island with bountiful and fruitful soil. It is a place which is blessed by The Great Mother Nature. Hughes established this Druid Order to celebrate and teach the wisdom and significance of the Island of Anglesey.

Whilst on tour of the United States myself, at the PSG Festival 2019, I had the pleasure of meeting this very larger than life character, although with his seriousness of what he was talking about he had a sense of humor that lifted everyone to a height of where he was coming from. He was a beautiful and happy soul with a lot of knowledge to share. He was a breath of fresh air and covered a subject that I knew little about. His writings are a must.

Kristoffer Hughes Works:

- *From the Cauldron Born*, 2012, Llewellyn
- *The Journey into Spirit: A Pagan's Perspective on Death, Dying and Bereavement*, 2014, Llewellyn
- *The Book of Celtic Magic*, 2014, Llewellyn
- *Branches of the Celtic Tarot – Tarot Cards and Boxset*, 2019, Llewellyn.

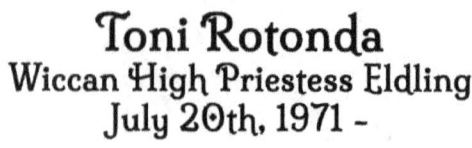

Toni Rotonda
Wiccan High Priestess Eldling
July 20th, 1971 -

Toni Rotonda at Buckland Museum

Toni Rotonda was born on July 20th, 1971, and had an early connection with the Divine Feminine. Rotonda recalls her earliest memory as a child whilst attending a Catholic mass with her father, remembering the Priest saying: "That our relationship is with God and Jesus and not with Mary". This always stayed in her mind as something odd to say, and for a second, she felt uncomfortable as it struck a chord within her that she was doing something wrong. Rotonda was always attracted to beautiful statues and figurines of the Virgin Mary as the Blessed Mother.

Rotonda when around the age of 7 or 8 always prayed to her, spoke to her, and shared her daily thoughts with her. The Priests words rang in her ears and her mind, where she did not like them at all, and certainly did not agree with them, so being rebellious and following her own truth continued her private relationship in secret with Mary.

Growing up in the Rotonda household with her mother was quite different as all things paranormal were welcomed subjects in her mother's household. It was normal for Rotonda to come home and see the Ouija board out in the dining table. They had a live-in nanny, Lester who introduced the incredibly young Rotonda to Spiritualism and various forms of divination. Lester would have his Tarot Cards out on the breakfast table every morning to divine how the day was going to play out.

Like many on a similar path, there was a need to know more and learn the secrets that are not spoken, which usually meant countless hours at bookstores, metaphysical shops, Libraries (pre-internet). This is how Rotonda on her path of searching came across the shop "The Cat and The Cauldron" owned and run by Kat Tigner. Rotonda continued to go to the shop and found Kat very approachable and helpful with a myriad of questions, and she was always given answers much to her surprise.

Rotonda was invited to a séance' at the shop, although a bit reluctant in attending and also a little nervous. She decided to go and walked in, and Kat Tigner introduced her to everyone. Making the rounds being introduced and speaking to everyone she was finally introduced to a white-haired, English gentleman standing in the corner. He affectionately reached out his hand and said "Hello, I am Raymond Buckland".

Rotonda had no idea of who this gentleman was and did not realise that this meeting, this incredible magickal moment, would alter her direction in life, as well as her faith. Rotonda went on the become Initiated in 2005 by Kat Tigner and Raymond Buckland, eventually to become and Ordained Minister who officiates as the last acting High Priestess of Raymond Buckland and his continuing coven "The Temple of Sacrifice", and also to become the keeper of his legacy, the custodian of his lifetime collection of artefacts known as the Buckland Museum of Witchcraft & Magick.

Rotonda has become a good friend of mine and is without a doubt one of the most genuine and beautiful souls I have ever met. The one thing about all the Priestesses of Buckland is that they are all gentle (hiding behind the scenes type people) and prefer their privacy, helping others to step forward into their truth.

Toni is a very strong and capable Priestess who has taken Buckland's museum to the next level, and since taking over the Museum, has expanded the museum incredibly with more and more artefacts and objects gifted to the museum for the history of Wicca, Paganism and Witchcraft and with the assistance of the Elders of the world, we can help keep and maintain the museum for all prosperity, that it remain a beacon to many to learn of and know the Elders of the Pagan world, who are the Keepers of the Inner Gates of our Past, present and Future.

Laura Gonzalez
Wiccan Priestess – Eldling
July 2nd, 1973 –

Laura Gonzalez

Rev. Laura González: Priestess of the Goddess, feminist, minister in training, podcaster, communicator, and spiritual advisor or Laura González: Witch Feminist Tarotologist.

Laura Gonzalez born in Mexico City on July 2nd, 1973, and is now a resident Bruja and professional Tarotologist. Laura came to the United States over 20 years ago, moving to the Chicago area, where she has built a loyal fan base among both Pagans and local community members. Laura is a practitioner of traditional Mexican Folk Magic, Native Philosophies, North American Paganism, and the Goddess Tradition.

A natural-born witch and psychic, Laura discovered her abilities at an exceedingly early age, sometimes at the apprehension of those around her. In addition to her work as a natural psychic and Tarotologist, she also does consulting with a variety of deck types, including Spanish cards and Oracle deck cards. Laura, a Bruja in tune with the cycles of nature and the Magic within, she is always willing to help those in need. Laura is a dedicated community activist, advocating for Pagan, LGBTQIA, and women's rights. She has passionately worked towards suicide prevention, supporting such organizations as The American Foundation for Suicide Prevention and participating in their Out of the Darkness walks.

Laura is co-editor of the e-zine, El Caldero (en Español), and the Founder of Boletín Pagano en Español, a meeting place for Spanish-speaking Pagans. Her writings have been featured in El Caldero and Circle Sanctuary Magazine. Laura is an influential leader in the Latin American Pagan community; she facilitates open discussions and teaches Spanish-speakers Pagan theory and practice across four continents. I was lucky to have got to know Laura on my last US tour, and we spent time chatting and also singing Spanish songs, as she discovered that I speak Spanish. I found her a very warm and giving person and very approachable.

Laura has presented workshops privately and publicly at such events as Chicago Pagan Pride, Fort Wayne Pagan Pride, St. Louis Pagan Picnic, Circle Sanctuary, and Pagan Spirit Gathering. Ms. Gonzalez has been featured in several popular Pagan podcasts and radio shows and has also served as a guest presenter on Saber Sanar and Pagans Tonight Radio Network where she conducted a couple of bilingual shows since 2011. She also has her own popular Spanish-English weekly podcast, Lunatic Mondays – Lunes Lunáticos on Circle Sanctuary Network Podcasts.

In 2017, Laura began the Ministers in Training Program at Circle Sanctuary. In 2018, she was Ordained as a Priestess of the Goddess from the Goddess Fraternity (Fraternidad de la Diosa) with Christian Ortiz. Laura is also a co-founder and Priestess of the Fraternity of the Goddess Chicago – Fortuna Temple.

In 2018, Laura participated in the international interfaith art project "PRAYER" with artist James Webb, the exhibition opened on September 6th, 2018 "James Webb's PRAYER" at the Art Institute of Chicago. In addition, Laura is a level two Reiki practitioner and is the only bilingual Advanced Therapist of Freedom Healing™. She also volunteers teaching ESL at the Aquinas Literacy Center.

BrujaLauraGonzalez@gmail.com
www.BrujaLauraGonzalex.com
@TarotbyLaura (X)

TarotbyLaura@hotmail.com
www.facebook.com/TarotbyLaura1
Tarot.by.Laura (Skype)

Jason Mankey
Gardnerian High Priest – Eldling
January 4th, 1973 –

Jason Mankey

My first meeting with Jason was at PSG 2019 in the US, I found him to be a wonderful free spirit who like all the guest at the event was always on the move, he spoke well and new how to get people's attention, I see Jason as a perfect Pagan to be an Elder of our future, and believe that with young people like him our Future Craft and Pagan Traditions are in safe hands. Jason Mankey read his first book on Witchcraft in the seventh grade, and at age 22 dedicated his life to the Craft. Today, Jason is a third degree Gardnerian High Priest and helps run two Witchcraft covens in the San Francisco Bay Area with his wife Ari.

Jason is a popular speaker at Pagan and Witchcraft events across North America and Great Britain and has been recognized by his peers as an authority on the Horned God, Wiccan history, and occult influences in rock and roll and heavy metal music. He is the channel manager at Patheos Pagan, the world's most read Pagan blogging site, and writes there at Raise the Horns, and at the magazine "Witches and Pagans."

Jason Mankey Books:

- *Transformative Witchcraft: The Greater Mysteries*
- *The Witch's Wheel of the Year: Rituals for Solitaries, Circles, and Covens*
- *The Witch's Athame*
- *The Witch's Book of Shadows*
- *Llewellyn's Little Book of Yule*
- *The Witch's Altar* with Laura Tempest Zakroff

Jason authors and publishers his books through Llewellyn Worldwide.

Alfred Willowhawk

Alfred Willowhawk, DMsc, DD is a 20-year veteran of spiritual counselling, coaching, and training. Willowhawk is an Ordained Metaphysical Minister by the University of Metaphysics with a Doctorate of Metaphysical Science. Willowhawk is also Ordained by the Assembly of God, previously licensed by the Church of God of Anderson Indiana, and was a member of a team of individuals who assisted in Morocco to enhance their own spirituality.

Willowhawk has earned a Graduate Certificate in Psychology – concentration Life Coaching from Grand Canyon University and has just completed his Master of Science in Psychology, with a concentration in Life Coaching. Willowhawk has been helping people manifest themselves to their highest potential for over 20 years. Also being a Reiki Master, and creator of the healing system "Celtic Transformational Healing". His work with men and women embraces the "Warrior Spirit" within. Willowhawk is an MKP brother and has facilitated the initiation of men and women into the Warrior of Spirit. Willowhawk has been an ordained minister and High Priest of the White Rayvn Metaphysical Church both in Kansas and Missouri.

Willowhawk is the assistant dean of education and a Professor at Woolston-Steen Theological Seminary ATC. Also, a practicing Reiki Master (1995) and also a chartered member of the World Metaphysical Association. Willowhawk hosts weekly on a radio show – "Up Close and Personal with Alfred Willowhawk" on WCAS-DB, Friday nights at 9 PM Eastern.

Alfred Willowhawk's Books:

- *Manifesting True Desires, Learning from Arianrhod and the Tree of Life*
- *Hawk Sightings*
- *I am Healer, Storyteller, and Warrior Priest – Second Edition*
- *Creating Guided meditations for Yourself and Others*
- *Shadow Relationships and How to Avoid Them*

- *Warriors of the Millennium*

www.witerayvnatc.org
www.wiccanseminary.edu

Brian Cain
Alexandrian High Priest – Eldling
May 15th, 1975 –

Brian Cain

Brian Cain born the 15th of May 1975 is a Witch and High Priest of the Alexandrian Tradition. He has been a devotee of Traditional Witchcraft since his early teens and was first Initiated in 1994. Today he is the High Priest of the New Orleans Coven, the only practicing Alexandrian coven in Louisiana. He maintains strong ties to the magical roots of Witchcraft in the United Kingdom and follows the teachings of Alex and Maxine Sanders.

His focus is on strong training in both Priesthood and the Arts Magical. With his husband, Christian Day, he co-hosts HexFest, a Weekend of Witchery held each August in New Orleans, as well as Festival of the Dead, a monthlong event series in Salem, Massachusetts that includes the Salem Psychic Fair and Witches' Market and the Official Salem Witches' Halloween Ball. Together they own Witchcraft shops Hex and Omen in Salem and Hex in New Orleans. They are also the founders and publishers of Warlock Press. Brian has been featured on MTV, NBC, and the Boston Globe.

Brian Cain Book:

- *Initiation into Witchcraft*

www.initiationintowitchcraft.com

Other Events:

- Hexfest Festival – www.Hexfest.com
- Omen Store – www.OmenSalem.com
- Hex Store – www.HexWitch.com
- Festival of the Dead – www.FestivalOfTheDead.com

Adam "Tarquin" Barralet
Wiccan High Priest
Clan of Boskednan - Eldling
June 15th, 1979 -

Adam Barralet in the Foothills of Perth

Adam Barralet was born in Perth, Western Australia and has been observing and living in tune with Nature since his early childhood. Barralet grew up amongst the bushland and wildlife of the hills of Western Australia and residing in various locations around the world has presented him with diverse opportunities to access extensive and eclectic teachings of the sacredness and secrets of Mother Earth.

Barralet at the age of 17 wondered into a shop called "The Alchemist" in Fremantle, Western Australia and met Lady Tamara Von Forslun, he was looking for his first crystal to buy, and I showed him the crystal section, where he chose his first crystal. Through this first contact he also discovered the Church of Wicca Australia/ the Clan of Boskednan, and undertook its Outer Court training, which was an involved series of training that was theoretical and practical that went for 6 months. After which being involved with the Pagan community for a while in Perth, he asked for Initiation not only into the Church of Wicca, but into Lady Tamara's personal Coven, the inner Circle of the

Clan of Boskednan, on the Full Moon on the 9th of July 1997 and took the spiritual name Tarquin.

Due to Barralet's strong connections to Nature, and his eagerness for knowledge and learning, along with his deep passionate connection with integrating all aspects of Nature into his Wiccan practices. His yearning interest in bringing forth the ancient knowledge and wisdom into the New Age movement and his personal spirituality, he, being passionate about helping those that were interested in all aspects of the New Age and spirituality welcomed the traditional aspects of Wicca into their daily lives.

Barralet helps guide the Seeker who loves crystals, and how to cleanse each stone in tune with the four Elements, shows Essential Oil lovers how to summon the Elemental Beings with aromatic blends and work through the Chakras using the eight Solar Festivals and the Eight Paths of Enlightenment of the modern Pagan as benchworks throughout the sacred "Wheel of the Year".

Barralet has now established himself as one of Australia's premier spiritual teachers, adept at working with Essential Oils, crystals, animal guides (in particular Australian animals), the Tarot, astrology and mythology. Barralet as a true devout Wiccan Priest and mentor who has been assisting in bringing the old ways into a new Enlightened Age with his Earth centred spirituality, passion, engaging personality and his relatable style of sharing the Magick of Nature has helped and guided people all around the world to change their lives and aid them in reconnecting with the blessings of Mother Nature's gifts. He is an inspiring lecturer and if you ever get the chance to hear him talk, maybe he too can help you discover the secret messages that the universe eagerly wants you to hear.

Barralet is a true Seeker of the ancient ways, and now an Ordained Priest of the Clan of Boskednan, he is an Eldling of the future who takes what the Elders of the past started, into the New Age world of the 21st Century with fun and knowledge under the guide of the Great Mother Earth and her gifts to mankind, this is one person who has surpassed the teacher.

Adam Barralet Works:

- *Essential Oil Message Cards*
- *Essential Connections – Guided Meditations*
- *Crystal Connections – The Book*
- *Crystal Keepers Oracle Cards*
- *Crystal Connections Message Cards*
- *Crystal Connections – Guided Meditations*
- *Gifts of the Essential Oils*, with Vanessa Jean Boscarello Ovens

www.adambarralet.com
www.facebook.com/mycyrstalconnections
www.youtube.com/adambarralet
www.instagram.com/adambarralet

Tarquin as a Priest in Circle

Kat McDonald
Pagan Elder & High Priestess of the Guardians

Kat & her senior Guardians

Throughout all my travels there has been certain people that have stood out more than others, not only because of their incredible presence in the community but due to their energy and time given freely to help with the red cross tents at all open festivals and everyone's medical safety but also as the Pagan Protectors and Guardians. They are the Guardians, much like our Covens "Men in Black" who are our Protectors and Security at our events, but also are Pagan community Coven Cops.

When I was a guest at PSG festival by Selena Fox, I was in a beautiful cabin next door to Selena's cabin and camped all around me were my beautiful Guardians, who were the security at the venue. They were so friendly and such a Magical experience knowing that they were there for not just mine, but everyone's safety and for any and all medical issues that may arise at these large events. This event, the PSG is one of the biggest in the US and is run by Circle Sanctuary.

I was told by them that many of the guests never even took the time to chat with them nor associated with them as they were classed as staff, although they offered their time and energy 24/7 for service to the community at a cost to themselves with no payment at all. They were incredible manning the gates, walking around the entire campsite on all three levels where hundreds were camping and where many had stalls, workshops, and authors booths etc. They were a strong presence which made everyone feel safe and comfortable.

I found them absolutely enchanting and beautiful people, each and every one of them, at night before retiring I invited them to my cabin where we sat out under the stars, and shared drinks, and my very own vegemite and cheese on crackers for all to experience the Australian social chitchat. I will never forget their courtesy and respect, and most importantly their beautiful High Priestess Kat McDonald, who was a graceful Guardian Elder (Shining One) and held all of their respect fully as their mentor and Lady. Thankyou Kat for making my stay one of the most pleasurable I have ever had in all my tours around our Pagan World.

As we performed our ceremonies and rituals especially the Summer Solstice Festival, I also discovered that they were always on the outer of the Circle as Guardians, and never actually participated in the ceremonies, so I brought part of the ceremony to them. If anyone feels that this is where their path can lead them, please get in touch with the Guardians to assist in your journey.

Kat, Me & The Guardians

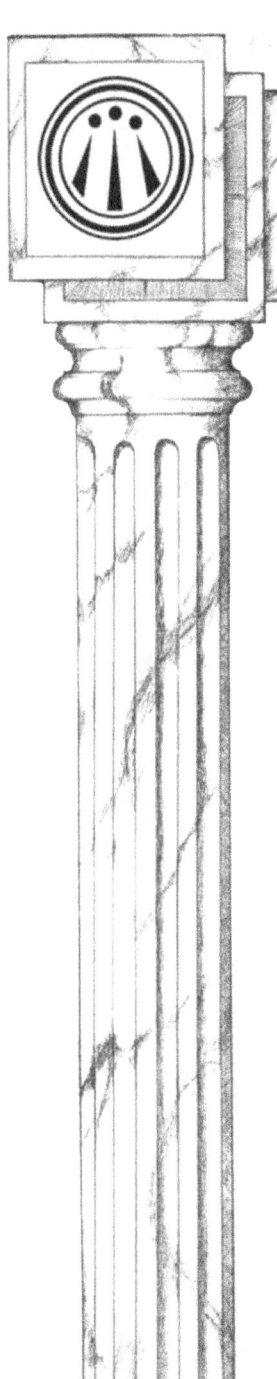

Shane Orthmann
Pagan Elder

Shane Orthmann is an artist, storyteller and spiritual leader, serving as Gothi with the "Daughters and Sons of Yta" since 2010. From fall 2015-Spring 2016 Orthmann was an artist in residency at the Creek, retelling the Norse Myths with an emphasis on their place in the seasons and the natural world. Collaborating to create three children's puppet theatre productions.

In 2014 Orthman travelled to Iceland where he was invited to participate in Summer Blot hosted by the "Asatruar Felag". Orthmann presented at World Peace and Prayer Day 2011, 2014 and 2015, an international conference of First Nation environmental and spiritual leaders, hosted by the Wolakota Foundation.

Shane Orthmann states:
"My life is a life of dreams, not ambitions, but dreams of the night."

Annie Waters
Goddess Elder

A child of nature, since 1970, Annie Waters has been called and immersed in service to the Goddess, organizing events and sharing her teachings of the Moon Circle, Sweat Lodge, Chants and Talking Circles, and a day-long Goddess Festival in Topanga, CA in 1984. In 1985 Annie began making Goddess Image jewelry, and her avid studies of Sacred Sites and the Ancient Divine Feminine became the background for her artistic work and business. In order to better serve and share these images, she continued to learn about the Goddess all over the world, and over and over has discovered Her to be the same Lady of 10,000 Names. Annie still creates sacred imagery in the context of her ongoing business – Ancient Circles Designs, and Open Circle, Inc.

Annie joined the "Church of All Worlds" in 1989 and began studying ritual form and the possibility of bridging the world of private group ritual and sacred public ritual-theatre. She was privileged to learn from some of the great ritualists of our time – Anodea Judith, Oberon and Morning Glory Zell, and many others who came through the Church Gatherings. Annie was honored to be chosen as May Queen for the "Isis Oasis Heretics Circle" in 2000, and in that year created a number of rituals and sacred theatre pieces for that group, still doing so annually. In October of 2002, she was Ordained in the "Fellowship of Isis" and the "Temple of Isis" as "Priestess of Brigit – the Multi-tasking Rainbow Goddess of the New Millennium". It was a pilgrimage to Brigit that took Annie to Ireland in 1992 – meeting Lady Olivia Robertson, co-founder of the "Fellowship of Isis" – for the first time.

She has danced as Priestess of the Goddess in Her many names, in theatre and ritual…Brigit, Inanna, Pele, Kali Ma, Hecate, Persephone, Sarasvati, Hathor and Sophia. She now uses wonderful masks for these dances, handmade unique art pieces by Lauren Raine – their presence is a blessing for our entire Goddess community here in California. Annie has a B.S. degree in nutrition, chemistry and biology from Michigan State University, and has continued to study and use nutritional and herbal healing to this day. Her other spiritual studies have included Crystal Healing, Chakra Balancing, the Lakota Pipe way, Hatha Yoga since 1970, a black belt in Aikido, and the close-up study of Grand parenting – Annie's most favourite of all... To learn more about Annie, and read an extended bio, visit: www.ancientcircles.com/anniesbio.html.

Sama Morningstar
Priestess Elder

Sama Morningstar

Sama Morningstar is a Womb Priestess devoted to Bio-Mystical Embodiment, sensual expression as worship in the Body Temple of the Goddess. Through her work as a Massage Therapist, Yoga and Dance Therapy instructor, Herbalist, and Poet, she loves to help women and men activate their creativity, recover from trauma through somatic healing, and grow into their purpose in service and devotion to Mother Gaia. Let us dance together, integrating Goddess/Womb guidance into the eco-practicalities of life.

She is deeply influenced by the fierce mercies of Kali, the compassionate fire of Quan Yin, the revolutionary kindness of White Buffalo Calf Woman, the comforting flow of Yemaya, and the ethical guidance of Ma'at. She is the answer to her ancestors' prayers and a devotee of the future priestesses that we are preparing the way for, who are reaching back through time and guiding us as well. Sama is a healing instrument of Gaia, an ingredient of the medicine she is mixing up, the balm for her scars, the elixir of renewal and change that we are all hungering for. She is a Priestess of Presence, flowing with the Waterfall of Words, sharing mud between the toes with you as we ignite fierce passion dedicated to embodying all our exiled parts. Inhaling, gathering, drawing us whole, breathing us home. Exhaling into rest, renewal, re-integration, restoration, revolution, and rebirth of ourselves and all humans on this precious Earth. Sama Morningstar is honored to offer compassionate, nourishing support for your sovereign blossoming on this journey.

Sama Morningstar Book:

- *Goddesses, Lovers and Dreams: Alchemical Poetry*

Deirdre Pulgram Arthen
Pagan Elder

Deirdre Pulgram-Arthen is the executive director of the Earth Spirit Community and has been involved with the organisation since 1980. Deirdre has an M.A. degree in Counselling Psychology from Lesley University. She is a trained Pagan Priestess, a spiritual counsellor, an educator, a writer, a community organizer, a singer, a certified Death Midwife, and an experienced ritualist and composer of sacred chants.

Since the birth of her first child in 1987, the theme of spiritual birth, both literal and symbolic, has become a major aspect of her work. In 1990, Deirdre helped to plan and execute an interfaith service for 250,000 people which opened Boston's celebration of "Earth Day". She has offered presentations for a number of civic and religious organizations, including the National Organisation for Women, the Unitarian-Universalist Women's Conference, and several universities. She has been featured in local and nationally syndicated television and radio programs and interviewed for numerous publications, notably Woman of Power magazine, the Time-Life Books series "Mysteries of the Universe", and the book "Stepping into Ourselves: An Anthology of Writings on Priestesses." Deirdre is a member of the Women's Task Force of the Parliament of the World's Religions and serves as one of the Parliament's Ambassadors. She has been a presenter or performer at every Parliament since 1993.

Eric Leventhal Arthen
Pagan Elder

Eric has been involved with the Earth Spirit Community for over thirty years, and he has been on the Board of Directors for much of that time. He has participated in many Earth Spirit activities which include attending, offering workshops, and helping with various staff positions at Rites of Spring. Eric has led clans at Twilight Covening since the first one was held in 1986. These include topics such as intuition and perception, haiku as a way to connect to nature, and dreams.

Eric has been part of the Earth Spirit delegation at the Parliaments of the World's Religions in Chicago, Barcelona, and Salt Lake City. Professionally, he is a software engineer and has worked at a number of high-tech companies in the greater Boston area. He also served for ten years on the Board of a privately owned retail apparel chain of stores. Eric lives in the Hilltowns of Western Massachusetts and can occasionally be found riding his tractor to help maintain the boundaries between the fields and the encroaching forests.

Moira Ashleigh
Pagan Elder

Moira Ashleigh is part of the "Glainn Sidhr Order" and is a longtime contributing member of the "Earth Spirit Community" with clergy credentials. She has taught at Rites of Spring, Twilight Covening, A Feast of Lights, Free Spirit, Pagan Pride, and was the coordinator of the Earth Spirit's "East" events for 20 years. Moira has a master's degree in Theatre and Dance from Emerson College, and during her tenure as a member of Mother Tongue, she held many creative roles including lyricist, choreographer, costumer, vocalist and CD cover designer.

She is also a storyteller with her long-time partner Duncan Eagleson and is the embodiment of the character Rag Root at the New York Faerie Festival. Moira is passionate about clean water and wildlife. She volunteers for the Mystic River Watershed Association and has won awards for her nature photography, which she uses to emotionally engage the public in the beauty and welfare of the natural world. Moira is a professional Web designer who began her design work for EarthSpirit with the Web pages for Rites of Spring in 1995 and has continued to grow and build the EarthSpirit online presence for 22 years, including this latest redesign. Moira is also on the Board of Directors for WRAM the Wildlife Rehabilitators Association of Massachusetts. She is involved in the local WordPress Community and is on the volunteer organizing committee for Word Camp Boston.

Katlyn Breene & Bob Gatrix
Elders Desert Moon Circle

Katlyn Breene

Katlyn Breene Las Vegas, Nevada, USA. My first knowledge of Katlyn was through her store Mermade Magickal Arts back in the 90s, when I had the Alchemist Store, and wanted unusual items and inspirational Magickal items for my store to sell. It was through Katlyn that I purchased much of her small books on Shell Magick and also all her many hand-crafted artisan incenses and oils.

Here is their story and the story of Desert Moon Circle of Las Vegas, Nevada, USA.

We know- really?? Here is the sharing of a story of Gods and Goddesses, Elemental Energies, the Faery Realms and the Magick of the desert. As unlikely as it may seem, a thriving community of artists, musicians, priests and priestesses, ritualists, and spiritual merry makers have found their way to a desert home. They hold the heartbeat of the Goddess in their ever-growing circle of friends and stand inspired and actualized by her presence. This place is not what you might think, and there is something about it that has drawn so many of them to stand in the light that shines there, oh so strongly. To tell the story of Katlyn Breene and Bob Gratrix is in part, to tell the story of their coming together, dedicating themselves to sacred work, and acting upon their better impulses and instincts to create the vessel of all that has flowed forth, Desert Moon Circle (DMC).

DMC has been coming together in ceremony and ritual for over 25 years. 25 years of gratitude, celebration, joy and connection and it still shines and smiles like the new light of the breaking dawn. They are not a coven and share the voices of the expressions they make with one another. They believe the Gods have infinite faces and they honor all of them. They design rituals to bring focus to the feelings and suspicions they have of what Truth is. They come together and share these many perspectives in the most delightful and creative ways. The sacred does not necessarily mean somber and the tone of their offerings echoes across a broad spectrum of expression. Sometimes, silly is sacred too!

Bob Gratrix has acted as the Priest of DMC for almost 25 years. He was drawn to the fledgling group, and Katlyn, by mystical forces in early 1995. Bob lived in Syracuse, NY and studied the Craft there in a coven experience with his lovely wife, Norma. Bob had spent a goodly part of his life in search of something that would soothe his aching heart that longed for something pure and unjaded in the world. When the Goddess came to him, he stopped in his tracks and privately vowed, and made a pact, to follow wherever she may lead. Up to this point in life Bob was a most unlikely candidate to receive the blessed light that the Goddess shines. He was neither mystic nor shaman, artist, alchemist, astrologer, or poet. But that did not stop him from reaching for the hand of the Goddess and asking for her guidance when it was offered to him. So, what followed was that as time passed, he felt drawn more and more to a pinpoint of light in the darkness that was Las Vegas. As you can only imagine, his friends advised him in disbelief about pulling up stakes and moving to the realm of Elvis!

As it worked out, little did they know! The Goddess guided Bob to all manner of the truly good things that life had to offer. She opened so many opportunities for him to lovingly serve and grow in wisdom and peace. When Bob first arrived in Las Vegas, not knowing anyone, one of the first places he visited was the Goddess Temple of Spirituality dedicated to Sekhmet in Cactus Springs, Nevada. There was to be a poetry reading that day where everyone shared their work. Bob met the Temple Priestess at that time, Patricia Pearlman, and they became fast friends. She called him "New York Bob". The structure of the Temple was built entirely by women. Imagine how honored he felt when, a few years later, Patricia asked Bob to reset the central fire pit with stones he carried from the desert and then to create a daisy chain of four linking wrought iron Goddesses to circle the central fire! What happened next was utterly amazing!

Bob hung around the Las Vegas metaphysical shop, "Bell, Book, and Candle", for a time and became friends with Scarlett, a practitioner, and very cool woman, who knew her way around the energies of a Woman Warrior. Scarlett invited Bob to a gathering of a group she worked with, which was DMC. Now here is where the story really begins, where Bob and

Katlyn meet. Weird facts first – Both Bob and Katlyn were born in Long Beach, California in the same year, and at the same hospital. Bob's birthday was January 4, in the sign of Capricorn, and Katlyn's on July 4, in the sign of Cancer!

Back to their story - Bob loved the vibe of all of it, the place, the people, and most of all Katlyn who knew all manner of things, the least of which was her power to speak the words and emanate the light of the Goddess. When Katlyn invited Bob to serve in the group as Priest, he was both honored and grateful. He was unsure of his worthiness to be chosen to do something this important. The best adventure he ever had was just beginning! Even better is that both Bob's wife Norma, and his beloved friend Samina Pitrello (an original founder with Katlyn) were both on this journey with him as Priestesses of DMC. When the time was right, Katlyn arranged for a very special Initiation for them by her dear friends, Oberon Zell and Morning Glory!

Katlyn has been involved with Magick in one form or another her entire life. She achieved one of her early goals of travelling the world performing as a beautiful and exotic stage magician, spellbinding audiences with her illusions and dance. She is an accomplished professional graphic artist who creates commercial illustrations and images for a variety of clients. Katlyn created Mermade Magical Arts in 1984, which is popular worldwide for its unique artisan natural incense blends. Katlyn lived in Los Angeles, among other places, prior to her move to Las Vegas in the 90s. She was a co-creator and facilitator of an amazing experiential event that was a re-creation of the Eleusinian Mysteries. Participants were drawn into an immersive four-day event that was transformative in the truest sense of that term. This event was presented for many years in Southern California. Katlyn has delved into many traditions, both old and new, and has experienced several Initiations on her path. Katlyn is Priestess of DMC and acts as a mentor, teacher, (and personal adviser when necessary). She is committed to creating sacred ritual space that is open to all who seek a spiritual experience…. Creating an earth centred spiritual community.

Early on after their meeting, Katlyn and Bob discussed what kind of group they really wanted to create, with several options before them as to structure and traditions. They wound up deciding on none of the obvious choices, and instead, chose to break free of any limitations or existing structures and follow their better impulse to create something that was new. Running the risk of failure, they settled on a group that would explore many traditions and celebrate a spectrum of Gods and Goddesses. It was not to be a coven. Hierarchy and "rules" were avoided. Their goal was to share sacred space with others who were free and self-motivated in their own individual paths. People who were not just looking to "follow" the leaders. What a trip it's been!

DMC has celebrated the Sabbats in the Wheel of the Year for over 25 years - consistently. Think of that - all the hundreds of gatherings, celebrations and ceremonies! For a long time, they celebrated the Esbats as well, and almost each of the rituals have been based on their original, scripted, rituals written specifically for the particular gathering. Hundreds of scripts with presentations committed to memory in honor of the Gods and Goddesses they serve. Their service to the Goddess has been truly remarkable and inspiring. DMC has performed handfasting's, baby blessings, ceremonies of Dedication, ceremonies that mark the changes in the lives or status of men and women (including LGBTQ), and ceremonies of passing over.

DMC follows the celebrations of the Wheel of the Year. In the past, they created experiential "Portal" events which focused on exploring, in depth, aspects of the Elemental energies. Portal of Air, Portal of Fire, and so on prove to be memorable events which were held in nature. They were three-day gatherings that took place at appropriate locations and featured innovative ritual work. DMC evolved, and in general, many of their presentations could fairly be labelled as "Ritual Theatre". Which brings us to the next thing - The "Vegas Vortex".

At many junctures, the work (and play) the DMC were doing crossed over into connections with the larger community. Early on, as invited guests of "Festival of Paths" in Las Vegas, members of DMC met some of their most dedicated future members. They admired each other's ritual style, and a union of the new friendly groups seemed like a natural fit. Later, the group opened itself to collaborate with a larger association known as the "Vegas Vortex", that creates and facilitates larger gatherings three times a year. DMC contributes opening ceremonies and a variety of ritual offerings in the course of their work together.

The Vortex is primarily focused on an Alchemical model of spiritual transformations and its events are attended by people across the U.S., and the world. DMC once worked together with the Vortex to create an immersive experience that followed a journey through planetary stations designed to theatrically present each of the energetic processes associated with the stages of alchemy. It's a fair claim to make that DMC bears the heart fire of the Vegas Vortex.

DMC is known for its work with the Goddess Temple of Women's Spirituality in Cactus Springs, Nevada. The beautiful temple where Sekhmet reigns. DMC has been blessed in the sense that it has managed to survive, drama free for the most part, for as long as it has. (and it is still going strong!). They routinely host ritual events at the "Mermanor", an oasis of green, and home to Michael and Katlyn Breene. They are attended by 40 -100 people each month, sometimes more. There is a modest $5 donation request made to help upkeep the beautiful garden like site where they meet, but no one is ever turned away. The group has been hived off to locations other than Las Vegas. "Ocean Moon Circle", "Silver Moon Circle", and "Mountain Moon Circle" all claim DMC as their origin.

DMC is not a business. It has never been "monetized" or acted as a source of income for its priesthood. DMC has never tried to advertise itself or made any wholesale attempts to increase its membership. It is priesthood has chosen not to promote itself by book or media and their philosophy is that the group will attract those who are meant to join with them. DMC is the real deal, and the secret is that there is no secret. The group is doing this out of pure love and devotion. It is their appreciation for all the miraculous things that flow forth from a loving God and Goddess, and the natural world which is present to help us all on this beautiful journey of life.

Christopher Penczak
High Priest Witch Elding
1973 -

Christopher Penczak

Christopher Penczak, born 1973 is a professional author in the fields of Paganism, Magic, and Witchcraft. Penczak was Ordained a Minister in the Universal Brotherhood Movement, Inc. in 2000. He is the Founding member of the Gifts of Grace Foundation, a non-profit organization in New Hampshire which is a collective if diverse people from varied spiritual backgrounds who are all dedicated to the service to the local communities. Penczak is a faculty member of the Northeastern Institute of Whole Foods Health.

Penczak is the proud author of many acclaimed titles on Witchcraft and healing. In 2002, City Magick won Best Magic Book from the Coalition of Visionary Retailers. In 2003, he won the same award for The Inner Temple of Witchcraft. In 2004, Penczak received multiple awards from the Coalition of Visionary Retailers, including a tie for Best Book of the Year for The Outer Temple of Witchcraft.

I have never had the pleasure of meeting with Christopher but have heard from many sources how assertive and positively sporting he is in the path of Paganism and Witchcraft and speaks his truth even though many may not find it welcoming. He is a true Elder of the future and with his knowledge, set of skills and power of direction can assist in leading the Seeker through the 21st century.

Christopher Penczak Works:

- *City Magick*, 2001, Red Wheel/Weiser
- *Spirit Allies: Meet Your Team from the Other Side*, 2002, Red Wheel/Weiser
- *The Inner Temple of Witchcraft: Magick, Meditation and Psychic Development*, 2002, Llewellyn
- *Gay Witchcraft: Empowering the Tribe*, 2003, Red Wheel/Weiser
- *The Witch's Shield: Protection Magick and Psychic Self-Defense*, 2004, Llewellyn
- *The Outer Temple of Witchcraft: Circles, Spells and Rituals*, 2004, Llewellyn
- *Magick of Reiki: Focused Energy for Healing, Ritual, & Spiritual Development*, 2004, Llewellyn
- *Temple of Shamanic Witchcraft*, 2005, Llewellyn
- *Magia blanca al instante: Descubre el poder de tu intención y tu palabra*, 2006, Llewellyn
- *Instant Magick: Ancient Wisdom, Modern Spellcraft*, 2006, Llewellyn
- *Sons of the Goddess: A Young Man's Guide to Wicca*, 2006, Llewellyn
- *The Mystic Foundation: Understanding and Exploring the Magical Universe*, 2006, Llewellyn
- *Ascension Magick: Ritual, Myth & Healing for the New Aeon*, 2007, Llewellyn
- *The Temple of High Witchcraft: Ceremonies, Spheres and The Witches' Qabalah*, 2007, Llewellyn
- *The Living Temple of Witchcraft Volume One: The Descent of the Goddess*, 2008, Llewellyn
- *The Living Temple of Witchcraft Volume Two: The Journey of the God*, 2009, Llewellyn
- *The Witch's Coin: Prosperity and Money Magick*, 2009, Llewellyn

Discography

- The Inner Temple of Witchcraft Meditation – Meditation 4-CD Companion Set, 2002, Llewellyn
- Outer Temple of Witchcraft – Meditation 4-CD Companion Set, 2004, Llewellyn
- The Temple of Shamanic Witchcraft – 4-CD Companion, 2005, Llewellyn
- The Temple of High Witchcraft: Ceremonies, Spheres and The Witches' Qabalah – 4-CD Companion, 2007
- The Living Temple of Witchcraft Volume One: The Descent of the Goddess – 5-CD Companion, 2008
- The Living Temple of Witchcraft Volume Two: The Journey of the God – 5-CD Companion, 2009

Luisah Teish

Luisah Teish (Iyanifa Fajembola Fatunmise)

Luisah Teish (also known under her spiritual name of Iyanifa Fajembola Fatunmise) is an African American, born in New Orleans, Louisiana. Her father, Wilson Allen Senior, was an African Methodist Episcopal whose parents had been two generation servants and only one generation away from slavery. Her mother, Serena "Rene" Allen, was a Catholic, of Haitian, French, and Choctaw heritage. Teish' original ancestry also includes Yoruba (West African). She is an Ifynifa and Oshun Chief in the Yoruba Lucumi Tradition.

Teish was a dancer in the late 1960s in Katherine Dunham's group, where she learned and performed Traditional African and Caribbean dance. After Teish left the dance company, she became a choreographer in St. Louis. In 1969 she joined the Fahami Temple of Amun-Ra, and it was here that she took the name "Luisah Teish", which means "Adventuresome spirit". Teish led the dance troupe of the Black Artists Group (BAG) in St. Louis after the departure of BAG's first dance teacher, Georgia Collins.

Teish was Initiated and Ordained a Priestess in the late 1970s in the Lucumi Religion and studied for seven years before finally teaching as a Priestess in 1977. Teish currently resides in Oakland, California. My first knowledge of Teish was in the documentary "The Occult Experience" when she was with Zsuzsanna Budapest's circle.

Teish once said in an interview "my tradition is very celebratory there's always music, dance, song, and food in our services-as well as a sense of reverence for the children. It's joyful as well as meditative". Today in the 21st Century Teish is probably the most well-known and respected Yoruba Priestess in the San Francisco Bay area (2010). She is internationally acclaimed for her Goddess circles and as a writer and ritual-maker.

Luisah Teish Books:

- *What Don't Kill is Fattening: Poems by Luisah Teish*, 1980, Fan Tree Press
- *Jambalaya: The Natural Woman's Book of Personal Charms and Practical Rituals*, 1988, HarperOne
- *Carnival of the Spirit: Seasonal Celebrations and Rites of Passage*, 1994, Harper Collins
- *Soul Between the Lines: Freeing Your Creative Spirit Through Writing*, with Dorothy Randall Gray, 1998, Avon Books
- *Eye of the Storm*, 1998, E P Dutton
- *Jump Up: Good Times Throughout the Season with Celebrations from Around the World*, 2000, Conari Press
- *What Don't Kill Is Fattening Revisited: Twenty Years of Poetry, Prose, and Myth*, 2002, Orikire Publications
- *Zulu Shaman: Dreams, Prophecies, and Mysteries,* with Vusamazulu Credo Mutwa and Stephen Larsen, 2003, Destiny Books (New Edition of Song of the Stars)

Jeff McBride
Elder of the Arts

Jeff McBride

Jeff McBride, named Magician of the Year by The Magic Castle in Los Angeles, is recognized as a foremost innovator in contemporary magic. His magic performance art combines mime, Kabuki Theatre, world-class sleight of hand and grand illusion to create a completely unique performance experience. New York Times columnist Glenn Collins writes, "What Mr. McBride give his audiences is a mesmerizing performance… a magic show that is at once a celebration of mystery and a struggle to understand powerful forces."

McBride is a regular headliner at casino showrooms in Las Vegas and Atlantic City and has been seen on every major US television network. McBride plays the role of Joran on Star Trek: Deep Space Nine. Most recently he has been a special guest on Criss Angel's Mindfreak, and the subject of the Canadian TV documentary: Jeff McBride-A Magickal Life on the "Enigma" series.

He runs the McBride Magic and Mystery School in Las Vegas and has created some of the bestselling teaching videos in the world of magic. In addition, he is a popular lecturer and workshop leader for both magicians and corporate audiences around the world. With his wife, Abbi, he hosts transformational fire circle events around the world.

The Vegas Vortex is an international community of friends, artists, musicians, performers and wisdom-keepers, centred in Las Vegas, NV. They host an exciting fun series of magickal events, concerts, playshops, drum circles, dances, and empowering retreats. Their mission is to bring people together, in community, to explore and share, to inspire positive transformation, to support and celebrate each other through various life-enriching experiences. They welcome all seekers of truth and beauty. Please consider this your invitation to participate in their growing magickal community.

The Vegas Vortex is invested in creating family-friendly events, in safe and sacred space. Together, they embark on journeys of transformation through purification, temperance, and sustained creative engagement. While they understand that the use of alcohol and other substances may be a part of an individual's spiritual practice, their intention is that the events are best served by a crystal-clear, attentive and open participation that is unaffected by mind-altering substances.

This video tells their story: www.youtube.com/watch?v=pfpwPt0a2Tk

For more information, visit www.mcbridemagic.com

Antonio "Papa Tony" Battistessa
Shaman & Wizard of Fire

Antonio Battistessa on his Dragon Chair "Draconis"

Antonio Battistessa and his family settled in Herne Hill, Swan Valley, (yes named after the Horned God) Western Australia, from southern Europe, where his parents cleared the land by hand and created a vineyard of grapes and vegetables on their large property, I use to come and visit and watched his mother in her 70s still pulling weeds out of the large acreage by hand, as she always connected with the earth in every way possible.

Antonio has always been creative and was taught by his parents to honor Mother Earth and how to connect with Her on a daily basis. But he went one step further with taking what was offered from nature, and making it into a masterpiece, and artwork that was not only raw and pagan but a living piece like none other.

Antonio from a young teenager learnt to be a blacksmith, which was a dying trade, but worldwide has always been a talent respected by all communities, where he worked with the raw elements in nature and created pieces of art from tress, branches, metals, recycled metals and timbers that nature had released for him to find and give it a new sense of life and beauty.

Antonio was so intuitive with his gift and connection to Mother Earth that each piece he designed had a story and a living life that he with the power of magic and fire breathed life into it. His motto "We welcome you to come and view the Magical World of Battistessa Studios", has reached the farthest points of the earth where his works can be found from Russia to Buenos Aries. His huge showroom is filled with sculptures, furniture, architectural pieces, water features, spiritual art. And creative lights including his famous Candle Holders for small tables to grand hallways in mansions.

Antonio has been a friend of mine for over 30 years, and through his passion of nature and the art, found that it led him on a path to Shamanism, where he eventually created large tepees, from the smallest that slept 10 people to the largest that slept over 80. Together we used to hold Shamanic weekends for a select few (maximum of 25), where we created and erected the Tepee for all to sleep, and a nepee (sweat lodge), and had a weekend of ceremony and cleansings.

He used to teach my Seekers and Initiates how to forge and make their very own ritual daggers (Athames) and spent a full 1-2 days in a workshop aiding them in creating their personal Witch Tools. He was a great teacher and shared much of his passion with everyone, he became Papa Tony to many as a storyteller and creator of Pagan Art for the world. He is a beautiful soul and a person well worth meeting and seeing his great works of art.

www.battistessastudio.com
www.facebook.com/Antonio.batistessa

Rebecca "Kundra" MacNess
Wiccan High Priestess Elder – Clan of Boskednan

Rebecca "Lady Kundra" MacNess

When I first met Rebecca MacNess, she was Initiated into a Lothlorien Coven ran by High Priest Manannan and High Priestess Lady Neith, and she although loving them decided to come over into the Coven of Boskednan. This incredible lady came from a troubled past but grew into a more positive and magical future. Kundra as I prefer to call her, has worked harder than many that I met over the years with her dedication, self-discipline, and totally immersed into the Covenstead and its members.

Kundra became my Maiden, and she was the perfect Maiden that anyone could have, she was the discipline that I never had. She helped all the members and also the outer community to be the best that they could become. She studied hard and went through the degree's until she finally after many years became a 3rd Degree High Priestess, sadly this meant leaving my coven to form her own. Kundra was my Maiden and the Church of Wicca Maiden for many years. When I started to step back Kundra stepped forward not only with her coven but with the entire Wiccan/Pagan Community in Perth, Western Australia.

Kundra now runs the "Combined Covens" and also runs the annual "Spring Equinox", which is a public annual event for all who wish to attend along with many other smaller events. Lady Kundra is a true and dedicated High Priestess who has earned her title through decades of training and teaching. I place her at the end of my book not because she is the least important, but to me she is the most important, as it is Lady Kundra who can carry on what I started, and be a beacon for many who seek out the Craft in whatever tradition or path they are searching for, whether they be Pagan, Wiccan, Witch, Shaman, Alternative spiritualist or any earth centred follower of Nature and the Goddess.

With my last lines of this book of Respected Elders of the World, I salute and honor her in every manner. Blessed Be my dear daughter who always called me "Lady Mum", may the Goddess hold you gently in the palms of her hands and always close to her heart.

Pagan Elders Past & Present

Abramelon, The Mage
Achrer, Jakub "Zahrada" (Czech)
Adaire, Gwen and Cairril
Adler, Margot (US)
Adunas, (Syrian)
Agrippa, Cornelius (Italy)
Ahern, Donata (US)
Alsace, Lady (US)
Algirdas, Lithuanian Grand Prince
Alli, Antero
Amairgill, The Bard (Czech)
Anderlini-D'Onofrio, Serena
Anderson, Larry
Anderson, Oz
Anderson, Melissa (US)
Anger, Kenneth (US)
Antinous, BDX (France)
Antonych, Bohdan Ihor (Ukraine)
Ardinger, Barbara
Arianna, Lady (US)
Arkhipova, Maria (Slavic)
Areianna, McColl (Ire)
Arthen, Andras Corban (US)
Arthen, Deirdre Pulgram (US)
Arthen, Susan Curewitz (US)
Arthen, Eric Levanthal (US)
Ashleigh, Moira (US)
Asgartha (Greece)
Arkana (Ireland)
Barralet, Adam "Tarquin)
Bardon, Franz (UK)
Barnes, Michael & Julie (NZ)
Barnes, Ray   (US)
Barnett, Judith (Mama Maureen) (US)
Barrett, Ruth
Barrett, Sir Francis (UK)
Baudino, Gael (US)
Beattie, Bill

Bennett, Rhiannon
Benner, Rebekah Rev. (US)
Benoist, Alain de (France)
Benoo, Michael (Aust)
Berthou, Gwilherm (UK)
Beyerl, Rev. Paul (US)
Biletsky, Andriy (Ukraine)
Billinghurst, Frances (UK)
Bishop, Conrad & Elizabeth
Black, Susan Morgan
Blight, Tamsin (UK)
Bloodwine, Gareth
Bone, "Lady Olwen" Eleanor (UK)
Bone, Gavin (IRE)
Bonewitts, Isaac (US)
Bonewitts, Phaedra Heymann (US)
Boni, Giacomo (Italy)
Boswell, Granny (Cornwall)
Botting, Dr. Heather (CAN)
Bracelin, Jack L. "Dafo" (UK)
Braese, Francine
Brastins, Ernests (Baltic)
Breene, Katlyn (US)
Bruegel, Pieter (Belgium)
Buchanan, Angie
Budapest, Zsuzsanna (US)
Buckland, Raymond (US)
Byrd, Roger & Jan
Cabot, Laurie (US)
Cane, Brian (US)
Camire, Arlynne
Carnahan, Wolf
Carpenter, Dennis
Carr-Gomm, Philip (UK)
Carson, Jo
Cat, Grey
Cau, Jean (France)
Celms, Valdis (Baltic)

Cherney, Darryl
Christensen, Olse (Germanic)
Christie, Ricard Lance (US)
Clark, Carolyn (US)
Clark, Jimmy
Clifton, Chas
Close, Del
Cluthin (Aust)
Coleman, John "Roger" (US)
Cox, Zachary
Cornett, Larry
Corrigan, Ian
Coyle, T. Thorn
Coyote, Jesse
Cropley, Pete & Cesily (Aust)
Crowley, Vivienne (UK)
Crowther, Patricia (UK)
Crowley, Aleister
Cuhulain, Kerr
Cunningham, Scott (US)
Curott, Phyllis (US)
D'Arc, Joan (France)
Dalton, Cate
Darling, Diane
Davis, Teri
Davey, Craig (Aust)
Davis, Pete Pathfinder (US)
Day, Gillian (Aust)
Day, Christian (US)
Day, Philip (Aust)
DeGrandis, Francesca (US)
DeCles, Don Jon (US)
Dearnaley, Roger
Dee, Dr John   (UK)
DeForrest, Jay & Jadzia
De Grandis, Francesca (US)
De LaBarthe, Angela (UK)
Devlin, Sharon Sean
Dexter, Miriam Robbins
Dexter, Raymond (Aust)

Diamond, Susan
Dickens, Samm
Digitalis, Raven
D'Montford, She'
DiZerega, Gus (US)
Dominguez, Ivo
Donohue, David
Dragonari, Stargard (Czech)
Dragonari, Illeana (Czech)
Dunwich, Gerina
Dyer, Moll (UK)
Earthwise, Astarte (Aust)
Ellison, Skip   (US)
Eason, Ankou (Germany)
Ely, Richard
Elspeth, Granma (US)
Epona, Julie
Erna, Sully
Fae, Peter
Fairgrove, Rowan
Fallingstar, Cerridwen
Farrar, Janet (IRE)
Farrar, Stewart (UK)
Fahrenkrog, Ludwig (Germanic)
Failain, Grainne Ui (Ireland)
Fink, Jason
Firefoz, Lasara
Fitch, Ed (US)
Flowers, Stephen (Germanic)
Forslun, Tamara (Aust)
Fortune, Dion (UK)
Fox, Farida
Folsom, Sean
Fox, Selena (US)
Foxsong, Breid
Foxwood, Orion
Fraser, Sir James (UK)
Frenssen, Gustav (Germanic)
Frew, Don
Freya Aswynn (EUR)

Frost, Gavin (US)
Frost, Yvonne (US)
Gaal, (Norway)
Gaalnorn, Yasmine
Gardner, Gerald (UK)
Garr, Carol (US)
Garland, David (Aust)
Gentille, Francesca
Gerard, Chjristopher (Belgian)
Giger, H. R. (Swiss)
Glassman, Sally-Anne (US)
Goheen, Arthur
Gondola, Alessandro (Italy)
Gonzales, Laura (US)
Goodwin, Peter (Scotland)
Goodwin, Colin (Germany)
Goodman, Simon (AUST)
Goody, Penny (US)
Gorman, Michael
Goudy, Isobel (UK)
Govannon, Taliesin
Gratrix, Bob "Gray Tricks"
Grand, Lady Brianna (Aust)
Grandis, Francesca de (US)
Grandma, Elspeth of Haven (US)
Grass, Herb de
Gray, William G. (UK)
Gray, Bob (US)
Greymere, Joanna Fink (US)
Green, Marian
Grimassi, Raven (US)
Gunther, Hans F. (Germanic)
Guerrero, Tony & Marie
Guiley, Rosemary Ellen
Hanson, Krista Rev. (US)
Harbaugh, Sea & Lindsay
Harbaugh, Krista (GER)
Hardin, Jesse "Wolf" (US)
Hatfield, Wil
Harlender, Zdzislaw (Poland)

Hartridge, Timothy
Hauer, Jakob Wilhelm (Germanic)
Hauer, Elga (Germanic)
Haugen, Andrea (Germanic)
Haukur, Halldorsson (Nordic)
Heimgest, Odinic Rite (Nordic)
Hennes, Mama Donna (US)
Hildebrand, Jerrie
Hilmar, Orn Hilmarsson (Nordic)
Homolka, Ayesha
Hopman, Ellen Evert (US)
Horne, Fiona (AUST)
Hubbard, Ed
Hughes, Kristoffer (WALES)
Hume, Lynne (AUST)
Hunter, Rowan (Aust)
Hunke, Sigrid (Germany)
Huson, Paul (US)
Hutton, Ronald
Iasky, Alexander
Ingal, Marianne
Ingersoll, Jack
Imakhu, Queen Mother
James, Tamara (CAN)
James, Richard (CAN)
Jansdotter, Maret (Sweden)
Janis, Dorothy (Austria)
Jay, Wendyl
Jennings, Pete
Jensen, Kris
Jonina, Kristin Berg (Nordic)
Jones, Prudence (US)
Jormundur, Ingi Hansen (Nordic)
Judith, Anodea
Jung, Fritz
K, Amber (US)
Kaldera, Raven
Kalash Tribe (Afghan)
Karr, Todd
Karen "Jade" Dunn

Karen Leone
Katz, Tzipora
Kelly, Aiden Snr
Kelly, Sir Edward
Kennealy-Morrison, Patricia (US)
King, Francis (UK)
King, Donald Michael (US)
Kiteler, Dame Alice (UK)
Klages, Ludwig (Germany)
Knight, Winter & Sharon
Knowles, George
Kolodziej, Wladyslaw (Poland
Korn, Anna
Koziara, Colleen
LaFond, Christopher A. (UK)
LaMond, Fred (UK)
Leland, Charles
Latham, Cassandra
Laveau, Belladonna (US)
Laveau, Marie (US)
LaVey, Anton (US)
Lee, Barbara (Ireland)
Leek, Sybil (US)
LeFaye, Debi   (US)
Lerner, Lawrence
Lewis, Don
Levi, Eliphas
Light, Deborah Anne
Liqankevich, Andrei (Argentina)
Lipp, Deborah
Littlewolf, Eldri
Logghe, Koenraad (Germanic)
Lola, Mama (US)
Lombardo, Nagia
Lord, Claire
Ludendorff, Erich (Germanic)
Lord, Simon
Lord Pilgrim
Lord Palin
Ludendorff, Mathilde (Germanic)

Lyngvild, Jim (Denmark)
Lyotard, Jean-Francois (France)
Lyncurium, Alder (Spain)
Mama Maureen (US)
MacKenzie, Jacquie Omi Zaleski (US)
MacKenzie, Don (US)
Maiello, Guiseppe "Dervan" (Czech)
Mallard, Alice (UK)
Mallard, Graham (Aust)
Marchal, Moryan (UK)
Martelle, Joe & Jacquie
Martello, Leo (US)
Maureen, Mama (US)
Mayhem, Monica (AUST)
Mazda, Colleen (Aust)
McBride, Abbi Spinner
McBride, Jeff   (US)
McCollum, Patrick (US)
McCoy, Edain (US)
McFarlane, Michael
McLennan, Bruce Appollonius
McNallen, Stephen (Nordic)
McNess, Rebecca "Kundra" (Aust)
Miller, Richard Alan
Miller, Mark
Mills, Alexander Rud (Nordic
Modrzyk, Stanley
Montgomery, Professor Jack (US)
Montgomery, Jillian (UK)
Moondog, (US)
Mooney, Thorn (US)
MoonOak, Rev. Alder (US)
Moonshea, Lady (UK & NZ)
Moontree, Lady (AUST)
Monvoisin, Catherine
Morey, Stan (US)
Morningstar, Sama (US)
Morris, Susan "Chasmodai" (US)
Morrison, Dorothy (US)
Morgana & Merlin Sythove (Netherland

Mortico Bali (Indonesia)
More, Alva (Portugal)
Murphy, Anthony
Murton, Ray "Eyramon"
Murray, Dr Margaret (UK)
Moynihan, Michael Jenkins (US)
Nemenyi, Geza von (Germanic)
Nichols, Mike
Nichols, Ross (UK)
Niven, Anne Newkirk
Nightmare, Macha
Novack, Penny & Michael
Norton, Rosaleen (AUST)
Nowicki, Dolores Ashcroft (US)
Nybor (US)
Okulam, Frodo
Oma Hexen, Melanie
Opsopaus, John "Apollonius" (US)
Opa Forslun, Wilheim
Orthmann, Shane (US)
Owen, Trish
Ozpagan, Tim (Aust)
Pagan, Dawn
Paredes, Xoan
PatternDancer, Lyryal Thea
Patterson, Elizabeth (AUST)
Paxson, Diana (Germanic)
Penszak, Christopher (US)
Pessoa, Fernando (Portugal)
Pickingill, George (UK)
Pitrello, Samina (US)
Pitzl-Waters, Jason
Platten, Ahrianna
Posch, Steven
Potrzebowski, Stanislaw
Povetkin, Alexander
Priest, Prudence (US)
Pwyll, Avilynn
Pythia, Lady (Marybeth Witt) (US)
Quinn, Lady Margaret DeLille (UK & Aust)

Raes, Roeland (Flemish)
RavenWolf, Silver (US)
Ravish, Gypsy Enchantress (US)
Read, Ian (UK)
Regardie, Israel
Reghini, Arturo (Italy)
Reinman, Adrian (Germanic)
Reith, Velvet (US)
Restall Orr, Emma (UK)
Reventlow, Ernst (Germanic)
Rhea, Lady Rivera (US)
Rhiannon, "Roberta" Lady (US)
Rigakis, Evangelos
Riley, Terry
Robbins, Trina
Roberts, Hunter
Robertson, Lady Olivia Durdin (Ire)
Robertson, Lord Lawrence Durdin (Ire)
Romany, Sharadon (Aust)
Romany, Diva of magic
Ross, Scarlett & Green
Rothenberg, Joseph
Rotonda, Toni (US)
Rucker, Paul. B.
Rudgley, Richard (UK)
Rule, Wendy (AUST)
Runyon, Carroll "Poke"
Run, Vera (Ukraine)
Rhyall, Rhiannon (Aust)
Rivett, David (Aust)
Rivelle, Marion (NZ)
Sala, Luc (US)
Sambal, Lady "Isabel" Olga
Samson, Agnes (UK)
Sandgrael, Lord (GER)
Sanders, Alex (UK)
Sanders, Maxine (UK)
Santee, Dr Frederick La Motte (US)
Sassman, David Rev. (US)
Serpentmoon, Bane (Philippines)

Serpentine, Ralph (GERM)
Sargent, Denny
Schaffer, Athena
Scott, Marylyn "Motherbear" (US)
Scully, Nicky (US)
Seigfried, Karl E.H. (US)
Selvik, Einar, (Norway)
Shaian, Volodymyr (Ukraine)
Shallcrass, Philip (UK)
Shah, Idries (UK)
Sheba, Lady (US)
Sherbak, Chris
Shirley, Larry
Short, Mike
Siegle, Frank & Mary
Silversong, Aeona
Silverstar, Phoenix Rev. (US)
Sintana, Lady
Sinnamon, Grace (Aust)
Seren-Ddaear, Caridwen
Serena, Lady (Aust)
Sherbak, Chris
Shipton, Mother Ursula
Simpson, Don
Siannan (France)
Songdog, Talyn (US)
Southeil, Agatha
Sprouse, Dylan (Germanic)
Stachniuk, Jan
Starhawk (US)
Stewart, Daniel Blair
Stewart, R. J (UK)
Stone, Barton
Svarte, Aske (Russia)
Sveinbjorn, Beinteinsson (Nordic)
Sweyn, Blot (Sweden)
Tatja, (Finland)
Tannen, Holly
Tanith, Lady (Aust)
Tauring, Kari (US)

Teister, Malcolm (Aust)
Teish, Luisah   (US)
Telesco, Trish (US)
Theitic, Andrew (US)
Themis, Michael (Greece)
Thomas, Kirk
Tigney, Kat (US)
Triplegood, Herman, B. (US)
Tripple, Reginald (UK)
Trinkunas, Jonas (Baltic)
Trinkuniene, Inija (Nordic)
Thrinkuniene, Romuva
Thunen, Erif
Tucker, S. J.
Tullou, Raffig (UK)
Tully, Caroline
Utu, Witchdoctor (US)
Valliente, Doreen (UK)
van Doorn, Mario (Netherlands)
VanBecelaere, Joan
Vic, Mama (US)
Victor, Arisa (Rainbow Granny) (US)
Victoria, Lady (UK)
Vikernes, Varg
Venette (Sth Africa)
Vega, Selene
Vejonas, Raimonds (Latvia)
Veleslav, (Russia)
Vitezslav (Czech)
Voigt, Valerie
Vydunas (Lithuania)
Waite, Arthur Edward (US)
Waites, Rhiannon (Norway)
Wakefield, Tony (UK)
Walker, Patricia
Walker, Wren
Waluburg, Seeress (Egypt)
Washburn, Loren Lightbeam
Waterhawk, Don & Daniella
Waterhouse, Agnes

Waters, Annie (US)
Weatherstone, Lunaea
Webster, Samuel
Weinstein, Marion (US)
Weller, Ann
Weschcke, Sandra K.
Wesche, Carl Llewellyn (US)
Weyer, Johannes
White, Joan (UK)
Whitehorn, Carolyn
Wigington, Patti (US)
Wildgrube, Donald
Wildman, Laura "Spellweaver"
Willey, Hawk/Helen
Willey, Thermal/Bruce
Williams, Russell
Willowhawk, Alfred (US)
Williamson, Cecil
Williams, Tom
Willowroot, Abby (US)
Wilson, Monique (UK)
Winges, Angel
Winter, Lady (Aust)
Winters, Pat
Witwer, Steve
Witt, Marybeth "Pythia" (US)
Witter, Ronald (UK)
Wizard, Jim "Fish" (US)
Wolfe, Alexander (Ger)

Wolf, Shimmering
Wolfwomyn, Joi
Wood, Robin
Woods, Julie
Worthington, Madge & Arthur (UK)
Wynne, Darla Kaye
York, Michael (US)
Yronwode, Cat
Zakrov, Laura Tempest (US)
Zell-Ravenheart, Morning Glory (US)
Zell-Ravenheart, Oberon (US)

Dates of Elders to Remember

Elders Day – November 23rd
(Day to Honour All Elders)

Name	Birth	Death
Joan d' Arc	January 6th 1412	May 30th 1430
Cornelius Agrippa	September 11th 1486	February 2nd 1535
Agnes Waterhouse	1503	July 29th 1566
Sir Edward Kelley	August 1st 1555	November 1st 1597
Tamsin Blight	1788	August 16th 1856
Marie C. Leveau	September 10th 1791	June 15th 1881
Eliphas Levi	February 10th 1810	May 31st 1875
George Pickingill	1816	April 10th 1909
Charles G. Leland	August 15th 1824	March 20th 1903
Sir James G. Fraser	January 1st 1854	May 7th 1941
Arthur E. Waite	October 2nd 1857	May 19th 1942
Dr. Margaret Murray	July 13th, 1863,	November 13th 1963
Aleister Crowley	October 12th 1875	December 1st 1947
Gerald B. Gardner	June 13th 1884	February 12th 1964
Dion Fortune	December 6th 1890	1946
Adrian Reinman	July 18th 1892	June 6th 1967
Lady Margaret D. Quinn	June 18th 1892	March 21st 1995
Dr. Frederick L. Santee	September 17th 1906	April 11th 1980
Israel Regardie	November 17th 1907	March 10th 1985
Cecil Williamson	September 18th 1909	December 9th 1999
Eleanor Bone	December 15th 2010	September 21st 2001
William G. Gray	March 25th 1913	1992
Stewart Farrar	June 28th 1916	February 7th 2000
Rosaleen Norton	October 2nd 1917	December 5th 1979
Olivia Durdin-Robertson	April 13th 1917	November 14th 2013
Sybil Leek	February 22nd 1917	October 26th 1982
Lady Sheba	July 18th 1920	March 2nd 2002
Lawrence Durdin-Robertson	May 6th, 1920,	August 4th 1994
Doreen Valiente	January 4th 1922	September 1st 1999
Francis X. King	January 10th 1934	November 8th 1994
Idries Shah	June 16th, 1924,	November 23rd 1996
Alex Sanders	June 6th 1926	April 30th 1988
Patricia Crowther	October 14th 1927	-
Delores Ashcorft Nowicki	June 11th 1929	-

Name	Born	Died
Carl L. Weschke	September 10th 1930	-
Leo Martello	September 26th 1930	June 29th 2000
Laurie Cabot	March 26th, 1933,	
Raymond Buckland	August 31st 1934	September 27th 2017
Pete Pathfinder Davis	August 14th 1937	October 31st 2014
Marion Weinstein	May 19th 1939	July 1st 2009
Michael York	September 15th 1939	-
HR Giger	February 5th 1940	May 12th 2014
Oberon Zell Ravenheart	November 30th 1942	-
Nicki Scully	1943	-
Richard L. Christie	April 7th, 1944,	October 28th 2014
Rev. Paul Beyerl	September 2nd 1945	-
Mama Donna Henes	September 19th 1945	-
Margot Adler	April 16th 1946	July 28th 2014
Maxine Sanders	December 30th 1948	-
Amber K	July 9th 1947	-
Zsuzsanna Budapest	May 30th 1948	May 13th 2014
Morning Glory Z. Ravenheart	May 27th, 1948,	May 13th 2014
Selena Fox	October 20th 1949	-
Isaac Bonawits	October 1st 1949	August 12th 2010
Carol Garr	December 27th 1949	-
Janet Farrar	June 24th 1950	-
Rev. Patrick McCollum	April 11th 1950	-
John "Apollonius" Opsopaus	August 4th 1950	-
Kat Tigney	November 24th 1950	-
Raven Grimassi	April 12th 1951	March 10th 2019
Starhawk	June 17th 1951	-
Donald M. Kraig	March 28th 1951	March 17th 2014
Simon Goodman	September 16th 1952	March 22nd 1991
Ellen E. Hopman	July 31st 1952	-
Morgana Sythova	April 15th 1952	-
Prof. Ronald Hutton	December 19th 1953	-
Rev. Velvet Reith	November 15th 1954	January 4th 2017
Phyllis Curott	February 8th 1954	-
Dorothy Morrison	May 6th 1955	-
Tamara Von Forslun	November 23rd 1956	-
Scott Cunningham	June 27th, 1956,	March 28th 1993
Silver Ravenwolf	September 11th 1956	-
Edain McCoy	1957	March 22nd 2019
Gavin Bone	January 19th 1964	-

Rev. Belladonna Leveau	August 18th 1965	-
Utu Witchdoctor	July 26th 1968	-
Christian day	December 25th 1969	-
Laura Gonzalez	July 2nd 1973	-
Jason Mankey	January 4th 1973	-
Brian Cain	May 15th 1975	-
Adam Barralet	June 15th 1979	-

Merry Meet, Merry Part and Merry Meet Again!

This book contains many acclaimed people who were either Witches, Pagans, Wiccans, Shamans, Occultists, Magicians or just being accused of one of these titles. Now in the 21st century new Seekers of these traditions and paths have no idea of the amount of hard work that it took all these people in one way or another to bring these very traditions and subjects out into the open. They were open to ridicule, abuse, attacks, torture, imprisonment, and in some cases death.

With all this in mind they fought on to create the path that we no take for granted, they made it possible for you to just say "I am a Witch", and not be burnt alive. They fought for what you now take as an everyday aspect of your life. Yes, it may still be hard for some in some of the areas that you may live. BUT you must stand up and be counted and be free enough to acknowledge what may be taken for granted.

In just 50 years the world has changed because of these brave Elders who fought the establishment for their and our right to be free and believe in their true calling. We are free and protected by governmental charter no matter where you live, we are human and have the rights of choice and freedom of religion and speech, no matter how many may disagree it is your choice. You do not have to walk in their shoes as they do not have to walk in yours.

When you have your Full Moons, New Moons, Festivals, or form a Magick Circle for a set reason, pay homage to the Elders, offer all the ancestors and Elders past, present and future your prayers to give them strength so they may stand up in front of the world on your behalf, and on behalf on many who have not yet found their voice and say "I am a Woman", "I am Black", "I am Asian", I am Pagan", "I am a Wiccan", "I am a Witch", "I am a Shaman", I am Homosexual", "I am Free", "I am Alive", I am Me", "I am What I Am", "I am everything that has been, that is, and that shall be!"

When you can stand up with your heart open and your spirit revealed then this world will not be filled with a variety of different people who cannot accept others in their ways, but a society of humans first who will honor all diversity with respect and honor, knowing that they have the courage to be who they are and where they are meant to be, and do it with Pride, Dignity, Love, Respect, Tolerance and Forgiveness.

When this happens, we will no longer be English, European, American, Australian, Asian etc. we will be HUMAN! When this happens, we will no longer be white, black, yellow, etc. we will be FAMILY! When this happens, we will no longer be Christian, Islamic, Buddhist, Pagan, Jewish, Hindu, Wiccan, Pagan, we will be DIVINE LOVE! Then and only then can we bring back the Garden of Eden, and "The Golden Age" and live as we are intended, together in Peace and Truth. Again, I would like to thank all the Elders who assisted me with sending their Biographies and photos for this book.

www.ingramcontent.com/pod-product-compliance
Lightning Source LLC
Chambersburg PA
CBHW051206290426
44109CB00021B/2364